291.1
M36   Martin, Malachi.
           The encounter.

Temple Israel Library
Minneapolis, Minn.

———

Please sign your full name on the above card.

Return books promptly to the Library or Temple Office.

Fines will be charged for overdue books or for damage or loss of same.

The Encounter

Books by Malachi Martin

The Pilgrim (under the pseudonym, Michael Serafian)
The Encounter

Malachi Martin

THE
ENCOUNTER

FARRAR, STRAUS AND GIROUX

New York

CONTENTS

v

CONTENTS

Foreword

For several years The Harry Frank Guggenheim Foundation has been interested, upon the initiative of its President, in fostering studies on the general theme of Man's Relation to Man. The perspective of the Foundation is long: perhaps in a century or two there may come some amelioration of man's inhumanity to man. Perhaps, as it is hoped, the Foundation may assist in the process of amelioration.

Early in 1965, before my time as a Trustee of the Foundation, Mr. Guggenheim wrote a letter to the Board indicating a possibly fruitful line of activity. The letter follows:

> The great prophets of all religions have preached gospels with much in common for human progress. The apostles of the prophets have created religious sects dividing mankind into contesting, and often power-hungry, groups.
>
> A world-wide educational project, with a simple explanation of the common ideology of the great prophets, might be of some benefit in improving man's relation to man. Such education should be completely objective and must reach the masses for effectiveness.

The Trustees deemed Mr. Guggenheim's suggestion a good one and a search was instituted for a scholar who would be qualified to deal with the indicated subject matter. In 1967 he was found in the person of Dr. Malachi Martin.

Dr. Martin for several years had been a student of the three greatest Western religions—Judaism, Christianity and Islam. He had studied them not only from the point of view of their doctrines and internal organization, but also from the point of view of the interrelations of Judaism, Christianity and Islam. Besides, it was clear to the Trustees of the Foundation that he was an able expositor and writer.

Accordingly, funds were granted to Dr. Martin to enable him to complete his studies and to write the book, *The Encounter*, now being published.

Like Benjamin Franklin, the Trustees of the Foundation are searching diligently for new truths and they keep all hypotheses tentative. Dr. Franklin's way was to foster the gathering of evidence and the making of observations: he tested them, rejected them when proved wrong, and settled on others, expecting that they, too, would fall before new evidence.

In his time, Franklin was dubbed "the doubting Doctor, who has been remarkable for skepticism from fourteen to four score."

In this spirit, Dr. Martin had complete freedom to write his book. We know that the basic condition which makes possible any advance for the greater good of mankind is freedom for men, as individuals, to find new paths to new truths and be given full freedom for their expression.

Without advance to new truths, new meanings, we shall be finished; and we shall have failed our Founding Fathers in their purpose to secure the blessings of liberty and of the good life to themselves and their posterity, to ourselves and our posterity. For, very obviously, the past is not good enough to lead either the present or the future. There can be no development, in any line or along any line, without freedom to think, to explore, to doubt, to criticize. There must be freedom even to be wrong. It is such an amplitude of freedom that has enabled individual men to make us what we are today—as individual people, as a nation, even as an industrial society. Our defense against every totalitarian enemy is, at bottom, a defense of our freedom.

That wise lawyer and judge, Learned Hand, has stated what are the principles of civil liberty and human relationships: "I answer that they lie in habits, customs—conventions if you will—that tolerate dissent and can live without irrefragable certainties; that are ready to overhaul existing assumptions; that recognize that we never see save through a glass, darkly; that at long last we shall succeed only so far as we continue to undertake 'the intolerable labor of thought'—that most distasteful of all our activities."

Dr. Martin ventured on his long labor of thought in the spirit of Judge Hand's declaration. As he has stated it to us, *The Encounter* is a study of the claims of Judaism, Christianity and Islam, each to possess exclusively the explanation of man, of all that man signifies, and of all that signifies man; and then to assess the merits of such claims in the light of present-day scholarship and thought.

We hope he has succeeded in his important endeavor and that *The Encounter,* in Judge Hand's words, indeed does "overhaul existing assumptions" in the interest of liberty and human relationships. And we expect to learn, from reading his book, that Dr. Martin has succeeded.

HENRY ALLEN MOE

Introduction

Few historians of the 20th century would deny that Judaism, Christianity, and Islam stand at a crucial crossroads in their history. Not many would assert that any one of these great religions is in danger of imminent collapse and dissolution. All three present a flourishing appearance and a certain promise of continuing growth and future expansion.

Judaism not only surmounted the Hitlerian onslaught on the ancient Diaspora homeland in Europe; it has, in addition, found a national homeland on the historic soil of Palestine from whence it emerged over three thousand years ago. All over the Western world, particularly in the United States, Judaism is recognized as a constituent part of modern life. Anti-Semitism in a sociological and political sense exists—but as an exception. The rule is that Jews and their Jewishness no longer provoke the storms they have experienced in the past.

Christianity, on the other hand, also seems to be flourishing. The most promising turn of events is the apparently universal desire to seek a common Christian unity. Ecumenism, or the science of regaining Christian unity, is almost everywhere in vogue and, for the first time in three hundred years, the Roman Catholic communion is on official speaking terms with other

Christian persuasions and churches. Twentieth century Christianity is, apparently, centripetal. And this, seemingly, is a sign of genuine health and a living spirit. Christianity, too, has come through a dark period during which it almost succumbed to a cataclysmic event—the onslaught of the atheistic principles of Leninist-Stalinist Marxism. Neither the Greek Orthodox Church, the Russian Orthodox Church, nor the Roman Catholic Church has become extinct behind the Iron Curtain. On the contrary, they seem to be endowed with a fresh strength and a new life.

Islam, above all others, seems to have regained a new lease on life. The countries in which it is the primary or sole religion have regained or won their political independence recently, some within the framework of the United Nations Organization. In addition, they are the recipients of special treatment in the shape of foreign aid and international guarantees. Thus, their political and economic framework seems to be established and guaranteed. And, thus, the argument could continue, they are untrammelled by foreign ideas or the presence of an Occidental dominance and Christian culture; they can continue to develop their own institutions within which Islam can flourish. Besides all this, Islam is now enjoying a new period of efflorescence in many newly independent countries of Negro Africa. If any religion is acquiring new adherents, it is Islam.

If one's analysis of Judaism, Christianity, and Islam stopped at these and analogous circumstances, we would have falsified our concept of these three religions today. We would also have nurtured an illusion which carries its own peculiar bitterness. Judaism, Christianity, and Islam claim the whole man and all his spirit. They are built on the principle of spiritual allegiance to an ethos and a dogma which, they claim, should rule all of man's life. It is the thesis of this study that as doctrines of man and as ways of life they have received dismissal notices from the evolving world of today; all three are resisting the peremptory orders; all three seem incapable of making the necessary leap into the modern world.

Even to the most superficial observer it is clear, on the one hand, that all three religions individually make an exclusive claim to a certain authenticity, authority, and leadership—a certain dominance, in fact, as an inborn right. On the other hand, it is equally clear that none of them has an effective voice among the sons of men as they parley and dispute over their global destiny. More than that, this very claim to a certain dominance is not only disputed among themselves; it is being continually refuted and coldly silenced by the apparently growing inability of any one of the three religious systems to speak coherently and intelligibly about this global destiny, according as the lines of the latter's development become more and more complex.

Even within their traditional areas and increasingly for their own adherents, they are ceasing to be relevant. Their claim to uniqueness is contended; the three no longer straddle the age. They tend to be regarded retrospectively, like figures receding more and more into the past. The main consideration of this book is that all three religions are caught for the same reason in an inescapable dilemma that offers no discernible alternative. The dilemma is briefly as follows: each of the three religions exclusively possesses, so runs its claim, the only answer to all man's questioning, and it alone can provide man with an explanation of his life. But such a claim to dominance is utterly unacceptable to modern man's mind.

Five hundred years or a thousand years ago, these religions were making the same all-inclusive claims—but man's world was different then. In the last 500 years it has changed more radically than over the previous 100,000 years. Chiefly, a global crisis now affects all men alike on the very issues which these religions once claimed as their exclusive concern. They, like man himself, have been overtaken by the logic of history.

In this last third of the 20th century, there is something shaking the human race. It is as if the latter had carried strange unwanted dreams in its head for millennia, only to wake up brusquely and try to live the dreams. There is abroad on the human scene a spirit that cannot be caged. Something that has been compressed, held down, distorted, and enchained for a long time has now coagulated, boiled up, and is in the process of explosion. There has also been a shaking off of shackles, a repudiation of traditional molds of thought, as if man had suddenly decided to be himself—to see himself as he really is, or perish in the attempt. He is intent on encountering himself in the raw, not through the colored glasses of ancient mythologies or modern ideological presuppositions. This is *the encounter,* the central theme of this book.

It is a presupposition of this book that none of the three great religions can be considered in abstraction from its history, and that one's assessment of a religion today would be falsified if we considered it only as we find it in the modern world and as proposed by some of its modern adherents. Thus some Christians now reject the notion of sacrifice; yet such a notion is integral to Christianity in its classical form. Many Jews today reject the idea of personal immortality in a life after death; they would claim that it is alien to Judaism. The truth is rather that this belief is alien to the type of Judaism such Jews have chosen, but not to the classical form of Judaism. They all therefore have a debt to pay off, and all three are already touched by the irrevocable sanctions that life imposes on such venerable offenders.

Jorge Luis Borges, in his story about man's quest for meaning, describes it as a journey without an end that always returns in a concentric movement back to man. Man, he mythologizes, has lost a face and is ever seeking it: he by-passes the "temple, devoured by an ancient conflagration, profaned by a malarial jungle, its god unhonored now of man," eventually finding a fire burning in the forest into which he walks calmly, "with relief, with humiliation, with terror," knowing that "he too was all appearance, that someone else was dreaming him." Modern man rejects the image of him imposed by exclusive-minded religions. He may never find his God. He may encounter only—himself.

A textual note: the device referred to in these pages as the "scenario" is used with the same purpose as it was given in the Jewish Bible, the Gospels, and the Koran—that is, the intelligent imagining by a modern mind of events described as irretrievably past and unverifiable. It is also used prospectively to foresee and understand possible future developments.

M.M.

Book One

THE PRICELESS
MOMENTS

PART I

Israel and the Law

1. An Old Man's Dream

He is an old man of ninety-nine, according to the Semite reckoning.[1] He is standing on a mountaintop beside a long stone altar. Before him lie three carcasses: a three-year-old heifer, a three-year-old she-goat, a three-year-old ram. Each carcass has been sliced evenly down the middle from chin to chine; each equal part is laid on opposite sides of the altar. On the ground, their feet tied with a leather thong to a stone, a dove and a pigeon flutter spasmodically and helplessly. From time to time, a carrion-crow or vulture moves down in a sinister glide toward the carcasses; each time the old man's immobility is galvanized. His eyes open. His voice breaks the silence. His right hand splits the air in a menacing gesture. The bird rejoins its companions on a tree to continue the vigil.

The carcasses have been rubbed with honey and oil, sprin-

[1] See *Genesis*, chapter 15.

3

kled with crushed petals and leaves of cyclamen, acacia, celandine, and wild roses. The old man has sweated and worked for one whole day in a specially dug trench preparing them, until the armature of his body ached and he emerged at evening blood-stained and splattered with mud.

> *"Lord,*
> *Who livens all that lives,*
> *How am I to know?*
> *Shall I inherit this Land?"*

he had queried with the brazen piety of the desert and an old man's petulant desire for immortality. The exchange had taken place at Bethel. The All-High had there promised him the entire Land. Further, his family and descendants would be as numberless as the dust of the Hejaz, uncountable as the stars in the seven heavens. They would possess this Land forever in blessings.

The All-High had commanded the age-old ritual performed in vain so many times for Sumerian princes and Egyptian Pharaohs: the surrender of the present life in order to be assimilated to the being of the Undying One. A whole-burnt sacrifice of three animals, one for each primal element: earth, fire, water. Each animal slit evenly in two equal parts, each part laid so that a narrow channel is formed in between them. Thus the soul and life of the offerer will run in the channelled blood. Is blood not life? If the offering is consumed by sacred fire, soul and life will fly arrow-sure to the house of the Eternal to be united with his unchanging eternity. The dove and the pigeon are to be released at the moment of burning. Innocence and strength bear soul and life to Heaven. The ritual of immortality as old as Olduvai.

Toward evening, the old man quivers. It is still warm, however, and clear. The sun is visible in the west, low and waning. In the east, which he faces, the mountains of Moab are hunched against the sky as indistinguishable masses of dark purple fruit. The moment of terror passes. Reddish light falls slantingly on the staring eyes of the dead animals evoking their glassy smiles. The drying rivulets of blood glisten in the channel and drip to the ground. Some minutes later, the hush falls on all things, and the old man again shakes. This is the loud pause between the time we see the shadow of the expected visitor fall across the doorstep and the moment when he takes the first step

into our view. The old man feels the gentle stir of presence,
firm and definite as one hand placed in another, soft and warm
as the cloak around his shoulders.

> *"Lord,*
> *Who livens all that lives,*
> *How shall I know?*
> *Shall my children possess this land forever?*
> *Shall I live forever in them?"*

The fears, hopes and reverence of the old man, poured out in
his words, mingle with emotions as leaves are carried sodden
on a stream. The language, Western Semitic, which he speaks
to his god, still possesses the mimation endings to words. The
liquid sounds, blending narrow and broad vowels and diph-
thongs with resounding labials, make a flowing mosaic of his
utterances. Moses, Isaiah, Ezra, will all speak a clipped, lap-
idary language as different from Abraham's as blocks of gaunt,
angular Syrian limestone on a desert landscape contrast with
eastern sunlight filtering through purple lattices. The former
will be hieratic, solemn with Levitical purity, a careful formulation of mysteries accepted but not understood. The latter will
be untrammeled, clear with realization that man still possesses
the power of immemorial laughter at every new dawn and of
tears for the desolation of every night.

In an instant, the sun disappears. Each black shadow thrown
by tree, rock, mountain seems to run over at the edges, to coag-
ulate with its neighbor in a veil quietly and deftly thrown
over the face of all things. It is night. The wind rises from the
seashore and blows fresh and strong across the plains and hills.
The watcher struggles against his desire to crouch, to hide, to
flee, to scream out, to call on the fellowship and comfort of
all living things, to summon even the departing carrion-birds
in defense against the paralysis now weighing on his eyelids,
gripping his limbs. Men are never so unwilling to enter awake
the limbo where their insubstantial wishes lurk, where the
brotherhood of sleep and death is consummated, as when they
feel detached from color, from sights, from sounds, from the
touch of things. His shoulders shake as under the blows of a
whip. Death and sleep are entered with closed eyes.

> *"This is my pact with you,*
> *said the Lord in that day.*

From Nile to Euphrates,
From the Great Sea of Water,
To the Great Sea of Sand,
This Land is yours and your posterity's.
Look!"

The stream of fire pours from nowhere, from the surrounding darkness, in between the separated pieces on the altar, fanned by the wind, licking the red lips of the separated fleshy edges, melting the blood, burning the hair and skin and meat, lighting the old man's eyes with crimson gleams, blackening the stars which a moment before had quietly shone. The old man's knife convulsively slashes the leather thong; dove and pigeon rise, flash white and grey for an instant, then disappear into the upper blackness. Fumes of burning flesh and sickening smells of sizzling blood stop his nostrils.

"I liven all that lives.
God of a single family, now.
God of a race, hereafter.
God of a nation, then.
God of all nations.
God of man.
You will live and die a tribal wanderer,
But father of blessings for all.
The world is mine."

Who were this man and his god? And when and where did all this take place? The teachers in the pan-Israelite federation of the 11th century B.C. and the Biblical writers of the 9th century B.C. had one set of answers. The man: Abraham, born Abram, late of Ur in Mesopotamia. The All-High: Yahweh, meaning I Am Who Am, Lord of Hosts. The place: Mambre, near Hebron, today in southeastern Israel. The hour: twilight of an early spring evening. The time: the dawn of sacred and secular history, some 1500 years after the creation of the world.

But we today, lacking the faith but having the science, know otherwise. The man: probably called Abraham, patriarchal head of a nomadic clan, of Aramean stock. The All-High: from surviving evidence, a tribal mountain god, El Elyon. The place: somewhere in the steppes of Syro-Mesopotamia on the fringe of modern Palestine. The hour: when an old man nods and dreams of finding a lush pasturage ground for the flocks he must ever drive on in search of water. The time: one day, probably in the 18th or 17th century B.C. A Sesostris or an Amenemhet rules as Pharaoh in Egypt; the first dynasty of Babylon has begun; the Aryans are pushing the black Dravidians and Austro-Asiatic Munda tribes back from the rich alluvial plains of Northern India; the Hele Stone of Stonehenge is already in place at the avenue entrance to the Ring; the world is already some five billion years old; no man has yet looked on the earth from space or walked on the surface of the moon; and the only infallible motions known to men are the revolution of the stars and seas, the rushing seasons, and their own mortal existence from birth to death.

Other and later times would each say they knew the significance of Abraham's revelation; different voices would claim that same moment as the authentic, primeval precursor of their various beliefs; all would attempt to explain it in their own terms. "Abraham was carried to the seventh Hall of Paradise, as Paul was," explained Augustine, in the 4th century. "The Father saw the Prophet with Allah's angels leading all Muslims into Paradise," Mohammad teaches in the Koran of the 8th century. "Our Father Abraham," writes Rashi in the 11th century, "was given a vision of all Israel's sins; he swooned." "The Patriarch was granted a foresight of Jesus and his sufferings," commented Thomas of Aquin imperturbably in the 13th century. "Traumatization of the senses with obfuscation in the afferent nerves leading to the central cortex, causing temporary coma and aphasia," says Sigmund Freud in the 20th century.

It was none of all this. The fire was gone. The stars looked down on Abraham now lying unconscious across the smoking altar, an old nomad with hardened arteries, burnt skin, scrawny body, scraggy hair, and a fierce desire to live forever. The vastness of the vision, the fullness of the response was too much for him. No more can we understand what pan-galactic consciousness could be. What would happen to us if we lived it for one moment? For such a vision is like a meeting-point where time ceases to flow, space does not extend, all physical dimensions are nullified and reduced to a point, the restlessness of detail is frozen and veiled by mists of unknowing, and the thin line of division between the human and the non-human is blurred with brightness. It transcends history because it includes it. It impregnates the merely material with transparency, because it renders the latter intelligible. Beside it, the exoticism of a psychedelic trip is but foolish double-think and a dangerous pathology, the intuition of poets an exercise of highly organized biologies, the flight of lovers a sublimation of self-destructive acts.

Today we know that Palestine was submerged in the water of the Tethys Sea during the Mesozoic Age. When it emerged again into the glacial sunlight of the Tertiary Age, some 50 million years ago, violent tectonic thrusts and upheavals split its face vertically with a deep jagged wound in which the Jordan's waters run today and threw up piles of rock to form the hills and mountains. Some 12,000 years ago, the first food-producers, the Natufians, appeared from the north. Slender, long-headed, averaging five feet in height, these remote invaders moved through the land, fishing, hunting, sowing crude grain, carving on their bone sickle-hafts the images of the fawns, gazelles, fish, and palm leaves they worshipped mystically. They came with the dogs they domesticated, buried their dead in "flexed" postures, and left us as principal monuments their bone awls, pins, pendants and beads, their flint blades, and the permanent mystery of their origin, their language, and their final fate about 6,000 B.C. What gods they worshipped were embodied in the animals, the monsoon rains, the sun, moon, stars, the suffocating hamzin, and the silent death of the arid wadis.

More than four thousand years later Palestine west of the Jordan River was occupied by the Canaanites. Palestine east of the Jordan was occupied by nomadic and semi-nomadic Semites who had arrived from the south and southwest, slowly becoming sedentary and occupying the land. These nomads were divided into independent clans, tribes, and families. Their principle of existence was simple: find pasture for their flocks, some suitable ground for grain crops and vegetable gardening, and sufficient water. The aim of all: a final resting place, a land of their own, where flocks would produce milk, where the hardness of life would be sweetened with honey, enriched by wine. The land of milk and honey. This was the theme of their music, the object of their prayers.

The society they lived in and formed was patriarchal. Their leaders were heads of families. Their gods were the gods of their fathers. And although they never remained long in any one place, their elders and their fathers found time to worship the particular god who had protected them in their searchings. The descendants invoked these gods of their ancestors. Thus it was that Abraham's story started. And Isaac's. And Jacob's. Not father, son, and grandson—at least in physical descendance. Each, within a corner of some forgotten valley, or on a mountain ledge above the plains, or in the middle of a winter storm on the steppe, had prayed for survival and for an end to wandering. Each one had prayed in his own way, as seen from the traditions of their descendants: Abraham for immortality, Isaac for living, Jacob for blessings.

Sometime between the 14th and 12th centuries B.C. these tribes began to move west. From the meager data at our disposal, it would seem that the tribes of Rachel, consisting of Benjamin and the House of Joseph (Manasseh and Ephraim) were the first to cross the Jordan into the middle area of Palestine of which Sichem was the center. They carried with them the Jacob tradition. After them in slow spasmodic succession came the House of Lea (Reuben, Issachar, Zabulon, Simeon, Levi, Juda); they had long been sedentarized in eastern Palestine; now they settled in the Negev. They brought with them the Abraham-Isaac tradition. Then came Aser, Dan, Nephtali. All eventually conquered their territories—all except Aser (the "mercenary"), Zabulon, and Dan; they sold their independence for security and served the coastal kingdoms of Sidon, Tyre, and Byblos.

By the 13th century B.C., a central grouping of tribes already had formed an amphictyony of six (Reuben, Issachar, Zabulon, Simeon, Levi, Juda) in the central and southern regions of Palestine. We do not know the origins of its very particular religious idea, or the original motives of the participating tribes, or the federation, or the surely complicated process by which it evolved. Some profound religious experience stood behind the socio-political web of interest. But a mystery probably will always shroud it.

Central to this mystery is that element which must be admitted; for to deny it would be to render illusory all talk about religion. That element is a definite religious experience had by individuals at a certain time, in a certain place. Every major

religion adduces such a claim. A vision. A visit. An ecstasy. An
Abrahamic revelation. In Israel's case, this initial experience
had then taken the form of a contact between Yahweh, invisible
and unimaginable god of the heights and depths, master of all
the elements, and the men who had later entered Palestine and
formed the federation. The essence of the contact had been a
pact: Yahweh became their god, they became his people. A
pact with conditions: Yahweh would preserve them, would be
"with" them; they would observe certain laws, the chief of
which is a unique exclusive devotion to him. "Hear O Israel!
the Lord our God the Lord is One." This had been the heart
of the experience.

We will probably never know at what date this mysterious
contact and pact had taken place, or where it had happened, or
the identity of the participants, or the occasion. Later Hebrew
tradition would attach it to Mount Sinai in the Sinai peninsula,
and place Moses as the central personality, the mediator with
Yahweh and the supreme legislator. The reality is probably
quite different. Certainly the date had been remote and had
nothing to do with an escape from Egypt; it could have been
at any time between the 20th and the 15th century B.C. The
participants had been members of one of the Semite tribes
which had joined with the other tribes arriving from other
places by other paths. Among them all the news of the pact
had been disseminated and for imponderable reasons had taken
hold of the population. The occasion, as clearly as we can discern it, had probably been a particular ceremony in connection
with the yearly fertility rites for men, animals, plants, and crops.

Whatever the facts of their past, by the 13th century B.C. the
Semitic nomads in Palestine had formed a sacred federation
based on this primordial experience and the ensuing pact.

The federation does not seem to have been a mere political
or military expedient for self-defense or aggrandizement, or an
institution organized for purely commercial and economic purposes. Yet, at the same time, it had no central cult, no temple,
no priests, no fixed sanctuary, no prescribed sacrifices, no written book, no codified law. It was something unique in history.
Calling itself "Israel" it rested on a historical choice: the participants had submitted to a divine law which was spelled out
in precise moral precepts and detailed ethical prescriptions. Observance of these precepts and prescriptions guaranteed the
existence and salvation of the group by Yahweh. He was held

to be intangible to the point of being utterly beyond all human representation in wood, stone, or metal, and beyond any of man's imaginings. He was present to them invisibly. The Ark, originally a throne and the portable altar of a nomadic people, signified his presence.[2]

The central functionary of the federation was the "judge," or teacher of righteousness. The judge was not essentially either warrior, king, or priest. He was there to remind "Israel," the federation, of the alliance with Yahweh, and to interpret the laws that preserved that alliance. The true character of classical Israel lies in this alliance with Yahweh and in certain historical happenings at which we can now only guess. The alliance was a juridical pact; the federation was a foundation in proclaimed law, in the ethical and moral sphere, aimed at preserving the pact. The historical happenings centered around the finding and occupation of a land to be Israel's own, under the protection of Yahweh. For the rest, "Israelitism" did not connote miracles, messiah, redemption of a transcendental kind, heaven, hell, sacrifice, kingship, dictatorship, democratic process, theological speculation, liturgical worship, or hieratic privilege. The original Six Tribes, rather, built their federation on their oral traditions of the vital historical happenings linked with certain religious ceremonies of a juridical and prescriptive kind. This was Israel.

About 1250 B.C., certain Semite nomads penetrated Egypt. There the price of admission was the work of their hands. They constructed granaries for the city of Pithom and built a royal residence for Ramses II (1292-1225 B.C.) in the eastern Nile delta. "Who works for another, lives for another and dies for another," runs an Arabic saying. Surveillance became repression. Repression became oppression. Within a century the Semites finally fled the country and escaped their masters, passing by the water and through the desert, and entering Palestine again. There they mingled with those of their race who had by now become sedentary and prosperous. With them they brought the theme of salvation. They claimed to have been saved miraculously, marvelously kept alive by their ancestral god. The

[2] In the late 12th century B.C., at the time the greater federation was formed, the Ark was at Sichem. Later it was shifted to Bethel. Later still it was placed at Shiloh, where it remained until the Philistines captured it and destroyed Shiloh in the middle of the 11th century B.C.

ancient themes concerning the Promised Land flowing with milk and honey, and the blessings from on high thus became fused with the "Sinaitic" themes of salvation, punishment of the oppressor, the triumph of faith. It was in this enriched ambient of group consciousness, established territorial presence, and centralized ethical norm that a new assembly of the Six Tribes was summoned by the Judge.

Late in the 12th century B.C., at Sichem, a town west of the Jordan River in central Palestine, there took place an assembly of the Six Tribes.[3] Sichem possessed an ancient sanctuary whose hoary, evil-smelling history stretched back into the unrecognizable past. It had once entertained the gods, goddesses, she-devils, and animal spirits of 20th century B.C. nomads, of Egyptians, Hurrians, Indo-Aryans, and Canaanites. Astarte, Baal, and various goat and heifer gods had been worshipped there at the high place, in the holy cavern, and at the sacral springs beneath the branches of the sacred terebinth tree. In their honor, men and women and children were put to death, to sanctify harvests, to avert droughts, to obtain victory in war, to celebrate the death of a chieftain. The federation now adopted this Sichem sanctuary as its own center. The Six Tribes then summoned six other tribes, the three tribes of Rachel (Benjamin, Manasseh, Ephraim), together with the northern tribes of Dan, Naphtali, and Aser. For, according to the written record, Joshua, son of Nun, an Ephremite, had been haunted by a new dream. Now Joshua was the Teacher of Righteousness and the Judge chosen by divine lottery at Sichem. On behalf of the God of Israel, Yahweh, he spoke and interpreted "commandment and right" for the tribes.

Joshua's dream was, indeed, new: a greater federation of 12 tribes, ruling from Dan in the north to Beersheba in the south, from the Syrian desert in the east to Carmel on the Mediterranean.

The swearing in of the confederates took place at sunrise. Joshua sat beneath the terebinth. The men of the twelve tribes stood around, helmeted and armed as for battle. One by one, starting with Reuben, each tribal chieftain came forward to lay his hand beneath the thigh of Joshua and to swear by their forefathers that Yahweh would be the god of "Israel," for so the new federation would be called. Then Joshua, aided by the strongest, set up a heavy, blunt-nosed stone as symbolic moun-

[3] See *Joshua*, chapter 24.

tain of Yahweh's high dwelling place. Chosen men entered the
sanctuary and brought forward the Ark of Yahweh's presence.
Joshua stood and intoned the laws and prescriptions by which
Israel would live: Yahweh would be their god; they would be
his people.

2. Israelitism and Judaism

These were the characteristics of Israelitism as it had developed by the 12th century B.C. from its tribal origins some 800
years earlier. But this Semitic stratum of Judaism was transformed over the next thousand years by certain influences.
Among these were the mythologization of the ancient themes
of Israelitism, the codification of the laws, the development of
the king and the Temple, the establishment of Jerusalem as the
cultic and hieratic center, the Babylonian captivity, the ascendancy of the law of Ezra in post-exilic Israel, and the arrival
of both Roman rule and Christianity. This chapter describes
the impact of these influences as they transformed Israelitism
into Judaism. But the destruction of Jerusalem by Rome in 70
A.D. presented Judaism with the necessity of choosing its future direction from among several alternatives. It was during
the critical years from 70-135 that Judaism was forced to
mold its new character, to prepare for its final stage of normative Judaism. It was then that Judaism faced its priceless moment. The alternatives, the possible directions, and the
projected results which gave that moment its great importance
will be examined in detail in the following chapters. Only then
will it be apparent how the religious dominance characteristic of Judaism also was present in fluid form in the tribal
years, was developed in the Israelitism federation, was transformed as Judaism emerged, and—faced with the options of
the priceless moment—was forced to choose its final aspect. It
will then be clear how the physical modes of that dominance
changed the face of Judaism.

It required the literary labors of many generations, the passage of over 800 years after the formation of the larger federation, and some fundamental changes before the basic truths of

Israelitism were interwoven with the current Near East mythologies of creation, redemption, flood, sin. Only then the classical Biblical presentation of Judaism emerged in full form.

A mythologization of the past took place. The narrations of miraculous escape from destruction with their god's help, of final arrival in the land of promise, slowly became part of the general religious patrimony. These elements were integrated into the already sedentarized tribes of southern Palestine. The shadowy figures of long-dead ancestors, an Abraham, an Isaac, a Jacob, who had lived and died on the periphery of Palestine, were introduced and integrated into place-names, local traditions, and national happenings. Abraham's experience, originally somewhere in the Fertile Crescent, was relocated at Mambre, and the Negev, as was Isaac's. Similarly Jacob was now associated with central Palestine, and with Sichem in particular. Their lives and experiences of divine help were reattached to the land where the people now lived. The god they had each prayed to was now worshipped at the very sanctuaries which had belonged to previous indigenous religions. All three were fitted into a catenation of physical descendance down which the promises and the fulfillment had reached Israel. Father, son, grandson. The various tribes of the federation later became rearranged as lineal descendants from Jacob, made inheritors therefore of all the blessings from Abraham and Isaac:

> *"How it breathes*
> *About this son of mine!*
> *The fragrance of earth*
> *When the Lord's blessing is on it!*
> *God give thee dew from heaven*
> *And fruitful soil, corn and wine in plenty.*
> *Let nations serve thee,*
> *And peoples bow before thee.*
> *Mayest thou be Lord over thy brethren,*
> *Receive obeisance from thy own mother's sons.*
> *A curse on those who curse!*
> *A blessing on those who bless thee!"*[1]

The compact mosaic of Biblical Judaism began to emerge: an original and basic religious experience taking place between Yahweh and some Semitic nomads somewhere between 2000

[1] See *Genesis*, chapter 27:26-29.

B.C. and 1500 B.C.; resulting contractual religious formula unique in the religious history of man; a nomadic dream of a promised land; a single adventure by a small group, who escaped bondage and returned to their own race. A powerful popular imagination kneaded and worked on these vital elements, fashioning formularies, creating would-be former historical configurations, elevating obscure personalities (such as a Moses and a Joshua) to superhuman stature, making of Yahweh the protector of a wandering race, and presenting Israel as a closely knit and coagulated body from the time of their origins outside Palestine.

To understand the full transformation that Israelitism underwent, in addition to mythologization, it is necessary to delineate the original nature of the other elements which were also changed. We have to discard any idea that either the land or the people of Israel about 1100 B.C. formed a political or national unity such as existed later or such as we know today in the idea of the independent national state. There existed at that time twelve tribes, the descendants of Semitic nomads, the majority of whom were ethnically related, but not by any mutual family kinship traceable to a common physical ancestor such as an Abraham or a Jacob.

Furthermore, what is most important, these twelve tribes formed a sacral unity. They belonged to a federation whose sole purpose and collective capacity was to preserve the exclusive worship of Yahweh among its members according to certain prescriptions and laws. This sacral unity centered around the chosen sanctuary; its guardian was a charismatic leader chosen by divine vocation and not by popular vote or acclamation. In all other things, each tribe governed itself, sought its own self-interest. The consensus, therefore, of Israel provided no framework for a political structure of the twelve tribes. This consensus rested on inner ethical persuasions, was entirely sacral, and made a deep division between the sacral and the profane or secular or lay. It was thus that Israel could boast that Yahweh had a nation not like any other nation. It was a grouping formed by this inner consensus, which, without any exterior political law, nevertheless dominated the thought and action of the federation.

Even this sacral "Law" did not exist in the extensively codified form in which it emerged in the 4th century B.C., and as we know it in the Pentateuch. The law, proclaimed periodically at the central sanctuary of Israel, was a list of practical and doctrinal prescriptions that depended partly on tradition, partly on the practical circumstances in which each generation found itself. Nor did there exist any accredited body of men whose professional function, resembling the later Pharisees, would have been to preserve a developing oral law and to explain a codified written law. The most we can assert is that at the beginning of the 11th century B.C. there existed a body of traditional narratives of the "patriarchs" and of the first efforts to occupy the land of Canaan. Written records or juridical prescriptions or any explicitly formulated "law of Yahweh" committed to writing is most improbable at this period. An official body of priests sanctioned by the federation did not exist; neither was there any detailed and pre-determined rite, ordinance, and liturgy for the offering of sacrifice, nor was there any central place designated as the only one where sacrifices could be offered to Yahweh. These activities were left up to the initiative of individual groups and individuals in different locations throughout the land.

In a few words, the religious consensus of Judaism, down to the beginning of the 11th century B.C., was other-worldly in its source, sacral in its function, occasioned by events in history, tribal in its ambit, lacked any unique geographical focus point for its cult, and was motivated by an ethical monotheism. Of this consensus, only a few elements remained essentially the same by the time Christianity was born. The rest were transformed.

The major changes in the original religious tradition of the federation were initiated under King Saul (in the last half of the 11th century B.C.), consummated by David (1010-970 B.C.) and permanently effected in the time of Ezra, during the last quarter of the 6th century B.C. About 700 years sufficed to translate and transform the original ethos and inner consensus of Israel.

The first indication of change was the declaring of Saul as King of Israel by the tribes at the sanctuary of Gilgal. It is important that, for the first time, this was not merely a charismatic appointment but a political office with military overtones. The powerful confederation of the Philistines had twice defeated the twelve tribes in pitched battle; Israel was in physical danger. Even though Saul perished in 1050 B.C. at the battle of Ebenezer, the change had started. For the first time the

12 tribes, once united only as a religious federation, acted as a political unit. In fact, it was the last time that all 12 would be bound together primarily by their religious traditions, for with the death of Saul the federation split into subfederations, each consisting of six tribes—Juda in the south and Israel in the north. The foundation had been laid for the later idea of the non-religious leader, and of the secular and profane, in opposition to the sacred and hieratic.

The actions of the nation of Israel were not to be dictated any longer by the inner consensus of its people, by the unity of sacred precepts, but rather, by the force of exterior political law. David was first declared king by the original six tribes of the federation. It was a political appointment. The remaining six tribes soon recognized his pre-eminence and acceded to his rule. Then at Hebron David was acclaimed before Yahweh as king. After the fact, the political appointment came under the protection of Yahweh.

An inherent contradiction was thus inserted in the heart of incipient Judaism, a contradiction that would be reproduced down to the 20th century in those politics and political systems built on a Jewish or Jewish-Christian foundation. Saul's political rule had necessitated an expedient functional unity of the sacred and the profane. History has proven, however, that these cannot work together. The present crisis in major religions, civilizations, and cultures is ultimately traceable to the presence of this irreconcilable contradiction in their foundational schemes.

Seven years after his acclamation, David stormed and took Jerusalem. There he established his royal household. David's political acumen immediately dictated the necessity of centralization. He brought the Ark to Jerusalem and installed it in an old Canaanite sanctuary in the city. Henceforth the priests were mere functionaries of his court. David thus succeeded in making Jerusalem his capital and the cultic center of the old federation. Jerusalem itself retained the status of a free, or independent, city; he did not attach it to Juda or to the other northern portion of his kingdom which by now was called Israel. Admitted to Jerusalem were the king, his mercenary army, his entourage, and his family.

David's achievements were far-reaching. In addition to the establishment of Jerusalem as the cultic center and the attachment of this cult to the house and the person of the king, he

also drew a division between Juda (where he had first been
declared king) and the rest of Israel. He then proceeded to
change the very essence of Israel as a nation—the people who
composed it. Whereas before Israel had meant the 12 tribes,
and the perpetuation of their pact with Yahweh, it now meant
acquiescence to the rule of David, not Yahweh. Israel was not
limited to the 12, nor were the 12 the exclusive possessors of
the right to belong to Israel. David amassed a territory which
included the small kinglets of Ammon, Edom, Aram, and Moab.
The original tribes found their new place and function to have
become narrower and not commensurate with the "Land of
Israel."

David thus established the principal of a secular power
ruling for reasons other than the preservation of the law of
Yahweh. He determined the full form of the new Israelite kingship. And, as this kingship was forced to deal with the realities
of the surrounding political situation and with the traditions
of the newly acquired peoples, it had to come to terms with
the prevailing concept of Near Eastern kingship. That concept
claimed divinity for its kings; it held that they were literally
the sons of gods and immortal in themselves. But, for Judaism,
this concept was not transferable. Yahweh, the invisible and intangible, could not have a series of human, immortal, king-
sons. David, therefore, proclaimed the king to be an *adopted*
son of Yahweh. The political expression of Israel and its sacred
theme could not become reconciled. Israelite kingship would
always remain on the periphery of the socio-religious element,
always subject to its censure, sometimes in collision with it.
Eventually it would lose both its own secular pre-eminence and
all influence on the religious life of its people. The new state
of David and Solomon contained the seeds of destruction for
kingship and for its religion.

Solomon (970-925) consolidated what David had accomplished. The temple which he erected (on the site of the present Muslim sanctuary, the Dome of the Rock) was merely an
elaboration of the Davidic policy of centralization. And the
magnificence of Solomon's reign, his harems, his alliance with
foreign kings, the triangle of commerce and economic exchange
which he established between Jerusalem, Phoenicia, and Spain,
merely emphasized the secular aspect of the new Israel.

During the Davidico-Solomonic period, the first efflorescence
of writing occurred, beginning with the royal annals written by

official chroniclers. At this time also a primitive form of the
present Pentateuch was composed. Scholars have called it the
Yahwist Pentateuch. It was a first and grandiose attempt to
envelop the historical themes and belief of the Israel of the
monarchy in a vast global panorama involving all mankind. In
the Yahwist treatise can be seen a trace of an important theme
later rediscovered during the Babylonian Captivity: universalism. The blessings of Abraham are intended for all men, not
merely for the former's descendants. Another aspect of universalism, the original unity of all Israelite tribes, would be developed after this period. The traditional accounts of the conquest
of the land of Canaan would be meshed together with the pan-
Israelite theme. Instead of the historical reality in which each
separate tribe entered at its own time, in its own place, and did
its own conquering, the acquisition of the land would be represented as the work of the entire people.

Of far greater consequence was the reign of King Josias
(640-609 B.C.). In the year 621 B.C., according to the Bible, the
high priest of Josias' court found an ancient book. He claimed
it contained the law that Yahweh had originally given to his
people when he made the contact with them. Scholars today
think that such a book could have been composed in the 8th-
7th centuries B.C. and would have corresponded more or less to
what is called the Deuteronomic Law. At any rate, at Josias'
court, this book was claimed to be the work of Moses, replete
with juridical prescription interwoven with narratives. Seemingly, it is from this document and this date that the position
of Moses as lawgiver of Israel was explicitly put forward.

Josias, as the king, as the head of the secular state, called an
assembly of his people in the Temple. There he promulgated
this newly rediscovered law of Yahweh, proclaiming it not as
royal decree or state law, but as the divine law of Israel. But
Josias did not just use his authority to determine the pre-
eminence of this law. He extended it to establish his own additional sacred prescriptions, thereby both strengthening his
right (as secular king) to do so and giving divine authenticity
to his rule. Jerusalem, Josias ruled, would not merely be the
center of the cult of Yahweh, it would be the *only* center, and
all other sanctuaries in Israel were to be destroyed. The first
among the priests was declared the head of all priests. Later,
under Persian rule, he would acquire the title of High Priest.
The priests of the outlying sanctuaries, now declared illegal,

would be allowed to ascend to Jerusalem, to offer sacrifice from time to time. There thus began a lower order of priests, *clerus minor*, the forerunners of the later Levites.

Perhaps, however, the most important influence working on the transformation of ancient Israelitism into Judaism was the Babylonian captivity and the subsequent themes which emerged from this experience upon the return of the exiles.

On August 9, 587 B.C., the Babylonian armies stormed Jerusalem, set fire to the Temple and confiscated its treasury. They deported the young King Joakin together with his royal family and his court functionaries. Mass deportation to Babylonia affected all, Jerusalem workmen as well as the military aristocracy. Because the cultic center was no more, the cult of Yahweh, as declared by Israel's kings, ceased. In Babylonia and until the return to Jerusalem the exiled Israelites began to perceive another dimension in their ethnic and tribal Yahwism. Yahweh, it was discovered, could be worshipped outside the central sanctuary and outside the land where the people of his choice lived. Moreover, their faith communicated itself to non-Israelites, and the system of proselytes and semi-converts began in embryo. There flourished therefore, for this moment, a universalism vying with the old tribal and ethnic particularism.

Persian theological ideas and doctrines made their way into the traditional beliefs of the Israelites. Chief among these were: the idea of a personal Messiah or Hero Saviour who would save the people from bondage, the final catastrophic end of the world, the inauguration of the millennial age in the world when peace and prosperity would reign and Israel's ancient glory would be restored, a system of angels and demons. The belief in the resurrection of the body and the immortality of the soul were not yet developed and would not be until nearly the end of the 3rd century B.C.[2] Of these ideas, the Israelite community knew nothing. They belong to the Jewish entity of the 5th century B.C.

The next stage of development completed the transformation to Judaism. It took place in the last quarter of the 4th century when the Babylonian exile was ended. Once more the people were back in the ancient land, Jerusalem was rebuilt. Its sanctuary, begun in 537 B.C. by virtue of an edict of Cyrus, was

[2] This belief appears for the first time in the *Book of Jubilees*, chapter 23:31.

completed in 516 B.C. Ezra, the priest and leader, proclaimed
the law of God—a law sanctioned, not by the federation's king,
but by the Persian sovereign. Furthermore, and most importantly, in order even to belong to Israel one had to accept this
sanctioned law. Thus the original idea of ancient Israel, of the
holy federation, was done away with forever. The binding force
now was not appartence to one of the tribes but adhesion to
the state-proclaimed law of Yahweh.

Israel now had neither king, temple, nor league of tribes.
The Israelites were at home both in their own land and dispersed abroad. The only focal point was the cult of Yahweh at
Jerusalem. As a result, the priesthood came to the fore. At the
time of Ezra and immediately afterwards the sacerdotal hierarchy was established under the leadership and direction of the
High-Priest. Beneath him ranged the Sadocides or Sadducees,
and beneath them the Levites, the successors to the country
clergy who were left without sanctuaries in the time of Josias.
The cult of the land of Israel began to assume a new aspect: it
was no longer a ritual and doctrinal life which a political leader
(the king) directed by means of his royal functionaries. The
divine worship of Yahweh was directed by the High-Priest. To
be a faithful worshipper of Yahweh meant identification with a
national group highly conscious of its ethnic and racial identity. Jewishness was identified with nationalism; faithfulness
to the Law became synonymous with political fidelity to a government. The universalism perceived in the Babylonian Captivity faded; religious and political particularism took its place.

The pivotal center of this new Judaism was the secular-
sacral, political-divine, Persian sanctioned law of the god of
heaven which Ezra had proclaimed to the returned and reestab-
lished exiles. We do not know today what form this law
possessed. Many scholars think that Ezra brought back from
Babylon a complete copy of the Pentateuch. This, however,
is not likely. The Pentateuch was probably brought to its
present form within the land of Israel. More probably still,
the law of Ezra was a composition of the Babylonian exiles
while in Babylon. Whether or not Ezra's formulation entered
into the final form of the Pentateuch, we do not know. We do
know that a century later the Samaritans possessed a complete
Pentateuch, and that shortly afterwards a Greek translation of
the entire Pentateuch was made in Alexandria.

The central cult of post-exilic Judaism was surrounded with

a new array of legalistic minutiae. Sophisticated rules, regulations, provisos, and an elaborate tissue of prescriptions for ritual purity were developed. These were the conditions of holiness and acceptability to Yahweh. The definitive redaction of the Law gave rise to a new body of officialdom, particularly in Jerusalem. These were the doctors of the law, the Pharisees of a later date. Jewish tradition of the time tells of the existence of men called Sopherim, or Scribes, who are regarded as the precursors of the Pharisees.

Controversies exist still among scholars as to the origin of the Pharisees. By the time they emerge into the full light of recorded history they are an established element of Jerusalemite officialdom, accepted interpreters of the Law and all its intricacies. Pharisaism was by then the dominant strain both in Jewish liturgy and Jewish theology. They were at one and the same time active at the highest levels of administration and among the people. They considered themselves the guardians of the Law and, therefore, of Israel in its full integrity. This led them, inevitably, to adopt nationalistic positions. They were engaged actively in the continuous efforts of the people to throw off any foreign yoke which impinged upon the integrity of Israel. The preservation of every aspect of their Law was synonymous with the preservation of the nationhood of Israel.

This new kingdom or state was, therefore, governed by the Law as interpreted and expressed by the effective ruling force, the priesthood. The relative positions of the various parts of the Law in the affairs of state caused endless divisions among the priesthood, particularly between the powerful Pharisees and the other main faction of priests, the Sadducees. Central to the controversy was the question of the place of the oral traditions which had passed from generation to generation: the oral Torah, as opposed to the written Torah.

It is clear that the era of Ezra marked the end of the Israelite period in the history of Israel and ushered in the Jewish period. For the first time since the 11th century B.C., when the dead Saul's eyes stared unseeingly from his body impaled on a sharpened pole on the wall of the Philistine fortress at Beth-Shan, the consensus of the people of Israel was irrevocably composed of a sacral element and a social-political-ethnic element. The law of Yahweh and its consequent liturgical and theological functions were wedded indissolubly to a political formula, a geographical center, an exclusively ethnic principle, and a hieratically organized theoretic officialdom. It was this Judaism which fell under the domination of Rome in 63 B.C.

Nothing that befell Israel under the direct administrative rule of the Roman Empire changed the form Judaism now had acquired. Even the building of the Second Temple by Herod the Great (37-4 B.C.) connoted nothing more than a more sumptuous central sanctuary and a greater consecration of the twofold Jewish officialdom composed of Sadducees and Pharisees. But it was both historically and morally impossible for the Jewish community of Jerusalem and Israel not to enter into a violent clash with their Roman conquerors. The newly formed consensus emphasized racial nationalism; it wedded the sacral with the socio-political complex; it provided an inevitable breeding ground for revolt and war.

Israel's steady course to a painful confrontation took momentum after the death of Herod Agrippa (grandson of Herod the Great) in 44 A.D. Earlier in the century, after the total annexation of central and southern Palestine by the Romans, the Zealot party had been founded. It was drawn mainly from Pharisee circles. These nationalists together with the more militant orders of the Essenians [3] and the Sicarii [4] now found fresh support for their cause among the common people and an ever-increasing number of Pharisees.

The situation was aggravated by a series of Roman procurators and governors who were either venal or harsh or incompetent. Incidents multiplied. The situation got out of hand. Finally it exploded in the year 66 A.D. The Roman Procurator, Gessius Florus, known for his shameless corruption and venality, extracted 17 talents from the Temple treasury in Jerusalem. A popular uprising started in Jerusalem. The daily sacrifice for the Roman Emperor was suspended by Eleazar, son of the High Priest. As the fighting spread, the Roman General Vespasian entered the country by the north. The end was inevitable.

When Vespasian became emperor in 69 A.D., his son Titus took command of the Roman armies. In the spring of 70, Titus began the siege of Jerusalem. The city was surrounded

---

[3] A great deal has been written about these since the discovery of the Dead Sea Scrolls. Most scholars seem to agree in identifying the Essenians with the owners of the Scrolls.

[4] So called from the *sica*, or short dagger, carried beneath their cloaks for the purpose of dispatching their victims.

with a ditch and trench. By August, the Temple had been taken and burned to the ground. In September, the rest of the city fell into Roman hands. By 73 A.D., all resistance had been quelled throughout the country. The central sanctuary was a ruin, the Holy of Holies had been profaned with Roman rites, and no more sacrifices could be offered there before Yahweh. Besides, the presence of Yahweh was gone. The priestly caste had been wiped out and the schools of Pharisees were abolished. All vestiges of national sovereignty and territorial integrity were taken away. Judaism and Israel were confronted with a dilemma of choices: assimilation? adaptation to the new environment? reversal to an Israelite form of its being? a new revolt?

3. A Watershed Moment: Three Scenarios

Judaism, with the disaster of 70 A.D., had arrived at a watershed of history. Old Israelitism had been transformed into contemporary Judaism. Although some 700 years in the making, this transformation had not yet consolidated itself; it had neither inserted itself into the ambient nor established those human bonds which ensure a relative permanency in history; it had not yet hardened into the normative Judaism of post-Talmudic times; it had not yet provided a well-defined catalytic agent for nascent Christianity. For, while there had been an Israelitism and now a Judaism without any influence of Christianity, without that Israelitism and that Judaism there would have been no Christianity such as we know it today. For Judaism in 70 A.D., change of direction was, therefore, still possible. And the fall of Jerusalem made imperative the choice of some direction from among the alternatives. For some 30 years a chaotic Judaism attempted to formulate its future.

In the end, it was the thinking of Akiva Ben Joseph, the great teacher of Yavneh, that dominated these attempts and supported the course of action leading to the final catastrophic failure of Bar-Kockba's revolt in 135 A.D. Even though Akiva then lay dead, his teachings, formulations, and students would continue to determine Judaism's future direction. His influence would extend as far as the compilation of the Talmud, as far as the codification of a Judaism animated exclusively by the Law, without Land or Temple or Priesthood.

What this would mean for the religious dominance of Judaism in the next, nearly 2000, years will be seen later. But at that watershed moment in Judaism's history, at 70 A.D., this was not the only course. For, faced with the destruction of their land, their people, and the physical modes of their dominance in the external world, the adherents of any such polity as Judaism consciously draw the plans for their future, deliberately choose their path from among the possibilities presented by the historical facts of the moment. Judaism could have also reverted to a Prophetic mode, attempted a spiritualization of its faith, or moved towards an ecumenism with Christianity.

Scenario A: Reversal to Prophetic Judaism

Suppose that within two years of the destruction of Jerusalem and the dispersal of the Jerusalemite Community, there are established in the Mediterranean coastal towns groups of surviving sects. Among these are the Pharisees, Sadducees, some Essenians, a few Zealots, and Hellenistic proselytes and semi-converts. It is clear to all of them that Israel and Judaism have suffered a devastating blow. The Holy of Holies, the only place in the world where Yahweh's presence was guaranteed, has been destroyed. The Temple, the only licit place for sacrifices to Yahweh, has been razed. The High-Priest's residence, the quarters for the priests and Levites and Temple guards, the schools, offices, libraries, storehouses, treasury, stables, record-rooms are all gone. The priesthood has been decimated.

In 75 A.D. the surviving Essenians gather for a meeting in one of these coastal towns. One faction is determined to organize another rebellion. They repeat tradition which says that once the Beast has violated the Holy of Holies, Israel will then hear the legions of angels marching thunderously behind the victorious Messiah to the Mountain of Megiddo for the final battle. However, other Essenians have lost heart and describe the revolt of 66 A.D. as a bad mistake. According to their chroniclers, the meeting breaks up in disagreement when one of the despondents cries, "We cannot do anything now. We should have waited for the Messiah, as the Teacher of Righteousness admonished us."

The Hellenistic proselytes and semiconverts are in bad condition. They never accepted the full burden of Judaism. Now they do not even try to organize their remnants. Most of them had been reassured by their mentors that the God of Israel would turn back the invaders and liberate the Jews. Faced with the present situation, some of them now doubt that the Jews *are* the Chosen People.

After the failure of the Essenian meeting, the Pharisees, in the late 70's, decide upon a general convocation of the leaders of all the surviving sects. Held at Yavneh, this meeting proves to be decisive. It is dominated by the two powerful groups, the Pharisees and Sadducees. They are, however, divided in themselves and between each other. In the first days of the meeting, the Sadducees blame the Pharisees for their preoccupation with legalisms and points of exegetical logic: "the spirit of Israel has thus been choked," they affirm. The Pharisees blame the Sadducees for their pride and lack of fidelity to strict observance of the Law. But all the various sects join in a general agreement on two cardinal points: Israel is faced with a seemingly inescapable dilemma which has arisen because of a profound error in Israel's behavior over the past few hundred years. The major effort of the convocation now becomes the delineation of that dilemma and the reasons for its existence.

This, they agree, is the dilemma. The worship of Yahweh must be carried on by the Chosen People. But the Temple has been destroyed, and it seems as if nothing short of another and successful revolt can affect the rebuilding of the Temple. But, despite the Essenian militant faction, most can see no hope of success in another revolt. The strength of imperial Rome is realistically assessed. Thus the dilemma of Israel.

This, they all generally concede, was the error of Israel. Through her priests, teachers, and the kings whom she has accepted, Israel has slipped from the purity of faith which the Fathers carried with them to the Babylonian Captivity in the 6th century B.C., and which Ezra endeavoured to pass on to Israel after the return from Babylonia in 536 B.C. Many, many days of discussion pass before they can all even agree to this, broadly stated as it is.

But daily disputes arise between Pharisees and Sadducees as they gradually try to clarify the nature of this slipping on the part of Israel. The prophets Isaiah, Jeremiah, and Ezechiel

are read attentively. From these writings, the Sadducees lead
the others to claim that they have refound a faith whose salient
elements have been obfuscated. They begin to censure themselves and their past decisions. The Maccabeans and the Has-
moneans are upbraided for their politico-military postures.
They re-examine their history and condemn the verbalizing
and literal interpretations of the early "Pairs" of teachers beginning with Simeon I, the High-Priest, and Antigonus of So-
coh in the 4th century B.C. In a heated moment, they even censure the arbitrary interpretations of Scripture which the Pharisees employed in order to bolster up their prescriptions and
laws for the people.

About three months after the beginning of the meeting, a
famous dispute arises between Rabbi Simeon Ben Yohannan
and Rabbi Akiva Ben Joseph. The latter argues impassionately
for the existence of the "120 Men of the Great Synagogue"
who, he claims, had carried the ancient law with them into
captivity and returned with Ezra to rebuild the Temple. They
embodied, Akiva continues, the true ancient traditions of Judaism as orally borne down through the ages from Moses himself.
Therefore, the all-important Oral Law which they transmitted
must continue to be observed. But Simeon Ben Yohannan dev-
astatingly demolishes Akiva's arguments. He calmly points out
that the only written proof of these men's existence which
Akiva can offer, chapters 8-10 of Nehemias, actually proves
nothing of the sort.

The Pharisees and Sadducees examine the arguments. They
note that they have already ascribed the cataclysmic events
of 66-70 A.D. not to a lack of observance of the Law, but to an
over-emphasis on the exterior formalities of that Law at the
cost of the spirit and true perception of Israel's message and
function. They decide that this over-emphasis found perfect
expression in the Oral Law. And there is now no proof that this
Law had anything to do with Moses. It was, they conclude,
probably the tangled result of hundreds of years of labor on the
part of many good men, who tried to justify every prescription
and precept with a text of Scripture. Even a staunch Pharisee
like Johanan Ben Zakkai expresses fear that many prescriptions and laws would be abrogated by future generations for
want of scriptural foundation. A historic moment in the discussions is reached when a majority of the Pharisees and Sad-

ducees formulate the first major point that will determine their new direction: continued adherence to the Oral Law would be harmful to the future of Judaism, and therefore it must be abandoned.

The survivors of Judaism now re-examine the entire basis of their religion. They realize that the Jewish people and their leaders have abandoned the core of the prophetic message for the mere outer rind. They have forgotten that purity and holiness are not fabricated by exterior actions but solely by Yahweh in the heart of man. The Essenians articulate what they believe to be the original prophetic message: Yahweh made a conditional choice of the Jews as his Chosen People so that they could prepare for the coming of the Messiah. He will affect a universal redemption for all men, and thus establish a spiritual kingdom on earth as a preparation for the kingdom of heaven. Nowhere in Scripture can the Pharisees or their students find any proof or assertion that the soul of man is immortal or that every man will be resurrected again, soul and body. Although they would like to believe this, they now decide to leave the question in abeyance. The Essenians then formulate the second major point: the decision to return to prophetic Messianism.

Toward the end of the long sessions the Sadducees demand the repression of the extremist nationalism of the Zealots and many of the Essenians. It is evident, they claim, that in the last forty years before the destruction of the Temple the teachers of the Law, the Pharisees, have been the prime source for the ideology which has animated the nationalistic groups. Legalism has transformed the original character of the Jews as the Chosen People of Yahweh in whose Land the Messiah will appear for the spiritual regeneration of Jews and of all men. A nationalism resembling in all things that of any other nation around them has resulted. Aware that such nationalism could only lead to another abortive revolt, they ask the assembly of leaders to reconsider the role of Judaism in its relation to the outside world. The Zealots finally agree that it would be impossible, and inconsistent with the prophetic message, to maintain the goal of re-establishing the secular rule of Israel over Jews and all others in the area now dominated by Rome. Instead, the Judaic Community should be limited to the Chosen—to the adherents of the sacral traditions of Judaism. The third major point is established: a revival of religious exclusivity and particularism.

With these three aims formulated, the assembly leaves to the Pharisees the task of working out the details of the fourth and final point: the rebuilding of the Temple, especially for the renewal of the sacrificial ritual by a revived and reorganized Priesthood. Having determined the major lines for Judaism's new direction, the historic session ends. The members return to their towns to implement their decisions.

By 80 A.D. the remnants of the priests are gathered and housed by the Pharisees at Yavneh. They are carefully examined and screened; the less worthy and the badly motivated are dismissed. The chosen candidates are trained in the details of Temple sacrifice and the spiritual meaning of Israel's offering. The Oral Law is abandoned as having nothing essential to do with Yahweh's revelation to Abraham or with the Law of Moses. By the year 140 A.D., the strength of the Yavneh community has become so great that a new order of Jewish scholars emerges, trained in the prophetic writings. Some of these, after ten years study of the Prophets, are then allowed to specialize in the written Law of Moses, and to give legal advice to faithful Jews in matters of conscience.

Economically, too, the Jewish community has prospered. The favor of the Roman Emperor increases as Jewish nationalism vanishes and civil and national prosperity increases in the peaceful towns. In 165 A.D., by decree of the Emperor Marcus Aurelius, the rebuilding of the Temple and its adjuncts is begun at imperial expense. Within seven years, there arises in Jerusalem à perfect replica of the old Solomonic Temple as described in the first book of Kings. Once more the Temple sacrifices are offered in Israel.

One prime result of such a policy, if it had been adopted, would have been the rebirth, perhaps, of a new spirit of inquiry in Israel among its doctors and teachers. Future generations of Jews and Gentiles would have found greater and greater areas of thought and activity in common. No ghettoization of Judaism would have taken place in the Western world. And in a later day, the two foundational religions of the Western world, though still essentially distinct, might yet have found so much in common that mutual good rather than mutual disadvantage would have resulted.

Scenario B: Spiritualization of Judaism

Suppose that the remaining leaders of the Jewish community gather together in a town called Yavneh on the coast in 75 A.D. Because five years have passed since the destruction of 70 A.D., many of these leaders have had time to consider what has led Israel into its present predicament. They find that many of the conclusions they have reached separately actually coincide in their basic elements. They all recall that after the Babylonian Captivity Ezra and his associates had insisted on a careful study of the Law as the means of reconstituting Israel. He had also labored to rebuild Jerusalem and institute the sacrifices in the Temple. Furthermore, he had insisted on racial purity. Because the restoration of Israel in the time of Ezra was due to Cyrus, the idea of a personal Messiah had taken on greater emphasis in Judaism.

Yet, these men of Yavneh now reflect, this policy of Ezra has had direct consequences. Some leaders, especially among the Sadducees, maintain that from this policy was born the isolation of the Jews as a race. Their pride in their geographical identity, and thence the return of kingship in Israel, was also greatly facilitated by Ezra's proclamations. If however, some Sadducees ask, Jews had been able to worship Yahweh in Babylon, why should it be necessary to live in Israel to do so—as was the common teaching of Israel's teachers during the Second Commonwealth? This initial contact between leaders is tentative—the group breaks up and its members return to their towns. In practical terms, it becomes clear to most of them with the passage of time that there is little or no hope of rebuilding the Temple or reinstituting the sacrificial rituals. This impossibility is believed not as due to the impiety of the Gentiles, but as Yahweh's will. A re-reading of Scripture reveals to many Pharisees that Moses and the Prophets insist on the inner man, on interior worship, on spiritual attachment to the faith of Israel.

Wandering from coastal town to coastal town, the leaders of the various sects keep in constant, if frictional, touch. Out of the controversies between diehard Pharisees, spiritualist Pharisees, disappointed Sadducees who desire a re-establishment of the Temple, and defeated nationalists, there emerge several dissident parties. The chief, and numerically the most important one, is the Orthodox Spiritualists who deny the nationalist interpretation of the law of Yahweh and Israel. Closely allied to them are the Gentilic Jews. Next in number are the moderate Traditionalists. Lastly, there is a group of diehard Traditionalists.

In 85 A.D. these extreme traditionalists, allied with nationalistic groups from the surviving Zealots and Essenians, separate themselves from the main body of Jews and retire together to Askhelon. They again set about the preparation of revolt and war. The group of moderate Traditionalists, who will have nothing to do with either the hothead nationalists or the Spiritualists, remove themselves by 90 A.D. to Bene Berak, under the leadership of Rabbi Ben Joseph Akiva. They send two delegations to Rome, one in 105 A.D., and the second in 127 A.D., in order to petition the Emperor that the Temple be rebuilt.

The first petition is turned down after fair promises are made. The second petition is a desperate attempt to avoid another revolt. When it is refused, these Traditionalists ally themselves with the extremists and nationalists and prepare for a common revolt. An uprising in 130 A.D. is easily crushed. The Romans' task is aided by the Orthodox Spiritualists who, representing the majority of the Jewish population, have disassociated themselves completely from sects espousing armed rebellion and other nationalistic aims, and they have assured the Emperor by a delegation in 115 A.D. that only a minority of the Jews support the Traditionalists' petition to rebuild the Temple.

By 150 A.D., it becomes possible for non-Jews to become members of the Spiritual sect in Israel without having to submit either to the rigors of circumcision or to the legal particularism of the former Jewish Oral Law. Circumcision for Gentile converts is abolished as the Spiritualist perception of the Prophets deepens. Physical circumcision is now seen to have originated as a racial mark: all the physical descendants of Abraham were circumcised when it was important that they be distinguished from the melee of tribes, clans, and nations occupying the land of Canaan in the second millenium before Christ. It is argued subtly that circumcision could not be the essential mark of a Jew. Women do not undergo this initiation, yet they are reckoned as Jews. In fact, only a man born of a Jewish mother can proclaim himself a Jew and therefore

undergo circumcision. A theological and logical contradiction
is thus uncovered. If circumcision has any value, it is concluded, it is because it indicates that the new member of
Judaism cuts himself off from evil. Now this must be moral
evil. And moral evil starts and ends essentially in man's conscience and heart and mind.

The abolition of circumcision for non-Jewish converts fa-
cilitates the admission of great numbers of Gentiles. But the
discontinuance of the rite for Gentiles eventually extends to
Jews also. A curious incident sparks this extension. Around 200
A.D., a shipload of black slaves from African lands west of
Ethiopia arrives in Caesarea for sale to Jewish landowners.
All the males are found to be circumcised. Inquiries show that
in their tribe circumcision is practiced purely for what they
consider aesthetic reasons. With such happenings and the developing teachings of Orthodox Spiritualists, it becomes normal practice to circumcise or not circumcise Jewish children
according to the wish of their parents. But because the
Graeco-Roman world looks upon circumcision as a mutilation,
the normal practice among Jews becomes not to circumcise.
By the end of the third century, Jewishness is no longer associated in the popular mind with any racial identification.
Judaism, too, has begun to spread to many upper Roman
classes.

Because the Jewish people are no longer identified with a
definite geographical area, a particular kind of temple cult or
sacrifice, or even with one race of people, the attitude of the
Christian organization toward them changes. By now, Judaism
has evolved a more refined idea of the Messiah. The Spiritualists had at first identified the expected Messiah with the Jewish
people. Gradually, however, as the concept of the Jewish people
enlarges (due to the transformation of physical circumcision
into spiritual circumcision) the racial element diminishes. So
also the messianic character of this spiritual "Jewish" people is
described in universalist terms: social organization and unity,
national peace and prosperity.

Although remnants of the Traditionalist group have continued to exist, by the end of the third century it is not they but
the Spiritualists who, in effect, are recognized as embodying
the faith known as Judaism. By this time all the main characteristics of the new Judaism have crystallized: a spiritual interpretation of the Law; a universalization of the Jewish faith due

to the mitigation of the racial aspect, the denial of the central function of Jerusalem as the only Holy City, and the abandonment of material sacrifices; and, finally, an identification of the messianic tradition with the "Jewish" people.

By the end of the fourth century, when the last military and political defenses of the crumbling Roman Empire are at an end, the "Jewish" people step naturally into the shoes of their Roman predecessors. The remnants of the Traditionalist Jews, however, and the Christian Church are always at each other's throats, and both are afflicted with a chauvinism in each other's regard: they hate each other; each claims to be the Chosen People of a God of Justice and Love; each claims a Messiah,—the Christian one has come, the Traditionalist Jewish one is yet to come.

The purpose of this scenario is to explore alternatives to the maintained racialism inherent in traditional Judaism. There is ample halakhic and haggadic evidence from Judaism of the first four centuries to prove that the distinction between physical and spiritual circumcision not only existed in the minds of Jewish theologians and Bible commentators, but that they insisted on the necessity of both. The reaction of the Christian Church to such a spiritualization of Judaism would have been a key factor in the resulting history of the two religions. The vitally formative period for the subsequent history of Judaism lay between the destruction of Jerusalem in 70 A.D. and the Second Jewish Revolt in 133-135 A.D. In this period, the opposition to the Christian Church hardened, the Christians developed their pro-Roman, anti-Jewish bias. Had any other alternative but this resulted from the 1st century A.D., the mutual relations of Judaism and Christianity would probably not have been riven with mutual hatred and jealousy. Furthermore, the Christian Church would not have been the only existent force in 5th century Rome capable of filling the vacuum left by the eviscerated imperial power.

Scenario C: Ecumenical Movement of Jews and Christians

For some 30 years after the fall of Jerusalem in 70 A.D., mutual relations between the Jews and Christians both in Palestine and throughout the eastern Mediterranean world are of the extremest animosity and the profoundest bitterness. Most of the Christians are Greeks or people of Greek culture, but their Greek wisdom has never prompted the Christians to get to know the Jews. Most of the Jews are practicing the Law, but the purity of that Law has never impelled them to accept the good in their adversaries. Jews and Christians are the stock-in-trade examples of born enemies, the eternal incompatibles.

A strange thing happens to the Christians in the year 100 A.D. Jesus does not return again to earth for the final judgement on all men. A majority of Christians have waited in fear and expectation for this second coming: it was to be the solution of all their ills. As strange an experience is undergone by the Jews: the Son of Man foretold in Daniel does not appear to rebuild the Temple. He should have done so; for the Beast— the Roman—violated the Holy of Holies 30 years ago.

At first, the Christians are nonplussed. In fact, they stop taunting the Jews with the failure of the Son of Man to appear. The Jews find little consolation, however, in this double failure. With the passage of some five years, the thinking men on both sides turn their eyes once more to consider their position rationally in the light of their basic teachings. In 106 A.D. a peculiar document is circulated through the Christian communities. Written in Greek, probably by a converted Jew who had become a priest, it contains a stinging denunciation of many past teachings. A few years later, its main points have been generally accepted and result in a proliferation of similar denunciations. They all unhesitatingly declare that the Christian teachers and writers who predicted the final end for the year 100 have deceived them. Some examine the four Gospels with a critical eye, discarding as fabrications all the words attributed to Jesus about an imminent end. Some even ask how Jesus, the most perfect of Jews, who preached love above all other things, could have indulged in some of the epithets and abusive language put on his lips? The original document had shown that all the Gospels represent Jesus as surrounded by crowds of hate-hissing Jews who incessantly sought his entrapment and who finally encompassed his death, in spite of the best efforts of a weak but humane Roman Governor. But the writer knew this was not true. From his pen and the mouths of Christians who survived from those days a blinding truth is revealed—and believed: Pontius Pilate was not only weak, he was a blood-thirsty, lecherous, cruel, merciless animal of a man.

The Jews, following their rivals' self-examination, suddenly find that their position resembles very much that of the Christians: the prophecy of Daniel has not been fulfilled, and they are surrounded by difficulties on all sides. It must be that Yahweh has reserved it for a later age and for a more worthy generation. Yahweh has withheld his mercy in the past only when obduracy and blindness have taken hold of his people. The Pharisees undertake a detailed review of their recent history to discover their mistakes and do penance for them. First of all, it became clear to them that they had been wrong in advocating the massacre of the Christian Jews in the revolt of 66-70 A.D. This realization leads them to a critical rejection of the nationalism which animated them from 44-70 A.D. And from this it is but a logical step to reconsider the once virulent Christian accusation that they engineered the crucifixion of Jesus. At this point, in the years 112-118 A.D., some first contacts take place between the Jewish and Christian communities living in Tiberias.

"Misery creates brothers," the old Arab saying goes. From being able to salute each other civilly in the streets, the two communities progress to practicing the ordinary politenesses and courtesies. Some years of this mutual truce finally culminate in discussions at the marketplace and in caravans—two places where they both have an independent right to be. Eventually, leaders on both sides meet informally for the first time at a pre-arranged spot—the trading house of an Armenian merchant. From then onward discussions multiply and with discussions mutual understanding increases.

By 118 A.D. the Christians are readily admitting that the original followers of Jesus had planned and intended revolt and sedition. In fact, the original followers thought Jesus was going to found anew the kingdom of David and rule over the whole earth. Jesus himself never intended this, however, they assert. The Jews agree, adding that it is common knowledge among the surviving Pharisees and Sadducees that the midnight arrest of Jesus in the Garden of Gethsemani and his subsequent scourging and crucifixion were all part of a plan necessarily followed because of the harsh threats of Pontius Pilate and the momentary weakness of two priests who feared for their positions.

Having disposed of any accusation against either the Pharisees, the priestly caste of Sadducees as a whole, or against the

Jewish community of Jerusalem, the Jews and Christians extend their mutual acknowledgments. The Jews affirm that Jesus was just, that he did work miracles, that he died nobly. They know that his body was buried and that it was missing on the third day afterwards. They do not know if God resurrected him from the dead. The Christians proceed to think out their position clearly. They know that the Jews are the Chosen People of Yahweh, and Yahweh does not change his eternal decision. The Jews still expect the Messiah. The Christians also regard much of what Paul wrote about the abrogation of Israel's right as inconsistent with the Jews' status as the Chosen People. An insurmountable illogicality exists in Paul's doctrine that all ascribe to his prejudice against his former co-religionists.

Both Jews and Christians experience a humiliating realization: it is noted that both Jewish and Christian doctrine is based on the love and the mercy of God, yet neither has practiced this love and mercy for the other.

When it becomes obvious that the Christians are going to undergo some persecution and the Jews are not going to receive permission to rebuild the Temple, the custom of using the same building as a Synagogue and as a Church comes into vogue. An audacious rabbi and a rather revolutionary bishop in Antioch do this for the first time in 120 A.D. The custom takes hold, especially since Christians lack Churches in some places, and the Jews lack Synagogues in other areas. Gradually, from praying before meals in common, they begin to pray together in the mutually shared building. Of course some traditionalist leaders on both sides issue edicts, condemnations, and ex-communications against the initiators of this daring move, but to no avail.

By 150 A.D., a profound change begins to make itself felt. Jews and Christians have been praying and working and talking together for about 30 years. A large minority of Jews believe that Jesus was the Messiah. Almost all Christian Jews maintain the rite of circumcision and observe Jewish ritual laws for purity in religious worship, in agriculture, in commerce, in traveling. There have been a few cases of intermarriage, but in general this is frowned upon because each side still claims that the children should be reared in its religion. Some think that the children should be reared in the religion of the father. A small handful thinks it should be left up to the children themselves.

A heresy starts with the influx of Greek concepts and Greek scholarship in the middle of the 2nd century. Until then, Christians have been calling Jesus the "Messiah." In their prayers the majority of non-Jewish Christians address him as the "Son of God." Jewish Christians address him as the "Son of Man." Very few Christians, only the very refined and subtle Greeks and Romans, address him as "God." This title is reserved by the Semites exclusively for the being who spoke to Abraham, Isaac, Moses, and who led the Chosen People out of Egypt. Even Paul in his writings rarely, if ever, addresses or describes Jesus as God.

Now, however, heretics arise among the Jews and among the Christians. The Jewish heretics claim that the Messiah, whether he has come or is to come, will be a mere man. Orthodox Jewish doctrine holds that he is not mere man, that he is more than man. The Christian heretics claim that Jesus was an ordinary man into whom God poured special gifts and to whom he gave special powers and help. Both orthodox Jews and Christians join together in stamping out this heresy, because both sides agree that it springs from the same heretical source called Naturalism. Naturalism was started in the early 2nd century by an Alexandrian Greek who held that man's nature was divine and was capable of all things. It later developed into full-blown Gnosticism.

The first formal council of Jews and Christians takes place in 184 A.D. at Alexandria. There the orthodox Jewish position is declared: the Messiah is not mere man; he is a man specially associated with God; that which is man in him is the same as the human nature in all men except the innate sinfulness of men. But the resident quality and endowment by which he is Messiah and the Chosen of Yahweh, this is from God, this is God in him. In other words, the Messiah is true man, and the true God is in him.

The orthodox Christian position is also affirmed: Jesus the Messiah is not mere man; he is true man in all things except in man's inherent sinfulness. God, however, united this human nature of Jesus with his own being so that it belongs wholly to him. Both sides condemn any teaching which would grant the Messiah (Jesus for the Christians) mere inspiration such as Isaiah or Jeremiah or Moses was granted. Messiah-hood is something more. And this is sufficient to condemn the heretics on both sides.

For more than a century the leaders of both religions are engrossed in the task of keeping stability in their communities and of inserting the orthodox creeds (mutually agreed upon at Alexandria, then at Antioch in 236 A.D., and at Jerusalem in 310 A.D.) into the fabric of their people's existence and thought. By the end of the 4th century, both Jews and Christians are installed in Rome and throughout the Roman Empire. They provide the only stabilizing element in an otherwise crumbling world.

Mutual love and collaboration between Christians and Jews could have resulted from a change of direction at the turn of the first century A.D. if logic, not partisan passion, had prevailed over men's minds, and if these men had been faithful to the basic principles of the religion which they defended so acrimoniously and so bitterly. A God of love is ill-served by hate and persecution. A God of truth and justice is insulted by deliberate blindness and wrongful attribution of evil motives. If God were God, in such a case, he would leave men to be punished by the lethal consequences of their own fanciful projections. The problem confronting the religious historian is really why relations between the Jews and the Christians did not take some such turn. If a network of interrelating interests had been worked out over a number of decades, say between the 2nd and 6th centuries A.D., it would be perhaps possible to speak of a truly Jewish-Christian foundation of Western civilization.

4. The Testament of Akiva

The man who made Israel's decision and Judaism's choice in their priceless moment was Akiva Ben Joseph. Akiva left a testament of biblical interpretation and legalism to Judaism which has remained with it for over 1800 years. That testament embodying his decision is now the heavy and cumbersome load under which modern Judaism stumbles and is threatened with failure.

When we examine the contours of Judaism about 130 A.D., some five years before Rabbi Akiva's death by Roman executioners, we find that Judaism, under the influence of his teaching, had definitively chosen what to snatch from the destruction and meaninglessness of total national defeat in 135 A.D. It chose the purifying and ascepticizing fire of juridical judgement and legal discernment into the requisites for survival according to the Law of its God. The second and last revolt against the Roman occupation would end in 135 A.D. apparently leaving Judaism politically and socially an eviscerated ruin. But, in reality, only its shell was shattered; the hard core of its being burned full for almost 2,000 years more.

That choice of moral judgement within biblical phraseology, in ethical discernment, guided by minute prescriptions in halakhic reasoning, based sometimes on three-word quotations from the Bible, fixed the character of Judaism into hardened molds. It defined Judaism primarily as a system of knowledge, only secondarily as a method of ethical behavior and liturgical procedure. It created the Talmud which, in its Babylonian version, runs into 18 printed volumes and millions of words. It bred a race of doctors, commentators, exegetes, philosophers, theologians, and lawyers, right down to our day. Finally it made inevitable the inescapable dilemma of Judaism today: locked in between Israeli nationalism and the assimilative Judaism of the Diaspora, its only alternative is to take refuge in the outworn and anachronistic stances of Orthodoxy.

But of immediate importance and preponderant influence was the Law which Akiva helped mightily to create. Thus consecrated by the school of Akiva, it became the center of Judaism's life and pains. It was torn from the hands of Jews by rampaging Crusaders in Cologne in the 11th century and was extracted from among the grisly remains of emaciated men in Dachau in the 20th. It has been elaborated, interpreted, formulated, refined, analyzed, with split-hair decisions, almost to the point of conceptual narcissism. It created the cohesion of the medieval ghetto in Italy, Spain, Germany, Poland, Russia, France, and the Balkans; and it was as much the reason for the Warsaw rising in 1940 against the Nazi oppression as for the prestige of the *rebe* in the central European *staedtl* of the 19th century as he resolved the scruples of a cobbler by candlelight in Posen and solemnized marriages in the ragged and forgotten communities of western Russia, thus conferring honesty and meaning on the pain of a life led in outlaw fringe status. It was the guiding light for disputant merchants in Venice of the Renaissance, for pinstripe-suited rabbis in mid-Manhattan temples of the 20th century, as it was for their counterparts in Tunis, in Algeria, and in Amsterdam of the 16th century. It has been studied, chanted, carried, fondled, at the Wailing Wall in June 1967, in London subways, on Boeing 707 strato-cruisers 30,000 feet over the Atlantic, with Israeli tank corps heading down the Mizpa pass in the Sinai peninsula to the Gulf of Aqaba, and on the Polar Cap at sub-zero temperatures. Every time the neon sign of a kosher delicatessen gleams on Broadway, or a bar-mitzvah takes place in Cincinnati or Caracas, or Yom Kippur is celebrated in Mea Shearim, Jerusalem, the shadow of Akiva stands in the background.

This persistence in being and that fire are the work of this gnarly patriarch of Judaism's winter. For him defeat was only a reason for greater exertion; when Judaism was riddled with doubts, death, desertion, rumors, intrigues, betrayals, faintheartedness, and exile in poverty, he erected the "fence" of Judaism, the Law. Thanks to his achievement, the Orthodox Jew of today is far nearer to the Diaspora Jew of 1800 years ago than the latter was to his predecessor, the Babylonian exile, three hundred years before that. But thanks to Akiva's choice, Israel need not worship the god of Israel and Judaism has logically become Jewishness.

Akiva's decision was made in great tranquillity of spirit and as the result of a long effort. He acted neither hastily nor in desperation. If we of the late 20th century could have asked him towards the end of his life for a commentary on his major achievement, he might have spoken somewhat as follows:

"I, Akiva, son of Joseph, now addressed as Rabbi by many in Israel, woke one morning, performed my prayers and ablutions before the Holy One. But on that day, all landmarks had gone: I could not turn with joy eastwards to participate in the daily sacrifice of the Temple; no presence of the Holy One hovered over Israel; no songs were sung in honor of his name. God had moved. The guiding landmark of all my maps, views, prayers, journeys, hopes, and fears, this had not merely been blurred by the garish glare of good men's corpses rigidly crucified in concentric circles. Nor had it merely diminished to less than a cloud no bigger than the palm of the hand. It had disappeared past the silhouette of human events, past the shadows of memory, into the unimaginable world of his being apart. Tomorrow and the day after and the day after, I would rise and go through the same motions. Yet I knew that something had passed away from our lives. You ask: 'Your house has burnt down. What have you salvaged from it?' I answer: 'The fire.' All else, brick, wood, gold, paper, victim, altar, priest, farmer, merchant, patrician, nation, is consumed. Only the fire endures."

By a tantalizing cruelty of history, we have utterly meager biographical details about this one man. We moderns, so preoccupied with personal psychology and addicted to factual descriptions of great personalities, are at a loss in Akiva's regard. We know very little, and legend has obscured much. His dates are approximate but sufficiently so. He was born about 40 A.D. and he died about 135 A.D. His birthplace and his tomb are not known with any certitude, but Lod in southwestern Israel and Tiberias on the lake of Galilee, respectively, are usually designated. His father was a laborer. His wife, Rachel, is unknown to us otherwise. He had two sons and two daughters.

He took up formal study about the year 80 A.D. at Yavneh, spending about 13 years learning and studying. At the age of 55, he set out to reconstruct the Law and to found his own school at Bene Berak. He undertook at least three great journeys for Judaism's sake: one to Rome, when he was about 55; one to Nehardea in Babylonia, at the age of 70, in order to regulate the calendar; and a third to Egypt, at the age of 90, in order to intercede with the Emperor Hadrian for the restoration of the Temple at Jerusalem. He was executed for refusing to cease his study and teaching of the Jewish Law.

Legend sparingly tells us of his physique: he was of abnormal height, prematurely bald, sharp-eyed, of an iron constitution. His spiritual qualities are given in greater detail: rigorous self-discipline and superabundant commiseration; practical good sense and a mystical perception; stubbornness of principle and adaptability to circumstances; deep humor and a stark intolerance of error. He was said variously to have had 12,000 and 20,000 disciples, to have been flogged five times during his early years at Yavneh for supposed misdemeanors, to have visited Paradise during his lifetime, to have been the counsellor of Roman matrons, to have paid his debts by miraculous supplies of money and, like Albert the Great, Thomas Aquinas, and Francisco Suarez in another age and religion, to have been initially impervious to all learning. The picture, vastly exaggerated in transmission, could not have come to us otherwise.

Yet the residue of accuracy in his story humbles the mind with
its towering performance.

Akiva was still a shepherd when the Roman armies captured
and burnt Jerusalem and its Temple, in 70 A.D. The surviving
leadership of Judaism, under the inspiration of Johanan Ben
Zakkai, settled in Yavneh, a coastal town. Here the conclave of
Israel met and functioned for sixty years until all was swept
away in the abortive revolt of 135 A.D. Akiva arrived in
Yavneh sometime about 80 A.D., when Judaism was still stumbling and reeling from the disaster of ten years earlier. It was
still wandering at the fatal crossroads of history, seeking a
reconstruction of its worship and a regrouping of its official
leaders who endeavored to see clearly in what direction salvation lay.

The damage suffered by Judaism was huge. There remained
no central sanctuary, no governmental contact with the mass
of the people, no revenues, a pitiful number of surviving
priests. Its leadership was reduced to a ragged nationalism
which now went underground in Galilee and the Negev. The
Roman fist held the sword of dissolution poised and near at its
throat. The burning question: what to do?

At Yavneh and other coastal towns, the surviving heads of
the nation gradually reassembled. It was a brilliant and motley
group of men: patricians such as Gamaliel II, Jose ha-Kohen,
Simeon Ben Nathanel, Johanan Ben Nuri, Haninah Ben
Teradyon, Tarfon who was Akiva's first teacher; plebeians such
as Ben Azzai, Simeon Ben Zoma, Pappias, Joshua Ben Hananya.
There were some groups of Sadducees bereft of dignity and
wealth; disorganized and disequilibrated patricians; single
Essenian pietists and extremist nationalists; Shammaite and
Hillelite students and followers of all the patrician and
plebeian factions which had participated in the revolt of 66 A.D.
and had escaped the shattering death of its cataclysmic end.

Many of the survivors, such as Zadok the priest-scholar,
walked alone with the long night of Israel's last moments and
with their god's universe, thus masking their own poverty of
alternatives. Some, such as Eleazar of Modin and Nahum of
Gimzo, due to an underlying parochialism, chose private
retreats, ivory-towers of piety and resignation, from which they
delivered themselves of opinions on dominant issues of the day
and then promptly fell silent. Some, such as Jonathan the Cobbler, Matthew Ben Harash, and Judah Ben Bathyra, essentially

private men *manqués,* shattered by the overnight destruction
of that world which had been built up on slow deposits of pride,
power and belief, now crossed the borders of Israel or travelled
over the sea into obscure exile. Others still permitted themselves
no luxury of a relevant decision, and lost either their reason
like Simeon Ben Zoma or their religious faith like the philo-
Roman Elisha Ben Abuya. Many, however, worked together to
find a solution. But no man in that scintillating congregation
of persistent survivors surpassed Akiva in his grasp of religion
at the grass-roots, in his knowledge of the artisan, the dirt-far-
mer, the hired laborer, the petty shopkeeper. He knew to what
tones they harkened, to what sensibilities they were prone, to
what ethical necessities they were exposed, to what extent the
belief of Israel still lay as marrow in their bones, fire in their
hearts, thoughts in their minds. Yet, as we noted, Akiva took to
book-learning late in life. He became a leader at a still later
date. What was the secret of his success? Undoubtedly, he had
a burning faith in Israel's destiny, and he had the gift of being
able to communicate this. But Akiva was more than a mere
memorial to undying faith. Chiefly, he was a triumph of innate
character.

Until the age of 40, he knew best the grazing habits of sheep
and goats and cattle. He was most skilled in the shifting pattern
of wet, dry, cold, warm, and stifling weather which determined
his daily location and activity. His judgement had been honed
and sharpened on the qualities of hoof and shank and sheep's
wool. Yet, when he died at the age of 95, he was not merely
adept in the subtle niceties of Pharisaic law and familiar with
the Bible to the point of total recall; he had formed an intui-
tional synthesis of where Judaism stood and of its road for
self-preservation.

There is no doubt that Akiva shared the general efferves-
cence gripping the coastal community; in effect, the defeat of
70 A.D. was not read as ultimate defeat. Many saw it as a preparation, a purification of Israel, and a prelude for the advent
of Elijah or the Messiah. All those who stayed and worked
understood it as just one more punishment from God. But they
kept faith in the Promises to the Fathers, and they believed
that the God of Israel would keep his pledge. Only the very
faint-hearted refused to reorganize. There is no great doubt
about Akiva's nationalism. It was inherent. This was one of the
great man's blind spots, his painful limitation, and the Achilles

heel of his solution. He resisted the clamor of extremist nationalism until the end, but a realistic analysis of the political situation would have saved him the fatal error he finally made. This nationalism led him to work and travel for the rebuilding of the Temple at Jerusalem and for the restoration of Israel as a sovereign nation.

The main lack in Akiva's analysis was that the normative Judaism, which he helped to develop and to give to his fellow Jews, envisaged a central sanctuary and a national independence. Mediterranean power-politics and the logic of history did not form any appreciable part of his education. But to grasp the significance of this weakness in Akiva's reconstruction efforts, we must review his achievement as a totality. Once Akiva had completed his studies, his thrust at leadership and dominance was ruthless, masterly, and overpowering. He deliberately challenged the established leaders, opposed and criticized Shammaite teachings, founded his own academy at Bene Berak, and fought unremittingly against interpretations of the Law which favored the patrician class and which differed from his own. Akiva was a supreme individualist.

His dominant preoccupation was with the Law; not merely with its written form as contained in the Pentateuch, but with the body of legal and moral rules which Pharisaism and the doctors of Israel had developed since the time of Ezra. It has often been said that Akiva and his followers stressed the Law to the practical exclusion of many other elements in the tradition of the Second Commonwealth. This would be both unjust to the men of Yavneh and inaccurate as a portrait of Akiva. Any evidence we have indicates strongly that Akiva envisaged a restored Temple and Temple worship, and this implied sacrifice and priesthood. Sometimes, it is implied that traditional doctrines were de-emphasized in the Akiva synthesis—the Messiah doctrine for instance. But this cannot have been true, and no shred of evidence is available to prove it.

Akiva did institute a fresh synthesis of theological speculation and doctrine with the ancient principles of ethical and moral behavior. Herein lay his innovation. Before, the late Israelitism of the time of Josias (7th century B.C.) and the Judaism of the last three centuries before Akiva's time had always contained two currents of religious activity. The two had vied for domination: neither one ever displaced the other, and both traced their lineage back in time and generations of believers past the reform of Josias, beyond the centralization of David and Solomon, to the 11th century form of belief. One current may be termed the *mystical* or intuitive current. Its main theme was immediate contact with the All-High, the thunder and lightning and gentleness of his periodic theophanies, the celebration of his beauty and his strength. The other can be termed the *rational* or discursive current. This issued in a moral code and a prescriptive list of ethical sanctions and duties touching on personal morality as well as beliefs and dogmas. When Saul proclaimed the Law of Yahweh at Gilgal to the assembled 12 tribes of the ancient federation, he was activating the rational current. When he stole at midnight into the cavern of the Witch of Endor to learn his fate on the morrow in battle with the Philistines, he was seeking to obtain direct, mystical contact with the beyond.[1]

We find these two currents reproduced throughout the history of Israel. It would seem that the mystical and intuitive current belonged to the same branch of tradition to which the Yahweh theme also belonged. They can be traced back among the teachers and the "pairs" who flourished during the period of the Second Temple, as well as in the Dead Sea Scrolls. The heterogeneous character of the *Manual of Discipline* becomes more intelligible in this light, as well as the well-known division of Isaiah's writings. Chapters 1-39 of the latter are the rational and discursive current; chapters 40-66 are a prolonged excursus into the mystical and intuitive. Once the first codification of the Law had been achieved, the opposition between the mystical and the rational could only be emphasized. But no clash took place between them until the whole story was over and Akiva with his generation were dead and gone. Continuous friction occurred throughout the Second Temple period. Generally, because of the growing importance of Pharisaical legal doctrine and its significance on the national scene, the mystical was relegated to the background. It flourished among the fringe groups, the Essenians, the Zealots, the Sicarii. Now, when Akiva was at his height at Bene Berak, and when revolt with

---

[1] The credit for bringing out the traits of both these currents in Judaism must go to A. J. Heschel, in his *Torah Min Hashamayim Bespeklarya Shel Hadorot.* It is obvious that the two are also present in the New Testament writings and throughout the theology and piety of Christianity.

his blessing was imminent, any one of the two currents could have prevailed.

The mystical current did not, and this for two main reasons. Firstly, the nationalists of Akiva's time drew their inspiration not from the legalism and precise moral definitions of Akiva and his Pharisaical colleagues, but from the intuitive vision of Israel's glory fraught with eschatological rewards for the Chosen People and apocalyptic punishment for their enemies. The motive was charismatic, not rational; it was not legalistic or based on prescriptive rights and canonical arguments. But the revolt of 133-135 A.D. meant the utter ruin of such groups. Rome was determined to hold Palestine; already the latter's geopolitical importance as a see-saw between North Africa and eastern Europe and Asia Minor was clear to them. With the end of this nationalism, the mystical current lost all claim to a deciding vote in Israel's fate. It lingered on in the scattered Essenians, had a small lease of life in Qaraism, and provided inspiration for the medieval Jewish Qabbala and the 17th century Hasidic movement. A strong argument can be made that it was due to this current that the world benefitted from the flashing volcano of Jewish creativity in European arts and sciences of the 18th century and onwards. One can trace the two currents also in early Christianity. The Fourth Gospel, for instance, belongs to the inner-directed tradition, whereas the Gospels of Mark and Luke belong to the cosmos-directed current and the rational consideration of man and his destiny. The Gospel of Matthew is of mixed character, thus betraying its composite origin.

The second and main reason was the Akiva emphasis. Akiva's emphasis must be understood. All his colleagues emphasized the importance of the Law, written and oral. The emphasis which Akiva communicated to it sprang from the brilliance of his treatment of the Law. A great teacher or expert in anything generally adds significance and importance to the subject or themes of his teaching and his expert knowledge. So it was with Akiva. He was the first legal expert, for instance, who insisted on applying the Law to the needs of the common people, the *am ha-aretz*, who had been despised by the former Jerusalemite community. His rulings and modifications were gauged to this grass-roots level of the population. When the upper classes were liquidated by war, and the priestly class was ended by Roman imperative, there remained as the stock of Israel only this *am ha-aretz.* There existed no proletariat in our modern sense; proletariat is an urban phenomenon and ancient Israel was essentially rural with small urban islets.

Akiva further emphasized the importance of the Law. He maintained that everything in the Pentateuch had been revealed; nothing was the result of mere human ingenuity or the effect of human weakness. He had an almost mathematical approach to what had become an amorphous mass of apothegms, *obiter dicta,* maxims, proverbs, proverbial rulings, analogies, allegories, and exegetical notes, all of which constituted the Oral Law of his time. In forming his own synthesis of teaching, he displayed the same characteristics of innovation, reliance on his own judgment, and a ruthless choice of alternatives, as before in the question of leadership. He did not hesitate to re-interpret the Bible freely when it suited his own opinions. He could produce hairsplitting distinctions as quickly as his colleagues. He replaced ancient norms and principles of Bible exegesis with his own newly-found ones. He developed an epigrammatic and apothegmatic form for principles of interpretation. He used dialectics as a rapier to destroy all opposition to his views.

It is generally admitted that the *Mishnah,* the *Tosefta, Siphra,* and *Siphre* originated in his teaching methodology. He had the added specialty that he could find a basis for any prescription of the Oral Law in the minutest jot, tittle, flourish, or element of the Written Law. His combination of dialectics, theology, personal reliance, intricate knowledge of the Law, and unquestioned integrity was irresistible. The Law itself could not but gain in prestige from such a prestigious master. But in so emphasizing the Law, Akiva prepared directly if unknowingly for the day that the Law would take over the whole weight of responsibility for the salvation and survival of Judaism. When finally all hope was lost of either a rebuilt Temple or of a regained national integrity and geographical independence, the Law took over their unitary and stabilizing functions. When the doctrines of Messiah, of afterlife, of sacrifice, of a spiritual Israel, had either been abandoned or watered down considerably because of the formidable onslaught of Christianity, there remained but the Law to be queen of Judaism's destiny. But this was after Akiva's death and well into the second half of the second century.

Akiva lacked an educated awareness of history. True to the tradition he represented, he built not merely his hopes but his very justification for his fresh theological synthesis on the hoped-for restoration of full national sovereignty, the rebuilding of the Temple, and the coming of the Messiah. But his acid analysis of law, morality, and the Bible did not exercise itself on historical events in a historical-minded way. He issued somber but non-historical-minded warnings. He refused the beckoning finger of the politics of violence. Power neither seduced him nor corrupted him, nor tempted him to exploit his gigantic prestige and masterful talents. Nothing was allowed to divert his time and energy away from what he considered to be the substance of things.

His travels to Rome to obtain from the Emperor Domitian a reversal of anti-Jewish legislation did nothing to enlarge his historical vision. In the small Christian sect he saw nothing but a bastard Jewish offshoot doomed to extinction on the periphery of religious reality. Akiva had keen, seismographic, almost preternatural insight into the importance of the Law. He relied on it, on the resurgence of the Jewish national state, on Yahweh's imminent punishment of the Roman invaders.

When the Trajan declaration of the years 110-112 A.D. promised the rebuilding of the Temple, he opposed the Nationalists who decried it as too little and the Christians who attacked it as too much. When Trajan's promise was retracted, he still refused to side with Ishmael and the other extremist nationalists who were bent on open rebellion. Even when Hadrian decided to rebuild Jerusalem as a Roman city, and to replace the Temple with a pagan shrine, Akiva still refused to sanction rebellion. In his eyes, the only necessary condition of Israel's persistence and final triumph, the study of the Law, was yet intact. Only when this study was forbidden did he turn favorably and support the military leader, Simon Bar Kokhba, who led the Second Jewish Revolt. "This is the Messianic king," Akiva is reported as saying, "the star which has come out of Jacob." Akiva cried for quick victory and hoped for divine intervention.

He was like a man shouting at the thunder. The expected victory did not result. The angels of Yahweh did not intervene. Simon Bar Kokhba was captured and executed; the main armies of revolt were decimated. The God of Israel had conferred no monopoly in inevitabilities on his chosen ones. All Jews, but not the Jewish followers of Jesus, were banished from Jerusalem forever. Akiva was first confined, then transported and imprisoned at Caesarea for three years. He was led out to execution in the dying autumn of Judaism, when Jerusalem had been sown with salt, and the plans of Aelia Capitolina were on the drawing-boards of the imperial architects; when schools, synagogues, rabbinical dwellings had been destroyed, ransacked, and pillaged, and the mass of the people were deported or fled into the long winter of exile.

This then was the paradox of Akiva's achievement and these were the limits of his greatness. He equalled the greatest in theological skill and dialectics. But his socio-political vision was myopic. Unknowingly he stood on the edge of two worlds, both his feet resting in the world about to dissolve forever, and his eyes unfocussed on the new world about to be born. Yet, at his execution, Akiva died unflinchingly as he had lived. As he sank up to the highest point of his consciousness of pain, and felt for the last time the heaviness of his old man's body almost freed of sensitivity and reaction to cold, to chains, to the quick lethal kiss of the death weapon, Akiva must have been in quiet, almost ecstatic triumph. The faith of Israel, if what he believed was true, was fenced around with a growing thicket of provisos and safeguards. It did not possess, for the moment, either Temple, priesthood, or schools. Nor was it bound to a shadowy Messiah or an imminent end to all things in a tremendous Last Day of conflagration. It was encased in a self-perpetuating Law, a traditional gnosis hidden from Gentiles but safe for the Chosen People; and it carried all the blessings of Yahweh with it.

By the end of the 7th century A.D., the work of writing down and codifying all the traditions connected with the Oral Law was complete. It was taught that both the Torah (Pentateuch) and the Oral Law came to Israel from the revelation on Mt. Sinai to Moses. The consecration of the Written Law went even further. Between the 7th and 9th centuries, a group of Egyptian Qaraites centered around the Asher family developed a new system of indicating the vowels of Hebrew writing.[2] Moses Ben Asher, and Ahron his son, elaborated the system. Within three centuries this had been adopted by normative Judaism, consecrated and considered as part of the revelation: to Moses had been revealed the vowel signs of every word of the Pentateuch. The Qaraites, on the other hand, were suppressed, and

[2] Cf. *The Cairo Geniza*, by Paul Kahle, Oxford, Clarendon Press, 1959.

their doctrinal heresies removed from current use. Qaraite manuscripts were altered and purged. Qaraism ceased to be a potential force in Judaism.[3] Judaism, however, had now completed the "fence" around the faith of Israel. The Law was not merely the sole guide of Israel's faith; but the material vehicle of the Law, the letters and the vowel-points, were now considered to be part of the Law of Sinai.

By far the greatest influence on the formation of normative Judaism, second only to the Akiva school of thought, was the early form which Christianity took. Treatment of this early form belongs properly in the next series of chapters on Christianity;[4] but the clash between Judaism and Christianity played a key role in the emergence of Judaism of the 2nd century onwards. We must mention here this clash and its main effects.

There can be doubt that at the beginning of the belief in Jesus of Nazareth, which we can date tentatively in the early '30s of the first century A.D., the first believers thought of themselves as Jews. Ethnically, the majority of them were Jews. This attitude, however, underwent a change. By the end of the first century, we find that the "Jews" are the enemies of truth, of salvation, of God—according to the first believers in Jesus. More importantly, the "Christians" have adopted the trappings of Judaism; they call themselves the Chosen People and inheritors of the spiritual and real Israel, in virtue of a new covenant written in the sacrificial blood of Jesus. The Messiah has come; all the promises to Jacob, Isaac, and Abraham are fulfilled. Despite half-hearted attempts of Paul to defend the title of "Chosen" for his compatriots, the overall persuasion of Christians was that they inherited the ancient title and all that went with it.

Judaism reacted violently against this attempt at usurpation. There is little or no record of the measures taken by the Jews of that time against the Christians; the former were under severe pressure politically and sociologically; besides, Christians were spoken of merely by coded names. We can measure, however, the violence of the Jewish reaction by noticing the change of emphasis in Jewish thought and teaching. There is, first of all, a diminution of emphasis on aspects of Jewish doctrine

[3] The most important modern Qaraite Synagogue is in Cairo, Egypt.

[4] See part II, seq.

which were thrown into particular relief by the beliefs and teachings of the Christians. The axiomatic roles played by the concepts of Messiah and of sacrifice are the most obvious. The failure of the Messiah to arrive in time to save Israel in 135 A.D. and the cessation of all sacrificial functions in Judaism due to the destruction of the Temple in Jerusalem, were merely circumstances which facilitated the diminution of emphasis on these two elements. The Messiah's era was thrust away into the very distant and unknown future. The personal character of the Messiah was diminished, to offset the Christian insistence on the person of Jesus. The divine affiliation of the Messiah which is clear in the latter-day writings of Judaism (notably in the Book of Daniel) was reduced to something little less than an option of Yahweh. Above all, Judaism acquired the consciously expressed principle that in its own framework of reference man needed no mediator whereby to reach his god. Modern-day writers such as Martin Buber and Leo Baeck have stressed this immediacy of the Jewish approach to the divine as contrasted with the Christian approach through Christ as its mediator. It is patently obvious, however, that throughout the history of Israel's religion, from the story of Abraham right down to the last book of the Bible, Judaism abounded in mediators: angels, prophets, lawgivers, judges, kings, even sometimes women. Moses, as he is depicted in the Judaistic writings of the 5th century B.C. was nothing more or less than a mediator, protecting his people from Yahweh's wrath, offering his own life in place of their safety, praying for the people's needs at the people's behest and request. The idea of mediation is inherent in biblical teaching. Normative Judaism practically abolished the idea of a mediator, as a reaction to the function which the followers of Jesus ascribed to him as supreme mediator between their god and man.

It is difficult now for us to assess the changes imposed on the old Judaism, in its worship, its prayers, and its synagogal liturgy, due to this willed differentiation from Christianity. Some idea can be obtained by comparing Samaritan prayers and liturgical formulae with both Christian and Jewish counterparts. We find that the Christian and Samaritan correspond on some essential points, but that the Jewish differs. This can only be because the Christians and the Samaritans preserve the original formulae and prayers, whereas the Jews changed theirs for the sake of differentiating from the Christians. The Samar-

itans never feared or clashed with the Christians; the Christians
never imitated the Samaritans; but both drew from a common
and ancient source. The most important effect which Christianity had on Judaism lies too deep for any verbal expression.
In such situations, it is difficult to make up one's mind which
inflicts the more profound wounds: the harsh bites of unwel-
come reality or the hidden wounds of conscience and broken
wills. There can be doubt that Judaism officially opposed Christianity, but neither can one doubt that the chief source of the
wound in Judaism was Christianity. Due to the ever more
straitened circumstances imposed gradually on Judaism by an
ever more victorious and dominant Christianity, there was
born in the Jewish soul an anguish of the spirit, a pain of the
inner self, which we can best and most sympathetically call
the Opposition.

Opposition to Christianity became seated in the very heart
of Judaism. At first, it was purely doctrinal. Rapidly in two centuries it became social and political. There was then born a
thing of beauty and pathos, of grandeur and misery, the inex-
tinguishable persistence of the Jew and his Jewishness, not
merely in spite of the oppressive Christian ambient, but because of that ambient. It is something which all men, despite
their prejudices and no matter what violences they have
wreaked on Jews, have recognized. Beauty, if we do not love it,
arouses opposition, anger, and even a desire to destroy it. But
it remains beauty. As we will note later, it is an irony touching
on fundamental blasphemy that a religion of love should have
officially fathered such a thing as the Opposition in the Jewish
soul.

The story of Akiva illustrates two principal lessons for students of religion. It reveals to us the source and the nature of
Judaism's fateful decision, when it stood at the crossroads of
history; and it lets us understand the total break with normative Judaism which the modern State of Israel made. Judaism's
decision is quite clear. Within five centuries, it had taken practical form in the Talmud and the tradition of rabbinic Judaism.
From these flowed its fundamental piety, its inherent legalism,
its non-historical attitude to the visible world of men and
things, its intransigence concerning all Gentiles.

The State of Israel, as we shall observe later, constituted not
merely a rejection of Akivaism and his legalism. Nor is it
merely an endeavor to break from the trammels of normative

Judaism. It is not a return to an Ishmaelism. It is, in a sense, a totally new experiment in Judaism. Israel is built on a mystical conception of the Land and of the People, their suprahistorical destiny and their transcendent unity. In this sense and this sense only, Israeli Judaism is a return to the preExilic type. It lacks, however, any of the religious beliefs or liturgical trappings which characterized Judaism in its early days. It is a secular state with no official god or temple or worship. It shares the nationalism, the mysticism, and the forthright daring of Ishmael but not his beliefs. It excludes his Judaism, but it jealously guards Jewishness as the sap of its being.

5. Children from Stones

We are now in a position to describe the physical modes of the dominance characteristic of Judaism. As explained earlier, dominance itself is defined initially in this study as an inner attitude, a mental posture. Inevitably this inner attitude gives rise to certain exterior attitudes. The people sharing this attitude look for and try to establish certain conditions in the physical world around them and, especially, in the social and political configurations of that world. Such conditions are called the physical modes of dominance. It is comparatively easy to enumerate the physical modes of Judaism's dominance: the *Land*, the *People*, the *Law*, the *Opposition*. But apart from a short analysis of what each physical mode connotes, the chief interest for this study is the evolution of these physical modes throughout the main periods of Judaism.

First Period: 12th-10th century B.C.

Initially during this period, all four of those physical modes were present in shadowy form. None of them had anything like the precision of later times. Some of them had a different or a smaller content.

The *Land* in no way coincided with the land of Israel as it was in Solomonic times or is today. Firstly, there was a total lack of geographical nationalism. The original six tribes and later on the twelve tribes within the federation were conscious in no way of the identification of all twelve with the land of each tribe. Each tribe, however, regarded its land as Yahweh's gift to it, as a tribe, as its promised land. No idea of a pan-Israelite land existed.

The *People* suffered from the same limitation. Lacking any national unity or common geographical identity, lacking also any fixed and unique sanctuary, there could be no concept of the People. The embryonic concept was that of those who bowed to the law of Yahweh. The later elaborated notion of the Chosen People did not exist.

The *Opposition* at that time concerned mainly the indigenous Canaanite inhabitants. But no wound to the soul resulted therefrom.

The *Law* was a series of moral and doctrinal prescriptions, probably some form of the Decalogue. We have no proof that a written form existed. Oral law existed vestigially in the explanations, judgments, decisions handed down by the Judges, the tribal Chieftains, and the Elders of the tribes. We cannot reasonably expect this to have been coded or subject to intricate legal procedures.

We should mention as two additional modes which existed then, the portable Ark and the vicarious sanctuary. Both had great importance. The ambulatory character of both was due to the nomadic and semi-nomadic origins of the tribes. The significance of these two modes is important: they signified a physical presence of Yahweh with the people who worshipped him. Both Ark and sanctuary implied a set of sacral functions: sacrifice, priest, prayers, offerings, fasts, etc.

Second Period: 10th-6th century B.C.

This was a period of evolution. The main cause of change was the institution of kingship. The four physical modes are described as they were at the time of the exile in 586 B.C.

The *Land* was now a defined geographical unit, the kingdom of David and Solomon. In David's day it had a somewhat greater extent. This land, however, did not correspond to the theological concept of the Promised Land of post-exilic times. As a land, it was considered to be the domain of the king, the product or result of his armies or his ancestors' prowess and power. It was not endowed with any charismatic character.

The *People* were divided into the northern and southern blocks ever since the accession of David. Again, their unity rested on the external institution of the monarchy, and not on any internal persuasion of an inherent unity due to the action of Yahweh. The notion of "Chosen People" was as yet vague and shadowy. Basically at that time, the people of Israel were united together under a king, and with that king they consented yearly to serve Yahweh.

The *Opposition* changed its content during these centuries. The old Canaanite threat had disappeared as did the Philistine menace. It was rather the threat of either Assyrian invasions from the north, or Egyptian domination from the south. It must be noted that this form of the Opposition is purely external, and threatened, not the very essence of Israelitism, but the external adjuncts of monarch and the new geographical nationalism—both elements not essential to Israelitism.

The *Law* had certainly been given some codification by the end of the 7th century and the beginning of the 6th. We have no proof that this codification coincided with the post-exilic Torah or Pentateuch. There was continuing tradition of oral commentary in ethico-religious matters, and one can presume that a semi-official group of men took care of such commentary.

The additional physical modes of this period are important. By the time of the Babylonian Captivity, the Temple in Jerusalem had been declared the only licit place in Israel for sacrifice, and the priestly class had been organized. The centralization conferred by this development was great indeed. But, thereby, Israelitism had united within it the two irreconcilables: the political system and the sacral system.

Third Period: 6th century B.C.—70 A.D.

The *Land* in this period was endowed with the charismatic quality of the Promised Land such as it is always described in post-Biblical writing and theology. It was now the only place where Judaism could subsist, because as a totality it had acquired the character of Yahweh's special gift to his people.

The *People* were no longer merely a matter of appartenance to a tribe or birth in a region. Membership was defined as belonging to the People who assented to the Law of Yahweh as it was promulgated by Ezra and the officials of the Second Commonwealth. There was thus conferred on this mode a new principle of unity. The excommunication of the Samaritans is a relevant example here. Ethnically Jews as much as Judeans or Benjaminites or Gileadites, the Samaritans ceased to belong to the People because they refused to accept the Law and the sacral center. No longer were Jews the people of Yahweh; they were his Chosen People whom he had brought out of the land of bondage into the Promised Land.

The *Opposition* again changes its content, and again it remains aimed against an external threat. The focal-point of the Opposition is, at first, the Persian domination, then Macedonian and Grecian rule, finally the sovereignty of imperial Rome. Because now the inner consensus of Judaism is associated, however ill-advisedly, with the external trappings of national identity and geographical unity, these threats are threats to Judaism. These are, however, external threats. None of them wishes to usurp the ethico-religious place of Judaism.

The *Law* now reaches ultimate codification. There arises, also, a body of men who set about the proper study of the Oral Law. Both Oral Law and Written Law are ascribed to Moses as the Lawgiver of Israel on Mt. Sinai. Because acceptance and observance of the Law is the qualifying mark of a true member of the People, the Law receives a sacrosanct character.

The additional physical modes are of paramount importance in this period. The centralization achieved by means of monarchical power is now confided to a priestly class flanked by doctors of the Law. Sacral and political are still united in one system. There is vast ramification of liturgical rules for ritual purity, for holiness, for Temple worship and participation. The entire Temple complex, Priests, Levites, Lawyers, is associated with the Sinai tradition and the grandiose figure of Moses. As his guardians and inheritors, these officials exercise a moral authority and control which is absolute. The doctors of the Law have become organized into the Pharisee sect with ramifications throughout the Land. Local worship and observance and knowledge of the Law are ensured by the synagogal system, which makes for unity of worship and orthodoxy.

Transition Between Third and Fourth Period

From 70 A.D. to 135 A.D. Judaism underwent its priceless moment. The physical modes of its dominance, while remaining basically the same as in the preceding period, were crystallized into the form they would take for the future until today. The transition has been documented in the past chapters; the final forms are summarized in the next paragraphs.

Fourth Period: 135 A.D. Onwards

The concept of *Land* and of *People* did not change from their status in the previous period. The value of both was emphasized, each one in a different way: the *Land* as that to which all aspirations tended, because only there could the true cult of Yahweh be instituted once more; the *People* because only they carried the possibility of true worship of Yahweh, and this was not completely possible in the lands of the Gentiles.

The *Law* achieved its full status. With the end of physical existence for the Temple, the priesthood, the geographical nationalism, the unity as a people, the only stabilizing and centralizing element became the Law. All the tendencies manifest in the last days of the Second Temple, and the excellence which the school of Akiva attained before the Second Jewish Revolt, came to the fore. We must understand in this term, the Law, both the Written and the Oral Law.

The change in the character of the *Opposition* was the principal catalyst of Judaism for the first three hundred years of this period. It was focused on the growing sect of the followers of Jesus. At first, the Opposition was aimed equally at Christians, Greeks, and Romans, among whom the Jews were exiled. Gradually and quickly, however, it shifted to focus almost exclusively on the Christians. For the Christians presented the first terrible threat to the essence of Judaism: they claimed to be the new Israel, to be the Chosen People, to have inherited all the blessings and to be enjoying all the promises.

This fundamental change in the character of the Opposition became only more ingrained as it took on social and political overtones. Christians exerted increasing social and political sanctions on the Jews whom they considered to have betrayed their heritage. The Church was Israel; the Synagogue was the Temple of Satan. The Christian was Jacob; the Jew was Esau. Christians started to use the very same terminology as Jews; both drew from the Bible, yet both interpreted this terminology in diametrically opposing ways.

Normative Judaism was now concretized within the four physical modes it would preserve for centuries to come. It had put into the background more ancient modes such as Temple, sacrifice, physical presence of Yahweh. It had mapped out its course and destiny for nearly 2,000 years.

PART II
Jesus and the Temple

6. *The Fisherman's Vision*

The four men set out to climb a mountain. It took them the best part of a hot summer day, and when they reached the top, they rested. Then, in the twilight, they knelt to pray. For this was the sole purpose of their visit. The mountaintop looked as if a great horse hoof had struck it in the dawn of time when all things were still molten. It was a rough, semi-circular, flat surface which rose towards the north, with zigzag fissures splitting its face. This tabletop mountain could be seen from the Mediterranean on a clear day. The local people referred to it as either the Devil's Trestle or God's Footrest.

The four men prayed in the positions which they always occupied on such occasions. One of them, Jesus, stood about twenty yards ahead of the others. The latter squatted, watching Jesus, whispering among themselves, and now and then praying. All four were Jews, had traditional Jewish names

59

(Simeon, Jacob, Johanan), and spoke Galilean Aramaic with
its split vowels and strongly accentuated gutturals.

Simeon was by far the most imaginative and impulsive, and
felt the mystery of this spot. Simeon sensed a change coming
over the place. Another world, dark and vast in outline, appeared beyond the flat rock on which they sat. The surprise of
it was as great as that of seeing a hairy husk concealing a
golden grain or a spotted anthill revealing the glory of a king's
grave. It seemed to Simeon that he was living on an island,
free of heaven and hell, unsponsored by any god, unharassed
by any demon. But it was not a godless world nor a desert.
From beyond the end of the rock there arose a medley of
flames, smoke, strange semblances, and nameless forms weaving in and out of sight—sharp Syrian profiles, flowing Bedouin
features, broad barbarian eyes, foreign faces, alien clothes,
which he knew were the marrow of his most unconscious
dreams. They snaked and trailed wordlessly in the smoke, appearing, approaching, melting, receding, dissolving, fainting
into shapelessness, disappearing like wax figures in a furnace
of phantoms touched by the sunlight. Then Simeon saw three
silhouettes. At first, what looked like three demonic figures from
some ancient etching, their eyes burning into him, marred the
godliness and shattered the evening peace. The sky was red-
dened by the dying fires of the sun. Gradually, the confusion of
detail melted away. The solid walls of the night sky parted as
curtains to admit a world of light and golden being. Flowing
shafts of brightness beat down like great archangels on the
tablerock. A hush possessed everything. Jesus stood, Simeon
could see, with Elijah and with Moses. Elijah he recognized by
the staff which he carried. Moses was marked by the twin
horns of light which sprang from his temples. The face of Jesus
had altered and now shone like the sun; his clothes glistened
intensely white, as no human light could whiten them.

Moses and Elijah were speaking with Jesus about his approaching sufferings in Jerusalem, his trial, his scourging, his
crucifixion, and the salvation which his death would accomplish, according to the sayings of the prophets of Israel. As
Simeon listened, only two incidents of the past kept insistently
racing past his memory in vivid flashes. One was the image of
an angry Jesus, eyes blazing, his voice raised in anger, his
words as cutting as whipcord on bare skin: "Get behind me,
Satan! You are not on the side of God but the side of men!" It

had happened on the road to Caesarea Philippi, about one week before. Jesus had foretold his death at the hands of the Priests, the Elders, and the Scribes in Jerusalem; and Peter had urged him to evade such an ignominious fate. How could Jesus become king of a restored Israel, if he died a criminal's death? The other incident was a now distant event, the moment Jesus had admitted him to his company: "Come with me and I will make you a fisher of men." Simeon had gazed at his nets, his boat, the waters of the lake of Galilee, its surrounding hills in their tranquillity, and the blue sky above them, for one last moment, and then turned abruptly and followed Jesus.

"Fisher of men," "God's side," "Satan"—the expressions traced a pattern interlocked with the talk of sufferings, crucifixion, resurrection, kingdom, Israel, salvation, glory now taking place between Jesus, Elijah, and Moses. All of a sudden he understood, and everything fell into place. Only one figure in all his religious knowledge fitted the picture of a suffering, triumphant king: the suffering but triumphant servant of Yahweh about whom the prophet Isaiah had spoken. A voice belonging neither to Elijah nor to Moses broke in on his thoughts: "This is my beloved son. Pay attention to his words."

Simeon, who was noted for his spontaneity of speech, could not restrain himself. "Master, I want to build three shrines here; one in your honor; one for Moses, and one for Elijah." Simeon said a lot more, but he knew that he was talking nonsense. Trying to express his feelings in words was like pouring water into too small a container; great drops of meaning kept splashing clear of the rim, running down and away from him. He seemed to be snatching out of bottomless profundities for the highest heavens, but the toiler in him, the fisherman, the digger of the earth, kept him in their toils. He remembered again the words of Jesus on the road to Caesarea Philippi: "The son of man must suffer much at the hands of the Elders, the Chief Priests, and Scribes and be killed, and after three days rise again. . . . Get behind me, Satan! You are not on God's side . . .". The rebuke hung in the air like an embodied question-mark, a sudden mystery of interrogation, initially refused recognition, because even to recognize it would transform it into a wounding shaft questioning his loyalty: "Do you wish to suffer with me and thereby enter my glory?"

Then its force became clear; it was an arrow against his breast. Whichever way he moved, it wounded him again and again. Simeon would remember this moment years later. He would spend lonely weeks pockmarked with little personal agonies and gnawing scruples. He had not assented immediately, —this was his self-reproach. Even at the end, when hanging upside down on a cross and dying, he would feel his failure and weep bitterly. Now he wanted to stretch his hands out to Jesus, to all the oppressed of Israel, to the unalives, the notalives, the impersons, the unpersons, to rid them of their shame in defeat and bondage, to snatch them free from the world of unlove and unbeing, to restore them to the happiness, prosperity, and the pride of a restored and glorious Israel. But his own self had become a riddle to him, a mystery he could not read. Then unconsciousness mercifully enveloped him, strains of singing, complaints, voices reached Simeon's ears, but he was already numbed and heavy with fear, with sadness, with suppressed sleep.

When Jesus woke him the following morning, Simeon saw no one on the flat tablerock but his companions. As they came slowly down the mountain, Jesus told the three of them not to reveal to any man what they had seen and heard until he had risen from the dead.

We will never know from any human resource whether the above event as recorded in the Gospels [1] is mythological or historical. It does not matter for the present context. All we need to know is that in the second half of the first century, sometime before the Fall of Jerusalem in 70 A.D., the writers and users of the Gospels believed, thought, and wrote in this fashion about Jesus of Nazareth. For there is perhaps no other passage in the Gospels which serves as well as this to illustrate the decision that the early followers of Jesus made within the life-span of those who had known and listened to Jesus or his immediate disciples. That fundamental decision concerned the attitude of Jesus' followers to the Jews, to Judaism, and to Israel. In the traditional thought of Christianity, since it became wholly a Western religion, this attitude has been, and is, one of two kinds.

Christians conceived of Christianity either as a total innovation in, or as a total transformation of, Judaism. As innovation, Christianity was thought to have taken what was valuable

[1] *Cf. Matt.* 17:1-8; *Mark* 9:2-8; *Luke* 9:28-36.

and true in Judaism; the rest was abrogated in its legality, nullified in its binding force, ridiculed as outworn and as God-rejected. As transformation, Christianity is said to have inherited all that Judaism was; all was then transformed from the crass, the material, and what was ineffective for reconciling man with God; it became spiritual, supernatural, a source of salvation. Underlying both attitudes is the judgement that Judaism as it was before the advent of Jesus no longer had any standing with God, any validity for human responsibilities. This was the decision made at Christianity's priceless moment.

The Transfiguration incident [2] described at the beginning of this chapter illustrates the mentality of Jesus' followers somewhat prior to the making and the implementing of that decision. But in order to grasp this mentality we have to abstract from all that Christianity subsequently became. We must travel back past the Christianity of the 16th century Reform; of the Renaissance; of the Medieval popes, emperors, and philosophers; of the Frankish Empire; of the 5th- and 6th-century Byzantine Empire; or even of the early Church of the 2nd and 3rd centuries, back to the state of things prior to the definitive rupture between Judaism and the followers of Jesus.

The early community of Jesus' followers did not conceive of themselves, and were not regarded, as either Christians or Judeo-Christians. There was no question of total transformation, much less of total innovation. As far as we can judge, those early followers believed that Judaism had culminated in Jesus: he would enable Israel to achieve its crowning glory. This was the Fisherman's vision. It would be replaced by another vision of Jesus, when Judaism formally rejected the followers of Jesus, and by still another when Christianity became a Roman-based and wholly Western religion. But this was the initial vision.

We conclude that this vision of the teaching and function of Jesus was merely one of many possible visions; that behind it as its source there stood a primordial religious experience undergone by those who associated with Jesus; and finally that the Fisherman's vision, as well as all the other and subsequent visions of Jesus, have only served to obscure that orig-

---

[2] The term "transfiguration" is derived from the Latin *transfiguratus est* used by the Latin translators to render the original Greek word in *Matt.* 17:2. The basic meaning of the latter is "transformed."

inal experience and the message of Christianity. A further conclusion developed throughout this book is that Christianity is in crisis today because it is unable to free itself from the obscuring effect of such visions. The contention of this chapter is that Christianity is in a crisis today from which there is an exit only if by an inner dynamism of its own it can divest its thought and behavior patterns of any remnant of its previous visions, including those of the Fisherman and his early companions, and develop a fresh vision of that original religious experience from which it claims to draw its origin and which, it maintains, is preserved intact as the living faith of the twentieth-century Church.

For in the long history of Christianity, as well as that of Judaism and of Islam, the vision entertained by their adherents was always particularized and confined. Each always claimed to have universal truth but excluded the vast majority of men from participating in it, except on conditions that sprang uniquely from the confined vision and which had nothing whatsoever to do with the truth and the religious experience that occasioned the vision. It was always and necessarily one-sided, permeated and infused with parochialism, cultural prejudices, regional characteristics, philosophical theories and presumptions, ethnic bias, linguistic particularism, political partisanship, personal ambition. No religious vision of these three religions was ever free from a note of exclusivity and of dominance. But today, it is precisely this element of the three religions that is irreconcilable with the spirit of modern man.

Here we are discussing the primordial Christian religious experience, not in order to prove or disprove the historicity of that experience, but to bring out the enormous difficulty which confronts Christianity in this century. Firstly, we must examine the meaning of the Fisherman's vision; then we shall place it in its historical context. The personalities of Moses and Elijah in this vision are of capital significance: Elijah was traditionally considered to be the herald of the Jewish Messiah; Moses was the Lawgiver of Israel. Their close association with Jesus, their discussion with him concerning his coming punishment and death, clearly indicate the mind of those who thought and wrote in this fashion: Jesus was the Messiah of Israel and the one to whom the Law was subordinate and who would fulfill the Law in all its promise and glory.

The other elements of the vision are of equal importance. The transfiguration of Jesus, his more-than-human appearance, the mysterious voice, presumably Yahweh's, heard by Simeon and which announced: "This is my beloved son; pay attention to his words," all these are the unmistakable signs used in Bible narratives to indicate the presence of Yahweh. The Transfiguration incident is presented not merely as a theophany; it intends to establish a super-human identity for Jesus, the Messiah. The final and distinctive note is the insistence on the death and resurrection of Jesus. Both are clearly associated with Jesus' role as Messiah and supreme propagator of the Jewish Law. Expressed in a modern way, the meaning of the vision would be: "Jesus is the Messiah who as the suffering servant of Yahweh will establish the Law."

This, of course, is a completely Judaic view of Jesus. It would be arbitrary and anachronistic to maintain that the vision clearly presumed and explicitly showed either that Jesus was the second person in a divine trinity of persons or was divine in nature. The vision is all the more Judaic because the Jesus represented here would in no way offend the religious susceptibilities of any believing Jew of the 1st century A.D. Provided that he accepted Jesus as the Messiah, he could accept the implications of the vision and still be a genuine Jew. Thus this vision illustrates the mentality, the religious status, and the outlook of the early followers of Jesus: they were considered to be Jews and held themselves to be Jews. More importantly still, they considered the function of Jesus and the message of Jesus to be exclusively and explicitly Jewish. The historical context in which this mentality flourished is to be sought between the death of Jesus (somewhere between 30-36 A.D.) and the final break of his followers with Judaism sometime between 66-135 A.D.

The Fisherman's vision is, however, only one of many possible visions. All of them are versions, conceptual and imaginative mental constructions, superimposed on an original religious experience. That religious experience can never be seized in a written or spoken word nor preserved in a monument of stone or metal. Christians are logically forced to maintain that, whatever be the vision enjoying a vogue in any particular age, this original religious experience is communicated down the ages from generation to generation by means

of the living faith of Christians. But the experience itself is
ineffable. Believers "live" it. They cannot "think" it, much
less verbalize it. We know that there is no such thing as a human experience without an expression, interior or exterior, of
that experience. In corollary, there is no religious experience
without an expression of that religious experience. Man in his
concrete condition cannot experience something or some one,
some thing or some other, even himself and his inner forum
where emotions and reason range, without immediately con-
ceptualizing his experience of that thing or person. He evokes
images, draws on symbols, forms words. He has a vision. A
description, an inner word, a *logos*, is born in him, spontaneously, connaturally.[3]

Once such a *logos* is born, however, the ingrained dialecticism of man's situation sets in. This *logos* is not man himself.
It is "other" than man. Faced with this "otherness" in himself, man becomes polarized in his choice; for the elements
offered to him are at that moment polarized; they repel each
other. These two dilemmatic elements concern the relation of
the self to the object known and expressed in his *logos*. Man
conceives this relation in two polarized ways: either the self
attains the object within its inner forum, thus excluding the
cosmos. The cosmos is shunned in this case. The object of
religious effort is considered attainable by withdrawal into the
inner sanctum of man himself, to be intelligible and compre-
hensible and to be finally embraced through the self. There is
no genuine cosmology. On the other hand, man can conceive
this relation within a cosmology: the supreme object is attainable primarily, and sometimes exclusively, through the cosmos. The cosmos is hierarchized according to a sacred cosmology, so that man's steps towards his object are clearly
marked out, hemmed in, guarded from errant paths, and di-

[3] At heart, this is the central logical fallacy of the Klausner
analysis of the success of primitive Christianity. It is all very well
to speak of Paul as the fashioner of the Christian *logos*. Yet there
must have been a *logos* from the very beginning, a description of
the religious experience that constituted the soul of early Christianity.
What Paul did by way of systematization prepared the way for the
Christological controversies of the 4th century and the later dogmatic
formulations of the Christian triune god. But both Jesus of Nazareth
and his immediate followers must have had a *logos* not dependent
on Pauline theological ramifications.

rected teleologically towards the end of his strivings and his desires.

What we learn from man's grappling with the dialecticism of his natural condition is that for man there is neither a middle way in between the self-directed and cosmos-directed systems, nor is it possible to pursue either extreme to the exclusion of the other. There could not be, unless man could forego his nature and its dependence on its inherent dialecticism. Buddhism, Confucianism, Christianity, Judaism, Islam, and the other major religions, whether they opted for one or the other pole, were necessarily driven from that pole to seek the opposite. If, however, they sought to follow a middle path, they were again caught in the polar configuration: they ended up with the choice of one pole, which in turn repelled them towards the other pole. In other words, not only does man's basic dialecticism involve two polar elements; it implies just as essentially a dialectic, a movement of attraction-repulsion-attraction, between the poles.

There thus arise the double tendencies of religious conception and feeling which were mentioned when the theological character of Akiva Ben Joseph was discussed: the mystical and the rational. These two currents are found in the religious tradition both of the West and the East. Augustine, Anselm, Duns Scotus, Bonaventure, Bernard, the Port-Royal School of the 17th and 18th centuries, together with the earlier mysticism of John of the Cross and Teresa of Avila, share the inner-directed view; while Aquinas, Albert the Great, Bacon, Maritain and others belong to the "other-directed" and "cosmos-directed" current. Some efforts have been made to identify the former with the Platonic tradition and the latter with the Aristotelian school. But the currents existed long before Platonism and Aristotelianism became developed and widespread philosophies. In eastern religions, we notice the same dilemma and analogous choices. Confucius, for example, in adopting the *li* concept as basic to his socio-ethical system, sought to find a balance between the emotional and the intellectual. Although this contrast is always and necessarily couched in dry, ethical language divorced apparently from theism or even metaphysics (in the Aristotelian sense), it is clear that what Confucius aimed at was a middle way between the inner-directed and the cosmos-directed. *De facto,* he and his successors ended up with a cosmos-directed ethic and religious index.

Buddha, on the other hand, met the problem head on. He recoiled in horror from the sacrifice-ritual aspect of Brahmanism on account of the moral corruption that seemingly accompanied this form of cosmological cultus of the deity. On the other hand, he had no use for the asceticism, the masochism, and the self-tormenting rules and behavior of the Jains and Ajivikas. He sought a middle way; he even decided to formulate such a middle way. Yet, in the end, the core of his teaching is self-directed. Subsequent Buddhism has undergone the dialectic. It has borrowed from the cosmology of Hinduism, created salvation machineries through the benign Boddhisattvas, reverted to the self-directed pole implied in social and political betterment, and recognized that, if one is in the cosmos with other living men, one must conform to the hard realities of hunger, disease, technological changes, and human evil. Thinking does not obviate their unpleasant traits.

Nowhere is the dialectic more obvious than in the history of Christianity, a totally western religion today. The choices open to primitive Christianity, once it had been liberated from the narrow optic of 2nd century Judaism, lay between a total flight from the cosmos to the self-directed way. It could have relied totally on an imminent return of Jesus to judge all men and to end the cosmos. It also could have chosen total immersion in the cosmos, adapting its *logos* to the law that was Rome and the thought that was Greece. We will never know in detail all the sociological and political factors which inclined Christianity towards its first choice, immersion in the cosmos. It may have been the fact that Christianity did not come equipped with a social theory and a political framework. It was, in a sense, anti-social. From this point of view it did not suffer as did ancient Judaism. The *pax romana* easily became the *pax christiana*.

The immersion chosen by Christianity was not total however; the force of the dialectic made itself felt. It tried to attain its own middle path: the bishop of Rome wore the crown and sat on a throne, but his strength was said to lie in the monks, the nuns, the recluses, the contemplatives. Celibates should make decisions about the morality of married people. The riches of this world should best be administered by those who had embraced Mistress Poverty. The master of all should be the Servant of the Servants of Christ. The power of death over men should be wielded by those who promised eternal life in the name of an eternal Master. The power of the world should reside in someone who had renounced all power in Christ's name. Obedience should be rendered to those who had taken a vow of obedience.

Augustine's personal choice was the inner-directed self within a cosmos doomed to nothingness. He conceived the self as luminous with the light eternal, and the cosmos as overshadowed by the darkness of sin and evil. This was translated into the power-structure terms of the two swords, the two cities, the two arms of the Lord—the secular and the spiritual. The Council of Trent in the 16th century was a reaffirmation of this Augustinian dialectic. The Second Vatican Council in this century refined this view in modern terms and according to the sociological exigencies of the times.

The same dialecticism is to be seen in the history of the Enlightenment and the Romantic movement. The former advocated total recourse to the cosmos, the latter total recourse to the self. Today, we have the curious and unexpected development of existentialism in philosophy and religion, in which a total recourse to the self is advocated without any hope or presumption or desire to find therein the object of religious search or of human hope. But even this intent and scope of the existentialist is frustrated by the dialectic. An advocate such as Malraux hastens to jump into the abyss of silence in which the ego lies clothed in the ultimate absurdity of a meaningless existence. What does he hear and what does he find? He hears, in short, the voices of the abyss clamoring for the ideal. He adopts history as his mediator, and takes destiny as the rule. He finds man in the *Musée Imaginaire;* and his esthetic goal once more attracts his gaze outward from the prone absurdity of the self, away out and over the human panorama, in which a certain triumph and a definite exaltation await man.

The operation of the same dialectic is noticeable in the inner history of Marxism and its Russian version. Starting with an utterly cosmos-directed viewpoint, Russian Marxism found itself face to face with the problem of the self during the Second World War. For there was no rallying against the onslaught of German National Socialism except by way of inner-directed appeal both to the mind of the Russian people and the minds of individual Russians. Nor has Soviet Marxism found it

possible to suppress or do away with the use, the utility, and
the pragmatic value of private ownership, which ideally should
be banished from the Communist state. Industry cannot function without some profit motive, which is self-directed. Advances cannot be made in science and technology without the
individual seeking to benefit by at least some advantages such
as television sets, laundromats, and automobiles. The cult of a
cosmic figure, such as Josef Stalin endeavored to become, cannot be attained without provoking the entire anti-personality-
cult and the rise of Khrushchevism, to be followed by the collegiality of the present regime. The dialectic is inevitable.
Maoism, the Chinese brand of Marxism, is caught in the same
throes of the human dialectic. A cosmos-directed revolution
necessarily leads to a self-directed ambition. We may be sure
that the personality-cult of Mao Tse Tung will inevitably lead
to an assertion of the individual and the emergence of a di-
alectically opposite force.

In view of this perennial dialectic affecting Christians, it
becomes imperative that the nature of Christianity's decision
in the 1st century A.D. be examined closely. This is done in the
following four chapters. Christianity's prime need is to re-
nounce not merely the Fisherman's vision, but all visions
formed in the past. For none are relevant to the present day,
and the increasing reaction of man is one of indifference.
For the vast majority of Christians and Jews, Messiah-ship has
no genuine relevancy, the Law of Moses has no application, the
function of Elijah is pointless. Completely removed from all
actual contexts of real life are any ancient notions concerning
the restoration of Israel in its Davidic glory as a beacon to the
eyes of the nations.

It is this irrelevancy of Christianity, paralleled by that of
Judaism and Islam, and the corresponding reaction of indifference to these major religions on the part of men today, that
cripples Christianity as it moves tortuously and laboriously in
the sphere of modern man's interests. Men only notice that the
religious visions of the past have been used to justify the degradation of man, the acquisition of territories, the division of
an entire globe, the enchainment of minds, the politicking of
priests and clergymen in the pulpit, the accumulation of wealth
in gold, securities, art treasures, million-dollar cathedrals,
mosques, synagogues, and shrines, hotels, apartment-houses,

factories, farms, ruby-studded crowns for statues, green land
and pastures and quiet gardens for the enjoyment of those
crucified to the world; pope's men in Wall Street, rabbis in
Cadillacs, muezzins fondling machine-guns, Emirs weighed
down by their weight in precious stones.

Mohammad of Islam never ceased to be anything more than
a South-Arabian. Moses was a Jew of the 2nd millenium B.C.
Jesus of Nazareth, a Galilean Jew, became and remained the
Messiah of the West. This is the burden of the past that Christianity carries, together with Judaism and Islam.

7. Jacob and Esau

All the evidence at our disposal inclines us to conclude that
between the years 30-36 A.D. the Roman Procurator of Judea
executed a man called Jesus who came to Jerusalem from the
small village of Nazareth in Galilee. If we lay aside the obvious
tendentiousness of early Christian writers and any religious
bias or interpretation on our part, it is clear that Jesus was put
to death on the charge that he was preparing revolt and sedition against the ruling powers. The charge was political, and
the penalty was decided by the dominant political power, Rome.
Jesus was crucified, was certified dead, and was buried. As far
as Rome and Judaism were concerned, the affair of Jesus was
finished.

Jesus had been but a momentary bother to the authorities of
the day. He did not rouse the attention of any Roman authority
outside Judea of the time. His figure did not stand out in contemporary Judaism either in religious or political emphasis.
He had not really come within the official orbit of interest until
he arrived one day in Jerusalem and was greeted by an enthu-
siastic crowd of followers who called him the Messiah.

The Jewish authorities could see no resemblance in Jesus to
the Messiah of their expectations. The Roman authorities took
cognizance of the obvious unrest and the publicly repeated
avowals that Jesus had come to restore the kingdom of Israel.
Already the Essenians, the Zealots, the Sicarii, and other
groups were causing enough trouble. A midnight arrest, an
identification process, an early morning arraignment and con-

demnation before the Roman Governor. His hands and feet
were nailed to a cross. He died in the usual fashion. Over his
head, the Romans hung their warning: JESUS OF NAZARETH:
KING OF THE JEWS. This was his name and thus ran the laconic
description of his alleged crime.

Concerning the period 36-70 A.D., most written evidence at
our disposal suffers from three limitations: it was written and
edited by men in the grip of highly-charged emotions; these
men were not writing history as our Western minds today
conceive history, but of the *meaning* of history such as the
Western mind cannot readily conceive; finally, when they
wrote, nearly 30 years had elapsed since the obscure life and
quick death of Jesus. Because of the first limitation, what they
wrote was given a humanly conceived slant in keeping with
prevailing emotions: emotions create their own reality, and the
reality changes with the emotions. Because of the second limitation, time was encapsulated and, indeed, transcended; events
were recounted not so much for their impact in time and
space as for their significance in an invisible world firmly
believed but not understood. Because of the third limitation,
we are not informed of the intricate and, for us, relevant
developments immediately after the death of Jesus, which would
now serve us so well: Jew and Christian at that moment in
history were twin brothers in the womb of one religious mother,
and the seed of our subsequent religious civilization was in
embryo. Today, with our simple lack of historicism and our
delightfully irrelevant prejudices, Jews would conceive of
Christians as Esau, Christians would regard Jews as Esau, both
thinking of themselves as Jacob, the recipient of divine blessings.[1]
For, as faithful and unthinking imitators of Christian writers in
the last third of the 1st century A.D., and of Jewish writers
during the first few hundred years after the destruction of the
Second Temple, we impose on this grave lacuna of our historical
knowledge, categories, emotions, and conceptions which would
have bewildered both the Jews who heard Jesus preach and
the followers of Jesus who saw him bleed and suffocate to death.

The most pernicious of these emotional categories is shared
by modern Jews and Christians alike. It is a two-edged sword:
it has afflicted their joint Western civilization with a primordial schizophrenia, causing a deep fission in the spirit; it has

[1] Paul was one of the earliest Christian proponents of this comparison. Cf. *Romans* 9:7-13. *Galatians* 4:22.

cursed them with those incoherent and illogical stances which today are alienating men and are the best proof that these two religions, at least, cannot solve man's dilemma. I refer to our neat conceptions of "Jew" and "Christian."

If any one thing is clear concerning the early years after the death of Jesus (say, 36-46 A.D.), it is that Christians as we know them did not exist either in name or in the guise we recognize as "Christian." [2] Whatever sources we have force us to form another idea, no matter what the consequences be for cherished conceptions, personal piety, or jealously guarded dignities and self-esteem.[3] We are forced to admit that during those years there was a Jewish community in Jerusalem and throughout the eastern Mediterranean basin, some of whose members believed that Jesus was the Messiah.

It is difficult to find a term that describes those believers; they were not "Christian Jews," for that to our categorized minds implies Jews converted to Christianity; nor were they "Jewish Christians," for that implies Christians who partook somehow or another of Judaism. They were full-blooded Jews, accepted wholly by Judaism, accepting all of Judaism, at first almost exclusively Jews by race. They were distinguished, like many more inner sects of Judaism at that time, by particular beliefs which cohered perfectly with Judaism and allowed them

[2] The relatively late term "Christian," supposedly an original nickname conferred by Greeks in Antioch on those who believed in Jesus, is chiefly valuable because it tells us what element in those believers' faith and statements most struck complete outsiders: viz. that *Jesus was the Messiah expected by the Jewish people.* These early believers in Jesus could just as easily have been called Nazarenes, Jesuits, Calvarians, Petrists, Galileans, Spiritualists, Servants, Resurrectionists, Yahweh's Witnesses, Baptists, Unitarians, Orthodox, Conservative, Reformed, Latter-Day Saints, Mosaics, Essenians, Love-Children, Crusaders, Episcopalians. In a later time they could have been called Greek Orthodox, Romans, Paulists, etc. Even at that time, aspects of their belief and practice could have provoked such appellations; but they were not so called.

[3] Mainly the *Acts of the Apostles,* Chapters 1-7. However, these are not totally free from the later conceptions of 60 A.D. onward. We have our source knowledge of Judaism between 30-70 A.D., but this also suffers from later contamination which continued for nearly 1000 years. Jews, no less than Christians, must be held responsible for changing their stance and their appreciation of the fundamental happenings in those days under the stress of events.

in conscience as well as in the eyes of the Jewish Community to live, act, and die as Jews.

Another basic flaw in our thinking vitiates our use of the term "Jew." For the "Jew" of the Second Commonwealth was as distinct from the "Jew" of today as their "Christian" counterparts are distinct from each other. The Second Commonwealth "Jew" was inspired by beliefs which no longer function in the life of a modern "Jew." Furthermore, he had not been wounded deep in his soul by the Opposition of whom we have spoken. With these limitations, we can speak more safely of the "Jew" at that time than we can speak of the "Christian." For the latter did not exist at all.

Furthermore, it is clear that Jesus was not tried and condemned either because he assured men that their sins were forgiven by him or anyone else,[4] or for supposedly making light of certain Levitical laws of purity,[5] or for healing on the Sabbath,[6] or for driving devils out of the possessed in the name of Beelzebub,[7] or for his attitude to fasting,[8] or for plotting the destruction of the Temple,[9] or for claiming to be the Messiah,[10] or for blaspheming by saying that he was the Son of

[4] Cf. *Ber.* 5a, where the current Jewish teaching of the time supported Jesus. "Sufferings wash away the sins of man." Cf. also *Ned.* 41a.

[5] Such laws only bound those who entered the Temple or who ate sacred food.

[6] Later Talmudic law permitted the healing of internal injuries on the Sabbath. cf. eg. *Yoma* 85b. This undoubtedly reflected the earlier latitude toward such merciful acts on the Sabbath provided they did not entail activity in preparing ingredients—not verified in the case of Jesus (cf. *Shab.* 108b).

[7] Such "ejection of devils and evil spirits" was practiced with impunity by the "whisper" therapy. Verbal therapy was always allowed.

[8] It is difficult to determine the fasting involved in the supposed accusation against Jesus. Cf. H. Mantel, *Studies in the History of the Sanhedrin*, Harvard Univ. Press, 1961.

[9] Such a crime was unknown in Jewish legal history. Jesus' actual implication that a heavenly Jerusalem would replace the earthly one was not new to Judaism; it is found in pre-Christian literature as well as after the time of Jesus.

[10] Claimants to the Messiahship appeared before and after the time of Jesus. They were never punished merely for claiming this role. Cf. *passim* Abba Hillel Silvers, *History of Messianic Speculation in Israel.*

Man,[11] or because the Pharisees were loyal to the Romans,[12] or because the Sadducees were corrupt,[13] or because the Jewish people as a whole clamored for his death,[14] or because the Pharisees and Sadducees were jealous of his power and popularity, or because Jesus proposed to abrogate the Law of Moses.[15] Such reasons are pathetically and patently fictitious, anachronistic, and fabricated in an age when some of them had come to be regarded by Jews as condemnable, not for any evil or anti-Jewish trait inherent in them, but because they backed up the tenets of a group who sought to usurp the heritage of Judaism. If the indictment of Jesus consisted exclusively of these, he would never have died as he did. Finally, it is clear, on the one hand, that Jewish courts at the time of Jesus did inflict capital punishment,[16] and, on the other hand, that Jesus was executed after a Roman indictment before a Roman official who imposed a Roman capital punishment for a crime against Rome and who entrusted the performance of this legal sentence to Roman subordinate officials and soldiers.[17]

What is as important as the proper assessment of why Jesus was executed, and by whom, is to determine the position in the immediate period after his death which his followers occupied within the Jewish Community. It is, again, clear that these followers considered themselves Jews, the best and the luckiest of Jews since they had found the Messiah. They held themselves

[11] This was merely tantamount to claiming to be the Messiah.

[12] The Pharisees regarded the Romans as wicked pigs. Cf. *Sanh.* VII, 5; *M. Ned.* III, 4. The nationalism of the Pharisees is so well known and clear that no demonstration is necessary.

[13] The Sadducees may not all have been everything their sacred office called for; yet we have no proof that demonstrates their treachery to Israel.

[14] The Jewish people as a whole were not present at the trial and execution of Jesus. Most of them did not know that he existed.

[15] Concerning Jesus' attitude to the Law, a controversy exists. The general body of unbiased evidence inclines us to conclude that all antinomian material in the Gospels is not attributable with safety directly to Jesus. Cf. Schniedel in *Encyclopaedia Biblica* II, p. 1839 ff, *sub voce* "B. Historical and Synthetical." Jesus and Pharisaism is studied by Riddle in his *Jesus and the Pharisees*, pp. 106-109.

[16] The best synopsis of the evidence for this is in Mantel, op. cit. pp. 307-316.

[17] Concerning the evidence for and against this, cf. *The Trial of Jesus* by Paul Winter.

as bound by the Law of Moses and as subject to Jewish officialdom. They worshipped in the Temple which included participation in Temple sacrifices and ceremonies. They did not actively or willingly seek to convert any Gentiles, or non-Jews, to
their particular beliefs. They could not and were not incrim-
inated either for believing that Jesus was the Messiah or for
professing belief in a man who had been executed by the Romans. Stephen was heard out and put to death by an inflamed
mob for what was regarded as blasphemy; Peter and John were
arrested, tried and punished because of the possibly seditious
interpretation of their preaching about Jesus as the Messiah
and because their public cures gave rise to the suspicion of
sorcery. It was not the chief Pharisee (who headed the Sanhedrin) but King Agrippa I who executed James, the brother of
John Zebedee; Paul was not tried by the Great Sanhedrin in the
Hall of Gazit but by a Roman tribunal on fundamentally the
same charges as Jesus and Peter and John: as a "mover of
sedition among all the Jews throughout the world." The world
at the time was the *oikoumene*, the Empire.[18]

But if we eliminate the elements touched on in previous
paragraphs from our picture of the immediate post-Jesus Jewish
Community, we are left with one principal conclusion that sits
well with neither Christian nor Jew of the traditional calibre:
"Christianity" of those years was acceptable to the Jewish Community as a genuine expression of Judaism and Jewishness;
and the "Christians" were, acted, and thought of themselves
as Jews.

The period we are considering (36-46 A.D.) was peculiarly
suitable for such a sub-group to emerge within the Jewish
Community. The various parts of Herod the Great's kingdom
had been in relative peace and for the most part united under
one rule.[19] The factional differences which split the Pharisees

[18] Concerning this and the other points mentioned in this paragraph, cf. Mantel, op. cit. pp. 290-300.

[19] His son, Archelaus, ruler of Judea, Idimea, and Samaria was
exiled in 10 A.D. His kingdom was attached to the Roman Province
with the name of Judea. Antipas, another son, was deposed in 39
A.D., and his kingdom (Galilee and Perea) was attached to that
of Agrippa I, grandson of Herod. Philip, the third son, died in 34
A.D. His kingdom (Trachonitis, Batanis, Aurantis) was given to
Agrippa I. In 41 A.D., Agrippa was given Judea; thus all the regions
were once more reunited under one ruler.

had been mended.[20] The mass of the people found their expression and direction in Pharisaism. Disruptive differences between Pharisees and Sadducees had been settled in a practical way. Both sides continued to teach and live as they wished; the Pharisees agreed to a Sadducean High-Priest. The Community was no longer under a double leadership—political and doctrinal power belonged to the Great Sanhedrin of the Gazit [21] and the political Sanhedrin of the kings and high-priests.[22] The principal leader of the Jewish Community was Rabban Gamaliel I,[23] grandson of Hillel, who bore the title of Nasi.[24] The High-Priest was the nominal head of the Great Sanhedrin which combined legislative and supreme court functions. But Gamaliel I, as effective head, regulated the calendar, issued edicts for Jews in Palestine and the Diaspora, and was the ultimate authority. His attitude to the Jews who believed in Jesus was typical:

> Men of Israel, think well what you mean to do with these men.[25] There was Theodas, who appeared in days gone by and claimed to be someone of importance, and was supported by about four hundred men. He was killed, and all his followers were dispersed and came to nothing. And after him Judas the Galilean appeared in the days of the registration; he persuaded the people to rebel under his leadership, but he too perished, and all his followers were scattered. And my advice is still the same: have nothing to do with these men, let them be. If this is man's design or man's undertaking, it will be overthrown. If it is God's, you will have no power to overthrow it. You would not willingly be found fighting against God.[26]

Gamaliel was here announcing a truly godly doctrine, one to which none of the followers of Jesus could take exception.

[20] After the fall of Archelaus in 10 A.D., part of the Pharisees formed the Zealot party.

[21] The "Hall of Hewn Stones."

[22] Concerning the rise of the Pharisees to political power cf. Büchler, *Synedrion* pp. 139-144, and his *Priester and Cultus.* pp. 56-58.

[23] Died circa 50 A.D., during Emperor Caligula's reign.

[24] Concerning the title *Nasi*, cf. Mantel, op. cit. pp. 1-53.

[25] Meaning Peter and other associates of his.

[26] *Acts.* 5:35-39.

They would add, of course, that time would prove them right. It was not, therefore, in the area of permission to live and practice their Jewish religion and be faithful to the admonitions of Jesus that his early followers found difficulty. They encountered it in another direction.

The religion of Israel, be it in its Israelite stage or the latter-day Judaistic stage, was essentially a thing of exterior action, of observance, of ritual, and of close performance of duties by which adhesion to the Covenant was signified. Abstract theological principles or, indeed, metaphysical thought is not connatural to the Semite mind. The Semite writes and speaks excellently, but his thought is structural and liquid. It has none of the static symmetry and attention to content which marks the Greek mind. The fullest flowering of religious development in the previous stage of Israel's religion was to be seen exclusively in juridical codification, lyrical expression, and historical chronology. The concept of Israelitism and of Judaism in its earlier stages was structural and dynamic, intuitive and visionary, rarely discursive and analytic. The place of abstract theological thinking and metaphysical analysis was taken by historical narratives in Israel's outlook. Its sacred books accumulated and united two elements: legal dispositions and historical narratives.

The followers of Jesus, on the other hand, were in this peculiar position: they accepted totally the legal and historical narrative elements of Israel's religion. Their belief in Jesus as the Messiah, however, added one more dimension to their outlook: a theological content and a body of thought which ultimately they would have to rationalize. The life, the acts, the preaching, the sufferings, the death, and the resurrection of Jesus were announced to and accepted by them as news, as a *kerygma*, portending hitherto undiscovered and undreamed-of meanings. The Judaism of their time in its essential character did not provide them with the concepts they needed in order even to think of the revelation of Jesus. Now Pharisaism fulfilled this vital function.

Over a period of 500 years after the return from Babylon, the Pharisees had developed schools of thought under Persian and, later, Greek influences in which abstract metaphysical rationale for exterior religious acts was elaborated. In their subsequent development, they had systematized a theological basis for their religion. Unconsciously, they thus arrived at establishing the need for an internal rationale, a consensus justifying the exterior actions of man. Jews and Christians today take such an internal forum of thought and rationalization for granted. But it did not evolve in Judaism until quite late in its history, and when it did it was the gift of Pharisaism to Judaism and to the Western world. The importance of this contribution cannot be neglected. The early followers of Jesus, who moved within the legal framework of Judaism, found in this Pharisaic development a ready and suitable internal rationale elaborated in a series of beliefs and teachings. Moreover, these beliefs and teachings were endowed with the authority of the doctors of Israel. There thus was born for the first time the idea that religion implied an official set of theological beliefs and an official formulation of those beliefs.

Between the teachings of the Pharisees and those of the followers of Jesus there existed an affinity that helped to identify the followers with the Jewish Community, providing them with a ready-made mode of thinking. The Pharisees, together with the Sadducees, had come into existence with the Maccabean revolt as a definitely organized politico-religious force. Pharisaic teaching had already been definitely influenced by Persian Zoroastrianism, particularly in its concepts of Satan, of angels, of an apocalyptic end to all mortal things, of final purification by fire, of the Messiah-Hero as a personal savior of Israel, and of the resurrection of the dead to life. These were either alien to or expressly denied in the Bible.[27] Greek Hellenism provided Pharisaism with the idea of the soul's immortality, something equally alien to the Bible.

The followers of Jesus believed both in the resurrection of Jesus from the dead and the resurrection of all men in virtue of his resurrection. They also believed in the everlasting reward and/or punishment of every man, in the personal forces of good and evil in man's cosmos, and in the imminent coming of Jesus for the second and last time. In Pharisaism they found a suitable formulation of these doctrines.

Where the followers of Jesus differed fundamentally with Pharisees and general Jewish belief at that time was in the question of Jesus. His followers believed him to be the Messiah and to be the Son of Man foretold in the prophet Daniel. They further believed that God had raised Jesus up from the dead

[27] In the Psalms, especially. But cf. Book Three, chapter 26, concerning immortality and resurrection.

and that he had subsequently been taken up alive into heaven. There is no one statement either in the Gospels or the Acts of the Apostles, at least in those portions that come from the early period of Christian history, in which Jesus is undeniably called God. The appellation, whether in Greek, Hebrew, or Aramaic, was reserved for the personal supernatural power from whom Jesus came, whose son he was, and to whom he had returned. Dominant in the minds of those believers was the Messiahship of Jesus and an association with, and relation to, God's divinity they did not comprehend but which they expressed by talking about the functions Jesus performed. Thirty or forty years later we find the divinity of Jesus asserted both explicitly [28] and by implication.[29]

But we must not attribute to these early believers the rational, pietistic, and theological preoccupations that have subsequently bedeviled Christians in trying to prove either that God exists or that Jesus was true God and true man. Formal and theoretic atheism was not a danger or problem for them. It was sufficient for them that Jesus was the Messiah. Reflection, controversy with their Pharisee co-religionists, and the Hellenizing work of Paul of Tarsus would refine these initial concepts entertained about Jesus.

Apart from this doctrinal difference with their ambient, the followers of Jesus had one other main difference. This was in the practical order of prescribed ritual. Jesus, on the night before he died, had eaten the Passover meal with them. He had adapted one part of the meal in a special way and instructed them to do this in commemoration of him. There grew up, therefore, the custom of performing this duty of commemoration. We do not know how regularly or how often. One could suggest that it took place weekly in the evening of the day corresponding to the occasion of the last meal together.[30] It might well have taken place on the day after the Sabbath, since Jesus had been resurrected from the dead on that day. We know somewhat

[28] Cf. for instance, *John* 20:28.

[29] The use of the phrase *ego eimi* placed on the lips of Jesus a number of times by the author of the Fourth Gospel can only be taken as an assertion of personal identification with God, and therefore of personal divinity.

[30] The date of the last meal Jesus had with his disciples is still a matter of controversy. Cf. A. Jaubert, *La Date de la Cene*, Gabalda, Paris, 1957.

more about the ritual of that commemoration. We know what it must have contained, while we cannot know all. The earliest testimony is to be found in a work of St. Justin Martyr (circa 100-165 A.D.). This, called *Apologia,* was written in Rome about 150 A.D. and addressed to the Emperor Antoninus Pius. In the third part of the *Apologia,* Justin gives a vivid description of how the commemorative ceremony was performed in his time: some portions of letters from the Apostles were read, then a portion of the Gospel was read, a small sermon was given, followed by an offering of bread and wine, a special prayer was recited, and then the bread and wine were distributed to be taken by all present. We know also that from the 3rd century onward the above ceremony was lengthened by the addition of a modified form of the old Jewish Sabbath synagogue service. This included recitations from the Bible interspersed with prayers, invocations, and a profession of faith. But this could not have been the original rite.

Such specifically Jewish elements were used in localities around the eastern basin of the Mediterranean from the first third of the 2nd century A.D. onward. Their use does not suggest, however, that the earliest form of the commemorative service was an imitation of the original synagogue service. For the followers of Jesus, this commemorative service must have been a thing apart; they worshipped in the Temple and they partook in the synagogue services. But they also observed this last injunction of Jesus.

We can say that the actual words and actions of Jesus must have been reproduced at these private rites. The actions of Jesus in taking wine and bread, blessing them, and distributing them to his companions is reproduced in completely non-Christian documents that preceded even the existence of Jesus, without, however, the operative words with which Jesus made the rite his own.[31]

Preceding this rite, or sacred meal, we can suppose that someone present described briefly what had happened that night and what Jesus had said. Doubtless, those present affirmed their beliefs in Jesus as the Messiah and as the Son of God, in his resurrection and ascension, and in their own hopes for his second and last coming, for the final judgement, and for life eternal in Paradise with God and Jesus. Whatever elements we suppose the original commemorative meal had, we cannot

[31] Cf. the *Manual of Discipline,* Col. VI, lines 1-8.

safely assume that it was modeled on the synagogue service, or
that the words of Jesus were explicitly interpreted as indicating
a sacrificial rite.

That the early followers of Jesus committed to memory and
to writing his sayings, injunctions, and directives, there can be
little doubt. Such was the custom for disciples and followers of
teachers and doctors and holy men. These, however, were only
notes and aids for memory. The chief source of factual memory
was the oral recitation of events in the life of Jesus. For the
Book was a sacred thing to Jews, and there was only one
sacred Book, the Bible.[32]

We will always find it difficult to imagine the mind, to
relive the thoughts, or to experience the emotions which per-
vaded the sect in this short space of time. They themselves had
no time—so short was it. They were not allowed to reflect long
upon it. For they lived in recent memory of a great pain, such
as we have never known; and they moved under the gathering
clouds of an imminent cataclysm that they desired. Their eyes
were lit by a transcendental glory which they saw touching
with magic the hilltops of Judea, the face of eastern waters,
the eaves and the towers of the Temple, the phylacteries on the
breast of a grave Sadducee in the market-place, the steel-
tipped lances of their Roman masters. Jesus had been executed. The Messiah was returning. Israel's millennium of glory
and peace was beginning with tomorrow's dawn. They were
the pick of the Chosen People.

As yet no serious hint of the struggle and Usurpation
appeared. Jacob's heel was not on Esau's head. Jacob's lie had
not become a mystery, as Augustine consolingly interpreted the
deception three centuries later. The Blessings were for Jews, the
Curses for the Gentiles.

Theoretically and practically, nothing great need have
resulted. History has an iron law; no event becomes a stable
factor in its pattern of human life or is prolonged into permanent existence unless it transits from the mind, from the inner
circle, unless it drives deep and separate roots within an ambi-

[32] An ancient prescription forbade the writing down of the sayings
and decisions of teachers in a published form. They could be written
either in letters, privately possessed rolls (made of skin, usually),
or on tablets. These were considered the equivalent of notebooks.
Doubtless the words and acts of Jesus were thus preserved at the
earliest times.

ent tolerant of its foreignness, open to its alien nature. The sect could have been simply absorbed in Judaism; it was not. Judaism saw the warning-signals, heard the hammer beating in its soul. The instinct for self-preservation cried out to it: do not try to hear this message through the restlessness of words or the wild syllables of a lost generation. Expel it! Because Jews understood life backwards but lived it forwards, the expulsion came. This was the saving of the sect. It could only blossom in an alien field. Christianity made one of several possible historical choices.

8. Three Scenarios

Scenario A. Total Identification with Judaism

Assume that between the years 30 and 40 A.D., the followers of Jesus are accepted as authentic members of the Jewish Community. Called Nazarenes, they observe the Law meticulously, worship in the Temple, require all male converts to undergo the initiation rites of circumcision, and enforce all the precepts and commandments. They identify totally with Judaism. They differ from official Judaism only in their belief that the Messiah has come. But they take literally the logion of their Master: "Not one iota, not one flourish must be omitted from the Law." By the year 49 A.D., the new group has surmounted its first crisis: a small number of its itinerant preachers attempt to get a ruling from its assembled members whereby non-Jewish converts need not undergo the rigors of the Law—especially in the matter of circumcision and abstention from the public handouts of sacrificial meat from pagan temples. This effort is defeated: "Jesus is the Messiah of Israel; Israel is God's chosen," is the motivating reason.

The Nazarenes are rapidly associated with the Pharisees: both are bent on absolute purity of observance, on the preservation of the traditions, on the doctrines of bodily resurrection and of angels, and on the sacrosanct character of the Law even beyond the Temple and the Land. Nazarene relations with the Sadducees are as sour as those of the Pharisees with that sect: a cardinal point in the Nazarene teaching concerns the resurrection of Jesus from the dead, and the consequent resurrection

of all men from the dead, when Jesus returns for final judgment on the world. The Sadducees deny this. Very few converts
are made in non-Jewish circles. The group draws heavily on
the previously existent Essenian communities throughout the
Land. Nazarenes become known for being as punctilious as
Pharisees in the interpretation of the Law.

When Jewish nationalism starts on the upward swing, after
the death of Herod Agrippa in 44 A.D., the Nazarenes are foremost in the ranks. They have an added reason for preparing
revolt and war: they expect as an article of faith that Jesus is
returning imminently from Heaven, to destroy the enemies of
Israel, to restore its ancient glories, to purify the Land, to
renew the whole earth, and to inaugurate the millennium of
justice, righteousness, and brotherly love.

As with the bulk of Pharisees, the Nazarenes participate in
the Zealot, Sicarii, and Essenian movements—all violently
nationalistic. The leaders of both Pharisees and Nazarenes try
to exercise a restraining influence, but to no avail. When the
revolt of 66 A.D. against Rome breaks out, Nazarenes participate
with the Pharisees and the remainder of the population. After
the destruction of Jerusalem in 70 A.D., the Nazarenes take
refuge in the coastal towns around Yavneh with the Pharisees,
where they are heart and soul with Rabbi Akiva in establishing
the Law as the one means of survival for Judaism. Many go
into exile overseas with other Jewish communities.

It is obvious that in such a scenario, Christianity such as we
know it at the end of the first century or in the middle of the
5th century A.D., could never have developed. Christianity
would have been doomed to ultimate extinction as a distinct
body—if it had accepted total identification with contemporary
Judaism and acquiescence both in the doctrinal trends of Pharisaism and in the socio-political trends of first century Jews. As
happened in Judaism, the Nazarenes would have diminished
their emphasis on the character of a personal Messiah, on the
effective redemption of man from sin, and on the universalist
character of Yahweh's religion. The inner contradiction of normative Judaism would have become theirs. It would have trans-
planted from Judea to a hostile world, separating itself from
that world not merely by ritual laws but by a doctrinal
attachment to one geographical center, rid of its official Temple worship. The best identity which it could have achieved

would have resembled that of the Qaraites in the 10th century or of the same sect in the 20th century. In the 10th century, Qaraism was a proscribed movement within Judaism, its books destroyed, its Scriptural interpretation condemned officially, its particular doctrines excoriated as heretical, its members ostracized from the Jewish Community everywhere in the Diaspora. In this century Qaraism is a minute Jewish sect, living on the periphery of mainstream Judaism, known only as an esoteric remnant of what once was a formative and dynamic element in Judaism.

Scenario B: Acceptance as a Formative Influence

Assume that by the year 40 A.D. the followers of Jesus have been accepted officially and popularly by the Jewish Community and that they assume a formative role in contemporary Judaism. Known as Nazarenes, they come rapidly to be recognized as the strictest observers of the Law. Religiously they are acceptable to the Pharisees. Socio-politically they are acceptable to the Sadducees and the Roman authorities because of their total abstention from all political activity and their purely spiritual interpretation of the kingdom of Yahweh.

By the middle of Herod Agrippa's reign (circa 42 A.D.), a new crystallization of religious thought has emerged in official Jewish circles. The Orthodox Legalists (drawn from Pharisees and Nazarenes) hold that nothing matters but the Law, the Land, and the Temple, however one interprets the fact of Jesus. The Orthodox Spirituals (drawn from Pharisees, Sadducees, and Nazarenes) hold that what matters is the advent of the Messiah and the intention of the spirit and the heart in man, leaving open the question as to whether Jesus was the Messiah. The Orthodox Imminents (drawn exclusively from Pharisees and Nazarenes) execute a holding operation: to decide the central question of Jesus, one must wait for his imminent return from Heaven. Finally, the Jerusalem Prophetics preach a return to the doctrine of the pre-exilic prophets and an abandonment of teachings which only emerged in the Maccabean and post-exilic periods—notably the dual rule of Israel by High-Priest and King, the apocalyptical and eschatological doctrines concerning the end of the world, the personal character of the Messiah, and the immortality of the soul and its resurrection with the body of man.

The reign of Herod Agrippa has a decisive influence in affairs. The king behaves both as a pious Jew in Jerusalem and as an ostentatious, fun-loving monarch in Caesarea, Tiberias, Gaza, and elsewhere outside the holy city. During his reign, a new life is breathed into a Hellenism which had declined in the Maccabean period. Schools, theaters, stadia, gymnasia, and Greek educational cultural elements take hold of the population. Added to this hellenization, there is the concerted effort of all parties to suppress and transmute the nascent nationalism of the population. By 55 A.D., the main leaders of rebellion, John of Gishala and Simon Ben Giora in particular, have been captured and executed. The more dangerous pockets of Essenian guerrillas, Zealots, and Sicarii, have been cleaned up in the southern and southeastern parts. This effective opposition to nationalism is due in great part to the pacifist influence of the Nazarenes.

A decisive transmutation of Judaism is effected by these three trends: the fragmentation of the original Jewish official duo (Pharisees and Sadducees) in Jewish life, the new hellenization under Agrippa, and the effective suppression of popular nationalism. Amid the national peace and consequent prosperity, the Nazarenes and the Orthodox Spirituals attract impressive numbers of converts. Many, however, are non-Jews. The latter object to such Jewish prescriptions as circumcision. Many of them are quite poor and, prior to their conversion, subsisted largely on the hand-outs of sacrificial meat which the priests of the pagan temples made on feast-days and on certain week-day mornings.

These questions are mooted in a council of the Nazarenes in 49 A.D. and in a general assembly of the Orthodox Spirituals, Orthodox Legalists, and Orthodox Imminents in early 50 A.D. The Jerusalem Prophetics abstain from the meetings, considering them irrelevant to ordinary life. The majority vote at these two decisive meetings is in favor of a greater liberalization. "Yahweh is the God of the living, not of the dead;" "neither foreskin nor circumcision are important but only faith infused with love;" "spiritual sons of Abraham cannot by mere circumcision become physical sons of Abraham;" "racial descent from Abraham cannot be effected by ridding a man of his foreskin, for who can return into the wombs of all his female ancestors and be born again of a direct descendant female of Abraham?"—these are the four motivating reasons for the majority rule.

As a result, between the years 55 A.D. and 135 A.D., a newly transformed Judaism takes strong hold not merely of the Jewish population, but throughout Egypt, North Africa, Syria, Asia Minor, Greece, and Italy. This Judaism, known as Nazarene Judaism, believes Jesus to be the Messiah. Under Greek and Latin influence, it refines its definition of Jesus as the Son of Man and the Son of God. The other parts of Judaism, the Orthodox Legalists and Orthodox Imminents sink into relative obscurity. The Jerusalem Prophetics disappear after the turn of the first century. The Emperor Hadrian visits the Holy City in 135 A.D. and elevates the new Judaism from being a *religio licita* to co-equal with the worship of the Roman gods throughout the Empire. The way is open for Judaism to enter into the arteries and sinews of the Empire and finally provide for its spiritual, intellectual, and social reorganization from the 5th century onwards, when the Empire was, in effect, no more.

As we know and recognize the logic of events operative in the fateful years 30-50 A.D., there is nothing fancifully impossible in the above scenario. Even presuming a minor nationalistic uprising on the part of Jewish elements, or projecting incursionary wars in Palestine, an acceptance of active Christianity into the bosom of Judaism could have been the decisive factor in transforming an otherwise explosive and lethal situation.

Such a Judaism would have suffered from a slight amorphism: the person of Jesus would have been acknowledged by the majority, but a strong minority would have refused such acknowledgment. On the other hand, the doctrine of the personal Messiah would have been preserved. The legalistic emphasis of normative Judaism which Rabbi Akiva and his associates gave inexorably to Judaism never would have succeeded. Judaism would have been purified from the tribal-ethnic-geographical trammels which were to choke its every socio-political move, and from the ritualistic and formalist barriers that were to make it inaccessible over the next two thousand years.

If no effective suppression of incipient nationalism and revolt is effected between 30-50 A.D., then we fall back into the previous scenario at its close. On the other hand, Nazarene Judaism probably could have avoided the romanist excesses of Christianity, the chauvinist imperialism of Byzantine Christianity, and a direct clash with Islam between the 10th and 15th centuries.

Scenario C: Acceptance of Total Separation from Judaism

Suppose that between the years 36-40 A.D. the clash between the followers of Jesus, the Nazarenes, and the leaders of Judaism had become doctrinally and socially acute. By 45 A.D. the situation has become grave. The death of Herod Agrippa in the previous year releases all the forces of religious nationalism. Before his death, Agrippa had executed Jacob, one of the main leaders of Nazarenes, under prodding by the Pharisee ruling circles. He had imprisoned another called Simeon. Later on, another Jacob, a blood-relative of Jesus, is executed by the High-Priest during the absence of a Roman Procurator. Even the nickname by which the Nazarenes are contemptuously described by their enemies (Balaamites) does not sound as decorous as the popular description of the Nazarenes as "Christians" which the Antiochean verse-writers derisively gave them.

It is neither these passing troubles nor the continuous harassment that brings the Nazarene leaders to a crisis. It is rather a combination of two other elements: their exclusion from Temple worship and from all the synagogues throughout the land by official decree of the Jerusalem Sanhedrin, and the ever-increasing pressure of non-Jewish converts. Both these pressures work to produce a greater and greater fission between the Nazarenes and the other Jewish sects.

The exclusion from participation in official Judaism has many effects. Previously, the Nazarenes have worshipped in Temple and synagogue. There they could participate in the use of the Holy Scrolls and benefit by the Blessings. At their own private prayer-meetings in commemoration of Jesus, they recall his acts and words. Since the death of Jesus, these acts and words have been written down in the form of notes in pinaces (codices).[1] To do otherwise would have been unlawful,

---

[1] Originally a writing-tablet of some hard material, such as wax; later softer material was used.

for, according to Jewish prescription, such notes are not to be written in the form of a book to be published. Now, however, the Nazarenes find it necessary to provide their own permanent meeting-places. In addition, they begin the practice of entrusting the records of Jesus not merely to disjointed tablets, but to papyrus (*diaphtherai*) and to the regular book form.

A more profound change is operated by these apparently simple adaptations. First of all, at the prayer-meetings it sounds more and more illogical to speak of themselves, the Nazarenes, as Israel, to think of Jesus as the Messiah expected by Pharisee Judaism, or to call themselves the heirs of the Temple and the Land and the Written and Oral Law. All these things are the possessions of the Jewish Community. Besides, the Temple sacrifices are considered pointless because Jesus has consummated all sacrifices by the supreme sacrifice of his human life. Daily, the words of Jesus, the oral account of his acts and the written records become of more importance than the written accounts of their Jewish forefathers and the codified Law of Moses. Besides, most Nazarene communities no longer possess any practical way of consulting the ancient writings of Israel.

The influx of non-Jewish converts merely pushes this incipient development to a logical conclusion. First of all, the major portion of the converts object strenuously to circumcision. It is, they assert, at one and the same time a mutilation of the body and merely a mark of physical descendance from a Jewish ancestor. Men protest for their own sake; wives, sisters, and fiancées protest for a variety of reasons corresponding to their interest. Because they are not Jews by race, and because their culture does not favor such mutilation, why should they be forced to undergo it? Besides, they are not allowed to enter either the Temple or the synagogues.

By the year 60 A.D., a profound change has taken place. Already in 49 A.D., the Nazarenes had decreed that all non-Jewish converts would be exempt from circumcision, from Jewish ritual laws and from observance of the 613 precepts. No convert need become a Jew. By the year 55 A.D., copies of the Nazarene records concerning Jesus had been circulated among the Nazarene communities throughout Judea, Syria, Galilee, Asia Minor, and Greece. These records are now considered to be on a par with the Torah. The solemn meeting of each Nazarene community is held, not on the Jewish Sabbath as originally in the early thirties, but on the day after the Sabbath, because

Jesus rose from the dead on that day. By 60 A.D., the major portion of Nazarenes are of Greek origin with a sprinkling of Romans, Lydians, Cypriots, and Arabians. Greek is the *lingua franca*. The popular name "Christian" is accepted by them as being a truer description of their identity. "Nazarene" sounds uncouth and provincial to Greek ears.

During the revolt of 66-70 A.D., the Jewish national leaders massacre "Christians" wherever they find them. When Jerusalem is taken by Titus in 70 A.D., the Temple is destroyed, the Jewish leaders are either executed or put to flight, and the major portion of the population is sent into exile. The "Christians" decide that this is the end of the Old Covenant between God and his Chosen People, the end of the Chosen People as such, the beginning of that renewal of sky and earth and man promised in the prophets and reiterated by Jesus.

The "Christians" gradually drop any claim to be a continuation of Israel, spiritual or otherwise. The writings of Moses and the Prophets are read for knowledge of the past and for lessons in how to avoid offending God. "Christian" doctrine and belief are gradually dejudaized. As Greek scholarship in philosophy and letters takes on the work of elaborating basic "Christian" teachings, a whole series of fresh concepts is evolved: Jesus is no longer called merely the Son of Man, nor merely the Son of God, but simply God. Greek concepts of *person, nature, relation,* and *cause* are employed to speak of God who has three distinct personal elements but who is, at the same time, one. The "Christian" doctrine of the Trinity is evolved.

"Christians," in dropping any claim to Abrahamic descent, spiritual or physical, and in renouncing any claim to be either a chosen people or the Chosen People, lose the inherent bipolarity of Judaism. By the end of the 4th century, Jesus has been de-individualized of his Jewishness and the notion of his supreme sacrifice has been rid of any resemblance to Biblical rituals. "Christians" are no longer saddled with the idea that God must be worshipped in one central shrine or that the authority of Jesus is vested in one principal man located in one particular geographical area.

This is, seemingly, the most improbable of all our Christian scenarios. Yet a careful reading of early Christian records, particularly of the *Acts of the Apostles*, shows us that even such thorough-going Jews as Paul and Peter and James came within a hair's breadth of this vision: a dejudaized Christianity and a Jesus de-individualized of his Jewishness. When the Council of Jerusalem (49-50 A.D.), under the persuasion of Paul and others, decided that non-Jewish converts need not become Jews, it was merely a small step in human logic to conclude that Christianity need not be Jewish in anything at all but its founder. And the Jewishness of the latter could be relegated to the geographical and historical dimensions of a man who was born, lived, and died as a Jew in a Jewish community, not to the Christ who rose from the dead and ascended into Heaven in supreme power. His spiritual dimensions were greater and grander.

We do know the thin, strong, psychological and social barriers which prevented the early Christian Jews from taking this decisive step: blind traditionalism, a pride of place, and a too slavish acceptance of the spontaneous forms of religious worship characteristic of all human reactions and activity.

But such a decision on the part of the early Christians would have voided any possibility of the later anti-Semitism that has marred Christianity socially and religiously for over 1800 years. It would also have prevented the rise of Romanism and the persuasion of temporal power which bedevilled the Christian Church for over 1000 years and finally brought on the splitting of its original unity by the 16th century Reformers. Jewish and Christian history would have been quite different. And humanity would have been the principal beneficiary.

9. The Usurpation

Cities, like women, can be classified according to the way in which they make an entrance. Constantinople and Alexandria, for example, can be likened to ravaged whores astride the seas, blackened by the usages and abuses of men, yet still commanding attention because of the suddenly impressive full view they offer with the traces of their original beauty. Damascus appears out of the sands at night like a scintillating jewel dropped in the middle of utter wastes. Rome appears as a thin rose strip on the distant horizon of the Latio plain, carrying the solid eminence of St. Peter's dome near its center. But Jerusalem is different.

When you approach Jerusalem in summer, walking from the coastal plain, the first indication of the city's presence is not visual but tactile. The air becomes progressively cooler and rarer, less stifling, as you climb. The effort of putting one foot in front of the other becomes increasingly laborious as the incline gets steeper. Poets sang of Jerusalem as a queen ringed around with hills. It is true. The Judean hills prevent you from seeing the hunched thrust of the city until you are almost near enough to hear the voices of the watchmen calling out the hours of the night. A traveler thus approaching one night in 49 A.D. would have noticed one house, still lit up at midnight, that stood on the western shoulder of a hill traditionally known as the site of a former Jebusite fortress stormed by David in the 10th century B.C.

Inside the house, a group of men sat around a table, listening to a small fiery man who was haranguing them in Aramaic. Paul, a converted Pharisee and trained rabbinical doctor, held the floor. The group of listeners included the original twelve followers of Jesus, together with the most prominent and influential of their converts.

The issue which had called the men together was a burning one: whether or not all non-Jewish male adults would have to undergo circumcision in order to join the New Covenant of Israel. Paul's stand on the issue was, like all he said and did, unmistakable. Peter had once complained that there were many hard things in Paul, and someone else had jokingly remarked that in Paul's language every needle became a two-edged sword, a simple spade became a Parthian shovel, and that Paul never presumed he could hand a hint to his audience: he always wrapped it up in molten iron and hit them over the head with it. In Paul's view, no non-Jewish convert should be held by any specifically Jewish law or prescription.

At the meeting in Jerusalem, the issue was quite simple in concept; but its solution required an effort of magnanimity and a breadth of vision which was capital. A wrong turning at this point would have condemned nascent Christianity to be hemmed into a provincial backwater, in which it would have been submerged and drowned, just like many a sect before and after it. The first substantial converts were arriving straight out of paganism, as the non-Judaic religions were later called. Should these converts be required to submit to all the ordinances and prescriptions demanded of born Jews? The question was a vital one, and it was not solved to complete satisfaction.

But a decision was taken. It was to the effect that non-Jewish converts should not be asked to obey all the Jewish prescriptions, they should "abstain from the meat of sacrifices" (partaking in such offerings implied worship of the pagan gods to whom the sacrifices were made), "and from fornication, etc." This decision, however, had one big implication: the members of the new creed were no longer *considered to be Jews* in the traditional and ethnic sense; nor was the new creed any longer considered to be the prolongation of Judaism. Whether any of those present at that fateful Jerusalem meeting formulated this implication consciously is something which we cannot now determine. It seems most unlikely that they did.

The rift that appeared between the majority of Jews in the eastern Jewish community and those Jews who believed in Jesus as the Messiah was due as much to the internal politics of the Jews (i.e. all Jews, "Christians" included) as to the dynamism released by belief in Jesus as the Messiah and the official reaction to it. Theoretically and practically it should have been possible to avoid such a painful division and the founding of such perpetual enmities. But when we have examined the situation thoroughly, we find that given the same circumstances and a chance to start all over again, the same protagonists would most probably make the same decision, act in the same way, and produce the same horrible result. We are at grips with the logic of history. Over a given period of time men dispose themselves, other men, and material resources into such configurations and stances that the complex of men and matter arrives at a critical threshold from which there is no drawing back. It merely requires the occasion, the instrument, the man, to set in motion an event already prepared in advance: a Luther to trigger the revolt against Rome in the 16th century; an assassination to justify Kaiser Wilhelm's war in 1914; the atomic bomb to render obsolete the totally independent nation-state in 1945.

So it was with the rift in Judaism over Jesus of Nazareth. It cannot be stressed enough that the vast portion of early Christian documents reflects the post-factum situation from the year 70 A.D. onward. We are again initially crippled by a matter of terminology. These early writings are usually called the *New Testament* as distinguished from the *Old Testament*. This nomenclature, however, can no longer be regarded as acceptable, even though by mere convention and by courtesy of understanding it is retained for want of a better one. But these names fit into the same category of odious and sectarian language to which the term "Christ-killer" has recently been relegated.[1] *New* and *Old Testament* are rather ancient expressions of the usurpation we are discussing in this chapter.[2] The proclaimers of the *New Testament* chose that adjective to indicate that the Judaism of the "other" Jews had been abrogated, and that the Testament of the latter was now the *Old*, the bypassed, that it had been legally, historically, and doctrinally cancelled by divine writ. But we will appreciate the extent, the pointless and the painful inevitability of this usurpation by the following considerations.

It is easy to approach this rift and usurpation with the sort of historicism which came into vogue only in modern times. Thus, we could say that "Christians" and "Jews" drifted apart because the "Christians" would not take part in the Jewish revolt of 66 A.D. This false historicism, however, neglects the socio-political framework of Judaism in which religious pluralism was inadmissible and whose consensus was uniquely religious. The peaceful insertion of the new sect within the bosom of the Jewish Community is described in one sentence by the *Acts of the Apostles:*

> Meanwhile, all through Judaea and Galilee and Samaria, the church enjoyed peace and became firmly established, guided by the fear of God and filled with encouragement by the Holy Spirit.[3]

This, however, could not have lasted long after the death of Agrippa I (44 A.D.). At that point, all the regions of Israel were consolidated into one Roman sub-province attached to the

[1] Since the Second Vatican Council, for Roman Catholics at least.

[2] The English term "testament" was chosen to translate the Greek *diatheke*, which in turn was often used to translate the Hebrew *berith*. But *berith* did not signify "testament."

[3] *Acts* 9:31.

province of Syria.[4] This sub-province was called *Judea*.[5] The stage was now set for a quick and deadly drama, a Götterdämmerung when Yahweh's heaven became a cavern of emptiness and longing for the Jews, when his glory departed from Israel. It ushered in the day of the long knives when death and destruction swept all in Israel.

The drama had a plot: Jesus versus the Temple. There was a painful conclusion: the pointless usurpation of name, title, heritage, books, traditions, promises, honor, and destiny. There were protagonists: Zealots [6] emanating from the mountains of Galilee; Essenians [7] training and praying in the desert by the shores of the Dead Sea and in the Negev; Sicarii [8] hiding the short lethal stab beneath their robes; there were the Roman legions composed of mercenaries; there were Roman Procurators, High-Priest, and Greek proselytes. Lastly, there were the followers of Jesus, standing, as it were, in the wings, seemingly excluded from the main developments but involved deeply in the plot.

We must try to realize the two threads of events which composed this drama. The two flowed alongside each other, intertwining, separating, knotting, cutting each other's path, never merging and uniting, one leading to the death of a polity, the other leading to a transformation and new life. The first of these was the religious nationalism of the Jews. The second of these was the development of the sect believing in Jesus as the Messiah. The final denouement took place over which was more important: Jesus or the Temple.

The first thread of the plot was set in motion by the death of Agrippa. Nationalism started to boil. By 48 A.D. the lurch towards violence was on.[9] Time only increased its viciousness

[4] Agrippa II received the region of Chalcis in 50 A.D. and the former kingdom of Philip, Herod the Great's son, consisting of Trachonitis, Batanis, and Aurantis, some years later.

[5] It was governed by a Roman Procurator resident in Caesarea on the Mediterranean and subordinate to the Roman Governor of the Province of Syria.

[6] Derived originally from the ranks of the Pharisees.

[7] Some controversy exists on the relationship of Zealots and Essenians and the people who owned the Dead Sea Scrolls.

[8] See footnote 4, page 23.

[9] The first two Roman procurators (44-48 A.D.) were passably acceptable to the Jewish Community. Beginning with Ventidius Cumanus (48-52) and ending with the execrable Gessius Florus, Roman rule became more and more intolerable.

and spread its afflictions. The list of causes, happenings, miseries, subplots, and violences during those days is endless:

Contemptuous treatment by Roman soldiery of pilgrims assembled in Jerusalem for the Passover; counter-riots; massacres of pilgrims; reprisal raids by Zealots; the rise and fall of the *sica* into the bowels and body of enemies of Judaism; the evermore frequent "incidents" between Roman garrisons and nationalist columns; the flowering of highway robbers and bands of brigands operating with the connivance of the highest Roman authorities on payment of "protection" money; the exaction of unmerited taxes; the breakdown of the caravan system of economic exchange; the profanation of the Temple by the Emperor's representative who grabbed 17 talents from Yahweh's treasure chest in the Temple. Mugging, murder, rape, penalization, mutilation, desecration of sacred books by the non-Jews living in the Jerusalem of the Jews; the slow disillusionment of the pacifist Pharisees in their majority; the increase of sectaries of all sorts hiding in the mountains, in the wadis, and in the desert places; the final act of rebellion in 66 A.D. Outraged by the porcine behavior of Gessius Florus, Eleazar, son of the High-Priest, managed to stop the offering of the daily Temple sacrifice for the Emperor. Israel thus rejected Rome. Death followed.

We must remember what animated the Jews: not the kind of nationalism that hurled millions of men against each other in the last two world wars, or embroiled the West in enormous brush-fire battles in Korea, in Malaya, in Vietnam. In the Jew there was no distinction at all between his love of Israel and his attachment to his religion. The Land was chosen by Yahweh for his people. Hatred, therefore, for the foreigner and the alien master drank strength and courage straight from the very vitals of Judaism. He was fighting for the Law, for the Temple, for the Chosen People, for Yahweh. Perhaps without knowing it, because Yahweh did not reveal his plans to mere men, he was fighting in the vanguard of the Last Great Battle before the coming of the Messiah to confront all forces of evil on the mountain of Megiddo.[10]

The second thread of the drama was the lifeline of the sect that professed belief in Jesus as the Messiah of Israel. There is

[10] Hence the "Armageddon" of later writings. *Har* in Hebrew means "mountain."

no doubt that they lived at peace in the heart of Judaism, that they shared the economic, religious, social, and political life of their co-religionists. They were in the Temple, in the synagogues throughout the land, in schools, and in the commerce of daily life. Yet they were awaiting a Second Coming. It was expected from week to week and year to year. Jesus had said that he would come back again for the last time to judge all men and to crown his work with eternal glory.[11] They remembered that his Second Coming would be announced by wars and rumors of war, by diseases, and persecutions. Meanwhile, as many chosen ones as possible must be saved, be led to know salvation in Jesus the Messiah.

The first serious abrasive criss-crossing with the thread of Jewish existence took place over a vital question: had Jesus saved non-Jews as well as Jews? If not, then in order to be saved by Jesus, all non-Jews would have to become Jews. This meant circumcision, submission to Jewish laws of ritual purity, and abstention from all things forbidden by the Law. All must become Jews.

Our main sources concerning this matter are not clear on the progress of events.[12] But they present the principal protagonists, some of their words, and their final decision. The whole affair could have turned out to be a sacrilegious Grand Guignol of their earlier dream. The first act was a tug of war between the cast-iron, unshakeable, Judaistic members of the sect and the slew of converts from non-Jewish sources.

The Gentile converts at the meeting objected: circumcision is a mutilation and an unbearable pain for adults; besides, it is a racial distinction; we are not of the physical descendance of Abraham. They objected further: if we do not believe in idols and if we mock and laugh at the foolish ceremonies performed in their honor, what harm is there in our eating the meat which has already been sacrificed to these blocks of wood and stone? The latter can neither speak, eat, walk, fly, much less save man. And they objected: meat without blood is tasteless, raw or cooked; will the eating of blooded or bloodless meat decide my entry into the kingdom of Jesus? The meat of certain animals is rarer and more delicate if the animals die by strangulation and not by the knife or drowning; what has this to do

[11] 1 *Corinthians,* 7:29.
[12] *Acts,* 15. *Galatians,* 2:1-10.

with the forgiveness of sins or purity of heart or faithfulness to Jesus?

The protagonists were chiefly Peter and Paul. James, Barnabas, Silas, and the others pass faceless in front of us. Peter walks through the pages of the *Acts* as gentle, slightly regretful, childlike, ever-learning—a man of narrow background and little education into whose spirit a huge light had burst and whose mind continually bathed in its reflection. Paul was the curmudgeon, the gnat, the gadfly of enemies, the fearless and outspoken companion of well-intentioned friends who disagreed with him and lived to regret it. Peter's double standards are exposed by Paul in a public letter: he found Peter, he wrote to the Galatians,[13] eating with Gentiles in Antioch until he was visited by associates of the straight-backed, Judaistic James; then Peter held himself aloof from the Gentiles, intimidated as he was by their presence. And Paul intimated that the "rest of the Jews" (he meant the other members of the sect) were not any less false to their professed Jewish principles. Paul told them so to their faces.

Paul had been scourged five times by the Jewish authorities, was beaten with rods three times, stoned once, shipwrecked three times, spent one day and one night floating in a shipwreck, grappled with innumerable swollen rivers, robbers, alien cities, unfriendly populations, unknown languages, wildernesses, treacherous associates, hunger, want, cold, and constant physical pain. Yet he never lost his capacity for pity, his ability to weep for the misery of others and the pain of life. He was bent forward all his life under the weight of the intuition of who Jesus was. He claimed to have seen him in a roadside vision. Tradition says that he was beheaded in Rome about the year 67 A.D.

The decision was made at the meeting of the apostles in Jerusalem without great difficulty. Peter had had two visions, and he was on the side of Paul and the new converts.[14] So was James. A letter was dispatched to Antioch where the difficulties had first arisen: no non-Jew need be circumcised; all should observe Jewish laws of ritual purity. The matter was closed. The decision constituted only a breach in the Jewish character of the sect. But it was enough. The motive alleged by

13 *Galatians,* 2:11-12.
14 *Acts,* 10 and 11.

the leaders proves this. "No burden should be laid upon you beyond these which cannot be avoided," ran the letter to Antioch.[15] "You must recognize that Abraham's real children are the children of his faith," wrote Paul some years later when discussing the Jerusalem meeting.[16] Followers of Jesus were still considered to be Jews,[17] but chiefly in a spiritual sense. Already Paul was instructing his non-Jewish converts that they need be Jews in no sense at all that conformed to traditional Judaism.[18]

As the fateful years passed and Judaism hurried to its appointment with destiny, the frictions and conflicts of the two threads grew more serious and more involved. In reality, the rivalry between the Jewish Community on the one hand, and the sect, on the other hand, grew more acute. Both believed that time was on their side. Both expected the Messiah and Yahweh to be their champions. The traditional Jews believed that they should arm for holy war. The sectarian Jews believed they should wait for Jesus to return.

Gradually, the new sect was excluded from religious ceremonies and the national cult. Synagogues here and there began to refuse admission to the local members of the sect. The increasing number of nationalist groups found the passivity of the sect intolerable; they even took it as a sign of complaisance in the face of Roman rule, and punished it severely. The day never arrived when the sect members were no longer welcome in the Temple, when they could no longer partake in the daily sacrifices or in the ceremonies. Even Paul worshipped in the Temple in the years immediately preceding its destruction, when tempers ran high.[19] But exclusion from synagogues and general disparagement of their beliefs led the believers to concentrate on their commemorative services and on the sacrifice of Jesus as expiation for all men's sins. The non-Jewish converts continued to accrue to the sect.

The picture which emerges of the believers in Jesus from the pages of their writings, particularly the Gospels, convinces us

[15] *Acts,* 15:28.
[16] *Galatians,* 3:7.
[17] *Acts,* 15:21.
[18] *Acts,* 21:21.
[19] Cf. *Acts,* 21:26-7.

that by the time Vespasian's army ringed Jerusalem with impassable military installations, the sect had, for all practical purposes, broken with official Judaism. In the Gospels, particularly those of Matthew, Mark, and Luke, we find mirrored a new state of affairs: there are obvious references to the destruction of the city, and there is an openly expressed opposition to the officials of Judaism, the Pharisees, the Scribes, and the Priests. There is, above all other elements, a permanent prejudice against the "Jews" couched in such determined language and so permeating the entire presentation of the primitive message that we can only conclude that something drastic had happened to human relations between traditional Jews and the sect since the early years of the forties, when the attitude of the latter had been that they were truly members of the house of Israel—but in its consummation.

We find, for instance, in the fourth Gospel that the parallelism and symbolism of the text is geared in what would justly be termed today as an anti-Semitic or Hebraeophobic way. The earthly career of Jesus of Nazareth is represented as the heightening parabola of Light which goes on increasing among the followers and believers of Jesus until the final flash of revelation on Calvary and at the Tomb. The darkness and error of his enemies, the "Jews," goes on in similar geometric progression to a nadir in the crime of deicide, putting the Son of God to death. It is difficult to reconcile this segregating of the "Jews" as the hardened core of opposition to the Truth and as distinct from the followers of Jesus, unless we assume that, for the writers of such texts and for those to whom the texts were destined, the term "Jews" had become a term not only of opprobrium, but a description of their mortal enemies.

When the Temple was destroyed in 70 A.D., the members of the sect took this as a sign that Jesus was about to return. In the years between that destruction and the declaration of the Emperor Trajan, in the early years of the 2nd century, that he would allow the Temple to be rebuilt, relations of the sect with Judaism became strained to the breaking point. Already, the followers of Jesus were spreading their beliefs abroad. Instead of worshipping with the other Jews they now concentrated on their commemorative service which they believed took the place of the Temple and its sacrifice. What need was there of sacrifices? Jesus had performed the supreme sacrifice.

The Christians rejected with horror Trajan's proposal to rebuild the Temple: this would be a setback of God's timetable. The Romans at this time realized that the Christians were not just another Jewish sect, but a separately viable and growing group. The persecutions began. But they served only to emphasize Christian alienation from the Jews. Simon Bar Kokhba led the Second Jewish revolt in 132. By 135 the heart of Judaism had been torn out, Jerusalem had been definitively profaned, only Gentiles were allowed to enter it.

For the Jews, desperately struggling to reconstruct Judaism and preserve it, the Christians became more and more apostates and not Jews at all. For the Christians, the omission of the Jewish burdens of Law and precept became imperative if they were to convert the Mediterranean world. They carried with them, however, the persuasion that they were the true inheritors of the promises of Abraham. And with the promises they took the Books, the Prophets, the honor, and the character of the Chosen People. The Jewish converts who believed in Jesus died and were not replaced.

Slowly, each side hardened in its position, each one emphasizing the elements that separated it from the other, minimizing those they held in common. By the fourth century, Christianity was proclaimed throughout the Empire as lawful and as the state religion. The break was complete. Christianity was now identified with a culture and a system of thought which were utterly alien to the culture and outlook of Israel and Judaism. By the sixth century, normative Judaism had emerged in its great Talmudic codifications, and Christianity had undergone its first major period of formation through its scholars and its councils. The Church, as we know it, had been born. The drama was over. Usurpation was complete.

For many Christians, it is practically impossible to realize the extent of this usurpation, much less to unthink its toils. For it is structured in a series of ancient and venerated thought-molds petrified and hardened by bimillenial age, encrusted with successive layers of Christian theology, philosophical speculation, and pietistic practice. To unthink the usurpation would be to ring down the curtain on an act of history still continuing, to call for a drastic recasting of vital roles in the drama of man's relationship to a Saviour-God. To do this would, in the eyes of many, threaten the essence of Christianity itself. Yet, we must formulate the Usurpation. It is the traditional Christian version of what happened.

When God's voice spoke to Abraham through the dusk of a far away evening in the Orient and conferred on him the paternity and origin of the Chosen People, the first and preparatory action in the drama had begun its inexorable course to Christianity—so Christian thought had always maintained. Judaism was supposed to pave the way for Christianity: Moses prefigured Christ, and the constant theme of Israel's salvation through her God-appointed leaders foreshadowed the final act of divine salvation which the God-Man would perform in his own blood on the rounded top of Golgotha. All was prefiguration, preparation, foretaste.

The stage-trappings of Egypt, Sinai, Jordan, of Jerusalem, Kingship, Temple, were God-appointed decor and background against which paraded and played the successive figures of Judaism: Patriarch, Seer, Judge, Prophet, King, High-Priest, Sacred Writer, Scholar, even the grandiose and central figure of Moses himself. Not without theological reason did medieval artists represent the light shining out of Moses' face, on his descent from Sinai with the Tablets of the Law, as a reflection of Christ's five wounds on the Cross. All was oriented, according to Christian thought, to the second and final act of the drama, the advent of Messiah, of the Nazarene, of Jesus the God-Man.

Theologically speaking, all that Judaism held as godly, true, noble, perseveringly valuable, was only so in virtue of Christianity, a valid form of pre-Christian belief because it was ordained to merge into the later religion. And no stage-director ever issued such peremptory orders to his actors as God issued to Judaism and to Jews on the advent of Jesus and the consummation of his redemptive sacrifice. It was not merely an *exeunt omnes,* an order to clear the stage, to huddle into the dark wings of history, to make room for the dominant and succeeding act. The Jews and Judaism had outlived their theological usefulness and their historical significance. They had not merely to get off the stage of history. They had to change costumes, to adopt new rules. For Judaism had now become by divine ordinance Christianity. The Old Testament had ceded to the New Testament. Ancient Israel gave way to the New Israel. The first Christians were to be the Jewish nation itself. *Exeunt omnes:* Priest, Prophet, Moses. Enter the protagonists of the final act: Apostle, Disciple, Virgin, Church, Bishop, Priest, all oriented to the Nazarene, God's son, dead, resurrected, glorified, triumphant, the leader of the New Israel.

Temple worship was abrogated—Christ was to be adored. The predominance of the Book was rescinded—henceforth the Spirit incarnate in a visible teaching authority was to enlighten man and to interpret the Book. Further persistence in life of a separate Judaism was nonsense in terms of history, for all history, including that of the Jewish race, had been re-polarized around the newly revealed mystery of God's incarnation and man's redemption by a cross. All that Judaism ever promised, all the good it ever presaged, every guarantee it gave of final salvation, all had been realized in cold historical reality. Judaism, in Karl Barth's pregnant phrase, had been consummated. Christianity replaced it as man's source of salvation, of divine knowledge, of human ethical wisdom.

10. The Ancient Beauty

Because of the Usurpation, there is a certain parallel between the physical modes of Judaism and those of Christianity. As in the case of Judaism, what is required is to outline how these modes acquired their final form. The physical modes are chiefly four: *Jacobism, Mission, Occidentalism,* and the *Two Cities.*

Under *Jacobism* is included the "christianized" forms and elements of Judaism which Christianity simply took over: the persuasion that it was the new Israel with a new Testament, that it was the Chosen People, that it was the Promised Land, that all the good in pre-Christian days was good in virtue only of Christianity. The mode of *Mission* implies that Christianity thinks of itself as possessing exclusively the truth about man and his needs and his destiny, and that it has received a divine mission to convert all other peoples. *Occidentalism* refers to the traits which Christianity adopted when it entered definitively into the cultures and the civilization of the West. To a certain

profound degree, Christianity molded and made those cultures and that civilization in the coming thousand years. But
it is also true to say that they in turn influenced Christianity.
The physical mode of the *Two Cities* has been by far the most
damaging of all the modes to Christianity. By these terms we
express the bipolarity of Christianity: as for Judaism, the world
was composed of the saved and the damned, the chosen and
the rejected, the believers and the unbelievers. Christianity,
however, decided early in its history to dominate both parts.
Included, therefore, in its Two Cities mode is a deliberate immersion of Christianity in the quest for and the wielding of
temporal power of a varied kind.

It will be noted that of these four physical modes of Christianity's dominance, only one, *Mission,* can be said to belong
essentially to Christianity. Even in this case, while the claim to
possess the unique truth about the life and death of man may
be a legitimate stance for a religious belief, the various ways in
which Christianity expressed this sense of *Mission* were sometimes very far removed from its ideals as proposed by other
principles. The Gospel of Love has not always been preached
or defended with love. Some comments on all four modes is
in order here. Prior to that, we must comment on the roles of
two men, Peter and Paul.

In the history of Christianity, the statuesque figures of Peter
and Paul have always been set up, sometimes as complements
one to the other, sometimes as contraries, always distinguished
from each other, never successfully disassociated. Certainly up
to the Reformation, they were regarded as the co-founders of the
Christian Church centered in Rome. Yet nature had rarely
wrought two characters so blatantly diverse; history has seldom smiled so mischievously or plotted so much like a pol-
tergeist of religion in human affairs, as when she flung Peter
and Paul into the same orbit.

For Peter was brother of stones and cousin of waters, a child
of the earth, of hard toil, of sustenance eked out in sweat, of
blood and bone and flesh hammered by the rudeness of generations among the mountains and the wild lake waters of Galilee. His wisdom was told him by the uncontrollable elements
which man has always sought to dominate with the spell of
mythology or the shining lever of technology. And his reactions to life and fortune were a healthy complex of peasant's

cunning and forgiveness, the unspoiled spontaneity of non-city folk. We have records of his petty fibs and his grand treachery, of his anger and his love. This sufficed for his greatness.

Paul was a hybrid, the best of Hellenism with its most provincial traits, the gleaning of a twilight Judaism with its most exaggerated myopia: heir to Pharisaism's patient religion, the gentlest tradition known in the ancient Mediterranean, modelled by Greek schools, indentured long to the finely shaped rigidities of rabbinic legalism, a walking theater of constant warfare within himself between the static symmetry of Atticism and the compulsion of a Semite's unarrested dynamism. His wisdom was a mixture: reason, intuition, passion, violent loves and hates, grandeur and misery. He was citified, cosmopolitan, megalopolitan. We can today read his syntheses, his perceptions, and his dead illogicalities and realize that, withal, he lived as he believed so fiercely and died for the love of a person who spoke once to him on a lonely road outside Damascus. This was the inspiration of his greatness.

Each of these men symbolized a different aspect of Christianity's coming high period of unity and life. The Keys and the Cross. The Revelation and the Commandment. The Glory and the Power. The Pain and the Kingdom. The Salvation and the Sin. The Kiss and the Handshake. Each of them affected history profoundly. But Peter approached it as a pet animal: he tugged at its dewlaps. Paul attacked it as a master-smith: he poured a molten stream of word and action over its settling surface. As such, they stood for different types. The Fisherman and the Scholar. The Mystic and the Philosopher. The Priest and the Rabbi. The Forgiver and the Lawgiver. The Ox and the Eagle. Both lived in obscure poverty and died in unknown pain. Yet it was they who settled beneath the arcades of the Forum and in the lengthening shadows of the Roman aqueducts carrying the baptism of Jesus throughout the centuries and the nations of the West.

They exercised key roles in the formation of Christianity's dominance. We must remark, first of all, that in the only written evidence at hand Peter undeniably is pictured as exercising a leading role in the nascent group of Jesus' followers after the latter's death. Many objections can be urged against what has come to be called the primacy of Peter and especially

the primacy of the bishops of Rome who succeeded him there.
It has been denied, foolishly, that Peter was ever in Rome. We
have as much evidence, direct and collateral, that Peter was in
Rome as we have that Caesar was in England, Alexander in
India, or Herodotus in Egypt. Without, however, insisting on
any primacy of a doctrinal and dogmatic kind for Peter, we
must admit his position of leadership according to the New
Testament. We have no other evidence but that for arguments
either way. And it is positive in this sense. The influence of
Paul is admitted by all, but exaggerated by some who would
try to rid early Christianity of any real connection with Jesus
of Nazareth.

Given this leadership of Peter and the predominance of Paul's
teaching, the molding influence of these two men was incal-
culable. In effect, it was Peter and Paul who supported the
decision at the first Apostolic meeting in Jerusalem to admit
non-Jews to the new faith but not to require of them that they
become Jews. Far more momentous was Peter's settling in Rome
and Paul's formulation of the new doctrine which seemingly
preserved the Jewishness of the religion but adapted it to non-
Jewish believers. When the Palestinian center of the new
religion was extinguished, it was replaced by the western
community in Italy. When the break with Judaism made it
impossible for Christians to think anymore with their former
religious brothers, it was Paul's teaching which made it possible for them to think of themselves as the new Israel inherit-
ing all that was good in the old Israel. Peter and Paul, therefore,
are directly responsible both for the Jacobism and the Occidentalism of Christianity. The sense of Mission was innate in the
new belief. The Two Cities mode was a much later development
that could never have entered the head of either Paul or Peter.

Jacobism

In speaking of the beginnings of Christianity, we noted that
in the first few decades of its existence very little remarkable
outer difference separated the early followers of Jesus from
their fellow-Jews. Even when the break came with Palestinian
Judaism and the Jerusalem authorities in the years prior to 70
A.D., a vibrant and representative body of Jewish followers of

Jesus subsisted in Palestine. We only know that between 112 A.D. and 150 A.D. the death knell of this Palestinian community was sounded. This community has wrongly been called Judeo-Christian: in its heyday it consisted of Jews who were accepted as Jews by their fellow Jews, and who believed that they were true Jews. By the time that the Christians formed a definitively separate and distinct religious group, the Palestinian community of Jews who believed in Jesus was no more. Christianity belonged to the people outside the ancient Land.

We find it impossible today even to outline the particular religious attitudes of that early Palestinian community of believers in Jesus. The destruction in Palestine was so great, the break with official Judaism was so sharp, the immersion of Christianity in its new surroundings in the Roman Empire was so deep, that when Christian voices are heard speaking from the middle of the 2nd century onward, the accents are recognizably un-Jewish. Christianity was henceforth plunged into a radically different society and caught up in a totally different political framework. It speaks powerfully for the transforming effect of sociological and political conditions of the Roman Empire that within three centuries there is absolutely no recognizable trace of the ancient formulation of Christian belief such as it was prior to 70 A.D. Traces of it lingered on for some decades in Palestine, in Asia Minor, and in some southern Italian settlements. Doubtless, the writings of *Hermas* and the *Didache of the Twelve Apostles* both contain elements of it. But we have no critical rule by which to sift this material.

In its stead, there emerged a community that cannot be explained merely on the basis of the outlook and beliefs described in the New Testament. In fact, the puzzling interval between 36 A.D. and 70 A.D. would remain inexplicable if we confined ourselves to that source. Something had been born; there had been a resurrection of the human spirit issuing in a community of men which Diocletian feared and Constantine finally acknowledged at the Milvian Bridge. There had been installed in the eastern Mediterranean a new economy of human life and a fresh creation of energy and hope which we cannot attribute either to the decadent Roman civilization of the Julio-Claudian house or to the synthetic formulas of the New Testament writings. A new faith had been born.

True, it had once formed part of Judaism, but only for less

than twenty years. When it broke with Judaism it was not through some fortuitous cause or chance error on somebody's part. The central theme of the new faith, originally formulated in a purely Jewish manner, was an explosive one: Jesus was the Messiah; he had come; he had redeemed. Neither Judaism nor the world would ever be the same again. Christianity, in other words, had to come to the fore. It does not seem to have been necessary for it to have broken with Judaism. Above all, it seems unnecessary for it to have usurped the trappings and honor, nomenclature and titles of Judaism. It did. This was Jacobism. And this mode of its new existence outside Judaism only added one more dimension to its already inherent exclusivity. It was now the Chosen People and inherited all that these chosen ones used to possess.

Mission

This mode implies two things: persuasion that the truth resides uniquely with oneself and conviction that one must communicate this to others. The first element of *Mission* was inherited by Christianity directly from Judaism. The second element is in no sense Jewish and was a new feature of the new religion. As far as we can judge, Christianity has always had this persuasion of its *Mission*. We find also that few religions in history, except perhaps Islam at its apogee, insisted so fiercely and devotedly on this mode.

Christianity claimed this mode and all that was necessary to live it authentically. It claimed absolute authority, just as it claimed absolute authenticity, in proposing man's way to salvation. It claimed that all other ways to salvation either were abrogated by its arrival on the scene, or could be justified only by virtue of its exalted function. It claimed further to be the only religion to which God had made inner revelations about his own nature. Finally, it was unique in that it claimed that each and every living member of its body could be in living mystical communion with God—in a way neither described, nor possible, nor suspected, in any other religion. Christianity, in a word, made the most demanding requests on its adherents. In return, it promised the ultimate of ultimates in religious surety, moral perfection, and after death, eternal happiness of the most elevated kind.

Occidentalism

When Christianity made its fundamental option against the Jewish people and the Judaism of its day and for the "nations," we must understand what it was that Christianity chose. The option was perhaps inevitable—one would like to think the contrary, but at all events it was fraught with consequences. With our modern mentality enlarged to the dimensions not merely of entire continents and the complete globe on which we live, but to the immeasurable distances that make up our cosmos, we are inclined to take it for granted that, in renouncing "the backwater of Judaism in Palestine," Christianity opted for that globe and that cosmos.

But this is an anachronistic interpretation. When the New Testament speaks of the early Christian Church turning out to the "nations," it does not mean that they turned out consciously to all men upon the five continents and around the seven seas, much less to the worlds we are now beginning to discover and assess beyond the sun. The "nations" meant the relatively small circumscribed peoples living in the Eastern Mediterranean, mainly, with vague references to the outlying territories of the Roman Empire to the north, west, south, and east. And it meant, above all, an option to permeate the Roman Empire as such. Thus the step from Judaism was not to a greater universalism, but to other forms of particularism.

In time, it came to mean a substitution of Occidentalism for the Semitism inherent in the Judaism they were leaving. In time, the Jews themselves would be forced to discard that Semitism and to cohabit the West with a malignant Christianity. And thus it has come about that Christianity in this century finds itself constricted to merely one mentality out of all the babel of mentalities of mankind that increasingly clamor for recognition, for development. In this matter, whatever form or kind of Christianity is discussed, whether it be Roman Catholicism, Anglicanism, Greek or Russian Orthodoxy, or any of the other major denominations, the state of affairs is the same: essentially, they are, one and all, Occidental expressions of the same Christian message. And essentially they do not appeal to the greater masses of Asia and Africa and Oceania. It thus happens that in our day Christianity finds itself in the almost exclusive possession of the European delta, of the Western

Hemisphere, and of other regions such as South Africa and Australia which were colonized by Occidentals. Its writ runs no further.

Two Cities

This mode goes back to the principle installed by Solomon, instituting twin arms of government. In modern terms, we would call these the sacred and the profane. The struggle between the Church and the State mirrors the same distinction. This physical mode of Christianity implies, however, that the profane, or secular, is subject to the sacred, is infused by the sacred with life, legitimacy, authority, and perdurance. The sacred, on the other hand, is maintained physically by and propagated with the active connivance and subservience of the profane and secular. And, in reality, there is but one source of government, the sacred. It, however, delegates authority to the secular. It also oversees the latter's behavior.

The expression itself, Two Cities, was made famous by Augustine of Hippo (354-430 A.D.). Under the pressure of the Vandal invasion of North Africa, Augustine formulated this doctrine, depicting the City of God as the kingdom of God, and pointing to this world as the City of Mammon in which, nevertheless, the City of God had to live and eventually dominate. There would always be an inherent opposition between these two cities, Augustine maintained, but the City of God would try continually to leaven and purify the City of Mammon. This leavening and purification was translated some centuries later into terms of ecclesiastical domination and the subservience of political powers to religious authorities.

The accession of Christianity to the position of actually wielding temporal power was not a conscious or a primary aim of the early Christian Church. It was an implicit result of the doctrine it preached. Christianity claimed to have the truth about all things, profane and sacred. The actual course of history helped it in its journey to power, because when all other authoritative government was failing, Christianity's representatives were there. More powerful than the pressure of historical lacunae in power blocs was the totality of the Christian teaching. A ruler who was Christian or who converted to the new faith found that not only was his interior and spiritual life governed by his religion, but his exterior actions also came under it and his decisions required its blessing.

Christianity claimed, in other words, to dominate the City of God on earth and to have all authority, all enlightenment, and all guidance necessary for the due government and consummation of the City of Man on the same earth. There was a time when it claimed absolute temporal authority over this City of Man. At one moment, it came near to wielding such absolute authority. Some of its worst excesses have been committed in the name of that absolute authority, just as some of its most poignant sufferings and most of its dazzling achievements have been witnessed in the same City of Man. But whatever be the degree of authority or respect it enjoys in the City of Man or the hierarchy of its powers in the City of God, one thing is sure: Christianity is obliged by its very nature to inhabit both Cities. By its very nature it cannot, or has not been able to, accept a secondary place in the City of Man. There is always a nostalgia in Christianity for the days when it was the sole accepted religion, when it ruled the City of Man as the sole legitimate representative of the City of God.

The complex stance adopted by Christianity due to these four physical modes must be seen as Christianity's "imitation" of its Jewish model. Indeed, one theme on which the Church theologians and writers of the first six Christian centuries are unanimous is that the Christian Church is supposed, by divine ordinance, to reproduce mystically the history of the Chosen People as it is recounted in the Bible. Churchmen, however, were inclined concretely to interpret this mystical aspect rather materially and literally. By Jacobism, the Church claimed all of Israel's privileges. By Mission, it asserted an aggressive uniqueness. By Occidentalism, it purported to be God's universal message. By the Two Cities, it claimed the Promised Land. Just as only in their Promised Land could the Israelites enjoy their privileges and be unique as a light to the nations, and just as that Promised Land of Canaan had to be cleared of its indigenous inhabitants, so Christianity entered the Occidental world to convert it. As remarked, the conversion was first conceived of mystically. Within two centuries of its exodus from Judaism, Christianity was on its way to real conquest and possession of the West.

There thus arose in Christianity its desire for temporal power. One often gets the impression that only the Roman Catholic Church was afflicted with this desire. Up to the 16th century, this Church was the effective leader and center of all other Christian churches. When the latter broke from Rome, we find no diminution whatsoever of this desire for temporal power as a spiritual means in the splinter churches. Nothing could have been more power-conscious than the Anglican Established Church, the Dutch and Swiss Calvinist Churches, the German and Scandinavian Lutheran and Evangelical Churches, the Greek and Russian Orthodox Churches. Whether it was the Vatican and the Spanish Court, the Moscow Patriarchate and the Czar's Court, the Anglican Church and the Court of St. James, the German Lutherans and the Junker class, the Swiss Calvinists and the Canton authorities, the Danish, Norwegian, and Swedish Churches and their respective monarchies, or the Pilgrim Fathers and the newly born American colonies, the story was the same.

Each one of these exercised the same political and social ostracism against members of churches other than their own; they applied the same rigid social barriers, made outcasts, declared heretics, put people to death and in prison and to torture, were just as virulent as any Spanish or Italian Romanists in their fervor and their bias, and indulged in a Hebraeophobia as degrading and unchristian as anything devised south of the European Alps. As Talleyrand is supposed to have remarked once apropos of heretic-burnings: "Be it Protestant or Roman, fire around my shanks is just as painful." Christianity as a whole sinned in this way.

No Christian church, however, succeeded in exercising and maintaining the same temporal sovereignty the Roman Catholic Church has even down to this day. In this sense and this sense only, we can take the latter's temporality as a paradigm of Christianity's weakness and faulty historical judgement. There is a photograph of the signing of the Lateran Treaty on February 11, 1929, which speaks volumes for the pathos of all Christian yearnings for temporal power. Dictator Mussolini, already seven years in power, had decided to make peace with the Roman Church. If Paris was worth a Mass to Henry IV in 1594, Italy is worth a small patch of land in the middle of Rome in 1929. Mussolini has one reason in mind: he will thus gain the Church's support, thereby unifying Italians behind him and giving Italian Fascism a sweet odor in the nostrils of Roman Catholics throughout the world. Fifty years before, the Piedmontese had taken Rome: the Pope had become known as the Prisoner in the Vatican. By granting the Pope a small, absolutely independent domain in Rome, he will effect all this. All prior negotiations for the Vatican were carried on by the aging but able Cardinal Gasparri.

Here now in the Palazzo dei Arti, on the Via della Conciliazione, Cardinal Gasparri and Count Ciano, Mussolini's Foreign Minister, were handed golden-tipped pens, smiles appeared, and the two signatures were appended each to six separate copies of the Lateran Treaty. The "Roman question" had been solved. The captivity was over. Mussolini had removed a thorn from the side of his nascent regime. And the Vatican had emerged in geographical security and independence with its honor unsmirched. It entered once more the comity of international diplomatic life as an independent power. This was the promise fulfilled. This was the triumph. And this was the tragedy.

No more fateful scene is preserved in official photographs of modern Roman Catholic Church activity than that group of Vatican and Fascist diplomats around the wide table on which lay the signed copies of the treaty. Staring out at later generations are the faces of men, all of whom have since died, some of them in a storm which they helped to create, such as De Bediglione; one before a firing-squad, such as Ciano; and others by the hand of the Great Witherer.

Gasparri is' obviously old, obviously contented, and quite clearly unwavering. Ciano is smooth, triumphant, grinning broadly, and feckless. None, seemingly, understands the full meaning of the act he has just accomplished. The politicians are saying with their smile: "This is the last foundation-stone of the regime. Now we can build a new *Pax Romana* in a new empire." The Churchmen are indicating by their ease, their insistent dignity, their diplomatic calm, that the irredentism of fifty bleak years has paid off in solid dividends, that a new era for the Church has opened up in continuity with the age-old stature of Rome. A battle was lost; but the war was won.

And this was the tragedy: there was a continuity with the Old Order. For the postage-stamp size Vatican City was more than a symbol of independence and power. It was the centerpiece of the most antique and profoundly rooted fiefdom in

Christianity's history, and when all else had perished of the former possessions, it had floated intact on the face of all the turbulent floods of change since the time of Leo the Great, carrying with it unchanged and unmitigated the City of God that Augustine had conceived, Aquinas had rationalized, Lepanto had saved, Luther had besieged, Loyola had defended, Napoleon had misunderstood, Hitler had underestimated as the product of subhuman peoples, and Stalin had derided as bereft of military divisions, which was to outlive them all and meet its biggest threat in the second half of the century, not at the hands of persecutor or heretic, but from the rising surge of internal dissolution.

The event now frozen in old photographs and modern memories is, as remarked, a paradigm of Christian dominance in its most pathetic form. For already the circumstances of world life were making the independent nation-state obsolete. Even a symbolic independence such as Mussolini granted and the Vatican accepted is outworn and pointless, emphasizing only the obsolescence of an ancient imperialism propagated in the name of eternal love and of an eternal god. When we examine the dominance crisis of Christianity in a later chapter, we will decide that all such trappings have become a hindrance, not a help, to Christianity.

PART III
Helpers and Emigrants

11. God's Last Offer

If you had been there at the end of the Ramadan month, in 610 A.D., you would have had difficulty in finding the man we are discussing. He was the man chosen by Allah, the supreme and only god, to convert his fellow-Meccans to the true faith. Meccans worshipped a bedlam of false gods among whom they numbered Allah. Now this man was chosen to restore the unique and rightful worship of Allah. For over a month, the holy season had reigned: all raiding parties had tethered their camels and horses; swords had been sheathed; women secluded; buying and selling restricted; feasting and rejoicing forbidden. Now all that was over. All the day and well into the evening Mecca was rejoicing as it always had rejoiced, as perhaps only it knew how to rejoice and live—drinking, dancing, buying, selling.

The man was certainly not in the marketplace where Greeks and Arabs and Egyptians and Persians and Abyssinians and Indians thronged, shouting and gesticulating, rubbing shoulders with plots and stratagems, selling bodies for metal, bartering silk with blood, exchanging camels for slaves, axeheads for sandals, perfume for onions and wild peas; haggling with hands, smiling with lips, crushing the lie between honey and dried figs. The man sought peace. Peace was not here.

No more than between the paws of a mountain lion was there peace among the hearts drained of mercy, the minds raging at the rattle of little coins, men choking at the stink of it, the misery of it, the heart of darkness blackening each one of them, as if the serpent gods of Egypt or the bull-headed python goddesses of the Abyssinians were laughing at men's squalor, laughing and enjoying it, and egging men on. The man had learned to escape from all that, before this aging evil world had pressed him down with the others, before it snuffed out the wick of hope in him, before the dead weight of mountains, of idol-crazing, of drunkenness, could break him apart. As Mecca reveled and haggled through the day, he sought entrance to the holy Ka'aba enclosure to pray.[1] Later, however, a path leading from the city would carry him—Mohammad, son of Aminah and Abdullah—to the mountains.

Once, three years before, he had tried to spend a whole night of prayer in the Ka'aba. Qusai, the keeper of the keys, had allowed him to stay for a consideration of some dirhams. But the whole experience had gone sour: some of his Meccan acquaintances had found him there toward sundown, and their behavior caused him agonies for weeks afterward. They had crowded at the gate, the lot of them: Abu Sofian, the burly blustering rug merchant; Ikrima ibn Al Waleed, the one-eyed supervisor of the camel pens; Umar ibn Abdulla, with his brothers Hamasa and Ali who controlled the city taxation on spices; the grizzly Abbas ibn Abi Mota with his hunched back, falsetto voice, syphilitic stumps of arms, and blasphemous sense of humor, all of them chanting a list of names of gods and goddesses interspersed with lewd remarks and suggestions as to why he was spending the night there.

The refrain of names had beat on his ears like a series of

[1] The Ka'aba, at the beginning of the 7th century, was a rectangular building about 27 feet in height, made of mud and brick, its roof supported on a double row of columns. It housed the famous black stone, probably a meteorite, an object of devotion in pre-Islamic Arabia.

well-aimed unavoidable pellets: "Manat, Uzza, Hobal, Tirtir," and so on right around the half-moon row of Mecca's 360 statues standing in the enclosure, ending with the vulgar satyr-goddess of *djinns,* Al-Lakti. He had finally given up and fled home, but the refrain stayed in his ears as irritating, as infectious, and as repetitiously gnawing as bits of red dust whipped up in a desert storm. What had galled him was that his tormentors were mainly townsfolk; very few of them hailed from the Bedouin tribes. "Manat, Uzza, Hobal . . ."

His wife Khadija had heard him repeating the words in his sleep for weeks afterward. She used to wake him up, bathe his forehead with water, and cradle him to sleep again. "Do not attempt to pray again in the city," she had later counseled, "go to the mountains, where your father and grandfather used to retire once a year for some weeks. Live with the Bedouins; you have many friends among them. They will feed you." Since then, he had taken every now and then to the mountains, searching patiently until he had found a cave which had obviously never been found by anyone.

On this particular evening, therefore, after praying in the holy enclosure, while Meccans rejoiced in the streets, he would, he decided, remain in his cave.

He found Qusai and requested from him a short time in the Ka'aba. Standing behind Qusai, who was laboriously undoing the seven sacred locks, it seemed to him that he was looking at the Ka'aba for the first time. For in his mind, an epoch of his life was closing. The black cube of the building had always before appeared to be clad in an aura of mystical power. But now the black brocade draping its walls seemed to be a demonic skin, not a miraculous covering to be touched in parched desperation by worshippers pleading for forgiveness, for salvation. From a nearby house came the strains of a querulous desert song: a girl chanting her love for the man of her choice.

Qusai left him in the silent darkness, stepped outside and pulled the door after him. As usual, the man prostrated himself in adoration on the mat and tried to pray. Prayer did not come. Instead, revulsion swamped his being. No matter how he tried to pray, no matter the tears of effort which stung his eyes, the sensation of being filled with impurity incarnate and with all that degraded him grew. He could not lull his mind and soul into peace with invocations. All the memories of past

prayers and meditations flooded helter-skelter in a jumbled con-
torted stream through his thoughts. His prayer stopped. He
lay there and struggled in silence. All his strength concentrated now on resisting.

A stench hit his nostrils. He fought it. A twisted image of
Allah bleeding oceans of hot, sticky red blood poured over
his mind. He repelled it. It was succeeded by a grinning rabbi
shrieking wordlessly at him. He blotted the image out. A
ragged rabble of Christians carrying naked dancing-girls, grinning rabbis wielding stone tablets, Moses drinking Allah's blood,
surged at him. Bleeding Allah, grinning rabbi, bleeding Allah,
grinning rabbi; the images whirled faster and faster out of all
control, like a hellish hurdy-gurdy beating balefully on the bas-
tions of his being. His body rocked and shook convulsively in
the silence. Then a burning taper crackled suddenly and went
out. It could have been a thunder-clap.

A stifled cry of fright broke through his teeth. His nightmare dream shattered like a cocoon. A stab of panic stiffened
his flesh. He was being pushed into a screaming fall as from
sanity. In an instant, he was on his feet, at bay now and staring
wild-eyed around the semi-darkness. The Black Stone embedded
in the eastern wall was a sullen tongue of some obsidian demon
stuck out at him in vulgar derision. For one moment his eyes
caught the glint of silver arrows, golden platters, bronze spear-
points hanging from the ceiling as votive offerings from Bedouins once cornered in a desert wadi by thirst or trapped on
the sand-dunes with a sword blade at their throat.

Then he dashed out into the sunlight past the waiting
Qusai, through the colonnade of white granite columns standing in a half-moon, past the frigid statues, past all the deities of
the Arabs, the phalli of Al-Uzza, of Allat, of Manat, the male
stone trunk of the Syrian Hobal, past the footprints of Abraham,
father of all the Faithful, frozen in the ground, past the blue-
white waters of the Zamzam well mirroring yesterday's mistakes and tomorrow's treacheries, out into the street and to the
city gate.

The path was one he knew well. It ran eastward past the
house of his birth, then northward parallel to the Taif road
for about three miles, branching eastward again through a long
gorge, then up the side of the Abu Qais mountain for about
800 yards. The last hundred yards was a stiff climb from rock
to rock, perching for breath on ledges, treading carefully over

thin, deep gashes and cruel clefts, the solid shoulder of earth and rock at his right, the open mouth of nothingness at his left, until he lifted himself up finally on to a narrow ledge which ran around a thick funnel of rock. The cave where he usually took refuge lay around a corner of the funnel. From it he could see all: the valley, Mecca, the mountains west of the town, and on clear mornings he could catch, so he imagined, the glint of the sea heaving anew for another day's struggle.

There was still an hour to sundown. He could not enter the cave until the night closed swiftly down on him. This was his practice. So he stood there, his skin tautened brittle beneath the Arabian heat, over his head a sky of fleckless blue shooting to eternity, fractured only by the furnace of the sun already dipping toward the western sea. Ache from the climb spread through his limbs, capsules of disgust swallowed at each labored breath. To climb up here was to revisit a disused hell in which slivers of sun had endlessly shattered rock, earth, sand, mudbrick, painted tile, short tempers, and human life, so that what remained of the spirit was scorched, strangled, seared. Beneath him was the small valley hedged by black-grey mountains, slashed with dry gullies and ravines, void of vegetation, empty of any life in bird or insect save for the scorpion and the desert-snake, burning during the day, cold and unwelcoming at night, shrouded always in the presence of demon and deity, man and slave, sand and sky, always the sand, the heat always.

He knew when the twilight was about to begin: an invisible cloak of oppressive heat slipped off his head and shoulders and away from his body and legs, as the sun weakened, and the mantle of blue above his head began to dim in luster because of the penumbral shades of bronze and maroon slowly and tacitly breaking the tautness of the sky. The silence was so profound that it spoke to him.

This was the hour when he knelt on the ledge and prayed, his arms outstretched. One pointed southward to Jebel Thor, the other northward to Jebel Al-Hour. His eyes gazed westward out over the arid-faced piles of eunuch sand seamed and sutured with a thousand lusts consummated and exploded, on nature so stark that it pained. It was easy then: the dimensions of every-thing were so great that vision automatically became a prayer. Once he had been granted a double sight: on Jebel Thor, Jesus, the prophet of the Christians, hung bleeding on a cross;

on Jebel Al-Hour, Moses, the prophet of the Jews, stood weeping with the Tablets of the Law in his hands; a faint cry echoed between both: "Salvation! Salvation!"

But the effect had been short-lived. Sometime after, at a Meccan feast, he had observed a Christian Greek merchant gorging himself on chicken sauteed with eggplant and onions, on roast quail simmered with pomegranate juice, getting drunk on red wine spiced with cardamom and turmeric, while he grasped a naked dancing girl around the waist and drunkenly dedicated her white teeth to his holy Trinity: the Virgin, Jesus, God. He had subsequently seen Jews, with their pride of race and religion, their stubbornness, their lust for money, their hypocritical rules for washing and cleaning their hands and feet while their hearts were sepulchers of rottenness. The next time he had knelt on the ledge, he had prayed only to a god flaming from heavens between the two peaks, and the cry echoing from one to the other was "Punishment! Punishment!"

Now his lips started to form the words of a prayer which had come to him spontaneously one hot morning as he sat with members of his tribe and watched them bargaining with foreign traders, Christians most of them, over a set of gleaming Damascus swords and shields:

> "They who hoard up gold and silver
> And spend it not in the way of Allah,
> unto them give tidings of a painful doom.
> On the day when it will be heated
> in the fire of hell,
> their foreheads, their flanks, their backs
> will be branded therewith.
> And Satan shall say to them:
> Here is that which ye hoarded for yourselves!
> Now taste well what ye used to hoard!" [2]

The long day was drawing to its close, languid and warm. The sky was a dark blue dome deepening in color all around the edges, blue, blue-red, reddish-brown, dun colored, black with golden streaks. The setting sun was now a blood-red knot tying the heavens together as a head kerchief. It always seemed to him that at any given moment the knot would give or draw

[2] Cf. Koran 9:34-35; vol. I, p. 211. All references to the Koran follow A. J. Arberry's edition, *The Koran Interpreted*, Macmillan, New York 1967.

the kerchief too tightly, and great slits would appear in the skies as the knot sunk slowly beneath the mountains, drawing the skies tighter. There was always a moment when he feared that such a ripping asunder and the hail of avenging angels would fall on his sinful brothers, on his beloved Khadija lying at home in their bed, on Mecca his city. But the moment had always passed. Darkness usually stretched a stealthy, soft hand over all until the danger passed and he breathed peacefully, alone with the night.

Contrary to what happened at all other times, fear now jarred him almost audibly. It was so distinct, it could have been a warning noise. Puzzlement, like a heavy drop, fell on to the motionless sheen of his mind, and little ringlets of questioning undulated outward through his five senses, appearing and disappearing, destroying his peace. It was too late to return home.

High up on that ledge at the mouth of the cave, there was nothing visible or tangible to fear. Yet ancient shapes were stirring in his mind, contorting his body into a sideward glance downward at Mecca in its valley. Time and time again in the last few years he had stood here at the cave mouth waiting for the night, stood and looked back at the Mecca he loved and hated. Loved it because of the Ka'aba, because of Allah's presence; hated it because of the dirt of hucksterdom, of drunken bargains, of unclean foreigners, of the filth of false gods. Each time, he had paused and asked himself: why? Because he was fleeing from some unholy garb Mecca had donned? Because he could not pray in peace there?

Always he had heard repeated distinctly in some unknown part of his being, as if it were by a voice from beyond the mountains, beyond the skies, the words he once heard a Jewish peddler quote:

> *"Gripped by the strength of God,*
> *By the spirit of God carried,*
> *I was placed in the middle*
> *of a plain carpeted with bones.*
> *All of them he let me see,*
> *the piles of them, their dryness.*
> *Son of man, he asked,*
> *can these bones live again?*
> *Can they stand and breathe?*
> *And be a living family of Allah?*

> *Can warm skin sheathe these bones?*
> *Can you fan these bones to life?"* [3]

All was still, cold, cheerless, without life. The moon was up and riding in a clear sky, licking the rocks and the cave mouth with passing silver. He turned and entered. Once he stepped over the threshold, the shadows of the cave began whispering to him: "Peace! Peace!" The dark gullet of the cave running, as he knew, deep into the earth, blanketed his vision with velvet nothingness, rendering all effort at seeing unnecessary.

He stood for a moment thinking of other times he had been here, then quietly dropped to his knees, sat back on his haunches, joined his hands on his lap, and remained still. Outside the sound of the wind had died down, and together with it all the running shadows it had spawned in his mind. Only a gentle rustle made itself heard in the distance, the sound you hear as you drift off to sleep on the leeward side of the shore when sky and sea are calm. If he tried to listen, he heard only the sighing children hear in the conch shell held to the ear. But while he knelt there, his mind slowly rid itself of conscious reflection on his body, on the hardness of the rock beneath his knees, on the night chill, on the desultory cry of a distant desert jackal defying the moon. He had withdrawn from the rim of the human cauldron; no sound from the living disturbed him. Without any images, without any motion, he was down again among the parched bones, the dry dead bones of a people. Would Allah make them live? Who was His prophet to tread among them, livening them with faith?

Quite suddenly, a shuddering took hold of his body, rocking him back and forth like a reed in the wind:

> *"Son of Abdullah!*
> *Clothe these bones*
> *In thine own skin!*
> *Liven them thyself*
> *With the breath of thy mouth.*
> *Thou art my prophet!*
> *Speak to my people*
> *The truth of truths,*
> *The good of goods,*
> *The beautiful of all beauties!"*

[3] Cf. Ezechiel, 37:1-6.

His entire body prickled with gooseflesh. The temptation now was to stand up, to shake himself free of the panic, to rub his arms and thighs, to get rid of the creeping itch running like so many scampering field mice over every inch of him. But he resisted and shuddered and the struggle was on. It seemed to him his skin was a parchment stretched between two poles— dry, taut, cracking in the noonday sun; now it was a fabric as thin as Byssos linen, four full folds of which the Tyrian merchants pulled easily through a marriage ring with one flourish of the wrist; now it became a gossamer-light veil between him and real knowledge but was torn by an army of eyeless skeletons with bony hands and horny nails, all seeking to be clothed in it and thus to live; now it was a leper's hide pullulating with sores and pustules, beset by flies, emitting worms and pus.

The crisis passed. He was calm again and praying. Only now his prayer did not concern a particular time, a particular place, a particular people. Allah does not live or move in certain times and determined places, he remembered. To him, all times are one. He sees yesterday, today, tomorrow, all like lines in a carpet, threads in a loom. For him no yesterday is dead, no tomorrow unborn, no today passing. In his vocabulary, the words "is," "was," "will be" do not figure. Nor is there a "present" or a "now." For both of these imply past and future. Nor is anything "continuing" or "static," because they imply either change or lifelessness. Allah does not change; Allah lives. At any given moment, all the past and all the future are "over and done with" for Allah, without his thereby having moved from one point to another.

It was near midnight. But Mohammad's spirit was moving from midnight to midnight to midnight, to evermore remote midnights, seeking, desiring, fearing, hoping, praying.

"All in the heavens and the earth
glorify Allah.
He is the Mighty, the Wise.
His is the sovereignty of the heavens and the earth.
He quickens or he gives death.
He is able to do all things.
He is the First and the Last,
The Outward and the Inward.
He is the Knower of all things." [4]

[4] Cf. Koran, 57:1; vol. II, p. 258.

He could not remember how long he had been praying or exactly where he was, or, for that matter, whether he was kneeling, standing, lying prostrate on his face or flat on his back. At times, he felt as if he floated in mid-air. Time and space had broken their recognized patterns and coordinated rhythm; they had shot off in opposite directions infinitely, until they were reduced to mere points, inconsequential specks in his consciousness.

"Son of Abdullah, read!"

"I cannot read."

"Read!"

"I cannot read."

"Open your eyes, see and read!"

Mohammad's eyes opened. The tunnel of the cave had become a long thrusting corridor running backward beyond the beginning of time. The mottled limestone face of the rock around him had become a galaxy of stars, countless galaxies. The scattered rocks on the cave floor mapped out a moonscape universe. He felt like the orphan of a long winter and a lonely journey who finally catches sight of home.

Gabriel, Allah's messenger-angel, was there. Rather, what he saw was Gabriel's face, for Mohammad could not see the angel's body. Try as he could, he could not unsee that face, calm and luminous, could not unthink its presence. Everywhere he turned his head, Gabriel's face appeared: Gabriel on his right, Gabriel to his left, Gabriel above his head, Gabriel on the rock floor, at the cave mouth, in the dark inner recess of the cave. In every niche and corner, every ledge and every nook, Gabriel's face. Thousands of Gabriels still luminous, unmoved, still calm, still gazing at him. Mohammad could not escape it. More than ever before, he felt what he was—a walking, talking, laughing uselessness of a man, a pigmy pain astride two femurs, a poor spirit burning in a spindly tenement of clay. Gabriel lived within the diadems of godhead; he, Mohammad was a burnt rag zigzagging through a piecemeal existence.

Then the vision was upon him.

"Read!"

"I cannot read!"

Quietly, without surprising him or jerking his body into horror and frozen awe, Gabriel's cloak fell around him, swathing him from chin to feet in a stream of black and magenta. He could see letters running down its length and disappearing and reappearing in the folds.

> *"I shall read for thee, Mohammad!*
> *In the name of the Lord who created,*
> *Who created man of blood coagulated.*
> *Read! Thy Lord is the most beneficent,*
> *Who taught men by the pen,*
> *Taught them what they knew not as men."* [5]

Now he appeared to himself as something outside himself. He seemed to be disembodied, to hang in the air, to be watching himself as somebody quite different from himself. A quickly changing kaleidoscope of selves passed in front of his mind's eye. Now he was suspended between heaven and hell. He recognized them because above his head angels wafted back and forth in peace, and below he could see the bared grin of Satan clucking his satisfaction and spreading out twin claws to catch him as he fell. Then he became a flea crawling on the rump of a she-ass on which the Prophet of Allah rode to battle, fighting his way through thick hairs, dirt, other fleas, smells, commotion, and dung. Finally, he was a breath of air; he was cold, very cold; nothingness greeted his eyes and touch. He tried to budge but only swung in space, as it were, like one of those cloth dolls which the traveling Persian tumblers managed on strings in their Shadow Plays. A sudden gulp of frigid night-air filled his lungs. His eyes opened. He was hanging on the edge of the cliff, his feet dangling in space, the sky above him, some thousands of feet yawning below him to the rocky riverbed. One more inch and he would be a sprawling mess of crumpled bones, shattered belly, blood and mucus and skin and intestines, staining the wind-swept rocks below. He had wished to kill himself.

Once more inside the cave, the voice and the vision returned. This time he was calm. In silence he heard the injunction:

> *"Preach to them, O Mohammad, the Prophet!*
> *Preach: we believe in Allah,*
> *And that which is revealed unto us,*
> *And that which was revealed unto Abraham,*
> *And to Ishmael and to Isaac and to Jacob*
> *And to the Tribes.*

[5] Cf. Koran, 96:1; vol. II, p. 344.

And that which Moses and Jesus received,
And that which the prophets received
From the Lord." [6]

Now the strain began to tell on Mohammad. His pulse beat faster. Beads of perspiration crystallized on his forehead. His breathing became heavier. His nightmare visions of bleeding prophets, recalcitrant rabbis, arrogant Christians, callow Jews, squabbling and mercenary Meccans, started afresh harassing his memory, flooding his heart with foreboding. The night was spent, anyway, and he was weak from thirst, from cold, from hunger, from strain. The cave began to swim in front of his eyes. His muscles relaxed and gave way. He tried to stand up, but failed. Then with gathering momentum he slumped forward, hitting the floor with a dull thump.

When he awoke, the sun was already halfway across the sky. Not until he staggered into his house in Mecca and fell on a couch did he learn from Khadija that he had been gone three days and three nights. He continued for some weeks to shiver and to laugh alternately. Then his normal equilibrium ebbed back with the return of bodily strength. The summer was almost spent before he ventured out again into the garden. All that time he had talked with his wife, meditated, prayed. Even she was astounded and somewhat frightened at the change in him.

There was the child Mohammad: waiting patiently to be fed, washed, lulled to sleep, clinging to her like an infant afraid of the gathering shadows and of every sound. There was the alien Mohammad: sitting on the edge of his bed, eyes blazing, talking soundlessly into the thin air, clenching and unclenching his right hand. There was the seer Mohammad: kneeling for hours, his eyes open and blank, his body cold and rigid. There was the preacher Mohammad: holding forth endlessly about the "middle nation of Allah," the nation which was neither "Jewish nor Christian," admonishing and chiding, unloosing verbal attacks of deadly vituperation against drunkenness, idolatry, infanticide, adultery. These states varied constantly for a period. Then their frequency diminished, and he would sit whimpering while she was absent, smiling and content when she was present. One act of devotion he imposed on her: each evening and each morning she had to stand with him facing the north-north-

[6] Cf. Koran, 2:120; vol. I, p. 45.

west: the holy City, Jerusalem, he said, lay up there, and they must pray in its direction. Finally, at the beginning of the autumn, Mohammad was restored in health. He walked forth in the streets. He met his family and kinsmen.

During his first forays forth among his townsmen and acquaintances, Mohammad felt as if he were the only man at home in Mecca: all the others were strangers, their faces bearing traits of evil, of ignorance, of wrong-doing, which he had never noticed before. As he talked with them, wonderment and a growing doubt assailed him: how shall such a people become the "middle nation" of which Gabriel had spoken? Furthermore, how shall he, Mohammad, become the Prophet to be "a witness over this middle nation?" Gabriel continued his education.

One night, lying beside Khadija, he was awakened. Gabriel was there beckoning him. He followed the angel outside into the covered garden. There in one swift motion, Gabriel slit Mohammad painlessly from his Adam's apple to his navel, inserted his hand and drew forth Mohammad's heart alive and pulsating. Heavenly waters appeared at hand's touch and Gabriel washed and purified that heart. All the while, Mohammad felt a new elixir being infused through his veins, throughout his mind. His heart beat more steadily to a new rhythm. When Gabriel restored his heart to his breast and miraculously closed up the flesh and bone again, Mohammad's knowledge had been enlarged: he now understood as never before.

That night Gabriel placed him on the back of the heavenly animal, Buraq, with the head of a woman, the body of a courser, the tail of a peacock, the coat of a panther. Buraq flew to heaven where Mohammad was greeted by Moses, a ruddy-faced man; by Jesus, a freckled smiling person of medium height; and by Abraham, who so resembled Mohammad as to be his double. Before the throne of Allah, he now understood fully his task: the building of a true Community of Believers at Mecca.

12. The Prophet's Progress

Before Mohammad started his preaching to the Meccans and the South Arabian tribes, the predominant religion was a nomadic polytheism. South Arabians worshipped a pantheon of gods which derived from earlier animism and nature cults. Christianity had made very little headway, mainly in the few large towns. Some Jewish tribes existed. This one man, Mohammad, in a short time abolished the old polytheism and established a virile monotheism possessing a sacred book, the Koran, a sacred law, the *Shari'a*, and channeled the wild energies of the Bedouin tribes into a huge potential. How did he do it? The most balanced answer relies on Mohammad's initial religious experience which he successfully communicated to his followers.

In the last third of the 20th century, over 1300 years since Mohammad lived and died, we have very little hope of ever directly knowing the thews and sinews of his religious experience. Our understanding, therefore, of how Islam succeeded under his hand and inspiration will always be deficient. All we have is the tapestry of legend woven posthumously by the devotion of his followers and the *mystique* he created around his personality. For the rest, there are the sudden quaking tremors of the entire Arabian Peninsula set in motion for ten years, and the breathing fire of the Prophet dying in triumph; then the violent clash and concussion of bodies, minds, peoples, empires, and spirits, a river of burning enthusiasms, and the emergence of a new world power within 50 more years.

The most we can do is presume that Mohammad had such an authentic experience. We can, perhaps, catch faint echoes of the voice which awakened all the Arabs, and one shadowy glimpse of the vision that flung them into a state of precipitation overrunning the known world from Spain to Sumatra. Yet, in the end we will fail. Only direct experience could have provided access to the knowledge we lack.

In the meanwhile, our understanding must not be obfuscated by pre-conceived ideas stemming from modern theories of group psychology. Nor can we, in the interests of sympathetic understanding, allow the statistical lore of the anthropologist to explain the centrifugal onrush of central Arabian tribes out beyond the periphery of their civilization. *Lebensraum* was not a problem; nor did problems of population control and nourishment bedevil the Bedouins of the 7th century. Finally, our modern sociological explanations, and particularly social Darwinism, must not be applied to those far-off events. No acute pressure system existed that would have evoked the "survival of the fittest" principle; nor do we know of any changes in the socio-political environment of Arabia which evoked an instinct for environmental adaptation.

With these provisos in mind, we can turn in the hope of greater and genuine understanding to some ancient relique such as the 16th century biography of Mohammad. It was executed in Ottoman Turkey to be read by Muslim nobles in the security and peace of great wealth and power. Fact is interwoven by the artists with fancy; in the exquisite miniatures which adorn the book, the face of the Prophet is always veiled —symbol of the opaque cloud of unknowing that intervenes between us and him. At least, the *Progress of the Prophet,* as the biography is called, is only two removes from the original reality. By a careful perusal, we can absorb something like the effect of the religious experience Mohammad signified. In it, we are not trying to cross the unbridgeable chasm that separates our modern mentality from the spirit of classical Islam. The Muslims of the 16th century were infinitely nearer to those of the 7th than we are to our great-grandfathers who witnessed Napoleon's exile to Elba.

Consider for a moment the salient facts and dates that a historian would underline in trying to find out "what really happened" in Mohammad's life. Born on August 20, 570 A.D., at the age of 25 married to a rich, already thrice-married Meccan named Khadija (595), 15 years later called to be a prophet by his first heavenly vision (610), he only began to preach publicly in 613. Within five years, he made merely half a dozen converts (all within his own family), compromised his new faith once with the idolators of Mecca,[1] and fled his hometown 4 years later in precipitate flight for his life,[2] leading

---

[1] Speaking with his fellow-Meccans, he acknowledged the existence and power of some idols: "Certainly he saw of the greatest signs of his Lord. And have you seen Allat and Al Uzza and Manat, the Third, and the 1st last? These are exalted females, and verily their intercession is to be hoped for." The Angel Gabriel appeared to him and chided him; whereupon he repented. Cf. Koran, Chapter LIII, verse 18. The verse was amended, the previous version being attributed to diabolical intervention. It now reads: "Nothing but names which you and your fathers have named them, on whom God has bestowed no authority."

[2] This event is called the *Hijra* or *Hegira.* The Muslim calendar is dated from this event. Thus 1969 is the year 1347 in the Hegiral calendar (Anno Hegirae), or 1347 *A.H.*

only 70 converts in exile (June 16, 622). Eight years later, he re-entered Mecca at the head of ten thousand converts and volunteer warriors armed with swords, spears, bows and arrows, as undisputed master (630). By the end of 631, Mohammad and his handful of Muslims were recognized as the greatest single power in Arabia; and when he died in June 632 at the age of 62, he left behind him merely an inchoate mass of individual tribal loyalties, mutually opposing clan covenants, inimical family alliances, with but one immaterial unifying factor: the ineradicable imprint of his personality and the unshakeable attachment to the faith he had preached.

Yet a dazzling progress awaited his successors who whirled triumphantly over three continents, engulfing at least four civilizations, three empires, dozens of states, innumerable cities and nations, all toppling over in quick, trip-wire succession like a row of very fragile and obsolescent dominoes. The Yemen in 633, Jerusalem by 637, Syria and Persia by 644, Egypt by 656, North Africa by 703, Bokhara in 709, Samarkand by 712, Kashgar in China by 713, Ferghana by 714, Sind and part of the Punjab in India by 715, Spain by 717, Narbonne in France by 720. By 750, Islam reigned from the Atlantic to the Indus, and its caravelles were exploring beyond the Indian Ocean to the east.

But a puzzling gap exists between the Mohammadan era properly so-called (622-632) and the Islamic era (750 onward), which we cannot readily understand. And the historian or student of religion would be at a loss to explain how it all happened. He could not explain it in terms of Byzantine weakness or Persian decadence (neither was weak or decadent); nor could he point to a socio-political consensus among the Arabians that led to a military venture of such magnitude.

This mystery is even more confounding when we consider Mohammad himself, for there is no evidence that proves he had imperialistic aspirations or that he believed the peaks of world power beckoned to him. The nearest he ever came to tackling a foreign power was in the shape of a ragged punitive expedition sent in September 629 against one small Arab territory which lay under nominal Byzantine control. His Muslims reached Mota, in southern Moab, to be decimated and repulsed ignominiously by the local Arabs and their Byzantine allies.

For all of his short public life as the Prophet of the One True

God, Mohammad had as his only vague political aim a desire to return to Mecca, to destroy the idols in the Ka'aba, to proclaim the sacred law which Allah had revealed to him, and to preach to his fellow Arabs. It is on record that in 628 he had letters written and sent to the four great rulers of his day: the King of Persia, the Emperor of Byzance, the Governor of Egypt, and the Prince of Abyssinia. Yet he summoned them, not to submit politically and to pay tribute, but to accept the Muslim religion.[3] It is as if, in the mid 1960's, the Dalai Lama had written to Mao Tse Tung, Lyndon Johnson, Charles De Gaulle and Leonid Brezhnev, telling them to join a Tibetan monastery. And it was just as effective.

For Mohammad never really ruled even Arabia. As far as we know, he never learned to read or write, never studied philosophy or letters, religion or government. He spoke one dialect of South-Arabian Semitic and did not know even the logistical size of outside powers and states or where their territories extended. We have no record of his having sailed on the sea. Like any Bedouin he could virtually live on horseback. The longest journey he made was to Tebook, about 500 miles north of Mecca. He had no grasp of military strategy either for open battle or for siege tactics. While he did have a practical turn of mind for commerce and barter-business, he never performed any act of statesmanship.

He listened and absorbed religious concepts and phrases, primarily from Jews but also from Christians. At his death, only a very small proportion of Arabians had accepted his teachings, and not all Meccans had converted. Shortly after his death, the majority of the Arabian tribes decided to cease paying taxes. He never organized a government, had no ministers, no council of state, no law officials, no police, no regular army, no public records, no written and officially sanctioned Bible for his followers,[4] had developed no clerical or priestly apparatus with analogues to either priest, bishop, pope, or rabbi, no central cult or sacrifice. He had not even appointed a suc-

---

[3] The Persian King tore up the letter contemptuously. The Byzantine Emperor inquired casually who Mohammad was. The Governor of Egypt declined courteously to convert. The answer of the Prince of Abyssinia is not on record, but the Lion of Judah must have reacted strongly.

[4] Cf. chapter 15, for the formation of the Koran.

cessor; nor had he considered setting up a mechanism for this purpose. He called his followers Muslims because they "submitted" to the law of Allah. Their religion was called Islam, the "submission," the "service."

During his lifetime he insisted merely on two things: the pronouncement of the Muslim formula [5] and the payment of a small tribute.[6] After his death, at least two self-styled successor prophets arose [7] in imitation of him, and most of the tribes offered to pronounce the formula if the taxes were abolished. He had established no hegemony, no dynastic house, no socio-political cohesion. There was only chaos. Later Arab historians called this period immediately after the Prophet's death, the Apostasy. But this was fancy on their part. The majority of Arabs owed no allegiance, religious or political, to Mohammad and his Muslim group. The religious and political framework of the tribes had not been changed. Only, deep in their souls, the light of Mohammad's faith in Allah had been kindled.

From eyewitness reports it is clear that Mohammad resembled any of the urbanized Bedouins of his day: medium in height; burly in build; an unusually large head with thick black hair; a wide forehead unspoiled except for a thick vein, which swelled uncontrollably between bushy eyebrows when anger swept him; big black eyes; scrawny face; prognathous chin; abundant beard; massive shoulders; large hands and feet; an impetuous walk characterized by an excessive forward thrust of his head. He had an ability to concentrate on one thought to the total exclusion of all else, a capacious memory, mesmeric voice, and an invaluable gift for pithy formulation clad in memorable assonances and impressive mystic fire.

As far as we know, because he did not read or write, he had absorbed half-formed reports on Judaism and Christianity by listening to travelers and merchants in Mecca, and was by

---

[5] "There is but one God, and Mohammad is his prophet."

[6] One-fifth was reserved for the Prophet's use; the remainder was devoted to the cause of Islam.

[7] Talha, chieftain of the Beni Asad tribe (in Northern Nejed), known derisively to later Arab historians as Tulaiha ("little Talha") and a certain Maslama (from the Eastern regions) known with equal derision as Masailama ("little Maslama").

nature meditative and original in thought.[8] He repressed harshly the Arabian habit of infanticide, fulminated against adultery, abhorred drunkenness. But he shared the pleasures of his fellow men. In addition to his beloved Khadija and, later, Aisha,[9] he took eleven other wives in the short space of ten years and had numerous concubines,[10] and he once remarked that what "I love most in the world are women and perfume, but the apple of my eye is prayer."

He brooked no opposition, could not stand ridicule, and used assassination unscrupulously as a means of ridding himself of both. In Medina, he had one poetess stabbed to death as she lay in bed with her children, another hacked to pieces in the blackness of the night by five chosen Muslims whom he accompanied and blessed on their mission. Both had lampooned him unmercifully in popular doggerel. At the battle of Bedr in January 624, his servant found the body of the Prophet's bitterest enemy, Abu Jahal, cut off the head, ran to the Prophet's tent, and threw the head down at his feet. "The head of the enemy of God," cried Mohammad triumphantly and fervently, "praise God, because there is no God but He!" Yet he ran out barefoot to meet the bloodied survivors of the Mota disaster crying: "No, these are not runaways, but come-agains, if God wills." He could be mindful of past favors and magnanimous in victory. His personal life and retinue were utterly simple. He wore ragged clothes, lived in a hut which would probably be condemned today as unfit for dog or horse, rarely bathed, ate and drank frugally, loved children, called his intimates by nicknames, allowed himself to be joshed and shouldered by the

[8] It is said that he believed the Christian trinity to be composed of Jesus, Mary, and God. His free-wheeling use of Biblical figures (Abraham's visit to Mecca where his footprints were preserved, for example) and his adaptations of both Christian and Jewish material, amply support the above statement.

[9] She was the daughter of Abu Bekr, one of Mohammad's companions in his flight from Mecca.

[10] Among whom was Mary who together with another girl, a horse, a mule, and an ass, had come as a gift to Mohammad from the Governor of Egypt. Mary bore him a son who died in infancy. It is said that Mohammad always hoped for a son and heir. Khadija bore him two sons, both of whom died in infancy, and four daughters, Zeinab, Rukaiya, Fatima, and Umm Kulthum. Mohammad saw his grandchildren by Fatima.

Bedouins, and died of pneumonia murmuring to Aisha, who held his head during a last raging fever: "Lord grant me pardon. Eternity in Paradise. Amen." That humble prayer would be replaced by the subsequent words of the Koran: "Lo! my worship and my prayers and my life and my death are for Allah, Lord of the Worlds. He has no equal. This I am commanded, and I am the first of the Muslims, first of those who surrendered to Him." [11]

A detailed factual account of the Prophet's "exile" between 622-630 does not throw any further light on the puzzling gap between the parochial, disjointed, non-centralized, disorganized regime of Mohammadanism and the monolithic, swift-hurtling comet of subsequent Islam. We are left wondering how the unenlightened and primitive enthusiasm of the small Muslim group Mohammad left behind him burst suddenly and, as it were, automatically across the skies of three continents with a brilliance unequalled by the riding hordes of Genghis Khan in the 12th-13th centuries and with a perdurance that has outstripped any other empire.

Those eight years, we find, are merely a baffling patchwork quilt of criss-crossing bitter failures and small successes, of caravan raids, and of massacres, ambushes, bloody battles, assassinations, personal feuds, hunger, persecution, plots, and final triumph. Mohammad's progress to power cannot be likened to the carefully thought-out and ideologically inspired expansion of Mao Tse Tung from the north, through the Great March on Pekin in 1949, to his iron grip on all the Chinas by early 1950, or to the meticulous establishment of a rural revolutionary infrastructure in South Vietnam by the North Vietnamese Le Duan between 1955-63. It resembles remotely the sudden success of Fidelismo in Cuba and Castro's meteoric rise to authority overnight on the carcass of the Battista regime.

In 615, the handful of Mohammad's converts, 11 men and 4 women, had to emigrate to Abyssinia. In 617, Mohammad's clan, the Beni Hashim, were boycotted and confined to their houses by the Meccans. In 619, the Prophet was stoned and insulted by the people of Taif when he went there to preach. In 620, he had received an oath of allegiance from 12 men of the Yathrib tribe. Then in March 622, he got wind of a plot to assassinate him. Asking a young convert, Ali, to lie in his bed and thus deceive those watching the house, Mohammad slipped

[11] Cf. Koran, 6:160; vol. I, p. 169.

out of Mecca, and took refuge in a cave at Thor for a few days. Thence he made his way to Yathrib, where the Emigrants from Abyssinia joined him. He now had followers composed of the Emigrants from Mecca and Abyssinia and his new converts from Yathrib. The latter were called the Helpers. A mosque was built. A written charter was drawn up: Mohammadans were recognized as a single group; all tribal loyalties were set aside; a Mohammadan believer could kill an unbeliever even though he belonged to the same tribe. The powerful bond of tribe and clan was thus abolished in the new community. Mohammad was at once prophet, leader, and military chief of the community. Yathrib was later called Medinat-an-nebi or simply Medina.

A blood-price of 100 camels was now laid on Mohammad's head. Keeping clearly in his mind his ultimate goal—return in power to Mecca and possession of the Ka'aba—Mohammad set out in three phases to achieve his purpose.

Firstly, he set about making it possible to return to Mecca with respect and safety. For this reason he had to inflict losses on Meccans and the Arabian tribes. In January 624, an abortive raid on a Meccan caravan took place, but other raids against Arabian tribes were successful. Booty and prestige became his. At Bedr, east of Medina and on the Red Sea coast, the Mohammadans clashed with the Meccans. The latter had 750 camel-riding warriors and 100 mailed horsemen. The former had 314 men—80 Emigrants and 234 Helpers. The Meccans were defeated. A year later in January 625, at Uhud, a mountain northwest of Medina, 3000 Meccans inflicted a withering defeat on 700 Mohammadans. The Mohammadans continued their policy of retaliation and plundering raids during the year. Mohammad had the chieftain of the Beni Lakyan assassinated and beheaded, but his plan to assassinate Abu Sofian, leader of the Meccans, failed. In September, he expelled the Jewish tribe of Beni Nadheer and enriched his community with their houses, gardens, fields, and furniture. Raids were made up to the frontiers of the Byzantine Empire during the following year.[12]

In 627, the Meccans sent an army of 10,000 to besiege Mohammad at Medina. The effort failed and Mohammad's prestige grew. He corrupted some of the tribes who made up

[12] Earlier, Mohammad had expelled the Beni Qainuq, another Jewish settlement, composed of silver and metal smiths.

the 10,000. A sandstorm arose which made life impossible for the besieging army. Above all, he had secured the engineering services of a Persian convert, Sulman, who had built breastworks and fortifications. Eventually, the Meccan army retired. In the same year, Mohammad attacked another Jewish settlement, the Beni Quaraidha. After taking the settlement, he had all 700 men led out. They dug a trench, were then beheaded, and buried in the trench. Those who converted to Mohammad's faith were spared. Few did.

By now Mohammad had finished the first phase: respect and terror had been struck into surrounding settlements and tribes in Arabia. It was time to undertake the next phase. He simply announced in February 628 that he and his followers were going to make a religious pilgrimage to Mecca to worship at the Ka'aba. He set out with 1500 followers, entered Mecca after some nervous moments, worshipped at the Ka'aba, and took up residence. In June of that year, Mohammad attacked another Jewish settlement at Kheibar, 80 miles north of Medina. This time, after taking it, he spared the inhabitants, and placed them under tribute. In February 629, 2000 Mohammadans made the pilgrimage to Mecca, and, most importantly, Othman ibn Talha, custodian of the Ka'aba, was converted to Mohammad's faith. September of that year was marred by the disaster of Mota of which we have spoken.

By the end of the autumn of 629, Mohammad knew that he had waited long enough; he was ready to deliver the *coup de grace*. Meccans had become aware of the respect enjoyed by the Mohammadans among the tribes of Arabia, the attachment of his followers for Mohammad, and the fanatic zeal of the new believers. An incident, probably manufactured by Mohammad, precipitated events and justified Mohammad's summoning 10,000 of his followers for holy war in January 630. By now, the Meccans were either divided among themselves or frightened by the force in their midst. Mohammad made a peaceful entry to Mecca, broke the 360 idols in the Ka'aba, declared a general amnesty, lined up the Meccans, and had them swear loyalty to him personally as the apostle of Allah. He established himself as sole ruler in the city. Phase three was completed.

Thus an examination of the "exile" and "return" of Mohammad merely confirms our previous conclusion. It was a pattern which in its outward manifestations must have been repeated a hundred times before and after his time. But it does not tell us much as to why Islam succeeded. The key to Islam's subsequent success is not to be found in a mere repetition of Mohammad's military and political success during those eight crucial years. Nor can the key be formulated simply by speaking of religious fanaticism and zeal. The fanatical sect of the Carmathians conquered all Central Arabia and the Yemen between 929-969. Yet after forty years, they ceased to be a force. At the end of the 18th century, the Wahhabis conquered all Arabia and threatened Iraq and Syria. The Wahhabi movement was one of the most fanatical the world has witnessed. It dissipated itself. In 1912, another Wahhabi uprising took place; it controlled Arabia until 1930. Again, it subsided. Mere religious fanaticism in itself does not rationally and satisfactorily explain the endurance of Islam and its beginnings in Mohammad.

If we turn now to the *Progress of the Prophet,* we find a completely different attitude and interpretation. The details of the Prophet's birth, exile, return, and triumph are related in terms of two basic assumptions: Mohammad by destiny was the focal point for a life-and-death struggle between Allah and Satan; at issue was the life or death of Allah's Community of True Believers, not merely in Mecca or Arabia but in all man's world and the cosmos for all time. The historical is transferred to a supra-historical plane. The 10 years of Mohammad's trial are stretched back retrospectively to the creation of the world in time and to Allah's life in eternity. They are projected forward for all the millenia of the earth's perdurance and, beyond that, to the endless eternities of Allah's life. The story is cosmic.

This is the point of view of later Islam, and its religious interpretation of the beginnings. But its validity and force must be sought in Mohammad and his religious experience. Some breath of this experience can be felt in the mythology of the *Progress.* As in the life of Jesus, so for Mohammad there is a Gospel of the Infancy.[13] Angels foretell his conception, name, and birth to a pious mother. His infancy and youth are marked by sanctity and wondrous things; Satan used evil men to attempt to extinguish the life of the child, but Allah and his angels thwart him. Like Abraham, Moses, and Jesus, he is formally introduced to his mission in the desert. From this point

[13] The *Gospel of the Infancy* is a phrase referring to Chapters 1-2 of *Matthew* and *Luke.*

on, Jewish mythological and haggadic elements predominate. Mohammad pays a midnight visit to Paradise, after a mysterious purification rite. In Paradise, he leads a procession (including Abraham, Moses, and Jesus, with all the prophets and saints) to worship Allah.

The *Progress* proceeds to recount his 10 years of public life in terms of the Allah-Satan struggle—Allah the All-Good fighting victoriously with the hosts of angels and saints against a highly personalized Satan and his ruthless forces of evil men and demons. At one point, the Prophet takes refuge in a cave from a pursuing enemy led by Satan. Miraculously, angels cause a cobweb to be spun over the mouth of the cave and a nest, complete with mother-bird and eggs, to appear on a nearby tree blocking the cave-entrance. Stupidly, Satan and his cohorts conclude that no one could have entered the cave. On another occasion, Mohammad gives his camel free rein; the animal, directed by Allah, carries Mohammad to the spot where he must build a mosque, famous later as his burial place.[14] After defeat in battle, a Mohammadan rout is turned into a victory by the sudden apparition of Gabriel bidding the Prophet turn and fight again.[15]

So it goes, from miracle to miracle, his enemies are fractured, confused, defeated; Mohammad and his group are fed, protected, and led supernaturally; the 360 idols of the Ka'aba spontaneously commit suicide by self-sundering; angels finally bear the Prophet's soul to Paradise. It is certain that this later mythologization of Mohammad's life was due in part to Mohammad's own interpretation and teaching. But its importance for us lies in this: its acceptance and Mohammad's apotheosis in subsequent Islam are the best testimony to the *effect* this extraordinary individual had on his contemporaries. His mind had been riven by some exalted experience. He succeeded in communicating the fire and life of this experience. This fire sufficed to overturn an entire geopolitical framework, to found a monolithic empire, to father a whole civilization,

[14] This was supposed to have taken place in Medina on the spot occupied today by the Mosque.

[15] At the battle of Hunain, in the spring of 630. Mohammad had gone to punish the men of Taif, a town that lay about 40 miles east of Mecca, for their insulting and injurious treatment of him some 12 years before.

to fashion a socio-political consensus for millions, and to give birth to a faith which still decided the daily life of over 400 million people in the late 20th century. In the logic of history, this was the right time, the right place, and the right man.

This communication by Mohammad can be traced in scattered incidents which bear the mark of authenticity. His battle-prayer at Bedr as he saw the waves of Meccan warriors appearing over the sand-dunes: "O God, here are Quraish [16] in their vanity and pride, fighting against Thee and calling thine apostle a liar. O God grant us help. O God destroy them." His rallying cry when a battle was going against him at Hunain: "Where are you going, men? Rally to me. I am the Apostle of God. O citizens of Medina! O Helpers! O men of the pledge of the tree." [17] His prayer in the day of utter humiliation: [18] "O Lord, I make my complaint to Thee of the feebleness of my strength and of my insignificance before men. O most Merciful! Thou art the Lord of the weak and Thou art my Lord." Of the respect and veneration shown him by his followers: "I have been to Chosroes in his kingdom, and I have seen Caesar and the Prince of Abyssinia among their subjects. But I have never seen a king among his people treated with such respect as Mohammad among his companions." [19]

When the Helpers grumbled after the battle of Hunain that they had received scarcely any battle booty, Mohammad assembled them and said: "Others may go home with camels and sheep, but you go home with God's Apostle. If all the world were to take one road and the Helpers another, I would go with the Helpers. O God! show Thy mercy on the Helpers, and on the sons of the Helpers." We are told that this outburst and the

---

[16] The clan of Quraish had dominated Mecca since the 3rd century A.D. They were of the northern, or Ishmaelite, tribes of Arabia, supposedly descended from Ishmael, son of Abraham.

[17] One Meccan hearing this cry said to a companion: "Now nothing but the sea could stop them." The "pledge of the tree" referred to a bad moment just before Mohammad entered Mecca in 628.

[18] This occurred when he was pelted with stones, wounded, and chased by the men of Taif to whom he had gone preaching in his early days.

[19] Words attributed to one of the Meccan emissaries who went out to make peace with Mohammad when he approached Mecca in 628.

force of his personality caused his audience to weep "until their beards were wet." We have no reason to doubt that he aroused such emotions in strong men.

It is in the light of such personal magnetism and confidence in his mission that we must understand the effect Mohammad had both on his contemporaries and their descendants. He was a combination of ruthlessness, iron nerve, and personal inspiration: to Abu Sofian, his enemy, one acute choice was given: "Testify that Mohammad is the Messenger of God before you lose your head." [20] Abu Sofian complied. Mohammad was a master in orchestrating the emotions of a group: once, before entering Mecca in 628, when he and all with him suspected that they would be ambushed and cut to pieces, he had all of 1500 men file past him as he stood beneath a thorny tree, each one putting his hand in Mohammad's and pledging loyalty to death. In this atmosphere of extreme tension and highly pitched personal devotion, he went on to enter the city successfully.[21]

Two incidents in the early years permanently captured the imagination of his followers. The first was the scene at Yathrib in 622. The Emigrants had arrived there with Mohammad. A small derelict palm garden had been bought. Aided by the Helpers of Yathrib, the Emigrants and Mohammad set at cutting and laying mudbricks intermingled with stones. All sang in unison:

> "Allahumma la aish illa aish al akhra,
> Allahumma irham al Ansar wa al Muharijira."

> "O God! There is no life but the future life!
> O God! Have mercy on the Helpers and the Emigrants!"

These rhythmic words and the otherworldly motif of the emotions combined the faith and the strong intent to conquer in Allah's name.

The other incident had occurred earlier in the same year. The place: a dry mountain water-course called Aqaba, about three miles east of Mecca. The time: an hour before midnight. The actors: Mohammad and his uncle Abbas, and 73 Arabs from the tribe of Yathrib. The action: the pledging of allegiance to this

---

[20] Said by Abbas, uncle of Mohammad, to Abu Sofian in 630 before they entered Mecca.

[21] This is called "the pledge of the tree."

single individual already under sentence of death and running
for his life. Mohammad and Abbas squatted on the gully floor
surrounded by silence. The men of Yathrib arrived in small
groups, stealing along "as softly as sandgrouse." Then, in the
darkness of the night, all filed past Mohammad, each man
striking the Prophet's palm. At the end, Mohammad concluded
the pact crying softly: "I am of you and you are of me. I will
battle against those who battle against you. I will make peace
with those who make peace with you." Historically, this was
like any other tribal pact. Neither Mohammad nor any of the
73 men could possibly know how world history had been decided
in that deserted and arid gully around the midnight hour.

At his death, Mohammad's sole achievement was the establishment of a *community* of *believers*. This was the essence of
his revelation and the result of his religious experience. Allah,
in pity for men, had always wished to found a community, a
people, in exclusive possession of the truth. The Jews had
betrayed his revelation as related through Moses. The Christians had betrayed his second effort made through Jesus.
Neither the Jews nor the Christians had become the community
of true servants of the One God. Whatever the imagery, the
borrowed symbolism, the transformed mythologies, the trun-
cated doctrines, with which Mohammad and later Muslims
clothed it, this was the core of his message. He fled Mecca in
622 burning with it. He returned in 630 to establish it. The
name of the Community was Muslim, literally "he who surren-
ders," "who inclines," "who obeys." The commander of the
Muslimin, the Servant, united in himself all political, religious,
and social power.

Furthermore, this community was centered around the person
of the Commander of the Faithful Servants, and it had as its
central shrine the holy Ka'aba, now purified of all idolatry.
Not only were the lives of the Faithful regulated in all things,
but their world and their cosmos were completely explained in
an all-embracing ideology. No room was left for personal idio-
syncrasy or volatile divagation. No distinction was made
between "church" and "state." Mohammadans lived in a theocratic idealistic state inspired uniquely by a religious ideology.

The Mohammadan world and the cosmos was bipolar:

Allah's center on this planet was at Mecca, was with the Community at home and abroad. The other pole was the remainder of men, their infidelity and refusal to embrace Islam. Even with all the limitations we have already described as affecting the Mohammadans at Mohammad's death, this was their cohesion and its correct formulation.

When Mohammad died, there was no historical guarantee, no logically compelling reason, and—as far as the world was concerned—no divine assurance that Mohammadanism would dominate even the tribes of its native Arabia. That it did achieve this domination and that it went on to become a great world power was in no way an iron-bound necessity or absolutely inevitable result.

In a certain sense, there was very little hope that an army of Bedouins could sweep out of the desert and, without any preceding experience either in pitched-battle tactics, in laying siege to fortresses and cities, or in statecraft, could defeat two huge organized and sophisticated empires such as the Persian and the Byzantine Empires.

But it was Islam's priceless moment in a deeper sense. The Muslim authorities of that time could have restricted their vision merely to Arabia, or merely to Arabia and its immediate neighboring territories where "Arabs" lived. Islam could have developed as a spiritual movement shunning worldly conquests and outside regimes. It could have foregone some of the more xenophobic and exclusive-minded traits of Mohammad himself, and thus left the world a heritage of a more universalistic religion and its modern followers a greater adaptability to change. It did none of these things. We must consider some of these possibilities in the following scenarios, in order to appreciate the particular line of development Islam followed.

13. Three Scenarios

At the death of Mohammad, his small community in Mecca and Medina could have developed along many lines: as a small Arabian sect eventually swallowed up by more powerful currents; as a purely political power in no way inspired by the religious ethos of Mohammad; as another expression of Judaism or Christianity. Or it could have succumbed and disappeared almost immediately after the death of the Prophet. That none of these possibilities became reality is due to many factors both within the community and in the world which surrounded it.

In the logic of history, the community was to grow: initial plundering and retaliatory raids were expanded into conquering expeditions, until the tiny theocracy founded by Mohammad had transformed part of that world and established itself as a formidable power. But its development was curtailed by the presence of the Byzantine Empire. Byzantium stood between Islam and Western Europe for well over 700 years. During that time, the West could develop politically, economically, militarily, religiously. When the clash came in the 15th and 16th centuries, Islam could make no headway. It was essentially confined to the areas of its earlier conquests in the 7th and 8th centuries. This expansion of the community from an obscure corner of Arabia to the status of a world power is described in a later chapter. This was its actual development. But the death of Mohammad was Islam's priceless moment.

The following scenarios are hypothetical accounts of other ways in which Islam could have developed from that moment. Because such alternatives were then real possibilities, an examination of them will illustrate the nature of Islam's choice and, consequently, the physical modes by which Islam's dominance expressed itself.

Scenario A: An Arabian Religious Sect

The Prophet has scarcely ceased to breathe when his lifelong companion, Abu Bekr arrives at the house, ascends to Mohammad's room, kneels by the dead man's bed, raises the sheet, kisses the face frozen by the agony of death, covers it again, rises, descends into the courtyard, and says to the Believers assembled there: "O Muslims, if anyone worships Mohammad, let him know that Mohammad is dead. But if you worship Allah, know that Allah lives forever and does not die." By this time all the prominent Muslims have gathered in the courtyard. The Community must now choose a successor to the Prophet. It is near midday, and the heat is practically unbearable.

Some wish to elect Saad ibn Ubada, chieftain of the Khazraj tribe, as khalif.[1] Others wish to elect Umar ibn Khattab. The majority vote for Abu Bekr. All file past this mild, humble, discreet, peaceful man putting their hands in his as a sign of fealty.

The first crisis facing the new khalif is the revolt of the Arabian tribes whom Mohammad had conquered and who now refuse to pay tribute. Two rival claimant prophets, Talha the chief of the Beni Asad, and Maslama who lived in the east, call for the allegiance of all Muslims.

Abu Bekr had been in a constant agony throughout the last year and a half of Mohammad's life. He realized that Mohammad was the prophet of Allah and that his message bore the truth about man and Allah and the world. Nevertheless, he could not abide by the worldly aspect of Mohammadanism. When the tribute used to arrive from all the petty sheikdoms of the Persian Gulf, from Yemen, and from Hadramaut, he had seen this money only as a source of corruption and greed. Bad men and self-seeking opportunists, he now concludes, had convinced the Prophet of the spiritual motives for these conquests. For Abu Bekr, the religion of Mohammad is a definite obligation for the tribes inhabiting Mecca and Medina: the holy Ka'aba belongs to Mohammadanism. The Prophet, Abu Bekr decides, is to be buried in Medina. For the rest, unless Allah himself converts the hearts of men, there is no use propagating the Prophet's message by the sword.

Therefore, after the Prophet has died in late June, 632, Abu Bekr assembles the two claimant prophets, Talha and Maslama, together with their followers in a peace parley in September. Abu Bekr's plan appeals to all: it leaves them free to follow their immemorial tribal customs of plundering and raiding and, at the same time, invites them to worship at Mecca and to pray to the Prophet at Medina. "There is but one chief prophet, Mohammad," states Abu Bekr, "but just as Moses and Jesus

[1] Mohammad's successors were called khalifs, which literally means "one who takes over from another," "a successor." Abu Bekr called himself the khalif of the Apostle. The next khalif described himself as the successor of the successor of the Apostle. By chance, someone addressed him as the "commander of all the faithful." The title stuck for more than 13 centuries.

were minor prophets, so you, Talha, and you, Maslama, may well be minor prophets closen by Allah. Go in peace, and may Allah make prosper your families, your flocks, and your tribes."

The assembly agrees that there is but one God and that Mohammad was his principal, but not his last, prophet. All obligations to pay tribute to Medina are dropped. All must contribute to the upkeep of the Ka'aba and of the Prophet's tomb at Medina.

The first undertaking of Abu Bekr is to gather together all the sayings and prescriptions that are ascribed to the Prophet. These are either preserved in people's memories or scribbled down on dried palm leaves, on bits of linen, wood, and dried goatskin. A committee composed of Abu Bekr, Umar ibn Khattab, Abu Ubaida, Ali ibn abi Talih, and Khalid ibn al Waleed supervises the collection and collation of the material. Two Greek scribes are employed to inscribe the words and wishes. They add to this an account of the Prophet's life from his conception to his death. The work is placed in the mosque of the Prophet at Medina. Muslims now swear by this book. It is not called the "life of Mohammad;" Mohammad is still alive in heaven, and ever-present to the community. They decide to call it simply the "Reading" of the Prophet. In Arabic, the word is "Qur'an," or "Koran."

Meanwhile, the Quraish tribe of Mecca has engaged in the usual tribal plundering raids and sporadic warfare with the Zubaid and the Beni Bajeela tribes of the Yemen. They also send expeditions against the borders of the Greek and Persian Empires to the north and northeast. The tribe prospers through these undertakings and eventually comes to control most of the South Arabian tribes in addition to some sheikdoms on the Persian Gulf.

The religion of the Prophet develops accordingly. Some efforts are made toward the end of the 7th century to change what had been lifelong habits of Mohammad. For instance, a certain Hassan proposes that instead of turning toward Jerusalem when in prayer, Muslims should turn to Mecca. The then leader of the Quraish opposes this fiercely: "The Prophet always turned toward Jerusalem, for it is the center of the earth where Adam 'the first man' was created. I will not allow any change in the Prophet's prescriptions."

Another tendency is to proceed so far with the glorification of Mohammad that, instead of being honored as a man whom

Allah had chosen to be his principal prophet, he is represented as superhuman, sinless, and all-wise, as having written down every word of the Koran himself, and not as having really died but as having been transported, living, in a fiery chariot to the seventh heaven by the angels Michael and Gabriel. By the end of the 9th century, this becomes the official standpoint of the leaders of the community who still dwell in Medina and Mecca.

By now, the Muslims are an intransigent, self-contained, xenophobic, fanatical group, slightly impatient with the progress of events. The Prophet had promised that eventually, but in the not-too-distant future, all men would have to submit to the new revelation of Allah. Men have not done so. This later generation of Muslims then undertakes a fresh religious war directed mainly against the Persians and the Greeks. Because they feel their religion, as promised, cannot but conquer, they decide to wage the holy war in direct battle confrontation. It is a disastrous decision. Muslims manage to overrun part of Palestine and devastate the land; they also cross the Euphrates and lay siege to the cities of Hira and the Persian capital of Medina. But they are only accustomed to desert warfare, and they have no expert knowledge in besieging cities or conducting pitched battles. Besides, the Greek fleets sail the seas constantly harassing Muslim encampments on the Mediterranean coast between Gaza and Alexandretta. The campaign is a failure. Both Greek and Persian empires are strong enough to resist the attack. The Muslims retire after much destruction and massacre on both sides. Arabia becomes their refuge. They will never attempt another outward expansion.

Anyone standing at the crossroads of history in 632 would have been sorely tempted to prognosticate the chances of Mohammad's little community in terms resembling the above scenario. If one remembers the congenital Arab inclination for rivalry, jealousy, tribal loyalties, and volatile resolution, the achievement of that community under the inspiration of the dead Mohammad appears all the more astounding and unexpected. History abounds in concrete examples of the above scenario; the Carmathians, the Wahhabis in Arabia; the numerous sects evolving from 16th century Protestantism throughout Europe; the Arians who beset the early Christian Church in the 4th century A.D.

Scenario B: An Empire without Religious Ideology

Mohammad has scarcely been buried when the leaders of the Beni Umaiya tribe enter the holy Ka'aba at night and make off with the sacred Black Stone. The Beni Umaiya are fiercely and irrevocably opposed to the Beni Hashim, Mohammad's tribe and the dominant one in Mecca. The Beni Umaiya had been opposed to the Prophet during his lifetime; once, they had even tried to starve the Prophet's tribe to death by confining them to their houses and not allowing water or food to cross the thresholds.

When the theft is discovered, the Beni Hashim and the Meccans set off in hot pursuit. They eventually catch up with the Beni Umaiya and slaughter them to a man. Unfortunately, the Black Stone is not to be found. The Beni Umaiya have given it to three members of the Beni Bajeela tribe from the Yemen. The latter are now beyond all pursuit and probably within the confines of their own territories. Nothing more is ever heard of the Black Stone. But the Beni Hashim return to Mecca vowing vengeance and promising to carry on the tradition of the Prophet.

Without the Black Stone, of course, the Ka'aba in Mecca becomes a heartless void. Its source of holiness is gone; the physical sign of Allah's blessing and presence is no longer there. Soon Meccans and others erect some idols of lesser gods. When they are attacked by more puritan Muslims and accused of not admitting the central truth of Islam ("there is but one God"), they respond that, in truth, there is but one God, that the idols represent servants, angels, demons, djinns of Allah, and that the Prophet himself has acknowledged the existence of at least Allat, Al Uzza, and Manat, all worshipped by the Meccans. The Muslims now split up religiously, some agreeing with the idol worshippers, some maintaining that all these things should be abolished in the name of the Prophet. Merchants, shopkeepers, hotel owners, side with the former group because it is good for business. The Meccans are a practical people.

Meanwhile, a successor to Mohammad has been elected: Abu Bekr. Outwardly mild and patient and soft-spoken, Abu Bekr together with Khalid ibn Walid and others have a dream: the conquest of the rich lands which border their beloved Arabia. They had already subdued all the tribes in Arabia itself, by the end of 632. This they had accomplished by a mixture of massacre and religion. Now, facing the Persian and Greek Empires, they lay out careful plans of attack, based not on a fanatical reliance in the ultimate success of Islam, but rather on Bedouin tactics they had refined over the centuries: as far as possible, the enemy will never be fought in pitched battle unless the Arabs have the desert at their back; they will not storm fortified cities and strongholds, but rather endeavor to buy their way into them by bribes and promises. They also foresee the day when they must build fleets and rid the seas of the superior Byzantine sea power. At this particular moment, the time is propitious; both Persian and Greek Empires are exhausted by a 26-year-old war; besides, their territories contain many Arab tribes who can easily be persuaded to fight on the Muslim side. But while their strategy is determined by the cold reason of military necessity and not religious conviction, it is agreed that they will use the tenets of Mohammad in order to give their soldiers a motive for fierce bravery in battle. "Empire or Paradise" becomes the motto of the Bedouin armies as they sweep northward and eastward in attack on the two great Empires at their weakest points.

By the year 680, the Persian Empire is at an end, and the Greek Empire is now restrained to its European possessions in Dalmatia and Greece. The Muslims now plan a two-pronged attack on Europe: one huge army streams across the straits of Gibraltar; its goal is to enter France, turn eastward, invade Italy by the Riviera coastal roads, overrun all of Italy, secure Sicily, and join up with the other prong which is aimed at Greece. The latter is then instructed to invade the Balkans and move westward to join with the first prong which by this time has occupied Italy. There is really no force left in southern Europe to oppose this onslaught. Within 30 months, the two armies are reunited on the plains of Lombardy. Strong cities such as Ravenna, Constantinople, and Rome still hold out, but they are isolated pockets of resistance soon to be picked off.

The whole of southern Europe from Bordeaux in France to the Dardanelles in the east is now in the hands of the Muslims. The Mediterranean becomes a Muslim lake. There is no religious persecution, because the conquerors themselves are not religious fanatics, merely empire-builders and ambitious men. The lingua franca of the area becomes Arabic. The Bishop of Rome, at the first threat of disaster, proceeds across the Alps and takes up his residence at Cologne where the bones of the three Wise Men who visited Jesus at his birth are preserved in a gold casket. Cologne now becomes the center of Christianity. The tradition of Roman imperialism is quickly lost as the papacy tries to establish itself as a spiritual power once more.

In the south, the Muslim conquerors are undergoing the influence of the subjugated peoples. The Muslims have no ethnic or religious isolationism to hamper them, because by now they have developed a religious syncretism composed of the tenets common to Mohammadanism, Judaism, and Christianity. For them, the world is really one—their own empire—with little pockets of resistance to the north and the east. Nowhere, either in North Africa, Europe, or Asia have they tried to impose a religious faith or belief on anyone. And throughout their empire Jews and Christians live on equal footing with all other groups. In fact, one of the marks of the Muslim genius is this capacity to weld differing communities together into a politically homogeneous group.

When we examine the extent and the limits of Islam's empire-building in actual history, what we most regret is the almost narcissistic isolationism and xenophobia that gripped its huge territories for so long, eventually excluding the peoples of these territories from the benefits of the advances made by Western European countries in science and economic growth. This isolationism and xenophobia were due directly and solely to the narrow vision of Mohammad and of the Islam that emanated from his words and his preaching. The physical modes of Islam's dominance, as outlined specifically in Chapter 12, are all rooted in the parochial intransigence, the religious fanaticism, and the political extremism of this one man. Islam's choice after Mohammad's death was for a fatal compromise: a theocratic lay empire. In other words, all the ambitions and power-instincts of man were allowed to roam as they willed within the myopic parameters of one person's conception of man and his cosmos. What saved Islam was the religious experience of Mohammad that somehow or other he successfully communicated to his followers.

Islam could have developed into a purely lay empire. It could have assumed control of all of southern Europe. It is safe to say that if that had happened, Christianity, and particularly Roman Catholicism, would not have developed its temporal power and imperialism, and the Christian animus against the Jews would have had little to feed upon. Christians would have found a totally different enemy to hate—the Muslims—and the face of Judaism in its dispersal throughout all European lands would probably never have resembled the ghettoized communities of the 18th, 19th, and 20th centuries in Central and Eastern Europe.

Scenario C: A Spiritual Religion

After Mohammad's death, his successor, Abu Bekr, is faced with a crisis: the tribes which Mohammad had subdued are in open revolt. Some of their leaders send a message to Abu Bekr offering to pronounce the sacred words: "There is but one God, and Mohammad is his prophet." They refuse, however, to pay tribute. Others state that they will agree to affirm that "there is but one God." As to the rest of it, they say, already two other new prophets, Talha and Maslama, have arisen since the death of Mohammad. These two are working miracles, enjoy the support of the people and are as genuine as Mohammad. Talha, in particular, has already had communications from Allah: the angel Gabriel visited him while he prayed in the desert. Gabriel showed him Mohammad with Jesus and Abraham and Moses before the throne of Allah. All were equal, Gabriel had told him. No tribute is necessary any longer, since the enemies of Mohammad are no more.

Faced with this solid refusal, Abu Bekr adheres to the admonition of the Prophet that Believers must not fight against Believers. Peace is established. The tribes return to their normal occupations—plundering and raiding. Meanwhile, Abu Bekr and the Companions of the Prophet meditate and pray for light on how they should propagate the message of the Prophet. They find the key to this in the Prophet's description of Allah as the All-Truthful and the All-Merciful. If Allah is really the embodiment of truth and mercy, then the Community of Believers should be first and foremost in propagating truth in a merciful fashion, mercy in a truthful fashion. Furthermore, the Prophet had always spoken kindly of the Christians and the Jews as the People of the Book, meaning that they possessed the Bible, the first source of revelation to man. True, Mohammad had been obliged to massacre one whole community of Jews and to subjugate a few others; but this was during the pressure of war when peace had not yet been established.

Abu Bekr sends three emissaries, one to Yemen where large colonies of Jews existed and prospered; another to Palestine to visit Jerusalem, and to Syria to visit Damascus; the third goes to Constantinople to visit the Emperor Heraclius. The purpose of these visits is to establish bonds of friendship with the Jews and Christians. Heraclius is overjoyed at seeing the emissary from Abu Bekr; for a long time he has feared an Arab attack on his very weak defenses in Palestine, Syria, and Egypt. Under his orders, the Patriarch of Constantinople assigns an archmandrite to accompany Abu Bekr's emissary all around the Empire. They eventually visit the Bishop of Rome. The latter suspects, of course, that Heraclius and the Patriarch are up to some trick, but he sees great advantages in striking up a friendship with the Mohammadans. Theological discussions are held in the Bishop's residence for over six months. At length, the Pope sends a special group of Latin theologians with the emissary who returns to Medina via Constantinople.

At Constantinople the Emperor Heraclius adds some of his own theologians, and the emissary returns to Medina. At Medina, it is clear to Abu Bekr and his counsellors that the Christians are utterly split among themselves as to how their Gospel of Love should be preached and practiced. In addition, the Greek Emperor wishes the Arabs to contribute soldiers to wage war on the Persians. Deliberations are held throughout the summer and winter of 636. Finally, in the spring of 637, the Mohammadan community sends a message to Constantinople and Rome, in which it states its firm belief that there is but one God of Muslims, Jews, and Christians (there cannot be two or three gods), that this God has sent Moses, Jesus, and Mohammad, and that all should live in peace and not make war on each other in the name of the God of Truth, Mercy, and Love. The community refuses to wage positive war, but will act in self-defense if the Persians attack.

Meanwhile, the Mohammadans have collected all the savings of their prophet and put them together into one book, which also contains an account of his life. This they do not regard as a sacred book since they themselves have put it together; but they do revere the sayings of Mohammad contained in it. They obtain copies of the Jewish Bible and the Christian holy books, and have them translated into Arabic. They now proceed to preach the doctrine of Mohammad based on his interpretation of these books. To them it is quite obvious that the Jews have strayed from the original message of Moses. Likewise, they see that the Christians no longer love their neighbors as themselves; they do not even love themselves; they are constantly warring for riches and territories and the exclusive right to preach the Truth.

The effect of this is to disaffect the Mohammadans from the current official expression of Judaism and Christianity. They revert more and more to the teachings of Mohammad, seen in the light of the original Christian and Jewish teachings as contained in the Testaments. There evolves a religion of contemplation and of charitable works. Its main obligations are prayer, pilgrimage, helping the poor and the hungry, and preaching peace and fraternal love. Gradually, also, it is realized that, although Mohammad was the Prophet of Allah, he was also human and therefore was fallible. Not all his doctrines are considered spiritual and godly.

This new spiritual religion, however, is surrounded on all sides by different religious beliefs and practices. After Mohammad's death, the tribes returned to idolatry; the idols have been set up again in the Ka'aba; some have even tried to set up an idol of Mohammad. Political trouble also attacks the Community of Believers. The Persians decide that they should extend their possessions to the Red Sea ostensibly to protect themselves from a Greek attack from the southeast. The Greeks understand the maneuver. War between the Greeks and the Persians devastates the area including Mecca and Medina. The Community is finally expelled by the Greeks who think that it has replaced Jesus with Mohammad, and massacred by the Persians who think that it has replaced Zoroaster with Mohammad. Thus, the Community finally perishes to a man.

The fundamental lesson of the preceding scenario is that no religion relying purely and simply on spiritual principles, eschewing force of arms, and refusing to be inserted in a living political structure could have succeeded in the 7th century A.D. Christianity apparently managed to dominate Europe, and parts of Africa and the Middle East, only because it willingly suffused political structures with its religious coloring, identifying its goals with the goals of those structures. In the scenario, the tangible continuation of the religion of the Mohammadans ceases because it attempted to be only spiritual and not rely on any material force. Whether this is an absolute rule of human existence is another and wider question. We touch on it later in discussions concerning the geopolitical situation of Judaism, Christianity, and Islam.

14. The Two Seas of Time

The path followed by the small Mohammadan community, and its transforming effect both on the community and on the socio-political and religious ambient of all Mediterranean lands, can be summed up very briefly. Between 632 and 680, the community changed from a theocratic idealistic group to a theocratically inspired lay empire and dynastic power; this empire and this power split the ancient Graeco-Roman world in two, thus modifying forever the geopolitical character of the Mediterranean land-mass from Gibraltar to the Persian Gulf. Henceforth Christianity would think of Islam as a sword thrust into its soft underbelly, as an insurmountable bastion hindering its access to Africa, as a Johnny-come-lately and poor imitation of its own self, as a golden whale lazing in southern backwaters. Islam, in turn, would consider Christianity as the enemy lying in wait beyond the wall, the alien and inimical country just across the water, the nearby threat of a hated and hating civilization, the cancerous crab clinging to its ancient pediment of dark and clammy earth in Northern climes.

Today, it is fascinating to reflect on the odds, in some ways seemingly insuperable, that faced the Mohammadan community. When we add to this the total unpreparedness of the community either to conduct pitched battles, lay siege to towns, build, much less sail ships, or administer the bureaucracy of an empire, the Mohammadan ascent to wide-embracing power assumes an extraordinary character. Nothing would explain it better than a favorite prophet of an All-Mighty God interceding efficaciously for success! The myth is almost uniquely sufficient. Withal, there is an element of chance, of undoubted bravery, and of the cooperation of history in its irresistible logic.

At Mohammad's death in 632, Arabia, the homeland of

Islam, was, for all practical purposes, an island. Surrounded by the waters of the Persian Gulf, the Indian Ocean, and the Red Sea, its northern frontier faced the fortified old man of the Persian Empire, horrendous to its contemporaries with the Glory of Ormuzd. Flanking it on the north and northwest stood the colossus of the Byzantine Empire. To the West, from the upper Euphrates down in a quasi-straight line to the Gulf of Aqaba on the Red Sea, was Greek possession. Everything from Egypt to Algiers also belonged to the Greeks.

The territories which today are divided into Algeria, Morocco, Tunis, Libya, Egypt shared the same culture, religion, governmental forms, commerce, art and literature as Spain, France, Italy, Greece, Syria and Palestine. All these lands formed the "world," the *oikumene*, of the West at that time. Successively conquered by Carthage, Rome and Germanic Vandals, North Africa was acquired by Byzance under the Emperor Justinian in 532. The population was a mixture of Carthaginians, Romans, Greeks, Vandals. The indigenous peoples such as the Berbers had been either driven into the hinterland or absorbed by some 400 years of alien rule and civilization. North Africa was part of the same cultural and civilizational world as its European masters. The Mediterranean was, truly, *mare nostrum*, for the Westerner of that time, the common medium or canal by which this world communicated with its various parts. Ethnic, religious, artistic, and socio-political homogeneity webbed the entire area.

The European possessions of the Greek Empire included all territories between the Danube and the Mediterranean, and extended as far as Italy. In Italy, Byzantine possessions included territories around Ravenna in the north, much of the land south of Rome, and all of Sicily. For the West and for the Byzantines, the "East" began at what today is approximately the common border of Iraq and Syria. A Syrian could travel from Syria to Spain and find himself at home. But if he turned east, he faced the Persian Empire, which stretched eastward from the Indus River, extending northward to the Caspian Sea, and the Caucasus.

In addition to their rather formidable Greek and Persian opponents and to their total unpreparedness and inexperience in the long-term logistics of a continental military venture, the Mohammadans surprise us further by the incidental, almost accidental manner, in which the entire venture started. Indeed, the initial actions and undertakings of the Mohammadans were purely and simply logical extensions of their normal behavior. The Community drove a short spearhead into a weak spot of the Byzantine Empire. It might have remained just that but, we must note in retrospect, the apex of that spearhead was a new fire—the ethos of righteous religion in this life and of Paradise in the next; its ultimate victory can be attributed to the monolithic unity imposed by Mohammad, on the one hand, and the momentary exhaustion of the Greeks, on the other hand.

For according to Mohammad, while a believer could kill anyone who disbelieved—whether the non-believer was of his own tribe or of another—the tribes of believers could not fight each other. Thus a perennial and sustaining activity of the Bedouin was forbidden; a way of life was altered. Inter-tribal warfare was prohibited. Something had to take its place. Raiding and plundering the fringes of the Byzantine Empire was that way of life. Secondly, the Byzantines and Persians had just finished a 26-year-old war that left both antagonists momentarily exhausted and susceptible to successful attacks. And one result of that war was that in both Empires, the local Arab dynasties on the peripheries were deprived of their local autonomy; government was centralized and emanated from Constantinople and from Medain, the Persian capital. Local Arab leaders, therefore, became disenchanted with these centralized governments and were ready to revolt.

What could be more natural, under these circumstances, than to carry out some typically Bedouin hit-and-run plundering raids on nearby Persian and Greek border settlements?

A prominent Mohammadan, Muthanna chief of the Beni Bekr tribe, suggested a raid on the Persian border. But it was decided that the Byzantine territories should be the target: rich caravans and prosperous settlements abounded between the Gulf of Aqaba and Damascus. Besides, the Prophet himself had raided up as far as Tebook, and memories of Mota were still alive. It is important to note that the Mohammadans went forth, not to punish infidels, not to convert them, not to acquire territory, but to loot and plunder. This was the way of life. They knew no other. Now a hurricane of fire whirled out of the desert, playing hide-and-seek with cumbersome armies and fortified strongholds like a lethal will-o'-the-wisp. It would not be contained for a century.

The fire burned simultaneously in two directions. The tongue snaked northward, up to Palestine under the joint command of Amr ibn al Aasi, Yezeed ibn abi Sofian, and Shurahbil ibn Hasana. The other, under Khalid ibn Waleed, spun across the desert in a northeasterly direction to the heartland of the Persian Empire. By 635, all of Palestine, except for Jerusalem and Caesarea, had been secured. They, together with Damascus and Antioch in Syria, were occupied by 637. The Byzantine Empire was mortally wounded.

By 637, also, a Persian army of about 75,000 trained warriors and 33 mail-clad elephants had been routed at the Battle of Qadasiya on the western bank of the Euphrates by a force of about 30,000 Mohammadans. "The Believers smote and slaughtered till the going down of the sun," wrote one Arab historian. The treasured banner of the Sassanids fell into Mohammadan hands, and Persia never recovered from the blow. In 638, the Persian imperial capital, Medain, was captured. Yezdegird, the last emperor, fled from stronghold to stronghold, until finally in 652 he was assassinated, stripped of his clothes and valuables, and thrown into a river. Persia was no more. "There is good news," exclaimed the messengers who had hurried back to Medina to inform the Khalif, "the Persians have given us the soil of their countries." Syria and Palestine were placed under the governorship of Muawiya.

On December 12, 639, Amr ibn al Aasi invaded Egypt. By 655, Babylon, Fustat (both on the site of the future Cairo), Alexandria, and Tripoli had been taken. The Greek fleet had been defeated in two major sea battles. North Africa was lost to the Greeks and to Europe. Henceforth, the gateway to Europe was open, and the Mediterranean ceased forever to be a Graeco-Roman lake. "Allah promised you great riches," were the reassuring words of the Koran, "you shall have it all." Constantinople was besieged unsuccessfully for seven years (670-677), and the Sudan was invaded disastrously. But the fire burned onward.

By 681, a Muslim general, Uqba rode his horse into the Atlantic near Agadir crying: *"Allah akbar!* If my course were not stopped by this sea, I would still ride on at the unknown kingdoms of the East, preaching the One God and putting to the sword the rebellious nations who worship any other god but Him!" By 750, Islam's writ would run from the Pyrenees in Spain to the Great Wall of China, and the Koran would note anachronistically that "Allah has brought the dream of his Apostle to concrete reality." Desert nomads had emerged from their black tents and endless sands to occupy the most ancient cities and most sumptuous palaces of man's world. They had established an empire on the ruins of two others, and Europe faced a completely new threat in the changed situation of Africa and the Near East. "The fear of the Arabs fell on all kings," was the description by one Arab chronicler. Indeed, it had.

The initial onrush of the Arabs was characteristically daredevil, and disrespectful of established canons in battle; their diplomacy was almost nonexistent. Moreover, as we have noted, they relied on tactics inspired directly by their former Bedouin mode of life in which their greatest ally was the desert. And in reality their vast conquests were merely extended plundering raids, until the weight of acquired territories and consolidated power wrought the inevitable changes.

In merciless warfare, they resembled the Huns and Vandals or, for that matter, the Crusaders marching across Europe and the Middle East. We have already seen examples in the life of Mohammad. It was not extraordinary for a triumphant Mohammadan force to massacre all the menfolk of a city and sell the women and grown children into slavery. Their rudeness was proverbial and shattered all norms of diplomacy. In 636, for instance, the Arabs sent an old Bedouin to parley with the magnificently attired Persian commander-in-chief, Rustem, who was seated with all grave pomp and imperial insignia surrounded by his retinue on priceless carpets. The scene was shocking to the Persians. The ragged Bedouin, armed to the teeth, rode his desert mare onto the carpets. Dismounting, he advanced toward Rustem, leaning on his lance and driving a series of ruinous holes in the lush surface of the carpets. Then standing before Rustem, he stated the situation grimly and laconically: "Convert and believe in Allah and His Prophet; subject yourselves to his successor, the Khalif, and pay tribute. Or you will be totally destroyed." In reality, two worlds were in confrontation here. One triumphed with its initial raw integrity, its ignoring of odds. One perished miserably, but with dignity.

In motivation, the world had not quite seen anything like the Mohammadans for a long time. Rushing into the Battle of Bedr in 624, they shouted "O Paradise of the Houris! Receive us!"

Death in battle against unbelievers was a sure guarantee of eternal felicity in Paradise. "O Prophet! Urge on the Believers to battle," were the words said to them before engaging the battle of Qadasiya in 637; "if there be of you twenty steadfast, they shall conquer two hundred. If there be one hundred of you, they shall conquer a thousand of the unbelievers." The Arab delegation which went to parley with Cyrus, governor of Babylon in Egypt, was led by a Negro named Ubada ibn as Samit. The latter told the governor that Mohammadans lived only to do the will of God and that money did not matter to them, adding, "this world is nothing, the next world is everything."

Their use of desert tactics was paramount in their success. As far as was possible, the Arabs refused to fight unless they had the desert at their backs: out of it they could pour with the immediacy of a sandstorm; back into its wasteless miles they could take refuge when necessary. "Fight the enemy in the desert," counseled Muthanna on his deathbed, "there you will be conquerors. If defeated, you will have the friendly and familiar desert at your backs. The Persians cannot follow after you there. From it you can return again to the attack." When Babylon in Egypt was secured in 641, one of the chief sources of satisfaction to the Mohammadans was that an uninterrupted line of desert now connected them with Medina and Mecca. They were always wary of fighting in the mountains of Syria and Palestine, always maneuvering for a battle site on the edge of the desert.

There was more than military strategy to this mode of conducting warfare. There was the regular mystique of the desert and the desert dweller. Ibn Khaldun, writing in the 14th century, formulated this:

> The inhabitants of the desert are sounder in their minds and bodies than the sedentary peoples who enjoy a softer life. Their skins are clearer, their bodies purer, their figures more harmonious and beautiful, their characters more moderate and their minds sharper in understanding and readier to acquire new knowledge than those of sedentary people. Compare the gazelle, the ostrich and the antelope with their counterparts who dwell in settled countryside. The former have more shining furs, more harmonious limbs and sharper senses.

The desert was the homeland, the natural habitat of the Arab, the source of his belief in demonic powers, with its vastness, its cruel aridity, its smiling oases, with its constant get-rich-quick opportunities on caravans, and ultimately the Arab's impregnable refuge from all onsets.

The *mystique* which thence evolved was that of two worlds: one was the island of the Arab, surrounded by sea and sand, where true belief and life flourished; the other was the "outside," the non-desert lying to the west, the north, the east. This pragmatic outlook was linked to Islam's belief in its own uniqueness: there was but One God, Allah; there was but one authoritative Prophet of Allah, Mohammad; there was but one authentic Community of Believers, the Muslims. All else, Christian, Jew, Western, Eastern, Indian, Chinese, and so on, were on the "outside," belonged to the "other world" the evil half of all humanity. A bipolarity thus arose. Even when the Mohammadans took on a vast bureaucratic framework of international government, lived in large urban complexes, and became a sedentary power, this mystique of religious bipolarity remained.

The comparison with the modern revolutionary theory of Mao Tse Tung and his Far Eastern version of Marxism is not merely inviting; it is quite valid. The Maoist configuration of the people's revolution emanating from the "countryside" and besetting the "cities," harassing the urban centers with untraceable and undefeatable guerrillas, the vulnerability and decadent character of sedentary forces, all these essential lines of the Maoist doctrine were the same ones that inspired the first far-flung successes of the Arabian tribes. The parallel is sustained also in the Mohammadan persuasion that its Community was the heir to the earth and the successor to a failing and blighted civilization. For Maoism, as for the early Marxists of Europe, the proletariat is the Community *par excellence*, the future possessor of the earth, once capitalism and all its works have withered away. The same bipolarity affects Maoism as it did Mohammadanism. The deep difference, of course, lies in the motivation and inner conviction. The religious doctrine of the Mohammadans was a pragmatist monotheism, oriented to the other-world of Paradise. Maoism is essentially atheistic and restrains its vision to the horizon of man and his perceptible cosmos.

The "desert" policy of the Arabs, on the other hand, served

them well in their conquests of Syria, Palestine, and North Africa, which were in Christian hands. Christianity was confined by and large to the urban centers; from the beginning it had been a religion of city-dwellers. The very name "pagan" (meaning the "village" or "country" dwellers) with which they labelled non-Christians, betrays this fundamental trait of Christianity. At the time of the Mohammadan onslaught, Christianity had absorbed all the area west of the vertical line formed by the Sea of Galilee, the Jordan River, and the Dead Sea Valley. East of this Christianity never got a foothold.

Even in Syria and Palestine and Egypt, where Christianity did gain strong support, it was hampered by two limitations. First of all, it was an urban phenomenon; the tribes living outside the cities and towns, whether sedentary or nomadic, were essentially untouched. Secondly, the local churches in Syria, Palestine, and Egypt (Copts) were placed in an inferior position ecclesiastically and religiously by their Byzantine overlords. Indeed, the Copts of Egypt had been so persecuted by Cyrus, the Byzantine governor, that they welcomed the ascendancy of the Arabs. The Christian Bedouin tribes converted with facility to the new desert religion. Christianity became confined to urban centers and, ultimately, to only small sections of the urban populations.

In changing the face of nations and lands, however, the Community changed. As was to be expected, the change came first outside Arabia in the conquered territories. At home, little changed essentially until after 670. Abu Bekr, the first Khalif, who is credited with starting Islam's outward expansion, died in 634, to be succeeded by Umar ibn al Khattab who was assassinated in 644. Othman ibn Affan, the third Khalif, ruled until 656 when he was murdered in a fierce inter-tribal feud. The fourth Khalif, Ali ibn abi Talib, cousin of the Prophet, was assassinated in 661. Thereafter, Muawiya reigned until his death in 680.

The first four Khalifs have been known as the "barefooted" Khalifs. Indeed, if any credibility is to be accorded to early accounts, all four lived in ordinary mud-huts, wore patched clothing, ate common food, accumulated no riches for themselves, and were determined to imitate the stark poverty and total dedication which had characterized the Prophet during his lifetime. In contemplating the transformation of the theocratic Khalifate with its threadbare, dedicated, frugally living Khalifs into a mighty, splendid, and hereditary empire, we put our finger on the historical choice or option that Islam made.

These Khalifs exercised absolute control over the armies and possessions of Islam. They lived in Medina and ruled from there. Again and again throughout the early years, we find instances of the autocratic rule they exercised in deposing generals, appointing governors, deciding strategy, ordering advances and attacks. The great Khalid was deposed at least twice; the second time, he was recalled to Medina to be accused by Khalif Umar of indulging in a bath of wine, of accumulating money and too many wives. When Amr ibn al Aasi had conquered Egypt, he received a letter from Umar informing him that he had accumulated too many slaves, silver and gold plate, and animals. The Khalif confiscated a great part of Amr's accumulated wealth. When Saad ibn abi Waqqas, governor of Iraq, built a fence around his house, he received a severe reprimand from Umar accusing him of having built himself a mansion. "It is not your mansion but the mansion of folly. Come out of it and close it and do not erect a door to keep the people out. . . ." Saad was dismissed from office. The spirit and outlook of these Khalifs, in spite of their jealousies, power-instincts, and limitations, remained until the advent of the short-lived Ali. In the meanwhile, a vital transformation was taking place abroad.

At the time of the Arab occupation of Syria, Palestine, Iraq and Egypt, the Arabs have been estimated to have numbered about 100,000. If the local populations are estimated to have been about 3,000,000, this would make the conquerors roughly one thirtieth of the total population. The Khalif Umar quickly decided that the Arabs had to be kept separate from the local peoples. He therefore organized huge encampments, one at Jabiya in Syria, another close to Hira on the Euphrates. The purpose was to prevent intermarriage and adulteration of the Arabs.

Adulteration, however, inevitably took place. By the concubines they took, by their commerce with surrounding peoples, and by the accession of large numbers of non-Arab converts, a change took place in the ethnological balance of the Mohammadan forces. In the passage of time, the majority were non-Arabs. In addition, the presence of non-Mohammadan communities throughout the Empire made the change even greater. No civil law existed for these communities. The Mohammadans were ruled by the *Shari'a,* the sacred law. The enclaves of Jews and Christians lived according to their own civil law while being subject to the Mohammadans. In Egypt, great numbers of Copts became Mohammadans. When Persia fell, it was impossible even for the Mohammadans to kill all the Persians who believed in Zoroastrianism. They should have done so, because according to the Prophet, only the People of the Book, i.e. the Christians and the Jews, could be allowed to continue in their own beliefs. Instead, the Zoroastrians were accorded the same privileges as the Christians and the Jews.

Gradually, it came about that *race* no longer differentiated the victors from the vanquished. The Arabians were no longer the only Mohammadans. Religion became the determining factor. Arab racial pride, therefore, disappeared and was replaced by Mohammadan religious superiority. Another mutating factor was that in the early years the bureaucracy of government in the Empire was peopled with Greeks (in the former Byzantine territories) and Persians (in the former lands of Persia). The Arabs had neither the education nor the training necessary for the "paper-work." Gradually the government took on forms and procedures which did not emanate from the Arab mentality.

The last factor contributing to the change was the inevitable rise of individual ambition uncurbed by any religious persuasions no matter how deep. Isolated examples occurred in the early years. Ibn abi Sarh, who won the battle of Sufetula in 647, retained for himself one-fifth of the loot taken in battle. This was contrary to all previously accepted practices. He was acting as an independent prince or general. But it was not such individual actions that precipitated the change, it was rather a breakdown in the central authority of the Khalif which split the Community and allowed the ambition of one man, Muawiya, to dominate over all.

Briefly, events took the following course. Discontent with some appointees of Khalif Othman led to sedition and uprisings in various parts of the Empire. At home in Medina, Othman was the object of criticism and attacks. He had been represented as a greedy, lecherous, tyrannical old man. He was finally beseiged in his house and murdered in May 656. The representative of the Prophet had fallen from his pinnacle, murdered by some of the Community. Islam would never be the same. The new Khalif, Ali, had no success in asserting his authority. Othman's blood-soaked shirt and the severed fingers of his wife, Naila, were smuggled out of Medina and brought to Muawiya in Damascus. Muawiya nailed them to the pulpit in the great mosque where they would remain until Muawiya ascended to power.

Muawiya then demanded that the murderers of Othman be punished, but Ali had already compromised himself with the assassins, and could not comply. Hostilities broke out between them. But Ali was assassinated in 661, and Muawiya was left as the sole claimant to the Khalifate. Although the Empire was once more reunited under one man, Muawiya reigned by the force of arms, not by the prestige of office, as the successor of the Prophet and the Commander of all the Faithful. The early tradition was dead. The idealism and the theocracy were impotent. Henceforth, a lay empire based on a theocratic idea and governed by hereditary Khalifs would rule Islam.

The total ideology of Mohammadanism was harnessed to the new imperial idea. The new Khalif was still regarded as the successor of Mohammad, as the Commander of Believers, governing them in the name of Allah and administering the sacred law. The wars he waged, particularly against the foreigner and the infidel, were still the sacred wars of the whole Community. But the Community was now welded into an imperial entity facing the outside infidel world. The essentials of Islam, as we know it, had been put together.

In the Battle of Yemama (about 632-33) many of the early companions of the Prophet had died. The Khalif of the time feared that the words and prescriptions of the Prophet would be lost as his early followers died. He accordingly set up a committee to gather all these words and prescriptions. The collection was finally put into written form during the Khalifate of Othman (644-56). We must remember, however, that this was merely a consonantal text: only the consonants were written; it lacked all vowels, and therefore no indication of the correct pronunciation was available. Mohammad was a Meccan of the Quraish clan, and his pronunciation was not pure. The Arabic spoken in Mecca had been influenced by the concourse of people who passed through it. It took over a hundred years before the text was finally provided with suitable pronunciation. The work was completed by people called "Readers," who travelled to the Bedouin tribes copying down their modes of pronunciation and incorporating these into the consonantal text of the Koran. The text was probably ready and complete by 815.[1]

By now, the attitude to Mohammad had changed. This was manifested in subtle ways. Mohammad himself had turned in the direction of Jerusalem when praying, for this was the Holy City *par excellence*. But slowly the attitude of Muslims changed. Worshippers now began turning towards Mecca. A magnificent mosque was built around the Prophet's tomb in Medina. The Koran was now reputed to have been revealed to Mohammad and to have been written down by him with the consonantal text and the vowel signs such as we find them in the 19th century. It thus acquired a sacrosanct character; it was believed that each word and vowel, each consonant and vowel-sign, had come to Mohammad from Allah through the mouth of angels.

Once the tradition of the "barefooted" Khalifs was transmuted into the glory and magnificence of Muawiya and his successors, the figure of Mohammad was correspondingly elevated. He never was divinized or considered to be supernatural. He was considered to have been superhuman. From being the Prophet of Allah, and the mouthpiece of Truth, he became the model, the inspiration, and the object of Islam's thought.

Thus, in the narrow span of 48 years and through a whirlwind cycle of battles, massacres, assassinations, sieges, seafights, endurance of heat, of cold, of hunger, enjoyment of vast power, of dazzling riches, of immense lands, the Helpers and the Emigrants became empire builders, conquerors of nations, dispensers of life and death to millions. Constricted in 632 to a little over one hundred Believers building a mud-brick mosque with their bare hands in a deserted palm garden in the middle of the Arabian desert, they became heirs to a sprawling complex as unlike Mohammad's crude, pigmy, idealistic power as the Taj Mahal differs from a wigwam.

The modest, amorphous, and parochial community left behind after his death changed from its narrow, other-worldly, tribal character, intent on achieving the delights of the *houri*

[1] Much remains obscure in the whole process. Cf. Paul Kahle, *The Arabic Readers of the Koran*, Journal of Near Eastern Studies II (1949) pp. 65-71, and his *Cairo Geniza*, Oxford, 1959, pp. 142-149.

Paradise promised to all true believers. When Muawiya, the fifth Khalif died, it was an island-like empire, broad as three continents, bent taut in a soaring posture of worldly conquest and human achievement. The eternity of Paradise was reconciled with the transient glory of time. Islam saw itself as one island and a variegated archipelago surrounded by two immemorial seas of time, the water and the sand. The island stretched from the Red Sea to the Atlantic, hemmed in between the sea of the Mediterranean and the impassable sea of Saharean sand.[2] The archipelago of Islam was the vast sea of sand and water from the Nile River over to the Caucasian Mountains, to Kabul in Afghanistan and Lahore in Pakistan, dotted with the islands of Islamic settlements, cities, lands, and possessions. The Community of Islam now floated triumphantly on the two seas of time toward an eternity of Paradise.

The axis of this Islamic world balanced between Mecca with its holy Ka'aba and Medina with the tomb of the Prophet. In another hundred and fifty years, the sacred book of Mohammad, the Koran, and the sacred law, the *Shari'a,* would receive their definitive form. Islam would proceed further in its conquests of land and peoples. Yet it would never again know that burst of power and overwhelming force it had enjoyed hitherto. Later it would retire behind the shelters of its seas, the water and the sand, dominated always by suspicion, sometimes by hate, of an infidel and evil world outside doomed to eternal damnation, eventually to be attacked and sliced up by latter-day empires. Thus the physical modes of Islam, which are discussed in the next chapter, had been established before the end of the 8th century. Nothing essential would ever change in Islam until the second half of the 20th century. For a time, the existence of Islam would seem in doubt. Muslim culture would be driven back and cornered in Egypt by the Mongol invasion of the 13th century until the battle of Ain Jalut in 1260, when the invaders would be displaced within two centuries to reside with the Turks, remaining there until the early 20th century. Yet Islam continued to hold sway over the same lands with the same perennial force.

[2] The term Maghrib (meaning "West") is used to designate either the eastern lands of Islam from Egypt to Algeria, or Morocco in particular. Originally, this term was part of an Arabic title "The Island of the West."

15. The Evening of the Magician

Even today, about 1,400 years after its abrupt birth in Arabia, Islam (and the Arab) still evokes in the Western mind a romantic idea as fascinating, as redoubtable, and as unrealistic as that of the Wandering Jew and Prester John in the Middle Ages, that of Gog and Magog in the 19th century, and of Tarzan of the Apes, James Bond, and the Abominable Snowman in the 20th century. This romantic idea is multi-faceted. It is not merely that Islam is erroneously identified with the Arab as such. It is, rather, a *mystique* of Islam as seen by an outsider, which is perpetuated by a series of syndromes as attractive as they are distant from reality. Effectively blotted out of our mind is the burning vision of man and his cosmos that constitutes the heart of Islam and springs from its total religious experience.

In speaking of Islam, therefore, it is especially difficult to realize the actual physical modes of its religious dominance. They are obfuscated by the romantic and wishful images constituting the Western mystique of Islam's being. Before describing the physical modes, various syndromes of this *mystique* must be pinpointed, thereby dispelling confusion between them and the actual picture of Islam.

One may be aptly termed the *Gibran syndrome*—after its most recent exponent Khalil Gibran, the Lebanese artist-poet whose leap to fame started in a Greenwich Village cafe meeting in 1916 with the young publisher Alfred A. Knopf.[1] Gibran's *The Prophet*, illustrated in one edition by Gibran's own sketches of idealized nudes, enjoys a wide cult whose devotees are always increasing.

As with all impressive messages, the messenger and his decor are reduced to the simplest terms undisturbed by the restlessness of details: Almustafa, about to leave Orphalese, answers the pious questions of the Villagers who wonder about Work, Freedom, Pain, Children, Love, Sorrow, and other basic human issues that normally rack any social group. Almustafa is Islam-Arab personified. Orphalese is redolent of Grecian sorrow at human weakness, and Grecian hope in the face of fate

[1] Knopf published Gibran's *The Prophet* in 1923. *The Prophet* was selling at 5,000 copies weekly in the summer of 1965. Gibran authored more than a dozen other works.

and the elements. As with all universally popular messages, the content of the message is unhindered by any partisan trait, any reference to a worshipped deity—Christian, Muslim, Jewish, or otherwise, or any formalistic obligation encased in an outward organization demanding conformity. The Gibran syndrome stresses man's inner union with the Good, the Beautiful, the All-Powerful, the Inevitable, those four pillars of Islamic mysticism.

Gibran's creed and aphoristic teaching is taken as a distillation of the wisdom of the East, of Islam. It is supposed, like stored essence, to reflect a philosophy of life and a theology of man enabling the beleaguered Western urbanite to taste the free leap of the spirit to Truth, to the All Good.

Included in this syndrome would be variations such as that sung by Omar Khayyam and "translated" by Edward Fitzgerald with its mixture of fatalism, esthetic joy, human pathos, sapiential reverence, and acceptance without prejudice of the Good wherever it is found.

All the wonder stories about Arabia and the Arabs, the Thousand and One Nights, the Thief of Baghdad, Ali Baba and the Forty Thieves, Aladdin and his Lamp, are also part of the syndrome. This mythology had an acutal source in Arabic and Islamic romanticism, but the ensuing picture is far removed from reality: lands of wondrous beauty and paradisiacal tranquility carpeted with magic lawns, seeing roses, perceptive fruit, walking mountains and chanting rivers, side by side with veritable hellholes planted with devil trees that strangled and tempted, strewn with dragons and evil genii, shrouded in mists of undoing and subject to volcanic upheavals, palatial halls filled with ravishing women whose beauty was measured by exotic tests; lands, in sum, where the law of Great Expectations, contrary to the Dickensian theme, fell on mortal heads according to the nutum of an invisible but nonetheless capricious deity and without the Western conception of merit through hard work, moralistic living, or heroic behaviour.

In this area, too, arose the persuasion of Arabic wisdom, its precis of much thought in telling apothegms and the short story with the punchline. "The fish always starts to stink at the head." "Vengeance is a dish which one should eat cold." "You never know in the Middle East," (the Scorpion to the Camel who had been stung by the former while transporting him over the Red Sea).

The second powerful syndrome may be termed the *Ibn Saud syndrome*. It is, at one and the same time, the most terrifying and the most romantic. Ibn Saud in the thirties of this century carved out a veritable empire for himself (Saudi Arabia) and lashed it together indissolubly by the twin ropes of loyalty and forthrightness. He had the single-mindedness of Peter the Great and a lot of his ruthlessness. But he had a supreme quality possessed by no Westerner: he understood the Arab Bedouin. The loyalty sprang from his inspiration as their traditional leader, and from the iron-handed domination he exercised. The forthrightness he practised left friend and foe in no doubt as to his intentions.

The cities and the countries of the Middle East since the time of the Crusades have held an unspeakable charm for the Western mind. All Muslims were Arabs, it was thought. Their land was Arabia, a land beyond description, full of strange and breathtaking things. This conception was chiefly based on ignorance arising from the officially sanctioned separation of the Christian West and the Muslim East. From being a religious thing, however, this mutual exclusivity became a social and political habit. There arose the powerful syndrome concerning the Arab ruler, his land and his people. The syndrome has many variations but only one accepted exponent—T. E. Lawrence ("Lawrence of Arabia"), who rallied the kings and sheikhs of the Arab world [2] against the Central Powers during World War I, and was killed in an accident at the age of forty-seven. Writer, politician, military strategist, mystic, masochist, and always alone, Lawrence consecrated this image of the Arab and of Islam.

The Arab, so this idea runs, lived surrounded by limitless desert sand, exposed to a merciless sun and to the whipping hand of headlong whirlwinds and sandstorms whistling out of fathomless silences with treacherous suddenness. Whether he chose to dwell in palm groves and at oases or in large white stone cities and towns which were inevitably full of towers, minarets, and palaces, the Arab wore flowing white robes, had a swarthy beard, sported flashing eyes as black as obsidian, never washed, possessed decades of wives, concubines, and slaves (Christians), and spoke an unutterably guttural language resembling the angry bleating of the she-camel in travail,

[2] Cf. *The Seven Pillars of Wisdom*.

with phonetics beyond any Western palate and a constant recurrence to throaty screams and rather threatening growls.

Nature had further endowed the Arab with the sensitivity of a German sheep dog and the instincts of a homing-pigeon: he could tell by smell and at a distance of anything up to 20 miles how many men, with or without guns, on how many camels were coming against him; could "feel" water at comparable lengths; could hear the sound of a truck or the clomping of the army boots on the desert floor long before his adversaries knew of his existence; could, in addition, see with the extra-fine vision of a hearty young eagle; and, in Mark Twain's immortal but hardly complimentary words, as a nomad carried many nomads on him.

Cruelty and rapacity and, further, an unbending attachment to a funny religion, were ascribed to the Arab. His rulers were either Sultans, Emirs, Khalifs, Imams, or Sheikhs; and they were just as ready to utter a fantastically wise aphorism, which Confucius would have envied, as they were to slice off somebody's head at a moment's notice. Their palaces were incredibly luxurious: marble halls and corridors, blue-green indoor swimming pools, domed bedrooms with circular beds of a spectacular hugeness, capricious luxury, ebullient richness and fascinating mystery that sent the head spinning, all serviced by huge dumb Nubian slaves and docile Negro eunuchs, amid the ringing sounds of all-night banquets on such unheard of delicacies as stuffed sheep's eyes, basted quail's livers, pickled swallows' tongues, the sweetened blood of unborn lambs, and mountains of brilliantly colored and luxuriant fruit—pale reminiscences of which appear in Western apples, pears, grapes, bananas, pineapples, and oranges.

Every palace held three essential elements according to the myth: the dungeon in which (a) Christians, (b) British and French officers, (c) princeling hostages from enemy tribes, and (d) uncooperative women captives (in that order) languished in hideous darkness, thirst, hunger, and hope; the treasure-house replete with fabulous mounds of rubies and chests of gold and silver and precious stones; and finally, the harem—an assemblage of beautiful, winsome, ravaged, shrinking, well-born, enslaved feminine beauties, who spent their days gazing sadly out of barred turret windows panting for freedom, and their nights in bestial torments on the couches of their ravening and insatiable masters back from the slaughter of a raid or the carousal of a celebration.

The mass of the "Arabs," of Muslims, were conceived of as living in humble servitude to the ruler and the elements of his world. Living on such hardy things as goat's milk, dates, the odd slab of camel cheese, and drinking water or native whiskey, the ordinary Arab bred innumberable children, honored strangers (as long as they were within the confines of his tent or house), and awaited the frequently recurring summons from two people: the muezzin calling in a high-pitched voice from the minaret five times a day, and the ruler bellowing for legions of followers on camels and black unmanageable Arabian steeds to rush out of the desert and descend on a tiny detachment of the Foreign Legion singing the Marseillaise, or on a lone, brave British Army column with, above all, a stiff upper-lip, or upon a really defenseless outpost manned by five walking wounded and a brutal sergeant-at-arms, finally retiring into the black womb of the night as barbaric as they emerged.

The third syndrome worthy of note here may be termed the *Aga Khan syndrome*. And its theme is very simple: the Muslim (or Arab, or Islamic) ruler is fabulously wealthy, the people are all very, very poor—in fact they live in dire poverty and hardship. And this is the accepted order of things. The well-known image of the Aga Khan being counter-weighted with his own weight in wealth on an actual pair of scales every year has driven this syndrome home. But the conclusions drawn from this go much further. Because of this disparity, the ruler is highly cultured and civilized, the people are barbaric, uncultured, untrained, and intractable. And thus an image of the Arab or Muslim country is again concocted which does not correspond to reality.

A fourth syndrome relevant to the chosen context of this book concerns Islam itself, as a religion and a way of life. It might be called the *primitive-cult syndrome*. This must not be confused with the Gibran syndrome which concerns an adaptation of "Arab wisdom", of "Eastern mysticism", to the tired Western mind. This fourth syndrome holds up Islam itself, its religious practices, its holy pilgrimages, its sacred shrines, its fervent multitudes of pilgrims, its leap to the face of God over the heads of the mechanized masses of the 20th century West and their grovelling slavery to the computer, the switchboard, and the TV screen through the long concrete canyons of Megalopolis and the anthills of conformity in Suburbia.

Nothing is so attractive to Western eyes as the yearly pilgrimage, the *hajj*, to the Holy Places of Mecca. It all seems so idealistic, so otherwise impossible in any other area or clime or for any other people or creed. And the photographs published in the West together with the impressive statistics and the stark recital of Moslem penances, prayers, and practices only heighten this attraction. The arrival by plane, car, bus, boat, cart and on foot of pilgrims from all over the world, clad in simple seamless white robes leaving the right arms bare: Senegalese, Malaysians, Pakistanis, Americans, Lebanese, Jordanians, Egyptians, Persians, Iraqis, North Africans, Turks, Cypriots, Albanians, Syrians. The chanting of prayers along the road in the desert. The ritual at the Stoning Pillars of Mena. The visit to the Prophet's burial place at Medina. The sacrifice of sheep in a simple slaughter. The stark rectangular shaped Ka'aba in the courtyard of Mecca's Great Mosque that marks the site where Adam worshipped before he left Paradise: 300,000 white clad figures, kneeling and bowed in concentric circles overhung by electric lamps, by reverential awe, by the black satin dome of the Arabian night, and by the rustling silence of religious attention. Or the 1,000,000 pilgrims standing together in prayer before Ararat, the mount from which Mohammad proclaimed Islam as complete; around them a sea of white, brown, and black tents.

Nor does this syndrome fail to feed on some of the monumental achievements of Islam—which are truly impressive. More impressive than any of Europe's Medieval Gothic spires would be the 13 acre Mosque of Negara in Kuala Lumpur, Malaysia, with its slender 245 foot tower overlooking a calm, translucent pool, its variegated parasol roof, or the Prophet's own Mosque in Medina in Saudi Arabia adorned with minarets, domes, arabesque windows and lofty halls, or the Blue Mosque of Istanbul endowed with an interior coloring of blue so penetrating that Pierre Loti exclaimed on seeing it, "le ciel n'est pas le ciel, si ce n'est pas comme ça," or the Dome of the Rock in Jerusalem which was first among the three monuments Berenson once said would never be surpassed (the other two: the Taj Mahal and the Sistine Chapel).

A fifth and final syndrome to be considered here is equally

illusionary. The *Arabs-versus-the-West-syndrome* is based directly on a modern event, the birth of Israel, but its roots go back into previous history. The situation in the Middle East for most Westerners and for many Arabs and Muslims is summed up in the Arab-Israeli conflict. Sides are chosen according to one's ethnic origin, religious persuasion, national outlook, or historical bias.

For sympathizers of Israel, the entire problem resides in Arab obduracy in not recognizing the *de jure* existence of Israel, its historic right to the Ancient Homeland, its claim to a haven after the Hitlerian holocaust, its innate value to the region. Remove anti-Israel feeling and attitudes, they would say, and the Middle East is pacified and on the road to constructive living.

The Israelis, thus, are pictured as hardy warriors, organized citizens, marvelous husbandmen, and the undying stump of a race that has finally achieved national unity after 2,000 years of wandering and constant persecution. And besides, they are a Western enclave set down irremovably amid the shifting sands of Arab rivalries, inconstancies, nationalisms, dynasties, tribal differences, infighting, backwardness, and disunity.

For Arab sympathizers, Israel is a historical error of such magnitude that nothing can be done until the implied injustice to the Arabs is corrected and punished, until Israel ceases to occupy Arab territory, until the Arab soul receives rightful restitution for the historic wrong. Nasserite Egypt receives, in this optic, a particular *raison d'etre*. The political ups and downs of Syria, Iraq, and Jordan are seen as the patient sufferings that befit a beleagured outpost of the Lonely and the Brave. The Arab boycott of things Israeli and anyone having truck with Israel appears reasonable. And Arab economic difficulties and industrial failures are easily explained.

Thus the Arab-Israeli conflict becomes the Bridge of Asses for the Western mind: passing to one side means inevitably reneging on the other, and to remain in the middle is to occupy an untenable position on a narrow plank that is not secured on either side. In short, it is a distortion of the reality: if this were true, no solution would be possible without unbearable suffering and unforgivable injustice. It is not generally recognized, but it is still true, that this syndrome is merely a modern version of a very old attitude toward the Arabs and the Middle East.

Traditionally, the Arabs and the Middle East were regarded

by the West as a hotbed of factional disputes, fratricidal wars, and above all, of a beleaguered spirit always in arms against the outside, a house always divided in itself, an area ultimately incomprehensible, implacably disturbed and warring. At the same time, the onus of solving the West's perennial problem of conscience—the Jews—is conveniently transferred to another continent and to an alien climate. Yet the problem remains. And that climate has worsened since the introduction of Israel.

These five syndromes, arising from the romanticized idea of the Arab and of Islam, are pleasant and even amusing to contemplate in the abstract. Taken together as skeins in a thread of understanding, however, they create a pattern of thought that inhibits an understanding of Islam and a grasp of the developing situation in the Middle East. They induce a contentment that the Arabs are wise beyond any need of Western advice, are utterly alien to the West in needs, are oriented inevitably towards ethical, religious, and social horizons other than those that bind the Western world. These syndromes blind, in short. And thus the real issues escape attention.

While each of these syndromes has fed on some particular aspect of Islam as a religion or a civilization, the physical modes of Islam are of a more spiritual and stark nature. They are four, and taken together they define the stance that Islam's adherents have taken to life, to man, to all visible and invisible things.

The *Community* is the first physical mode. Fundamental to the thought of Mohammad and of Islam down through the centuries was their historical judgement on Judaism and Christianity: they, the Muslims, represent on earth a community of true believers who would transmit the truth throughout time, spreading it abroad, destroying the unbelievers, and eventually retiring to Paradise where they alone would be rewarded for their fidelity. Confronted with the corruption that both Jews and Christians had produced in the original message of Abraham, Allah decided on a final offer: the revelation of Mohammad in the 7th century A.D.

Mohammad, under infallible divine guidance, founded the Community. With Allah's guarantee, the Community cannot err, cannot fail, cannot betray the truth. More importantly, it is the only recipient and possessor of the truth. Others may possess a fraction of it; Jews and Christians certainly do. But the whole truth is only with the Muslims, and only Muslims are destined to enjoy the full fruits of heaven. It must be remembered, also, that it is primarily the Community of Believers that matters. Leaders may come and go, Prophets, Khalifs, Sultans, Imams, Teachers, Saints. Only the Community is guaranteed permanence and perdurability in faith, in life, in truth.

The second physical mode of Islam resides in the *Law,* or *Shari'a.* This is a body of rules and principles developed into a permanent constitution for Muslims. It defines individual and public rights and duties. No government may govern, no ruler may rule, no man is authorized to adopt or grant any privilege or facility to power except within the framework of the sacred Law. The Law is necessary in order to validate all man's social and private activities from house building to running a government ministry. The Law is sacred, because it is an expression of the original revelation made to Mohammad. It is not manmade; nor does it depend on man for its sanctions and obligation. In ordinary, strict Islam, the idea of secular or civil law or a democratic government, in the modern Western sense of the word, is utterly alien.

This character of the Muslim Law renders all relations with the outside world extremely precarious and difficult. A non-Muslim can satisfy the religious and ideological exigences of a Muslim with whom he wishes to contract an agreement or establish the basis of mutual trust and cooperation only within the framework of the *Shari'a.* The latter constitutes one barrier between Islam and the outer world; it implies difficulties for Muslims and non-Muslims alike.

The third mode of Islam is the *earthly axis* on which the ordinary life of the Community turns. This axis runs between Mecca and Medina. Both are associated with the beginnings of Islam. In both there are hallowed and sacred places: Mecca contains the holy Ka'aba with its Black Stone, with the footprints of Abraham, with its sacred spring, and with the permanent association of its walls with Mohammad who cleansed it, worshipped there, and consecrated it forever. Medina was the dwelling place of the Prophet; here his body is buried; from here Islam began its outward expansion, carrying the truth to the nations. It is difficult for Westerners, even for those who, like Roman Catholics, venerate local shrines, to realize this axial function of Mecca-Medina. One of the obligations incumbent on each believer is a pilgrimage, at least once in his lifetime, to Mecca and Medina; the entire undertaking is fraught with a mystique of communication with the beyond, a consciousness that in these holy places the might of Allah and his choicest Prophet, together with the great men of Islam, are present in a veiled fashion. The Ka'aba at Mecca and the Mosque of the Prophet at Medina are not analogues of the Madonna's Grotto at Lourdes or St. Peter's tomb in Rome. For neither have been given a cosmic significance. In modern existentialist language, Mecca-Medina is an incarnation of Islam; Islam cannot be conceived without them. Islam will forever be oriented to them.

The fourth physical mode can be termed the *Siege*. We have referred in an earlier chapter to the bipolarity of Islamic thought. The Community is the carrier of divine truth. Historically and geographically the Community has always been located in the two seas of time, the sand of the desert and the fringes of water. Outside and to the north has always stood its mortal enemy: the West and Christian powers. Islam, for its part, is the mortal enemy of infidels and disbelieving humans. After its failure to spread beyond the southern coast of the Mediterranean, Islam retired to its redoubt. As time went on, the continual empire-building and colonializing efforts of Europeans were seen as the efforts of the alien and condemned world to encroach on the inheritance of Islam and the lands of the Community. Islam was in a state of siege. As far back as the 7th century, the Khalifs had decreed that no non-Muslim could live in the Arabian peninsula. Much of the same mentality exists today in Saudi Arabia. The *Siege mentality* has only been fomented and become more ingrained due to the rise of the modern state of Israel. For this is seen as a direct breach in the defenses of Islam, an invasion of its sacred territory. Israel for the Arabs is a Western enclave set down by force and terror in the center of Islam.

Thus Islam today in its purity: a divinely protected and infallibly guaranteed Community possessing exclusively the truth and the means of salvation, guided by a divinely appointed Law, resting on a sacral Axis of worship and devotion, and maintaining itself uncontaminated from an outside alien world that is ever pressing, ever encroaching on Islam's possessions.

Book Two

THE DIMENSIONS OF DOMINANCE

PART IV

The Basic Structures

16. The Thought of Dominance

When we come to discuss the language of dominance, we are struck with one overall characteristic it displays: it expresses the identity of the religions in question and of their dominance by the use of a *dialectic of opposites*. The cosmos in which the three religions find themselves is described in terms of a basic polarization. These terms are drawn from the perceptible phenomena of the world. This usage of the dialectic of opposites, as we shall see later, is basic to the pre-scientific mind. A primary pair of opposites is *light-darkness*. In the Upanishads, creation is thus described in terms of opposites:

> *"The sun is brahma, this is the teaching.*
> *Here is the explanation:*
> *In the beginning, this world was non-being.*
> *This non-being became being.*
> *It developed.*

It turned into an egg.
It lay there for a year.
It burst asunder.
What was born of it, is yonder sun."

We find, furthermore, running through the thought and the literature of all pre-scientific peoples a gamut of such opposites: pre-scientific man is, as it were, an artist stringing beads of opposing colors on a two-string necklace; heaven-earth, creation-destruction, life-death, male-female, *yang-yin,* night-day, good-evil, sacred-secular, etc.

But the presence of opposites seemed to be essential in order that man express himself, in order that his cosmos be whole and entire, and be adequately described. Hence pre-scientific man described that cosmos in terms of a primordial struggle still continuing: sun against darkness, hero against dragon, height against depth, life against death, sanctity against sin. The mythologies and religious faiths of the Far East, the Middle East, of Africa, and of the Western Hemisphere all reflect this basic binarism. It is such a universal element in the early thought and language of man that one is tempted to speak of it as a constitutive element in his natural make-up. For profound reasons, one wishes that it were not, because it is in virtue of this basic binarism that he sets up his dominances, petty and vast, whereby he creates the divisiveness threatening his species with extinction.

As a constant phenomenon of previous human thought, the origin of this binarism can be traced back only to a primordial conflict in man, a consciousness of choice between being and non-being, between order and chaos. There seems to be in man's instincts a latent nihilism and an equally latent persuasion of immortality. They both lurk beneath the surface of our successes and our failures; they await just around the corner where we meet what is different, what is difficult, what opposes us. We associate consciousness with life and activity, unconsciousness with death and nothingness.

Instinctively, we explicitly translate the various situations into the archetypal opposites of our hidden dreams, and categorize men and things according to the clinging cobwebs of ancient myths whose words we have forgotten but whose message still prevails in our psyche. With this explicit translation and only with it, we are capable of experiencing, of having

experience. And this experience we express by means of opposites always gyrating in the dangerous dialectic of existence.
Thus we create systems of thought and produce verbal formulations of these systems in which order and chaos, the creative and the destructive, death and renewal, are locked
together in a dialectic of tension and delicate balance. By anything he says and on account of anything he does, man must
always fear the negative pole of that dialectic, the "heart of
darkness" in him, the possibility that he will cease to be conscious man, or that he will be other than the man he was, or
different from the man he plans to be.

Thus the achievements of man seem to arise from the tension
and successive balancing of dialectical opposites, and thus one
can explain the work of great artists and writers: Kafka fighting against the deadening 19th century society of Prague that
turned a man into a cockroach; Hemingway celebrating male
potency in the hope that he could thus exorcise the monster of
impotency; Joyce twisting language beyond all bearing into
senselessness, in order that language should escape senselessness; Ionesco, Pinter, Beckett, and O'Neill indulging in the
sensuality of loneliness and isolation, so that neither horror
would take hold of man's condition; Nietzsche and Sartre
endowing man with godly power to resist the gods, thus hoping
that man can live with them; Camus advocating a visit to the
home of Nihilism, because "it is not in ignoring nihilism that
we shall find the ethic that we need"; Malraux conferring a
voice on silence, because only thus can man live with silence.

The process of this binaristic thought has been fundamental
to human systematization of life hitherto. The basic unit of
man's thought-pattern has been the binary pair. This is of paramount importance when we come to examine the language of
dominance in Judaism, Christianity, and Islam.

To understand the privilege and the power, the weakness
and the tyranny of religious dominance, it is necessary to
describe the dimensions that dominance has assumed in all
three of the religions under discussion. By dimensions is meant
the extent and the directions in man's life along which these
religions claim and exercise absolute authority, ultimate
decision. For dominance, when exercised, fulfills that apt
definition of the snob: it brooks neither rival nor partner; it
tolerates no equals; it knows only inferiors and superiors.

These dimensions are analyzed in three stages: the basic

arrangement of religious ideas and of words used by the religions to express these ideas; the basic unit of thought-pattern which the religions employ; and the two-level view of all human happenings characteristic of these religions. None of these betrays anything of the white-hot intensity emanating from the original religious experience which fathered them. They are merely the cold steel struts of its unyielding selfishness, the solid pillars of its confident superiority.

Judaism, Christianity, and Islam think about themselves and each other within a certain limited perspective. All three have formulated this thinking in words used to express their thought. We find that both ideas and words fall into logical clusters. These clusters can be called the basic paradigm of the three religions. This paradigm of ideas and words, however, must be recognized for what it is: a logical formulation which in no way reveals the burning core of each religion. The latter—the living religious experience of the founders and followers—is wordless, ineffable, cannot adequately be clothed in thought or language, can only be lived.

At the same time, without these ideas and words, any one of the three religions in their classical form would be utterly unthinkable. In the course of their development, each religion modified this basic paradigm to a greater or a lesser degree. When, by such modifications, essential parts of the "classical" structure were jettisoned, these religions were either threatened in their existence and integrity, or mortally wounded. The more significant of these modifications will be examined later. This chapter will outline the basic paradigm in their classical forms, and note the variations from one religion to another.

There is a statement of belief, a credo form, which could be put on the lips of Jew, Christian, and Muslim. This statement does not express all the truths and modifications of belief professed by each religion. Included here are only those without which the classical formulation would be incomplete.

The Jew says:

I believe

that there is but one God, YHWH, Eternal, Immutable, All-Perfect, who dwells in Paradise; that He created the skies, the earth, and all things visible and invisible; that He created the angels and spirits, among which is Satan, the Evil One, who was originally an angel, but who fell from favor by disobedience;

that He created Adam and Eve, the first man and woman, each with a body and immortal soul; that they sinned against Him, and were expelled from Paradise; that He later revealed the true religion to Abraham who thus is the father of all true believers;

that after Abraham's death Moses was the chief of these and that he led the Israelites out of Egypt at the Exodus to the Land of Promise; that he founded the Law by which the true Community of Believers might be saved and so be YHWH's Chosen People living according to His spirit and awaiting His Messiah; that the Christians corrupted the original teaching of Moses by following the teachings of Jesus of Nazareth; that the Muslims corrupted the true belief of Abraham and Moses further by following the teachings of Mohammad;

that Jerusalem is the holy center of the world; that YHWH's revelation is only contained in the Jewish Bible; that henceforth men are divided into the Chosen People and the Gentiles; that YHWH's salvation is only with the Jewish People;

that there will be a Last Day in the history of the world; that all men of the past will rise from the dead for a Last Judgement by God; that only Jews can receive the final reward of Paradise; that on that day YHWH will admit the Chosen People to eternal rewards in Paradise, and severely judge the others; that the sinful and unbelieving will be punished forever in Hell.

The Christian says:

I believe

that there is but one God, Eternal, Immutable, All-Perfect, who dwells in Paradise; that He created the skies, the earth, and all things visible and invisible;

that He created the angels and spirits, among which is the Devil, the Evil One, who was originally an angel, but who fell from favor by disobedience;

that He created Adam and Eve, the first man and woman, each with a body and an immortal soul; that they sinned against Him, and were expelled from Paradise; that He later revealed the true religion to Abraham, who is thus the father of all true believers; that after Abraham's death, He sent a number of prophets to revive the true religion of Abraham;

that Moses was the chief of these, and that he founded the Law by which the true community of believers might be saved; that the Jews corrupted the Law; that finally God sent Jesus of Nazareth, His Son, to be the Messiah; that Jesus taught men the true doctrine and founded the Church to perpetuate these beliefs so that all Christians could live according to His Spirit; that Jesus saved all men from sin by His death on the Cross and resurrection; that Mohammad and the Muslims corrupted both the Jewish Law and the Faith of Jesus;

that Jerusalem used to be the holy center of the world, then later it was Rome, then still later various places in the world; that God's revelation is contained primarily in the Christian Bible; that henceforth men are divided into the Church of believers and the non-believers; that God's salvation is only to be found in this Church;

that there will be a Last Day in the history of the world; that all men of the past will rise from the dead for a Last Judgment by God; that only Christians can receive the final reward of Paradise; that on that day God will admit Christians to eternal rewards in Paradise, and severely judge all others; that the sinful and unbelieving will be punished forever in Hell.

The Muslim says:

I believe

that there is but one God, Allah, Eternal, Immutable, All-Perfect, who dwells in Paradise; that He created the skies, the earth, and all things visible and invisible; that He created the angels and spirits, among which is Iblis, the Evil One, who was originally an angel, but who fell from favor by disobedience; [1]

that He created Adam and Eve, the first man and woman, each with a body and immortal soul; that they sinned against Him and were expelled from Paradise; that He later revealed the true religion to Abraham who thus is the father of all true believers; that after Abraham's death, He sent a number of prophets to revive the true religion of Abraham;

that Moses was the chief of these and that he founded the Law by which the true community of believers might be saved; that the Jews corrupted his Law; that Jesus of Nazareth, the Messiah, was another prophet, but that the Christians corrupted his Gospel; that finally Allah sent Mohammad who left all he possessed at the Hegira in order to establish successfully the true Community of Muslims who could live according to His spirit;

that Mecca is the holy center of the world; that Allah's revelation is contained only in the Koran; that henceforth men are divided into Muslims and unbelievers; that Allah's salvation is only with the Muslims;

that there will be a Last Day in the history of the world; that all men of the past will rise from the dead for a Last Judgement by Allah; that only Muslims can receive the final rewards of Paradise; that on that day Allah will admit the Muslims to eternal rewards in Paradise, and severely judge the others; that the sinful and unbelieving will be punished forever in Gehenna.

Clearly, all three credos are built around three cardinal ideas: the *Group* (Jews, Christians, Muslims), the *Event* (Exodus, Crucifixion, Hegira), and the *Identity* of the Group (Chosen People, Only True Church, the Community of True Believers).

[1] *Iblis* is an Arabic form of the Greek *diabolas* (devil).

Each of these three ideas is explicitated under four chief headings. Throughout these cardinal ideas and main explicitations there is no essential difference among the three religions. It is only in the further development of the explicitations that differential factors arise. The differentiating power of these factors is chiefly this: they mutually exclude each other. If Moses together with the Exodus and the Law represents God's supreme act of salvation, then the Crucifixion of Jesus and the Hegira of Mohammad are meaningless. If God's Chosen Ones are Muslims, then neither the Christians nor the Jews can claim to be considered the Chosen Ones. The exclusive character of these differentiating factors is one main expression of religious dominance. The three cardinal ideas together with the four main explicitations can be represented schematically as follows. Some of the differential factors are supplied:

Cardinal Ideas	Explicitations	Some of the Differentiating Factors
	1. Father	Abraham
	2. Man	Adam & Eve; Soul & Body
I. THE GROUP:	3. History	Beginning-Middle-End
	4. World	Created; to end
	1. Personal God	YHWH; Trinity; Allah
	2. Hero	Moses; Jesus; Mohammad
II. THE EVENT:	3. Revelation	Bible; Koran
	4. Geographical Center	Jerusalem; Rome; Mecca
	1. Special Choice	Chosen People; Church; Muslims
III. THE IDENTITY:	2. Salvation	Exodus; Crucifixion; Hegira
	3. Sin	Satan; Devil; Iblis
	4. Punishment	Hell; Gehenna; conscience

(Fig. 1)

In short, each of the religions presents itself as primarily a societal unit or group of men historically located in the physical world by an act of creation on the part of an omnipotent and eternal god who exists apart; they owe their societal character and existence to a historical intervention by this thinking, decisively acting god, who confers on them a special group identity as the "saved"; their earthly history ends when eternal existence after death begins for them in another "world." The latter is divided into Paradise (Heaven) and Hell; there is a direct relationship and continuity between life on "earth" and life "hereafter."

Each of the differentiating factors could be expanded almost indefinitely. Completeness is not a requisite in this context. Rather we must notice the way in which the particular elements of the religions are to be classified.[2]

Just as each of the religions claims a human father-figure, Abraham, so this has been extended in other father-figures: the priest, the pope, the rabbi, the teacher, the Khalif, the mufti, the imam, the marabout, the theologian.

Personal god is elaborated into the anthropomorphic god of the Jewish Bible, the "Father" about whom Jesus speaks in the Gospels, the Trinity of later Christian theology, the Allah of the Koran with his innumerable divine traits. In all three religions, the god in question is considered to act in human history with a rational plan which he has devised, and to be a "person" in the same sense that an individual human being is, without, however, the constricting limitations of man, *viz.*, his birth and death in time, his bodily and mental fallibility, and so on.

Revelation is expanded into the Jewish Oral Law, the Ten Commandments, the Muslim *Shari'a*, the Roman Catholic Canon Law, infallible teachers and popes and churches, theophanies, visions.

Geographical center is prolonged to the ideas of synagogues, churches, basilicas, mosques, statues, altars, sacred relics, holy cities, and graves.

Special choice is elaborated into Circumcision, Baptism, Confirmation, Bar Mitzvah, Covenant between god and man, monasticism, celibacy, systems of belief.

Salvation is involved further with sacrifice, worship, prayer, resurrection from the dead, the Mass, the assumption of holy men into heaven, millenniar theories, heaven, angels, spirituality, piety, mysticism.

---

[2] The following is only a partial list. *History* is discussed alone in Chapter 18.

Sin is elaborated into entire theologies, rituals, original sin of Adam and Eve, actual sins of men, forgiveness and expiation for sins, role of conscience, the Roman Catholic Confession, the Yom Kippur of Judaism, penance, pilgrimage, the Devil, Hell, Last Judgement.

It must be stressed that the close structural similarity among the three religions is not due to mere factors of geography, to the original Jewishness of Jesus, or to a fantastic desire on Mohammad's part merely to imitate Judaism and Christianity by borrowing from both. The similarity has a far more tragic basis: each of the three religions vociferously and steadfastly claims to possess *all* the elements that the others claim.

Abraham, according to Christians, was a pre-Christian Christian. According to Mohammad he was consciously and explicitly a Muslim. The Jews naturally claim him as their own. According to the Jews, salvation is primarily in the Exodus from Egypt and the observation of the Mosaic Law. Christians maintain that it was the beginning of salvation and that this held until Jesus came. Then all was changed. Exodus, Law, Promised Land, all these lost validity. Only the sacrifice of Jesus gives salvation now; the Exodus, the Law, and the Promised Land were mere symbols and foretastes of what Jesus brought to men. The Muslims maintain that this was true until Mohammad came. By that time, Christians had corrupted the Gospel, and Jesus' sacrifice was useless. Now only Mohammad's religion and teaching can give men salvation; both Moses and Jesus were really pre-Muslim Muslims who failed to accomplish God's purpose on account of man's perversity and weakness.

According to Judaism, God chose the Jews and never changed his mind; [3] they have the true and unique revelation about man's destiny and about God's nature; they know what Hell is,

[3] Paul never overcame this difficulty. He "solved" the problem by posing another one. The Jews, he stated, are still the Chosen People in the sense that the promises of God to them cannot be abrogated. For God is faithful to His word. But the Christians are the chosen people in the sense that they now possess salvation and the Savior. How explain this seeming contradiction? Paul proposes a mystery: not until the end of time and the fullness of God's plan will we know the answer. Then the veil of blindness which prevents the Jews from embracing Christianity will be lifted away from their eyes. This Pauline doctrine has given rise to the traditional view of the Jews. Cf. *Romans* ch. 11.

what Paradise is, what goodness is. According to the Christians, God chose them, revealed to them all he had originally revealed to the Jews (discontinuing ethnic habits such as circumcision, for example), and gave them much more besides. According to Muslims, these claims are farcical and blasphemous; Jews and Christians have a portion of the truth, but God has now chosen the Muslims to whom he has revealed all he ever revealed to Jews and Christians, in addition to much else besides.

Judged merely from a scientific point of view, and abstracting from the validity of any religious belief, man, in elaborating such a basic paradigm, appears as a magician. Through his mind and imagination, by his words and rituals, man casts a spell over the stuff and matter of his being; magically, he clothes the nakedness of his animal existence with the fine raiment of religious conception. Lifeless stones and shining distant stars and all between are made translucent with higher meanings. But the magician operates where man is in greatest danger: in the encounter.

The encounter is a clash of irreducible and irreconcilable beings. It is a head-on collision of independent interests. It is man as a highly developed organism gyrating with other such organisms within an enclosed whirlpool of lethally opposed drives, interests, and instincts. It is man in the raw against man in the raw. On neither participant in the encounter does a law of behavior descend from outside the human ambient; either one may impose such a law by force and survival. Within neither participant is there an inner law that transcends the exigencies of flesh, blood, brain, senses. There are no absolute duties to others, no absolute rights for the self, no sanctions on all and sundry.

By thinking the thoughts, speaking the words, and living according to the principles of the basic paradigm, man enables himself to avoid this clash in the raw, this encounter. He can bypass the biological reality. He can look beyond intellectual values, esthetic symmetry, political grandeur, social complexity. He can define duties, establish rights, enforce sanctions. He may do all this sincerely, insincerely, cruelly, kindly. He may submit freely or merely under constraint to such a system. The point is, he has from such a paradigm the possibility of a mode of thinking; and this illustrates for him a mode of acting. Man need not be forced into the encounter. He need never threaten himself in his own name with self-destruction.

Man, in Henry Cardinal Newman's words, founds states, fights battles, builds cities, plows the forest, subdues the elements, rules his kind. He creates vast ideas that take a thousand shapes, and undergoes a thousand fortunes. As a being of genius, passion, intellect, conscience, power, he indulges in great deeds, in great thoughts, in heroic acts, in hateful crimes. He can submit gracefully, dominate graciously, or advise wisely. He can kill guiltlessly. He can build avidly without fear of failure. He can fail without despair. Death is no longer mere putridity and oblivion. Immortality is not merely life in the memories of one's descendants. With this magic, he can thus avoid the fateful encounter, whether it be on the ancient morning in the forests of his dawn, at the brilliant midday of achievement within the complexity of urban civilizations, or at the eventide of the magician when the hour is late and the encounter inevitable.

But one special trait of this magic, dominance, appears in man's history to break the spell, to render the magician impotent. The thorough effect of this magic, however, is only further understood in the basic unit of thought-pattern. This is examined in the next chapter.

17. The Language of Dominance

From their beginnings, both Christianity and Islam made their own the Hebrew account of how man and his world originated.[1] Each of them adapted this account to suit their own particular belief and outlook. The adaptation, however, did not affect either the mode of thought of the Hebrew account or the interpretation of human history which it implied. Hence all three religions are identical on these two capital points. This chapter deals with the mode of thought. The interpretation of history is discussed in the next chapter.

According to the Hebrew account, God the Creator is above and outside everything. The formless matter of things to come is below and inside the world. God's spirit hovers *above* the *deep*. The contrasts are clear. Other contrasts follow. *Light* is contrasted with *darkness; life* and *living* things are con-

[1] *Genesis*, Chapters 1-3. It is to be noted that the Hebrew account in Genesis is an adaptation of earlier accounts preserved in Sumerian and Accadian texts.

trasted with *lifelessness*. To be alone is contrasted with *companionship*. Man is *raised* from the *dust* by God. Cursed by God for his disobedience, he will return *down* to *dust*.

As the account progresses, light and life and what is high are clearly associated with God and with what is good. Contrariwise, what is low and dark and lifeless is related to what is bad. The serpent, symbol of evil, is condemned by God to crawl low on its belly in the dust. Toil with hard ground which produces only thorns and thistles and hot sweat is contrasted with the ease of soft fruits and the cool of the evening in which God walks with man in Paradise. Immortality to be gained by eating the fruits of the tree of life is contrasted with death.

This binary framework of contrasts is used throughout the Jewish Bible to express the totality of all things and of all possible happenings. God is the Lord of heaven and earth, therefore of all things. Full knowledge is the knowledge of good and evil. In each binary set of concepts we find one (the positive), associated with what is good; and another (the negative), associated with what is considered evil.

God is associated with heights, high mountains, high heavens, high-riding clouds. The Psalmist states that he was drawn "out of a cheerless pit" (39:3) and tells God that "the light of Thy presence" is his escort (42:3). He expresses his spiritual wants in terms of thirst, hunger, disease, weariness, dirt and dust, while lauding God's loving care as providing him with fresh water, with food, rest, cleanliness, health and life. He prays that he may even walk in the valley of the shadow of death but that God will send his light from on high to revivify him. He trusts that God will smooth his path and entrap his enemies on rough and arid wastes, while he himself retires to green pastures. He claims to be protected by the right hand of the Almighty, while God smites his enemies with his left hand.

For the coming of the Messiah, the prophet Isaiah bids a straight road be made through the desert, all crooked paths be straightened, all rough paths be smoothed, every valley be bridged and levelled. When evil men oppose Moses, the earth opens and they sink down to punishment. At the end of his mortal life, the prophet Elias mounts up to heaven in a flaming chariot.

This random list of such binary concepts in the Bible could be extended almost indefinitely. We find that what is good and godly is always associated with certain physical traits of man's environment; what is bad is associated with a series of other traits. High, smooth, round, soft, sweet, laughter, food, health, and so on are paired off with low, rough, sharp, hard, bitter, tears, hunger, disease, and so on. However, these physical traits are not used merely as metaphors or analogies. The Bible does not indulge in any metaphysical or speculative concepts about God and his religion. It knows no other realities but the physical world. The "other" world of God and of the spirit is therefore only understandable in terms of this physical world. Hence, any spiritual meaning is conveyed by means of that world's physical traits.

This binary formulation of religious truth persisted even in the later and more sophisticated concepts of God and religion which were developed within Judaism. From the beginning God was considered to be physically remote, to be outside and above all things human. This divine trait of being outside and above was refined into concepts of remoteness and inaccessibility. Yet Hebrew thought lacked any means of conceiving and expressing this remoteness and inaccessibility other than the physical traits of distance and height.

The Hebrew description of God's nature follows similar lines. In earlier Hebrew thought, human emotions of anger, disgust, change of heart, etc. were attributed to God. As Hebrew monotheism was purified, the idea of God's unchangeableness became more evident; changes of human emotion were seen as incompatible with such divine unchangeableness. Yet God was conceived of and expressed verbally as a person in the same way as human beings, but without the faults and limitations of the latter.[2]

Christianity, in adopting the Jewish Bible, accepted the binary formulation inherent in it. A fundamental document such as the Fourth Gospel starts off with the contrast of light (associated with ignorance and sin—and with the Jews). Indeed, this Gospel recounts the life of Jesus as a double process: as the light of Jesus' divine character and mission becomes more and more manifest, the darkness and wilful sin of Jesus' enemies, the Jews, become greater. Throughout the Gospels and other early Christian writings, the use of binary concepts is obvious.

[2] Anthropomorphisms in the Bible have been studied extensively. We find, in general, that the Jews who translated the Bible into Greek in Alexandria, Egypt, at the end of the 4th century B.C., mitigated much anthropomorphism of the Hebrew original.

From the 4th century onwards, Christianity initiated a gigantic process of refining its concepts of God, of man, and of his world. But in defining Jesus, his Father, and the Holy Spirit as persons, Christianity still clung to the original Hebraic concept. The philosophic explanations and expressions developed during the Middle Ages did not, of course, basically alter or eradicate the binary formulation. Instead, one of the great tasks of a medieval philosopher such as Thomas Aquinas was to justify, mainly by his theory of analogy, Christianity's claim that man could say something intelligible and accurate about God when using the binary formulation.

The concepts, however, with which men think their beliefs and the words with which those concepts are expressed, are rarely if ever purified philosophic concepts. Christianity uses the binary formulation extensively, for instance, in its various creeds and professions of faith: Jesus came down on earth; he died and descended into the underworld to preach to the faithful souls who had believed in his coming; afterwards, he ascended into Heaven and sits at the right hand of God. Hell is a place of torments chiefly by fire. All men rise from the dead on the last day; some will be thrown into Hell; others will go up to Heaven for all eternity.

Islam, no less than Judaism and Christianity, used and uses the same unit of thought-pattern. Thus God "is the light of the heavens." [3] He "sends down his Shechina on his apostle." [4] Of the just it is said that "when they are reminded of the signs of the Lord, they do not fall down blind and deaf." [5] The true believers are "the fellows of the right hand," but evil men are fellows of the left hand." [6] God in sending his revelation to men "quickened a dead land." [7] The fate of the evil is described as "an hour most severe and bitter." [8] Believers are men and women "with their light running on before them on their right hand." [9] The hearts of the unbelievers grow "hard." [10] Para-

[3] *Koran* 24:35; vol. II, p. 50. All references are to A. J. Arberry's edition of the Koran: *The Koran Interpreted.* Macmillan Co., N.Y., 1967.
[4] Cf. Koran 48:25; vol. II, p. 228.
[5] Cf. Koran 25:70; vol. II, p. 62.
[6] Cf. Koran 56:5; vol. II, p. 254.
[7] Cf. Koran 50:10; vol. II, p. 233.
[8] Cf Koran 54:45; vol. II, p. 249.
[9] Cf. Koran 57:10; vol. II, p. 259.
[10] Cf. Koran 57:15; vol. II, p. 260.

dise has a "breadth which is the breadth of the heavens and the earth." [11] The damned "are thrown into a narrow place thereof" (Hell); [12] when "the torment of the day of the shadow seizes them." [13] The just shall see "those who lied against God, with blackened faces." [14] On the last day, "God raises them all together from the dead." [15] Mohammad asks, "is he who walks prone upon his face more guided than he who walks upright upon a straight path?" [16] God asks whether he shall reveal the lofty practices of virtue, "shall I make thee know what the steep is?" [17] Moses, according to Mohammad, prayed, "it may be that the Lord will guide me to a level path." [18]

If we analyze and attempt a grouping of such binary sets of concepts used in Judaism, Christianity, and Islam, we find that they fall into three main categories. The simple binary of *good-bad* is used as a description of the positive and negative elements in all binary sets. We find a first category of binaries concerned with the self-identity of man. There are three of these: self-other, movement-immobility, and relation-nonrelation. Firstly, man is only considered to be in a good state, a true state of man, when the "other," the "alien," does not invade him, possess him, or dominate him. Man's self is considered to be a sacred thing. The stronger, the higher up, the more inaccessible man's self becomes, the more perfect it appears to be.

Secondly, poverty, disease, sin, punishment, death, and difficulties of any kind imply that man is not free in his movements, but he is restricted or even immobilized bodily, mentally, spiritually, even orally. Not to be able to praise God, for instance, is alleged as one objectionable trait of the dead; the just man, therefore, does not wish to die. Thirdly, relations with God, with other men, with nature, with things, is considered part of what is good for man, part of man. Conversely, a lack of relationships is considered bad, whether it be through

11 Cf. Koran 57:20; vol. II, p. 260.
12 Cf. Koran 25:10; vol. II, p. 57.
13 Cf. Koran 26:185; vol. II, p. 73.
14 Cf. Koran 39:60; vol. II, p. 172.
15 Cf. Koran 58:15; vol. II, p. 265.
16 Cf. Koran 25:45; vol. II, p. 60.
17 Cf. Koran 90:10; vol. II, p. 339.
18 Cf. Koran 28:20; vol. II, p. 88.

exile, which separates a man from his land; through solitude, which separates him from hearing, seeing, and enjoying his people; through disease, which cuts off friends; through blindness, whereby man cannot see God's glory in the heavens or in his children; through sterility, whereby a man will not have offspring; or through death, which implies an end to all man's former relationships.

The concept of a personal god, which all three religions possess, is expressed in terms of these binary concepts. Just as man is a "self" distinct from other men, opposed to what is alien, able to move and act in his environment, related to some elements in his cosmos, not related to others, so the concept of Yahweh, God, and Allah, has been evolved. The supreme being in all three is endowed with maximum selfhood (no other is comparable), maximum movement (omnipotence) and maximum relationship (creator and originator of all things).

A second category of binaries is based on the appetites and the five senses of man. The following are some examples:

Appetite	*Senses*
Air	Bright
Airless	Dark
Water	Audible
Thirst	Non-Audible
Food	Smell
Hunger	Non-Smell
Strong	Sweet
Weak	Bitter
Talk	Soft
No-Talk	Hard
Laughter	Smooth
Tears	Rough

We find a third category of binary concepts and their corresponding terms that do not result merely from man's appetite or merely from his sense-perceptions. Their value and meaning are relative; they are formed on the data of more than one sense and always imply a comparison. Some examples of such binary sets are as follows:

Up	High
Down	Low
Long	Big
Short	Small
Fat	Round
Thin	Square
Straight	Right
Crooked	Left

Before
After

It is to be noted that the use of binary concepts and terms is not peculiar to the three religions we are studying. Man, in speaking about the intangibles of his world and life, thinks and speaks in a fashion that reflects this basic binarism. *Death* is considered cold, airless, dark, bitter, low, weak; man sees it as implying a loss of sight, hearing, taste, smell, of relations with what he knows, and as the fullest expression of sorrow, thirst and hunger. But *life* is considered to be bright, smooth, warm, strong, long, as implying full use of man's senses, the enjoyment of air, food, water, laughter. What is *good* is straight, bright, big, to the right, up, high, sweet, round; whereas what is *evil* is small, black, to the left, crooked, short, bitter, down, low, rough, square. Thus man, instinctually, describes the transcendental values of his life. Such descriptions take the form of folklore, heroic tales, music, poetry, sculpture, painting, architecture, and so on.[19]

Judaism, Christianity, and Islam, however, have ascribed to the binary concept and term such a capital function that it is impossible to think or speak about their basic doctrines without recourse to such binaristic concepts and words. That function is to convey a message about the spiritual world and the afterlife to which man is destined. In heroic tales, in poetry, and other such activities, man is endeavoring to convey his ideas and impressions. In religious thought and verbal formulation man is trying to convey a concrete reality, a series of realities.[20]

Furthermore, these realities are not only believed to be ultimate, but to lie beyond the scope of ordinary sense-perception,

[19] Compare the structuralism of Levi-Straus.
[20] Compare Jean Piaget's psychology and development theory.

to belong to the "invisible world" and to man's "afterlife." [21]
This difference is fateful for religion. The binary sets of concepts are based directly on man's physical world and man's
characteristic reactions to the different aspects of that world.
Man, in fact, claims the privilege that he can describe this ultimate reality in terms of his physical world.

All three religions assert, for instance, that sin "stains,"
"deforms," "blackens," "alienates" man's soul from God;
that this soul of man, like any member of his body, can be
"beautiful" or "ugly," "deformed" or "pleasing" to God; that
man's body, having died, will be resuscitated by God again on
the Last Day in a resurrection that implies restoration of all
bodily powers.

In the history of these three religions, we find there is a
popular and a theological use of binaries in the business of
knowing and of talking about the "spiritual" world. The popular use relies on a direct relation between what is seen, heard,
touched, tasted, smelled, lived in man's physical world, and a
series of parallel realities in the invisible world, in order to
understand and to describe that spiritual world.

The theological use relies on mental abstractions, on a
reflective philosophy, in order to achieve understanding.[22]
The theological use, however, has never supplied the concepts
and the words with which the living belief of these religions has
persisted in the mass of believers. No sizeable group of Roman
Catholics has daily prayed to God in explicit terms of Aristotelian act and potency. Nor has any impressively numerous
community of Jews constantly participated in a synagogal service where the Law was interpreted in terms of Averroistic uni-
versals or Maimonides' teaching on good and evil. Muslims do
not pray with Ibn Khaldun's theology of history as their mental picture or pray to Allah in terms supplied by the Islamic
philosophers of the first four centuries.

The popular and theological uses of binary concepts, however, convey a two-level picture of man and his cosmos: on
one level man lives, moves, sees, hears, and dies; on the
other level, man's spirit lives, moves, sees, hears, but does not
die. The intersection of man's existence on these two levels

[21] See next chapter concerning the "invisible world" of the
religions.
[22] Compare John Smith's work on the theological firmaments.

constitutes the view of history which is peculiar to Judaism, Christianity, and Islam. In the next chapter this two-level view of history is considered.

18. The Tree of Good and Evil

Judaism, Christianity, and Islam, are absolutely categoric on one question concerning man: each one claims with unassailable authority and unshakeable certainty to know man's history, how he began, how he progressed and progresses and will progress, how he and his world will end. Despite the apparent similarity of structure and some details, the explanation given by each one excludes the other two. Each one brandishes a unique claim. Only one key opens the door of life and death. There is only one answer to the problem of good and evil.

According to the three religions, there was one beginning to Man's story: [1]

The Serpent's tongue licked a nearby leaf for added emphasis: "And why do you think HE said that?" The Serpent shot the question suddenly and shrilly at the Woman. The sunlight played tantalizingly along the purple-green scales, glinted suggestively on the half-closed eyelids. The Serpent was, indeed, the most cunning of all the animals. In six days, HE had flattened out the primeval stuff into a saucer shape called Earth, thrown a large bowl shape deftly over it and called it Sky, hung lights there, made all plants and animals, planted the wonderful Garden, and fashioned a Man and Woman from dust and nothingness. "Kick your heels; do what you like; but keep away from those two trees," HE had told them. The Tree of Life, and the Tree of Good and Evil. Now the Woman stood beside the Tree of Good and Evil fascinated by the Serpent entwined lazily around its trunk.

"And why do you think HE said that?" repeated the Serpent. "For the love of your beautiful eyes? To guard you from death? A mere caboodle of hokum!" From where she stood, the Woman could see the Man lying asleep in the grass, his body golden and soft and strong, flung as it were, nonchalantly in the shade.

The Woman's eyes travelled again to the fruit hanging

[1] Cf. *Genesis,* chapters 1-3.

heavily and ready to drop off its twig. An aroma of musk-sweet juice touched her nostrils. She glanced over her shoulders at the Man. The sense of something succulent ebbed in her saliva and her mind. Her spine tingled. "You know," whispered the Serpent confidentially, "you know what's up?" Her eyes widened. "HE just does not want any equals. Wants to dominate you. Eat that fruit, and both of you will be just like HIM! Imagine! Gods, both of you ! Able to do all things!"

The Serpent rested his head on a branch and waited lazily.

The Man stirred and opened his eyes. "Here, have a bite. It's so good," he heard the Woman say. She knelt beside him holding a half-eaten fruit, her other hand resting on his belly. The Man smiled as she placed the fruit for him to bite. "Tastes like nothing you ever gave me before," he murmured, "give me more."

Adam's eyes travelled from the Woman's eyes to her lips, her breasts, her navel, her thighs. "I never realized before . . ." he faltered. With a sigh, the Serpent slid noiselessly from the tree trunk, slithering along the grass towards a hole in the ground. It was past midday. He paused and glanced back before entering: the Man and Woman were strolling slowly, deliberately, hand in hand, towards the bank of the river, their bodies touching lightly. "Without the benefit of pessary or coil, mind you," the Serpent muttered satisfiedly. "So uncomplicated." He headed for the hole. As the darkness closed over his eyes, he heard a woman's cry.

As the sun went down, the Woman said lazily: "Let me make something to cover you." "It was never quite like this before." The words came from the Man involuntarily. Her hand caressed him. "No eyes must see you as I do. This belongs to me as my secret."

In the quiet dusk, they both could hear HIS voice carried by the cool wind of the evening across the treetops saying almost casually: "Where are you two? This is the first time you hide from me. Where are you?"

Although all three religions agree on the beginning of man's history, their explanations are quite different.

Judaism's God was a perfectionist from the start. He wanted all things just so. The Man and the Woman with their descendants would live in Paradise forever. But there was the Serpent. There was the Tree of Good and Evil. And there was the Woman.

Once Man ate that fruit, two inclinations entered his heart: a good inclination and a bad inclination. Evil dissolved the crystal walls of Yahweh's beautiful ideal. His perfect plan had gone awry.

But, besides his perfectionism, Judaism's God was persistent. At least, something could be salvaged. He would choose a special group, reveal the truth about good and evil to them. They would be his Chosen People, living according to his law and in His land. Land, Law, People. The trinity of toil.

Although man would not now live forever, there would always be on earth a group of people saved from sin and waiting for the end in worship and praise of Him. They would be heirs of the knowledge of good and evil. Theirs was the dominant position. The rest of the world, the Gentiles, will ever be subject to error. The world is divided forever. World history is polarized into an ever-unfolding drama of the salvation being effected and the wicked refusing wisdom. Those who die will be immortal in so far as they live on in their children and the memory of their virtuous actions. On the Last Day, the sky and earth will be purified; the members of the Chosen People living then will live in a new world free from labor and pain. The wicked living then will perish in the fire of judgment.

Christianity's God was a speculative philosopher. He had many possible choices and plans. "Create Man and Woman so that they cannot sin, and we have a race of immortal robots;" thus he formulated possible Plan A. "In such a world, I will only have playthings. Who wants playthings?"

"Create Man and Woman so that they can sin, and we court infinite disaster;" thus he formulated possible Plan B. "In such a world, I create beings just so they commit sin perpetually in this life and burn in flames eternally. They would be my picnic litter."

"Create a world to be saved, and I can demonstrate my greatest glory;" thus he formulated possible Plan C. "In such a world, I can exercise my mercy and compassion, not mere pity. Pity costs so little. Compassion takes a toll. Mercy only I can have."

Plan C it was. The greatest act of mercy and compassion would be to sacrifice His Own Son to save sinful Man and Woman. Man and Woman and their world will be created in view of a Cradle and a Cross and a Risen Savior's smile.

Man and Woman are made, tempted, seduced. There is now

need of a Redeemer. He is promised, this second Adam. The old Adam grasped at all power, the knowledge of Good and Evil. The second Adam, sinless, God and man, possesses that power. He comes. He teaches. He dies. He is brought back to life by God. He returns to Heaven leaving His Church. His Church now has His power and that knowledge of Good and Evil.

Forever, all is changed: human history now has one meaning derived from Christ's sacrifice and His final coming to judge all men. Forever, the world will be against His Church. Jesus will preserve His Church. His Father will bless it. The Holy Spirit will inspire it. The Trinity of Love. The world will stumble and split asunder on the corner-stone, Jesus.

On the Last Day, all the dead men who ever lived will rise from the dead and stand with all the then living to be judged by Jesus. The good will enter Heaven. The wicked will be punished forever.

Islam's Allah was a desperate idealist. Having made the Angels, the earth, the sky, and all the animals, He wished to appoint a "viceroy on the earth." [2] He created Man and Woman "of the dust, then of sperm-drop, then of a blood-clot." [3] Satan, however, tempted them, "revealing to them that which was hidden from them of their shameful parts." [4] Allah's enchanted spun-glass world was fragmented irrevocably. His initial plan was in ruins.

Allah decides, however, to send apostles and prophets. He sends Abraham with a new knowledge of belief, of virtue, and of Paradise. He sends Moses. He sends many others. The Jewish race corrupts the tradition of Abraham, betrays the Law of Moses, and abandons the teaching of the prophets. He then sends Jesus of Nazareth. The Christians successfully corrupt his doctrine. Men now walk in a hall of mirrors which do not distort, which merely reflect mercilessly man's ugliness.

Finally, he sends Mohammad, the true, the faithful. Mohammad succeeds. He founds the True Community of Believers. It now possesses the truth and all knowledge of Good and Evil. It has the power to save. Now the world will never be the same. All and every event in human history has a relevance only for Paradise. Otherwise it is meaningless. The True Believers know this and live according to the Law. The world is

[2] Cf. Koran 2:25; vol. I, p. 33.
[3] Cf. Koran 40:65; vol. II, p. 182.
[4] Cf. Koran 7:15; vol I, p. 172.

split between believers and non-believers. Human history is not
a story. It is a series of epiphanies.

On the Last Day, the unbelievers will be thrust into eternal
fire. The believers will reside in Paradise enjoying bliss untold
and pleasures endless.

For the three religions, human history began in time and
space on a First Day, when God created Man and Woman. It
will end on a Last Day, when God judges all men. Between these
two extremes stretches the human story. It is a peculiarity of
these religions that human history is thought of as a drama in
three main acts: beginning, progression, ending.[5] This drama
of human history revolves around the source of dominance:
the knowledge of Good and Evil. The traditional Christian name
for dominance is Original Sin. Man, according to each religion,
reached wantonly for the source of all power. God punished this
lust. Instead, each of the religions claims it has been given
authority to wield such a power, to wield that dominance.

As a consequence of these beliefs, the believers, Jewish,
Christian, and Muslim, look at human events on two levels.

A historian finding himself at Mount Horeb in the Sinai
Peninsula some time in the 13th-12th centuries B.C., would see
a scrawny Bedouin named Moses squatting in front of a clump
of bushes some distance from a grazing flock of sheep. At a
given moment, due perhaps to the overpowering heat of the sun
or a stray spark from the cooking-fire, the bushes burst into
flames. The Bedouin is seen approaching the burning bush; he
takes off his sandals, talking all the while to himself as soli-
tary men are wont to do. In a short time, the fire dies out. The
Bedouin rises, puts on his sandals, and departs.

A Jewish believer sees and knows all these "historical" facts,
yet he sees another series of events taking place in parallel
sequence and pattern. The Bedouin, Moses, is summoned by
Yahweh who speaks from the burning bush. Yahweh bids him
take off his sandals because he is standing on holy ground, and
to listen. While the bush is lit by fire of theophany, Yahweh
gives Moses the assignment of leading the Israelites out of
Pharaoh's Egypt.

A historian standing on the hill of Calvary in the spring of,
say, 30 A.D., would see a convicted criminal executed. His
name is Jesus. He has been beaten by lead-tipped whips and led

[5] Cf. Chapter 13 concerning history.

out to Calvary with a crossbar strapped to his shoulders, as was the Roman method. Some drunken soldiers have planted a wreath of thorns on his head for garish fun. On Calvary, he is stripped to the waist, thrown to the ground, his hands stretched out and nailed solidly and deftly to the crossbar. Then half a dozen Roman soldiers lift him up and drop the crossbar into the socket of an already standing upright. Jesus has been crucified. With him two other criminals also convicted of sedition are crucified. Jesus takes three hours to die. He prays to God, talks with those around him, asks for a drink, murmurs in his agony, and dies with a loud cry. The Roman officer drives a lance through his ribs to make sure of death. A late spring thunderstorm breaks out shortly after his death. Jesus' friends and relatives bury his body in a nearby tomb. An officer finds the Roman guards sleeping at their watch some two days later. The body of Jesus is nowhere to be found.

The Christian believer sees Jesus achieving the redemption of the world. He is scourged with whips for men's sins of the flesh. He is crowned with thorns to atone for men's sins of pride. He is crucified for all sins. While hanging there, he forgives his enemies, promises Paradise to one of the other two crucified with him, and dies with a cry of prayer. The blood and water that gush from his side, when the Roman officer runs him through, symbolize the purification and the baptism that Jesus has won for mankind. His death is the supreme sacrifice accepted by God, Who then considers all men as acceptable to Him. The storm indicates God's anger at the evil men who crucified Jesus. On the third day after his burial, Jesus rises glorious from the dead, stunning the Roman guards with the brilliance of his appearance and the triumphant thunderclap accompanying his emergence from the tomb.

In the late autumn of 637 A.D., Umar ibn al Khattab, the Khalif, takes possession of Jerusalem. He enters the Holy Sepulcher and walks around the church. Muslims believe that this is the spot where Allah had created Adam and Eve, where Abraham had sacrificed to Allah, and from where Mohammad himself had ascended on the back of a fabulous flying creature with the Angel Gabriel to visit with Allah in Heaven. Umar is watched by the Greek Orthodox Patriarch, Sophronius, who whispers in Greek to a subordinate: "Surely this is the abomination of desolation which the Prophet Daniel prophesied!" For a modern historian, here is a very ancient Bedouin leader, ragged and barefooted and armed to the teeth, inspecting one of the many spoils of a very successful war. The modern historian is thinking about history.

Both Umar and Sophronius and the modern historian are contemplating the same tangible, visible facts. But all three, the modern historian included, are interpreting it according to their presuppositions.

The historian wants to find out what happened. He moves within one frame of reference: the data of his senses, the material surroundings, the paraphernalia of the incident, the causes and consequences of the Muslim's actions. Sophronius sees the same facts but understands them as the fulfillment of a Jewish prophecy. He moves on another plane. Umar himself moves on the same plane as Sophronius, but he regards this victory as a sign from Allah: here are the Muslims back at the umbilical center of the cosmos and in communication with Abraham, with Mohammad, and with Allah.

This is the two-level view of history that the believer has. The non-believing historian records events, explains them in their causes and effects. His progress is horizontal through a series of events: Umar conquers, enters the Holy Sepulcher, circles the walls; Sophronius whispers to an aide; or Jesus is convicted of sedition, nailed to a cross, etc. or the bush catches fire, the Bedouin shepherd, Moses, tries to approach, cannot do so, takes off his sandals, etc. Taken with the accompanying causes and consequences, this is history.

But the believer, while following all the visible and tangible events, sees a parallel series of events and happenings taking place invisibly and simultaneously. His progress is vertical. For him the latter are the real events. The material events are only real because of the invisible ones. This is super-history.[6]

On the space where Moses squats, Jesus is crucified, or Umar walks, there is posed a superspace. On the time in which Moses talks and acts, Jesus suffers and dies, or Umar measures and decrees, there is posed a supertime. On each action of the people involved and each event that takes place, a superaction and a superevent are posed. The believer considers the mere exterior and visible fact as a sense-sign reaching his will, in-

[6] Compare Bultimann's theory of mythologization and his use of the terms *historisch* and *geschichtlich*.

tellect, and emotions. He relies on all the supersigns (space, time, event) to tell him the super-history, the real story. In this way, he ascends to the supernatural where he finds existence and reality. There space is lost in infinity, time explodes into eternity, events dissolve into absolute truth.

H I S T O R Y   A N D   R E A L I T Y

SUPERNATURAL	*Existence*	Infinity	Eternity	Truth
SUPER-HISTORY	*Super-Sign*	Super-Space	Super-Time	Super-Event
HISTORY	*Sense-Sign*	Space	Time	Event
	Inner-Sign			
	(will)			
	(intellect)			
	(emotions)			

(Fig. 2)

The world of the believer, Jew, Christian, and Muslim is irretrievably and by divine decree a *bipolar* one. The basic binary of "self" and "other" become "us" and "them," and "good" and the "bad." For Judaism: Jews and Gentiles. For Christians: Christians and non-Christians. For Muslims: Believers and non-Believers.[7] It is the belief of each individual religion that it and it alone has been given the absolute power arising from the knowledge of Good and Evil. Judaism reposes this power in its Law, Christianity in the Keys and the authority to bind and loose.[8] Islam in its sacred law, the *Shari'a*.

The "other" part of the world is evil and of itself, unsaved. Alone of all three religions, Judaism has no traditional or official policy of trying to save that "other" world. Both Chris-

[7] In each religion a further polarization takes place. In Christianity, for instance, Roman Catholicism and non-Roman Catholics. In Judaism: Neture Karta and non-Neture Karta. Each religion and religious sect has its own particular pole or "other."

[8] A conception not confined to Roman Catholicism.

tianity and Islam have used the word and the sword in order to "save" the bad part of the world. Entire theologies have been developed concerning this salvation and that "other" world.[9]

Furthermore, for the believer there is nothing in man's cosmos—micro-particles, solids, fluids, plants, animals, man, events, planetary bodies—that man can understand and explain in itself. No object is self-explanatory. Nothing can validate its own existence. The unbeliever uses his physics, biology, geology, physiology, psychology, etc., in order to analyze the things he finds. The unbeliever holds that all things can be studied and known adequately and fully in themselves. Each one carries its own validation and explanation. No intuitive leap of mind or heart is needed to understand it. But, according to the believer, his progress is, again, horizontal. The real explanation escapes him.

The cosmos of the believer is peopled with the same objects and phenomena as the unbeliever's: men, plants, animals, dead matter, forces. But all these objects receive an adequate explanation of their identity only within a higher synthesis. The believer subsumes all things into a higher order. His material world is a vertical one; every object is a Gothic spire shooting up to the heavens. All its contents point straight up, past the immemorial stars, high above the congregated particles blowing endlessly through space, out beyond the cosmos to an extra-cosmic being, an order of things that depends not on this cosmos, but on which the cosmos depends for existence, for explanation, for salvation.

In such a world, the unbeliever finds his skies are ever-expanding bronze and steel domes against which he can only hurl his partial explanations. The earth itself is a bottomless pit of discovery and unknowing: the unbeliever can only gaze into the endless depths. The believer sees in this the heartrending ineptitude and pathos of the "other" part of the world.

This is the spectacle of the three religions. Living and moving on the visible plane of earth and stones, of men and animals, of birth and death, the believer must live and move spiritually also on the plane of the invisible world, which has thrust itself from outside the cosmos into human affairs. Each one of the religions is based upon a central enactment of sal-

[9] The most noted exponent was the Christian theologian, Augustine of Hippo (354-430). His doctrine of the "Two Cities" is the archetypal embodiment of the bipolar world doctrine.

vation that, they maintain, took place historically in the past. But, at the cost of atrophy and decay, they must maintain that in super-history the enactment is never past, is always present. The Exodus is an ever-present mystery. The Crucifixion is renewed daily and hourly. The revelation to Mohammad and the purification of the Ka'aba is constantly performed. Salvation never ceases.

The force and the weakness of such beliefs must be examined somewhat further. In Part V situations in the history of each of the three religions will be examined where the principles of their beliefs were implemented or foresworn.

19. The Chains of Dominance

The notion of religious dominance that emerges from the foregoing chapters is not a very complex one. If we omit consideration of the historical factors that accompanied its emergence in Judaism, Christianity, and Islam, we can discuss its essential elements in a reasonably short context. One distinction is important: the dominance we have been discussing is a character trait of those who exercise domination of one kind or another—not the actual act of domination itself. This distinction between the dominance-trait and the dominance-effect (or domination) must be kept clear. The dominance-effect can take various forms, from naked aggression, to brainwashing, to social pressures, to passive resistance.

The dominance-trait of these religions is basically an attitude of the whole man (mind, will, emotions, physical existence) to his cosmos. It is primarily an "inner" thing, and not an exterior framework. Secondly, it claims to have *the* only explanation. It purports to tell man how he began, why he exists, how he should behave, and how he shall end. It proposes that man adopt a definite set of ideas and concepts, use certain words, phrases, and formularies, in order to verbalize this explanation. The explanation is within man, is supposed to affect primarily his mind and his will.

Thirdly, it is absolutist in two senses. It brooks no equals. On the one hand, it claims to be supreme. It does not stop at claiming to be first in a series that contains a second, a third, a fourth, and so on. It claims to be unique, to have no analogue, no second-best, no runner-up. It is no mere Alpha. It is the

Alpha and the Omega. The first and the last, the only one. On the other hand, its absolute claim includes all and every element of man's existence and man's cosmos from micro-particles to outer planetary spaces and bodies, from matter to spirit, from womb to tomb, from the beginning to the end. The domain of its domination is co-extensive with all reality: possible, actual, past, present, and to come.

Fourthly, the claim of these religions is based, its adherents say, on an event in human history: an intervention in human affairs took place at a given time, in a given place, involving given people. Furthermore, this intervention came from outside man's cosmos. It was an extra-cosmic intervention on the part of God (Yahweh, Allah). The precise meaning attached to the term extra-cosmic is of supreme significance for these three religions. It does not mean simply or simplistically that God was somewhere up in the sky or located outside the solar system of earth or even merely outside the entire universe with all its galaxies and all the billions of miles and light years by which man at present measures the immeasurable distances of space.

The distance between God and man is not in the order of space and time or any dimensional category known to man and measurable by his senses, aided or unaided by instruments. The distance is in the order of being. God (Yahweh, Allah) is believed to have an existence depending in no way on dimensional categories: he has no matter, no measurable quantity or quality. He is not merely "outside" man's entire universe. He is a totally different being. He is "extra-cosmic" and transcendental in this sense. The only words man has to express this belong to the binary concepts of distance, height, remoteness, inaccessibility, endlessness. None is adequate. And in their subtlest expressions the theologies of these religions define God more by negation than by affirmation: they can say what he is not, rather than what he is.

Fifthly, the dominance-trait of these religions imposes an iron law between this inner explanation and man's outer world. A believer must not merely register a knowledge and mental acceptance of the explanation; he must translate this into an outer framework of rules in his behavior. Each of the three absolutisms proposes minute and detailed rules for human behavior. On his environment man must impose this explanation and act accordingly. To do otherwise, to believe inside and not to act accordingly in one's normal life, would be hypocritical, according to all three religions. Religion, according to them, is not a private affair for the Sabbath, for Sunday, for Friday at the Mosque.

There thus issues from the inner trait of dominance an entire world outlook that involves personal morality and social mores, folkways and language, custom and law, socio-political institutions, a theory of good and evil, a cosmogony, a theology, and a way of life. This outer configuration is dictated by the explanation. Not to fit in, not to conform to this configuration is to reject the explanation. To reject the explanation is the sin. But even such sinful ones are located within the configuration.

For this total explanation explains man's world in terms of an invisible world: each object is ultimately and only explicable in the light of that invisible world. By object is meant either thing or event. And the explanation presumes that it will be rejected by the bad and the evil ones. The contents of this essentially vertical world are thus polarized into the good and the evil, the just and the unjust, the saved and the damned, the wise and the foolish, the elected and the rejected.

It is on the basis of this absolutism that we can understand and explain the historical forms that the religions took and the activities in which they have indulged. We cannot, however, excuse thereby their excesses. Their exclusivity is easily grasped: "we are Thy Chosen People; all the Gentiles are but dust;" "outside the Church there is no salvation;" "there is but one God and Mohammad is his prophet." We readily understand the immediate desire of these religionists to invest all men with their outlook: the theocratic state of ancient Israel, the theocratic state of Islam, the confessional state that Christianity propagated for the first 1700 years of its existence. The missionary effort of Christians and Muslims is also understandable.

As understandable but not excusable are the excesses: the persecution of Jews by Christians; the nourished bias to be found in the Jewish writings of the post-Talmudic period; the militant and harsh treatment used by the early Islamic conquerors in founding their empire; the internecine wars that sprang from the Reformation and Counter-Reformation movements of the 16th and 17th centuries in Europe.

Religious dominance (or the dominance-trait of these religions) can thus be defined as an attitude of the whole man demanding, under pain of extreme sanctions, a total adhesion and subjection of man to an absolutist explanation of man and his cosmos, for the duration of man's bodily life, and guaranteeing perpetuity of existence after his bodily life and functions have ceased.

Absolutist, unique, total, transcendental—these are four terms that fittingly describe the religious dominance of the three religions.

But because of this absolutism, these religions insist on transforming man and all of man's life. Man, no matter where he exists or at what stage of development he has arrived, displays a scheme of simple values based on his life and the world around him. His environment, first of all, is regarded by him as a *cosmos,* an array of details into which order has been introduced. In this cosmos, *history* takes place; the basic unit of that history is man's family, *man-woman-child.* This is the first dialectic which man knows. Certain phenomena he regards as integral parts of himself and his existence: *birth, father, mother, brother, home, his own kind.* He seeks certain objectives in this cosmos and throughout his history: *life,* its prolongation, preservation, and betterment; *law,* to govern that life, all that is *good* in his eyes; and an *ideal* constantly held in front of him. He relies on a *hero* figure who will give him the *key* to that ideal, who will guarantee him the *knowledge* he needs. He tries to avoid *death* in any form or gradation, as well as all that is *alien* to him and his, the *evil* that will destroy all he seeks and loves, and the *monsters* who have always threatened him from time immemorial.

These basic values can be thus schematized under various headings. Each of the three religions under study has taken all these values and transposed them on to its particular plane. Each one, thus, presents to its members a series of parallel spiritual and religious values. These are reckoned and understood, not as mere analogues or symbols of the original human values. They give meaning and significance to the merely human. The religions do more. They claim—and on the validity of this claim they stand or fall—that man can only be himself, can only attain his objectives, can only avoid mortal dangers, if he accepts the religious version of these values. Otherwise, according to these religions, man is left on the "purely natural plane" grappling with superior forces inside and outside him, and condemned to encounter other men and these forces in raw and naked collision. Religion claims it can save man this fatal encounter.

The schematization (fig. 3) of these human values and their correspondents in each of the religions is rendered more useful if we include the correspondents of the only other absolutism in history which has produced as complete a system as religion. Marxist Communism, in this respect, is a religion.

In the meanwhile, it is necessary to insist on a striking trait of all absolutisms and of modern absolutisms in particular. This is their close similarity, not merely in terminology, but in structure of thought. This can be brought home by considering the following excerpts from a speech (Column A) that could well have been given at the Second Vatican Council in Rome. The subject of the address is materialism and its dangers for Roman Catholic Christianity. The speaker is a firm conservative and has just outlined the teaching of St. Paul about materialism.

As a speech to be delivered to the Second Vatican Council, it is quite imaginary. Yet throughout, the sentiments expressed concerning Papal centralism, concerning the dominance claimed by the Roman Catholic Church over all and sundry, and concerning the ultimate victory guaranteed the Church because of its God-given dominance, are perfectly consonant with a certain brand of conservative Catholicism.

Throughout this text, certain key words have been put in Italics. In the original text (Column B), the actual terms used stand in place of these words. The original speech was delivered at midnight, February 24, 1956, to 1,436 delegates attending the Twentieth Congress of the Communist Party in Moscow. The speaker was former Premier Nikita Khrushchev. Khrushchev launched his historic attack on the dead Stalin. The burden of his speech concerns the cult of personality—a crime, Khrushchev said at the secret midnight session, of which Stalin was supremely guilty.[1]

[1] "We cannot let this matter get out of the Party, especially not to the press. It is for this reason that we are considering it here at a closed Congress session." The full text of the speech took many hours to deliver and occupies 165 pages of Bertram D. Wolfe's book, *Khrushchev and Stalin's Ghost*, Praeger, N.Y., 1957, pages 88-252. The speech excerpts are drawn from pages 88, 90, 116, 134, 228, 249-259, 252.

COMPARATIVE VALUE SCHEMES

HUMAN VALUES	JUDAISM	CHRISTIANITY	ISLAM	20th-21st CENTURY MAN	MARXISM
COSMOS	Heaven-Earth-Hell	Heaven-Earth-Hell	Heaven-Earth-Hell	Universe of Matter	Material Universe
HISTORY	Salvation	Salvation	Salvation	Evolution	Evolution
MAN-WOMAN-CHILD	God-Good-Evil	Trinity	God-Man-History	Communications' Media	Dialectical Materialism
BIRTH	Exodus	Calvary	Hegira	Managerial System	October Revolution
FATHER	Abraham	Abraham	Abraham	Technocracy	Marx
MOTHER	Synagogue	Church	Mosque	Technology	The Party
BROTHER	Jew	Christian	Muslim	Homo-ideologue	Communist
HOME	Jerusalem	Rome/Constantinople	Mecca	Technopolis	Moscow/Pekin
ONE'S OWN KIND	Jews	Christians	Muslims	Homo-Ideologues	Communists
LIFE	Heaven	Heaven	Paradise	Space Age	Workers' Paradise
LAW	Torah	Church Law	Shari'a	External Law	Communist Manifesto
GOOD	Spirit	Spirit	Spirit	Productivity	Matter
IDEAL	Justice	Holiness	Submission	Freedom	Work
HERO	Moses	Jesus	Mohammad	Scientist	Lenin/Mao
KEY	Circumcision	Baptism	Acceptance	Education	Confession
KNOWLEDGE	Bible	New Testament	Koran	Science	Das Kapital
DEATH	Hell	Hell	Hell	Slavery	Imperialism
ALIENS	Gentiles	Non-Christians	Infidels	Non-Man	Capitalists
EVIL	Sin	Sin	Sin	Want	Revisionism
MONSTER	Satan	Devil	Iblis	Oppressor	Capitalist

(Fig. 3)

COLUMN A

Reverend Fathers, in the report of the *Holy Office* of the *Church* at the *Second Vatican Council,* in a number of speeches by *Bishops* to the *Council,* as also formerly during the *public* sessions, quite a lot has been said about the cult of *materialism* and about its harmful consequences.

Allow me first of all to remind you how severely the classics of *Papal teaching* denounced every manifestation of the cult of *materialism.*

St. Paul had always stressed the role of the *Holy Spirit* as the creator of history, the direction and organization role of the *Church* as a living and creative organism, and also the role of the *Papacy.*

Collegiality of leadership flows from the very nature of our *Church,* a *Church* built on the principle of *theological* centralism.

Reverend Fathers, the cult of *materialism* has caused the employment of faulty principles in *Church* work and in *theological* activity; it brought about the rude violation of internal *Church* and *Papal government,* sterile administra-

COLUMN B

Comrades, in the report of the *Central Committee* of the *party* at the *Twentieth Congress,* in a number of speeches by *delegates* to the *Congress,* as also formerly during the *Plenary* CC/CPSU sessions, quite a lot has been said about the cult of *the individual* and about its harmful consequences.

Allow me first of all to remind you how severely the classics of *Marxism-Leninism* denounced every manifestation of the cult of *the individual.*

Lenin had always stressed the role of the *people* as the creator of history, the direction and organizational role of the *party* as a living and creative organism, and also the role of the *central committee.*

Collegiality of leadership flows from the very nature of our *party,* a *party* built on the principle of *democratic* centralism.

Comrades, the cult of *the individual* has caused the employment of faulty principles in *party* work and in *economic* activity; it brought about the rude violation of internal *party* and *Soviet democracy,* sterile administration, deviations of

214

tion, deviations of all sorts, covering up of shortcomings, and varnishing of reality. Our *religion* gave birth to many flatterers and specialists in false optimism and deceit.

Reverend Fathers, we must abolish the cult of *materialism* decisively, once and for all; we must draw the proper conclusions concerning both *theological*-theoretical and practical work.

It is necessary for this purpose: firstly, in a *Roman Catholic* manner to condemn and to eradicate the cult of *materialism* as alien to *Papal teaching* and not consonant with the principles of *Church* leadership and the norms of *Church* life, and to fight inexorably all attempts at bringing back this practice in one form or another; to return to and actually practice in all our *theological* work the most important theses of *Papal teaching* about the *Holy Spirit* as the creator of history and as the creator of all the material and spiritual good of humanity, about the decisive role of the *Papacy* in the *ecclesiastical* fight for the transformation of society, about the victory of *Christianity.*

In this connection, we will be forced to do much work in or-

all sorts, covering up of shortcomings and varnishing of reality. Our *nation* gave birth to many flatterers and specialists in false optimism and deceit.

Comrades, we must abolish the cult of *the individual* decisively, once and for all; we must draw the proper conclusions concerning both *ideology*-theoretical and practical work.

It is necessary for this purpose: firstly, in a *Bolshevik* manner to condemn and to eradicate the cult of *the individual* as alien to *Marxism-Leninism* and not consonant with the principles of *party* leadership and the norms of *party* life, and to fight inexorably all attempts at bringing back this practice in one form or another; to return to and actually practice in all our ideological work the most important theses of *Marxist-Leninist science* about the *people* as the creator of history and as the creator of all the material and spiritual good of humanity, about the decisive role of the *Marxist party* in the *revolutionary* fight for the transformation of society, about the victory of *Communism.*

In this connection, we will be forced to do much work in order to examine critically from the viewpoint of *Papal teaching* and to correct the widely spread erroneous views connected with the cult of *materialism* in the sphere of history, philosophy, economics, and of other sciences, as well as in literature and the fine arts. It is especially necessary that in the immediate future we compile a serious textbook of the history of our *Church* which will be edited in accordance with scientific *Papal* objectivism, a textbook of the history of the *Roman Catholic Church*, a book pertaining to the events of the *Early Church* and the *Counter-Reformation.*

Secondly, to continue systematically and consistently the work done by the *Church's Holy Office* during the last years, a work characterized by minute observation in all *Church* organizations, from the bottom to the top, of the *Papal* principles of *Church* leadership, characterized by the observation of the norms of *Church* life described in the statutes of our *Church*, and finally characterized by the wide practice of *confession* and self-criticism.

Thirdly, to restore completely the *Pauline* principles of *Roman Catholic theology*, expres-

der to examine critically from the *Marxist-Leninist* viewpoint and to correct the widely spread erroneous views connected with the cult of *the individual* in the sphere of history, philosophy, economics, and of other sciences, as well as in literature and the fine arts. It is especially necessary that in the immediate future we compile a serious textbook of the history of our *party* which will be edited in accordance with scientific *Marxist* objectivism, a textbook of the history of *Soviet society,* a book pertaining to the events of the *Civil War* and the *Great Patriotic War.*

Secondly, to continue systematically and consistently the work done by the *party's Central Committee* during the last years, a work characterized by minute observation in all *party* organizations, from the bottom to the top, of the *Leninist* principles of *party* leadership, characterized, above all, by the main principle of collective leadership, characterized by the observation of the norms of *party* life described in the statutes of our *party*, and finally characterized by the wide practice of *criticism* and self-criticism.

Thirdly, to restore completely the *Leninist* principles of *Soviet Socialist democracy,* exsed in the *Canon Law* of the *Roman Catholic Church*, to fight the arbitrariness of individuals abusing their power. The evil caused by acts violating *ecclesiastical and canonical* legality which have accumulated during a long time as a result of the negative influence of the cult of *materialism*, has to be completely corrected.

pressed in the *Constitution* of the *Soviet Union*, to fight the arbitrariness of individuals abusing their power. The evil caused by acts violating *revolutionary socialist* legality which have accumulated during a long time as a result of the negative influence of the cult of *the individual*, has to be completely corrected.

Reverend Fathers, the *Second Vatican Council* of the *Roman Catholic Church* has manifested with a new strength, the unshakeable unity of our *Church*, its cohesiveness around the *Papacy*, its resolute will to accomplish the great task of building *Christianity*.

Comrades, the *Twentieth Congress of the Communist party* of the *Soviet Union* has manifested with a new strength, the unshakeable unity of our party, its cohesiveness around the *Central Committee*, its resolute will to accomplish the great task of building *Communism*.

We are absolutely certain that our *Church*, armed with the historical resolutions of the *Second Vatican Council*, will lead the *Roman Catholic* people along the *Pauline* path to new successes, to new victories.

We are absolutely certain that our *party*, armed with the historical resolutions of the *Twentieth Congress*, will lead the *Soviet* people along the *Leninist* path to new successes, to new victories.

Long live the victorious banner of our *Church—Pauline teaching!*

Long live the victorious banner of our *party—Leninism!*

It will be noticed that the word-substitution effected above does not affect the essential thought-structure. In that structure, Communist Party orthodoxy corresponds functionally to Church orthodoxy, and the Communist Party to the Church; the People as the source of all power and transformation corresponds functionally to the Holy Spirit of Christian theology;

Papal teaching corresponds to Marxism-Leninism; the figure of Lenin to St. Paul; and so on. The substitution of cult of *materialism* for the original cult of *the individual* may seem an arbitrary one. Yet the greatest danger for the dominance of the Roman Catholic is materialism, because this saps the "spiritual" view of history and of men and things in history. So also, the greatest danger for the dominance characteristic of Marxism-Leninism is the cult of the individual, because this saps the exterior collective discipline and allows the individual to enter himself, to follow his own thoughts and decisions.

An important question arises immediately. Is the dominance-trait an essential characteristic or basic element of these religions? If they lacked or got rid of it, would they be identically the same in their essence as they are now? Are they viable as religions without the dominance-trait? Is the dominance-trait non-essential, a historical accretion due to mere historical development or, at least, is it an element due to human limitations and not issuing necessarily from the religions themselves? After all, these religions claim to be divine in origin, to be messages of salvation received by fallible men from a god who is deemed to be illimitable, eternal, faultless, perfection itself. Perhaps the message itself is free from the dominance-trait; only the recipients suffer from this limitation? Perhaps all three religions adopted physical modes at the priceless moments of their history, and these modes imply a purely human dominance-trait?

This question has a burning importance today when a deep crisis appears to be shaking these religions at their very foundations: one of the aspects of all three religions that seems incompatible with the mind of modern man is this dominance-trait of Judaism, Christianity, and Islam. Certainly the prejudice, bigotry, cruelty, the massacres and pogroms and persecutions, the suffering and the oppression to which this dominance-trait has given rise, have shaken modern man's belief in the authenticity of their absolutist claims.

It is certain that *exclusivity* is an essential note of these religions. If tomorrow, Judaism, Christianity, and Islam conceded that any one of the others was as good as or better than itself, they would fall apart as we know them. Their entire history would be negated. The Jews would cease to be the Chosen People. Jesus would cease to be God and Savior. Mohammad and his Koran could be pushed aside as historical accidents. Each of the three must singly and for itself claim to have exclusive possession of the one and absolute truth, to exclude the other two and all others besides. The most any one of them could concede is that the others have a fragment or a portion of the truth, that in virtue of good faith and good works, Yahweh (or God or Allah) will have mercy on them.

The pathos of their locked position is sharply focused by their professed belief in one god. There can be only one god, all three maintain obstinately. And this one god can have only one truth. Embedded in each religion, however, are mutually exclusive propositions about that one god: Jews and Muslims reject the divinity of Jesus; Christians and Jews reject the supremacy and final authority of the Koran as the last word of this one god to men; Christians and Muslims reject the Jewish Torah as the ultimate word of this one god; Christians and Muslims believe in the virginity of Mary which the Jews reject; Jews and Muslims reject the idea that the blood of Jesus wiped out all men's sins. The list is endless.

We will not be able to sift and examine the other elements of this triple religious dominance, and thus be able to decide in what measure dominance is essential to these religions, until we explore the predicament of these religions in today's world. Such an examination properly belongs there. We must note, however, a development in the religions that will help us to grasp the weakness of religious dominance today. The development is historical; each religion shows many examples of it since its inception. In the next three chapters, we will examine three such examples.

PART V

The Historical Evidence

20. Two Signs: The Cloud and the Spitfire

Once upon a time, men became very disenchanted with their lot on earth; they finally decided among themselves that something was radically wrong. Injustices abounded. The wicked prospered. None of the means men had adopted in order to worship God seemed to be of any avail. Their temples and offerings, their prayers and self-discipline, all these only seemed to increase life's burden. It did not affect any change for the better. Things had got worse in fact: the unscrupulous-minded preyed on the religious-minded and the just, and they got away with it. Finally, the unbelievers seemed to advance in knowledge and culture, whereas religion and its beliefs seemed to constitute so many hoary trammels keeping the observant from succeeding and being up-to-date.

Men finally went in search of God. They had one question to ask him: Why? Why did he make man and his world like this?

219

It could have been so different—if God was so powerful and intelligent, why was it not different?

They searched long and wide and finally found God at dawn in a forest; he was an old charcoal maker.

"You are God?" the leader of the delegation began, "it is you, isn't it, who are God?" The old charcoal maker looked up at them, confused. He spoke no word, but nodded gently and resignedly. "You sit there burning charcoal," the leader said incredulously, "while the world and man in it goes to the devil?" Then slowly plucking up courage, the leader continued. "Look, we are ordinary men. We have believed. We have been observant. In the middle of a thousand difficulties, we have never entertained one serious doubt until today. Now tell us why did you make the world as it is? Couldn't you have done better?"

God laid down his pannier of charcoal, wiped his forehead carefully and said, "Honestly, I thought it would work. But it's like rabbits in Australia: the idea seemed good, but something went wrong somewhere."

"Well, what are we to do?" asked the leader. "Must we go on doing the same old ineffectual things, or can you give us some sound advice?"

"I'll tell you," God said at last, "go on speaking and thinking as you used to, but change what you do. Keep what temples you have, but you needn't worship in them necessarily. Use my name as before, in oaths and curses. Especially, you can rely on my acts of kindness in the past. But you can go ahead and do as you will really. You see, when I created this world and man in it, I never really intended man to have everything he needed. He must always search, always make adaptations to new circumstances."

The Cloud

The Cloud descended from interminable blue skies, as if from nowhere. Yahweh was the Lord of Heaven and Earth. This was the sign of Israel's sacred nationhood. It came immediately after the Priests had placed the Ark of the Covenant together with the two Stone Tables of Moses in the Holy of Holies. They set it down between two gigantic Cherubim which overshadowed the spot with outstretched wings. Outside the central shrine, in the inner court, the outer courts, and in the purlieus of the Temple, the people of Israel were gathered around Solomon, son of David. Part of Solomon's being had already been corrupted by power, by money, by foreign wives. But he was the son of David. Now David had been beloved of Yahweh.

The ceremony began in Jerusalem, twenty years after Solomon became king, in the 10th century B.C. The day and the hour are now unknown to us. Immediately on seeing the Cloud, Solomon was inspired. The sounds of his chanted blessing on Israel rang out over the heads of the assembled Jews:

"Blessed be the Lord God of Israel,
Who has now fulfilled in act
The promise he made to my father, David.
So many years since he had rescued his people from Egypt,
And never a city among all the tribes of Israel,
Had he chosen
To be the site of his dwelling-place
Or the shrine of his name." [1]

The twelve tribes had taken over 400 years to come together as one people. With no tribal ties or family blood uniting them, it had taken the genius of David and the external pressure of enemies to unite them. The glory of the Lord now inspired all with a will to be one people in one land with one law. Solomon prayed:

"Listen to the cry of entreaty
Thy servant makes before you this day!
This I ask: that your eyes
Should be ever watching,
Night and day
Over this Temple of yours,
The chosen sanctuary of your name.
Forgive the sins of your people, Israel,
Restore them to the land
Which you gave to their fathers." [2]

This was the origin of the people's unity and this was the guarantee of its continued existence. The fundamental law of the State was the Ingathering of the exiled and the persecuted:

[1] I Kings 8:15-16.
[2] I Kings 8:28-29; 34.

> *"Maybe, You in your anger,*
> *Will let them fall*
> *Into the power of their enemies.*
> *As prisoners, they will endure exile*
> *In countries neighboring and distant.*
> *Before long, in their banishment,*
> *They will repent in their hearts,*
> *Crying out, poor exiles . . .*
> *You will relent towards your people . . .*
> *You will pardon their sins.*
> *You will soften the hearts of their captors*
> *To pity for them."* [3]

Israel was surrounded by enemies more numerous and more powerful than herself: Pharaonic Egypt in the south; the Moabites and Edomites in the south and southeast; the Aramaeans in the northwest; the Assyrians in the north:

> *"Sometimes, Your people will go out*
> *To make war upon their enemies.*
> *If they but turn in the direction*
> *Of the City You have chosen,*
> *Of the Temple I have built there*
> *In Your honor,*
> *You in Heaven*
> *Will listen to their prayer for help,*
> *Will maintain their cause."* [4]

But Solomon and his people desire peace with all their neighbors. They only pray that Yahweh will enlighten the hearts of all men to see His beauty and worship Him truly:

> *"Some stranger who has no share*
> *In your people of Israel,*
> *Will come here to honor Your name.*
> *For men will hear of Your fame,*
> *Of the dominating force*
> *Your power displays throughout the earth.*
> *When such a man comes*
> *To pray in this Temple,*

[3] I Kings 8:46-47; 50.
[4] I Kings 8:44-45.

> *Listen to his prayer and answer it.*
> *Thus, all the world will learn*
> *To fear Your name*
> *No less than Israel,*
> *They shall not doubt*
> *That this Temple I have built*
> *Claims your protection."* [5]

Solomon finally celebrates the fundamental *raison d'etre* of Israel, the reason it could hope for continual rebirth. This was the basis for its legal existence:

> *"Are they not Your own people,*
> *Your coveted possession?*
> *The men You rescued from Egypt's furnace of iron?*
> *Ever let Your eyes be watchful*
> *To look down—upon me, your servant,*
> *And upon Your people,*
> *When they cry for help.*
> *Grant all the requests they make.*
> *Have You not set them apart*
> *Among all the peoples of the world*
> *To be Your treasured possession?*
> *Was not this Your promise*
> *Given through Your servant, Moses,*
> *When You rescued our people from Egypt,*
> *O Lord, Our God?"* [6]

The above excerpts from Solomon's prayer bring out the type of dominance claimed by Judaism at that time. Firstly, the people of Israel are the only people chosen by Yahweh on this earth. As such they claim from Yahweh fulfillment of His promises: victory over their enemies, prosperity, peace, intact borders. Secondly, the Temple is the center of Judaism: Yahweh dwells only there; only there can the true worship of Yahweh be performed. Thirdly, only the religion of Israel is the true religion and only her law is Yahweh's law. Fourthly, the land of Israel is sacred.

These components are welded into a notion of racial supe-

[5] I Kings 8:41-43.
[6] I Kings 8:51-53.

riority, ethnic unity, unique religious truth, and economico-
military pre-eminence. This is the Jewishness of Solomon's
prayer. And this is the dominance claimed. But this dominance
is utterly dependent on an outside source, a religious source:
Yahweh. He is the centerpiece in the mosaic of Israel's glory.

The Spitfire

The Spitfires were manned by Arab pilots and came from
Egyptian airfields. This was the sign of Israel's nationhood.
They started coming after midnight. Their object: obliterate
the newly-born State of Israel, make impossible the return of
Jews as a people to the land they once occupied, and deny to
them this expression of their Jewishness. The Jews were clus-
tered around one, David, an unbendable little man, part of
whose being had been turned to granite by the pain of loss and
by half a century's wrestling with primal forces of good and
evil.

It began in Tel Aviv, on Friday, May 14, 1948. The sun's
rays were already slanting over the Mediterranean from the
West. The sea was blue and golden and red, the sky flecked
with some towering cumulus clouds to the south. Punctually
at 4 o'clock, the strains of an ancient Hebrew melody with
fresh words floated from the upper window of a two-story
building in Rothschild Boulevard out over the heads of some
thousands of people waiting in the street. Over the building
floated the Star of David in blue and white colors. A guard of
armed men occupied the sidewalk. Machine-guns bristled from
the roof-top and at every corner. Camera bulbs flashed.

It was the eve of Sabbath for Jews: the religious-minded
would soon be singing of that night above all other nights long
ago when Yahweh brought the Children of Israel out of the land
of bondage by the blood of a Lamb. Down in that land, Egypt,
mechanics and technicians checked the gas and fuel supplies
and started loading bombs and ammunition on the warplanes.
For England and America it was Whitsuntide: the religious-
minded would celebrate the Feast of the Holy Spirit whose gift
of wisdom, although bought by the blood of a Crucified One, had
not prevailed at Lake Success, in London, Paris, or Cairo. The
House of Commons in London listened to a desultory hour's
debate led by His Majesty's Minister for Defence, A. V. Alexander: an area of 10,000 square miles acquired for the Empire
by General Allenby in 1917 would be totally evacuated by

August 1; the United Nations would take charge of Palestine.[7] In Philadelphia, the new governor of Jerusalem was still packing his bags: when he did arrive, the city would be a pockmarked, smoking riven ruin occupied by bitter enemies.

At 4:06, the singing stopped. In soft steady tones, a man started to speak. David Ben-Gurion was dedicating the new State of Israel. It would be born at midnight when the British Mandate over Palestine ended after nearly 30 years rule:

> "Eretz-Israel was the birthplace of the Jewish people. Here their spiritual, religious, and political identity were shaped. Here they first attained to statehood, created cultural values of national and universal significance and gave to the world the eternal Book of Books."

In the upper room, David Ben-Gurion, born 62 years before as David Green, son of Avigdor and Sheinal, in Plonsk, Poland, stood on a platform behind a long table at which thirteen of the new State Ministers sat. He was reading from three typed pages of Hebrew. Some 200 people had crowded into the room to listen. Behind him hung a photograph of Theodor Herzl, the father of modern Israel, the man who dreamed it all and saw it all fifty years before the event, but who had died of a broken heart in 1904.

The Jewish people had a historic right to this land. They had never ceased to be a separate nation, a group of people distinct from all other peoples and nations, even though they were dispersed and persecuted among all nations. Now they were again returning to their own country. This is the fundamental

[7] Already the Arab nations had won partial or total nationhood: Iraq since 1932; Egypt since 1936; Syria and Lebanon in 1944; Transjordan in May, 1946. The British Mandate over Palestine had never worked, despite the 200,000 troops maintained there and the imposition of martial law. In 1947, Bevin, speaking for the Labor Government, wearily admitted that the Mandate was unworkable. On November 29, 1947, the *General Assembly* of the *United Nations* voted 33 to 13 that Palestine be partitioned between Jews and Arabs. An economic union was to bind both sectors. Jerusalem was to be internationalized. The Arabs, except for Abdullah of Jordan (who was then assassinated), rejected it. David Ben-Gurion, speaking for the *Jewish Agency* at that time, said that the Jews would abide by it. On May 11, 1949, Israel was admitted to the *United Nations*.

raison d'etre of Israel's rebirth and the sole basis for its legal existence and proclamation:

> "After being forcibly exiled from their land, the people kept faith with it throughout their Dispersion and never ceased to pray and hope for their return to it and for the restoration in it of their political freedom."

Down south, Jerusalem was under siege. The territories occupied by the Jews throughout Palestine were under attack from four directions by five armies: the Egyptians from the southwest; the Jordanians, Iraqis, and Syrians from the east; the Lebanese from the north. At the back of the Jews lay only the Mediterranean and destruction. The will to fight and to survive is part of Jewish heritage:

> "Jews strove in every successive generation to re-establish themselves in their ancient homeland . . . they made deserts bloom . . . created a thriving community . . . loving peace but knowing how to defend itself."

After World War II, Jews of the world were reduced from about 17 million in 1939 to approximately 11 million in 1945. The ancient homeland of the Jewish Diaspora was gone forever from Central Europe. The center of gravity was America. In Palestine, Jewish settlements numbered 600,000 people. Jews existed only in small numbers elsewhere. Both in America and Israel a new desire had grown up: to restore the Land of Israel in the form of a modern State.

> "The catastrophe which recently befell the Jewish people—the massacre of millions of Jews in Europe—was another clear demonstration of the urgency of solving the problem of its homelessness by re-establishing in Eretz-Israel the Jewish State . . . and confer[ing] upon the Jewish people the status of a fully privileged member of the comity of nations."

At a given moment, Ben-Gurion paused, stared for an instant over the heads of his listeners as if looking at a distant object or lost momentarily in far off memories from the past: some ghost from Plonsk, Warsaw, Paris, Belsen, or elsewhere, flitted noiselessly through the room. Then he continued:

"We, members of the People's Council, representatives of the Jewish community of Eretz-Israel and of the Zionist movement, are here assembled on the day of the termination of the British Mandate over Eretz-Israel and, by virtue of our natural and historic right and on the strength of the Resolution of the United Nations General Assembly, hereby declare the establishment of a Jewish State in Eretz-Israel, to be known as the State of Israel."

· This was the origin of the State, and these were the guarantees of its legal existence among the nations.

The fundamental law of the new State was the Ingathering of the exiles and the persecuted ones:

"The State of Israel will be open for Jewish immigration and for the Ingathering of the Exiles; it will foster the development of the country for the benefit of all inhabitants; it will be based on freedom, justice, and peace as envisaged by the prophets of Israel . . . and it will be faithful to the principles of the Charter of the United Nations."

But the new State has only one desire: peace. It desires that all men realize the value of the Jewish nation and come to respect its way of life.

"We extend our hand to all neighboring states and their peoples in an offer of peace and good neighborliness, and appeal to them to establish bonds of cooperation and mutual help with the sovereign Jewish people settled in its own Land. The State of Israel is prepared to do its share in common effort for the advancement of the entire Middle East."

When Ben-Gurion finished, there was celebration in the streets of Tel Aviv. People poured out of houses and shops and bars, singing, dancing, embracing each other, drinking together, congratulating each other. The immolations would start at midnight: bombings, shooting, raids, devastations, taking a toll of human life, of houses built with care, of farm settlements raised literally out of the arid sand.

At midnight of that Friday, the last British High Commissioner, Sir Alan Cunningham, closed the door of his hill-top

residence in Jerusalem, drove quietly to Haifa, and slipped away
on board His Majesty's cruiser, *Euryalus*. Eleven minutes past
midnight, President Harry S. Truman announced that the
United States had recognized the new State. On Saturday,
Guatemala was the second state to afford recognition. The
U.S.S.R. was the third soon after. At 5 o'clock Saturday morning, as Ben-Gurion spoke over the radio to America, the sky was
filled with the whining roar of the Spitfires levelling down over
Tel Aviv to drop their bombs. It was their fourth visit that
night. Israel was born under that sign in the sky. The war was
on. Officially, it was the 5th day of the month Iyar, 5708 years
since the creation of the world.

Ben-Gurion's speech ran to 650 words in Hebrew; translated
into English it contains almost twice that number (1,027). All
the key words and phrases with few exceptions came straight
from the Jewish Bible. All were replete with Biblical and theological connotations. Yet, it is possible to say that not one of
them was used by Ben-Gurion in the original sense nor even
with the later traditional connotation which the religion of
Judaism had attached to them. The Jew at this moment was
not acting to save a religion or vindicate the God of history who
speaks in the Bible. He was acting to secure his Jewishness
without further reference to something else outside his cosmos.

In the Proclamation, however, there was no appeal to the
Lord of Hosts for his protection. The proclamation was not
made in a Temple but on the 2nd floor of a museum. There was
no mention of the forgiveness of sin. When the Exiles were
mentioned, Yahweh was not asked to bring them back. The old
familiar physical modes of Judaism were there: the Land, the
People, the Law, the Opposition, Jerusalem. But the eternal
yearning of the Jew was no longer for the kingdom of heaven,
for the glory of Yahweh, for the observance of the Law, for the
beauty of his Temple. The kingdom was a modern state. The
glory was the glory of the Jewish people. The Law was the Law
of Return and Settlement. The Temple was, symbolically, the
Knesset (the Parliament), realistically the body of Israeli
Jewry. The Opposition was no longer merely between the Jew as
God-bearer and the Christ-bearing Gentile.

The Jew at this moment was at the entrance of an arduous
journey the end of which is not yet in sight. He fingered, as it
were, the outer shape of that mystery he must know or die: the
threat to his historical identity as a separate and viable mod-

ern nation. He had to enter this tunnel, face the beast of his millenniar nightmare, and either enchain him and pass on to glory, or be sucked back into the maw of primal elements, and once more be a pawn in the directionless maze of lost causes, of failure incarnate in a race.

David Ben-Gurion's proclamation speech must be placed side by side with Solomon's prayer. Only then can we point with some precision to the definite and fatal shift in the dominance professed by each one.

Firstly, the Jews are the Chosen People, not because Yahweh chose them, but because of a unique historical tie to one particular land, Israel. The religious and political identity of Jews was born here. The choice of Israel and Jews, therefore, is not the act of an almighty and personal God, but the historical development of a particular race of people.

Secondly, there is no religious center to Israel. The Judaism which it claims has no Temple and no sacrifice. The only center is the duly elected government of Israel.

Thirdly, there is no religious obligation on Israel or its Jews: it does not depend on the good will of Yahweh or the virtue of its citizens in worshipping Yahweh. Likewise, the territory of Israel depends on the historic right of Jews to defend Israel.

These components make up the complex notion of Israeli Jewishness: racial separateness, historical precedence over all nations in claiming this land, reliance on the inner force of Judaism to achieve the economic, military, and legal pre-eminence which Israel vindicates as her own.

As remarked before, Ben-Gurion uses Biblical language to express this dominance. But this dominance is now completely purified of any religious significance characteristic of traditional Judaism. At its roots, Israel is a state without any professed religion. As is clear from Ben-Gurion's thoughts and words, Israeli Jewish dominance is expressed in the words and thoughts of super-history; but there is no belief in a super-history, much less in a supernatural order or a personal God inhabiting that order.

We will see that this differs radically from the persistent religious view of Orthodox Judaism. For the moment, it is sufficient to note that the claims of Israeli Judaism are reduced to the plane of mere history, and that it is on this plane alone that its merits and demerits should be discussed and will, actually, be decided.

An inner difficulty, therefore, afflicts Israeli Judaism. The concrete example of Brother Daniel illustrates this contradiction. Born Oswald Rufeisen in Poland in 1922, this Jew was converted to Roman Catholicism in 1942, became a Carmelite monk in 1945, and emigrated to Israel in 1958. There he applied for an *oleh's* certificate [8] and an identity card showing that he was ethnically a Jew. He made this application under two Israeli laws: the *Registration of Inhabitants Ordinance Acts* and the *Law of Return*, both of which governed the status of Jews who migrated to the new State.

There was never any doubt that Oswald Rufeisen was ethnically a Jew, that his hardships resulted because of his Jewishness, and that he loved his people. His application was refused. But he was facilitated in a naturalization process according to which he could have become an Israeli citizen. This he refused, appealing to the Supreme Court. His appeal was refused by a dissenting Court [9] and the reasoning behind the judges' rejection of his appeal is illuminating.

All the judges agreed that ethnically he was a Jew. Nevertheless, as Justice Silberg remarked during his summation: "A Jew who becomes a Christian cannot be called a Jew." He emphasized this further by stating: "The concept of a Jew and the concept of a Christian cannot be united in one person, (this) is generally accepted by all." Silberg based his judgement on the mind behind the laws in question. If, he countered, Rufeisen's case was judged according to Jewish religious law, all would be well: "If we were to apply the concepts of Jewish religious law, as I have shown, then he would be regarded as a Jew."

Justice Landau concurred: "The Jew who cuts himself off from the heritage of the national past of his people, by changing his religion, accordingly ceases to be a Jew in that national sense which found expression in the *Law of Return.*"

Justice Berenson summed up for all when he stated: "The people, as is known, with its well-developed instinct for self-preservation, decided otherwise, generation after generation. For the people, a Jew who has embraced another religion has excluded himself not only from the Jewish religion but also from the Jewish people, and he has no place in the community

[8] *Oleh* is the legal term adopted to describe a Jew who participated in an *aliya,* a "return" (literally a "going-up") to Israel.

[9] The original judgements of the Supreme Court are to be found in *Piskei Din* (Law Reports of Israel), Vol. 16 (1962), p. 2428.

of Israel. Not for nothing is a Jew who changed his religion called *meshummad* (apostate); because from the national point of view, he was considered as one who had been cut away from the people, he and his children after him; and his family would rend their clothes as in mourning for their dead, and discontinue all contact with him. In the popular understanding, Jew and Christian cannot subsist in one human being and even less a Jew and a Catholic priest. The two are mutually irreconcilable. This, I think, is the spirit which permeates the *Law of Return*, and by the word Jew the Knesset intended to refer to a Jew in this popular sense."

When Moshe Sharett testified on behalf of the Jewish Agency before the United Nations Special Committee on Palestine, prior to the establishment of the State of Israel, he was asked who the Agency considered to be a Jew. He answered unequivocally: "I would say technically and in terms of Palestine legislation, that the Jewish religion is essential. What is essential is that a person should not necessarily be actively an observant Jew. He is still considered a Jew; but if he becomes converted to another religion, he can no longer claim to be considered a Jew. The religious test is decisive."

No more vivid illustration of the damage done to the Jewish soul by Christian anti-Semitism can be found than this deep-seated revulsion from Christianity which lies at the back of Israeli legislation. This is the Opposition born in the 2nd century A.D., now alive again and painfully operative in Jewish-Christian relations. Christians will not understand it unless they study the terrible price which the Christian West exacted from Jewry in its ancient homeland in Central Europe. The judgement passed by the Israeli Supreme Court on Brother Daniel is more than understandable; no other judgement could have been passed.

That the Supreme Court considered this discriminatory attitude to Jews who change their religion as a temporary condition is clear from the concluding remarks of Justice Berenson. He makes it quite clear that the attitude issues from the memory Jews possess of Christian persecution. When, at a later time, he concludes, the memory of all the bloodshed and the misery imposed by Christians on Jews has disappeared as a painful memory, then perhaps the Law may be interpreted differently.

It is clear from the summations of the Judges that Israel is considered to be a secular state. This concept of the State is, in itself, a perfectly justifiable and legally viable one. Between the Solomonic and Israeli concept of Judaism and Jewishness there yawns an unbridgeable gap. Israel has chosen a modern form of statehood. Logically, this should entail no pressure-elements either of an ethnic or religious kind. Yet, it does. One understands quite well the desire to create a Jewish state for Jews. This was the modern reality which issued in the *Law of Return* and lies at the back of the Rufeisen judgement. But religion has nothing essential to do with Israeli Judaism. Essential differences separate normative Judaism and Israeli Judaism.

One is God-centered, God-justified, God-preserved, God-exalted, oriented to the visible world. The other is self-justified, self-preserved, self-exalted, self-centered, oriented to the visible world. One presumes as essential an entire religious mythology, a divine history, and a determined set of rules for ethical behavior which depends on a god for sanction and reward. The other has discarded the mythology, reduced the history to a human plane, and determines its ethical behavior merely by man-made law. The presumption is that man no longer needs the mythology, the interpretation of history as the work of a supernatural being, or the ethical rules ascribed to the latter's personal desire and order. Like rabbits in Australia, the idea could have worked. All that matters is that it did not.

21. Two Meetings: The Christian and the Hun

It was the last day of the Great Year. King Minos stood at the entrance of the Cave of Eilythyia near the port of Knossos. Flanking him were his two brother kings: Radamanthys of Phaistos and Sarpedon of Mallia. In front of them, seven young boys and seven girls were ranged two abreast. A circle of priests and priestesses ringed the three kings and these young people. Around this central group, a hushed crowd of several thousand was gathered. The seven couples were about to enter the abode of the Blessed in order to be the Bull-God's attendants forever in bliss. Eilythyia cave was the entrance to the House of the Double-Axe, palace of the Bull-God. Beyond, hidden from mere mortal eye, lay Paradise.

Dawn had just broken over the Eastern Sea, tipping the

waves, the white sand, the sloping cliffs, the harbor jetty where the black-sailed boat rode at anchor, the upright lances of the royal guards, with a bright copper light. Over to the west, a slight morning haze veiled the sides of Mount Ida. Southwards, the Knossos palaces of Minos sparkled in the sunlight, its towers and pillars decorated for the Feast.

It was a gala crowd: children, farmers, merchants, shop-keepers, soldiers, courtiers, priests; the men with shaven heads and feathered dresses; the women coiffed, with topless skirts and carefully painted faces, their diadems, arm bangles, and leg bracelets scintillating in the sunshine. On the outskirts of the crowd, the lesser priests stood with an array of dwarfs, mon-keys, peacocks, elephants, tumblers, bull-leapers, acrobats, dancers. All faces were turned and lifted towards the gleaming bronze doors of Eilythyia. Each face was smiling. Every eye was wide with expectation as they gazed mutely on the sign of the Double-Axe spreadeagled over the bronze panels.

The rumbling roar started as a very distant echo, now in-creasing, now dying away. Then the earth and rocks beneath the worshippers' feet started to rock and groan while from the mouth of the Cave and the ground underfoot the noise rose in volume, until it was a steady muffled roar: the Minotaur, guardian of the Gates, was signalling the pleasure of the Bull-God. A delirium of joy seized all those waiting. The multitude sank to their knees; the priests blew loudly on their trumpets; the tumblers and acrobats and dancers gyrated in an ecstasy of devotion and thankfulness.

The Head Priest sprinkled lustral water on the heads of the Fourteen Dedicated Ones. Minos and his brothers approached the Bronze Doors, and with reverence began to open them. The Fourteen took up their lyres and started to play the marriage melody, accompanying it with the Song of the Bull. The pro-cession started to the slow wild rhythm of the trumpets and the lyres. All were now singing in unison with the Fourteen. The Bronze Doors opened slowly. The rays of sunlight stabbed the holy darkness, lighting up the white stalagmites and stalactites, and were then engulfed in the cave's depths. A skin-pricking thrill of awe and satisfaction ran like mercury through every-body from priests to people. All eyes were now on the lucky ones about to join the God.

One by one, the singing bridal couples passed by the doors which closed gently on the heels of the last pair. For a while, their chanting could be heard. Then the strains were dying. Then they were gone. By this time, the Priests had dropped three heavy lateral crossbars into their sockets across the panels. At a sign, workmen started piling up earth and stones to cover the doors, effectively sealing it off. For only the Chosen Ones could be betrothed to God.

Inside the Cave, it took most of the Fourteen over two weeks to die. Death did not come easily. They could not suffocate: outside air penetrated by scores of small channels. Wandering around in the darkness, realizing their real plight, madness seized most of them. Some committed sudden suicide by banging their heads on the rock walls or by falling on stalactite points which eviscerated them immediately. Some lived on little rivulets of water and the hope that God would appear. Some in their insanity and deathly hunger attempted to eat the flesh of the already dead.

Outside, the world was happy. Minos banquetted in the Hall of the Double-Axe. In his Great Courtyard, the female bull-leapers incessantly jumped and soared and defied the sacred bulls for fourteen days. The priests retired with the priestesses and Temple maidens to the sacred enclosure. All was well.

Christian and Hun

In the oppressive summer heat of 452 A.D., a meeting takes place on the southern bank of the river Po in northern Italy. The fate of Europe ·for 1500 years to come is decided at that meeting. Attila, king of the Huns and emperor of all the Scythians, meets with Leo, the bishop of Rome. Immediately at stake is the city of Rome, its life or death. But tied inextricably to the decision of the Asiatic is the continuance of a Western civilization.

Leo, seated on a mule, approaches the southern bank. Bearded, grim-faced, he is wearing the white robes of a bishop; on his head a simple mitre; in his hands a staff. Before him walks a black-garbed cleric carrying a cross flanked by two others with incense-burners. Behind him walk two lines of brown and white clad monks singing psalms. It is the late afternoon. This is Leo's supreme gamble, the gamble of a great belief backed up by supreme courage.

Leo, of Tuscan blood, a native of Rome, has come with the consent of the Roman Emperor, Valentinian, as a last hope.

Rome is defenseless. Since he became bishop 12 years before, everything in his life has prepared him for this moment. He has asserted the primacy of Rome's bishop over all other Christian bishops. More than that: he has declared the authority of the Roman bishop over all temporal rulers. He has asserted that Christian faith and belief mean not merely a hope of immortality in the next life but order and wisdom in this life. He is the first of the great exponents of the Roman bishop's temporal power. Now, his claim is being tested: can he by the force of faith save Rome from a blood-bath? He is unarmed. Rome is without armies. Can his belief dominate this Asiatic?

The northern bank is lined with Huns: small men, with grotesquely formed skulls, narrow waists, broad shoulders, long arms, large chests, faces flat, beardless, yellow; each one a bundle of fur bristling with bows, arrows, daggers, astride small skittish long-haired horses; each one's lance carries a rotting human head. The sky behind them is red with their flaming banners. Attila rests on his horse surrounded by his bodyguard as the Roman retinue approaches with Leo. At a signal, it stops. Leo continues alone. He urges his horse into the thin sluggish water. Attila's bodyguard finger their bows and lances, watching for the slightest sign of trouble.

Attila moves forward into the river from the northern bank. Both men are watching each other; Leo is now still, Attila advancing slowly. The distance narrows. Leo now sees Attila as an oldish man, with bent back, slanting eyes rolling restlessly hither and thither, a lined face, narrow-lipped mouth. He sees Attila's worn tunic embroidered with precious stones, the black fur cap pulled down over the eyebrows, the curving longbow and colored quiver of arrows, the battle-axe slung in the belt. Attila has a forceful quiet and primitive dignity. The distance narrows. Their eyes meet. Attila barks a sudden question:

"Your name?"

"Leo."

This question and answer are just about all that history has preserved with any surety of the words which passed between Attila and Leo.[1] Onlookers hear Attila's question pronounced in heavy nasalized Latin. They see his eyes glitter in challenge. Leo's head comes up, his eyes staring into Attila's. Men see his right hand raised for a moment in the Christian Latin sa-

[1] Many fanciful pictures of this meeting have been painted both in words and on canvas.

lute: the palm turned towards Attila, index and forefinger held erect and together, the third finger bent and apart, thumb and little finger joined. He speaks. Attila listens. Then the latter rides towards the cleric on the southern bank. The rest of the conversation has escaped us. For these moments, Leo is alone with Attila and with history.

At this distance in time, it all looks so simple. In reality, Leo's visit to Attila was as feasible in 452 A.D. as if President Lyndon Johnson had walked on foot through the DMZ between North and South Vietnam in search of President Ho Chi Minh during the Tet festival of January 1968, or as if Pius XII accompanied by cross-bearer and incense-burners and ten chanting cardinals had personally confronted Adolf Hitler in the Reichskanzellerei off the Wilhelmstrasse in Berlin at the opening of Spring, 1942. By human calculations, it was a piece of madness.

The Huns had appeared like scavenging hawks and carrion birds from nowhere: first on the borders of China, then on the Caspian Sea, then in the Balkans and throughout Europe. They were always rushing headlong, wandering at full speed, driving to the horizon, the men on small sturdy horses, the women and children in chariots, ever flying away from the edges of the great desert where, men said, they had been born of demons. But the Huns were running from the demons: the sand and the wind. Their gods lived above the sky, and an ancient legend admonished them to search for their Land.

Time and time again, they found a new pastureland, settled there, only to find the lithe, tawny toils of the sand monster descending on them in howling billowing storms, driving them onwards. Blasting desolation pursued them from Asia, slithering and searching the earth mercilessly for them. The Hun always senses the demons at his back hunting him now eastward to China, now westward to Europe, wherever he sought the land of his dreams. The Huns read the future in ruffled sand-dunes as the Romans had in the entrails of hens and cocks. They felt the will of the Bird-King in hot grains stinging their eyes. Thus by 374, they had crossed the Volga and advanced to the Danube.

They had no constructive laws, and intended to build nothing. They killed unmercifully, burned endlessly, raped as a matter of course, took no prisoners and few slaves, had an insatiable greed for riches, hated all that was stable, nourished themselves on goat's cheese, and raw meat carried between their thighs and their horses' flanks, and drank millet and barley wine. Their religion was animistic and simple: in air and water and earth and fire lurked demons and gods to be satiated with blood.

Attila, the son of Mundzuk, traced his lineage back through 35 generations to Schongar, the Bird-King, who ruled all flying things.[2] Born of mixed Mongo and Hun ancestry, in 395, on the floor of a Hunnic chariot standing somewhere along the plains of the Danube. Living, hunting, killing, on horseback by the age of six. A hostage in Roman imperial hands at the age of twelve. Back among his own people before his twentieth year. A onetime ambassador to the imperial court of Constantinople. Widely travelled through Europe and Asia. Almost unique in his knowledge of Hunnic, Greek, and Latin. By 434, at the age of 39, king of all the Huns. By 445, having killed his brother Bleda, he is emperor of all the Scythians and heir to an empire stretching from the Alps and the Baltic in the West to the Volga and the Caspian Sea in the east, an area roughly covering present Soviet Eastern Europe and southwestern Russia of today. Before his mysterious death in 453, he had expanded this empire to the Great Wall of China; thrashed Greeks and Latins in Turkey, Greece, Germany, France, and Italy; extorted peace money amounting perhaps to over 2 million dollars from two unwilling empires; assembled a gargantuan treasure by plunder; earned the name of "God's Scourge" (the grass never grew again where his horse had trod, men said); and threatened both Constantinople and Rome.

We do not know the correct form of his name. Western ears picked it up as Attila, Atli, or Etzel. It was the Hunnic name for the Volga. Even the name of his race is obscure: Chinese chronicles refer to it as *hioung nu;* Latins heard the brief nasal grunt *ioung* and they latinized it as *hunnus.* We know he was as bloodthirsty, as greedy, as ruthless, and as unscrupulous as any Latin or Greek Emperor before or after him. We know one trait

---

2 His genealogy ran: Son of Mundzuk, son of Turda, son of Sceman, son of Ethe, son of Opos, son of Cadicha, son of Berend, son of Sulthan, son of Bulehu, son of Bolog, son of Zambour, son of Zamour, son of Reel, son of Levente, son of Kulche, son of Ampud, son of Miske, son of Kike, son of Betzer, son of Rudli, son of Chanad, son of Buken, son of Bordofort, son of Tarkans, son of Othmar, son of Radar, son of Beler, son of Kear, son of Keve, son of Kelod, son of Dama, son of Bor, son of Nembroth, son of Chus, son of Cham, descendant of the Bird-King Schongar.

of his character which may be the key to his destiny: his super-
stitiousness, shared by all the Huns. Having overrun Rheims
with blood and fire and cruelty, this irresistible band was put to
flight by some loud sound emanating from the Cathedral. At
another time, Attila would not offend the Bishop of Troyes because the latter's name was Lupus: the wolf was a deathly
totemic symbol for the Huns, and "wolf" was the meaning of
this bishop's name.

Attila had an autocratic personality. Told by an envoy of
the Emperor Theodosius that the latter prayed for his welfare,
Attila answered: "May it be unto the Romans as they wish it to
me!" Asked by another delegation, come to discuss peace and
war, when they should return with a final answer to his demands, he retorted with one laconic Latin syllable: "Now." Offered 350 pounds of gold (approximately $250,000) as a peace
price at a truce meeting on the banks of the Morava river in
434, he casually answered: "Make it 700," and got it. To an
imperial legate starting his speech with the words: "My Lord,
the Emperor, has lived up to his promises and . . ." Attila
shrieked: "That is a lie!" Told that Orleans could not resist
beyond the 23rd of June, he replied: "On that day I shall arrive." On the eve of his onslaught against Rome and Constantinople, he sent couriers to both Emperors bearing the identical
message: "My master, who is also yours, orders you to prepare
his palace for him!"

Attila had a dream based on his descent from the Bird-King,
enlivened by this perpetual flight of Huns from the demons of
wind and sand, and fed by his hatred of Rome. All Hun warriors employed by Rome as mercenaries would return to their
people. Rome and Constantinople would be destroyed. The
Great Wall would be demolished, the Chinese Empire seized.
India and Persia would be overrun. The Bird-King would reign
from the China Sea to the Atlantic. The Huns would find the
land of their seeking and settle down in towns and cities of stone
and wood. They would live on the spoils of nations, dominate
all in the name of their ancient gods, and impose the law of the
Huns on all men. But he had sworn a special oath to destroy
Rome. It was the object of his living hate. His night bodyguard,
Edecon, often heard Attila grind out the name of Rome hoarsely
in his dreams.

It was this man and his hordes who had appeared on the

banks of the Rhine in 451. In quick succession he had taken Worms, Windisch, Spires, Mayence, Basle, Strasbourg, Colmar, Besançon, Troyes, Arras, Metz, Rheims, Laon, St. Quentin. At Orleans he had been stopped and driven back. He lost a battle at the Catalaunian Fields near Châlons. He had returned to Etzelburg, his stronghold, and reorganized his forces. In a quick change of methods, he had replaced the fur clothing of his warriors with armor bordered with metal. He had employed Roman tacticians and trainers. The rough flying hordes are drilled and disciplined in military formation and tactics. Huns learned the use of siege weapons: scaling-ladders, ballistae, catapults, onagri. He decided to march on Rome. He invaded Italy. By 452, he had taken Aquileia, Padua, Verona, Bergamo, Brescia, Cremona, and Mantua. He was now camped north of the Po and was prepared for the last leg of his southward conquest to Rome. No army capable of stopping him stood between him and Rome. Yet all he could now hear was the singing of clerics.

In threatening Rome, Attila threatened not merely an ancient imperial city. At stake was the loose coagulation of nations, now settled throughout Europe, which formed the basis of her future civilization and greatness which the Occident would achieve over 1500 years. The Visigoths in Spain and Southern France, the Franks in Northern France, the Lombards in Northern Italy, the Saxons and Thuringians in Germany, they and the indigenous populations would have fallen under the Asiatic blight of Hun rule thus nullifying all the West possessed of her past.

There was more at stake: Christianity had become a center of unity and a hearth of rekindled hopes for the already disintegrating Roman Empire. The Christian faith had happened, and it presented acceptable alternatives either to the dead works of effete religions or the mortal necessity of death. Rome and the eastern Mediterranean is strewn with broken funerary inscriptions representing every cult known to man at that time: Mithra, Serapis, Isis, Osiris, Zoroaster, Greek mysteries, Oriental rites, the Roman gods and the Greek Pantheon. Yet the universal message carried by all was set forth succinctly and poignantly by Horace in his famous lines to Torquatus. Turning his eyes from the contemplation of Spring, he looked at the human condition and wrote to his friend:

"Do not hope for immortality,
This is the message of the passing year,
And of the hour which snatches our happy days.

Swift months renew the heavens and the earth.
But we, when we die,
Just as when our father Aeneas died,
Just as when divine Tullus and Ancus died,
We are but dust and shadows.

Torquatus, when once you die,
And the underworld has claimed you,
Nothing, not your family,
Not your accomplishments,
Not your piety,
Nothing will restore you to life."

In contrast, the Christian faith offered a hope and a guarantee of eternal life after death. The epitaph of one Petrolanus, found on the Aventine overlooking the Vatican hill, sums up this hope and that faith in five simple words: *Petrolanus, Deum videre cupiens, vidit* [3] We know that it was under the tutelage of this belief that Medieval and Renaissance Europe with all its faults and successes evolved from the post-Roman period into modern Europe. All this, however, would have been rendered impossible, if the Hunnic Empire had engulfed Europe of 450-500 A.D. That it did not is due to Leo. Christianity had just begun to insert itself throughout Europe as the way of life. Radiating from Italy, it had spread long lines of communication through Gaul, Belgium, England, Ireland, Germany, Spain, and eastern Europe. If unimpeded, it would in 300 years dominate the entire Continent.

Leo's conversation with Attila lasts a few minutes. Did Attila superstitiously fear the priest in Leo? The totemic symbolism of Leo's name ("lion")? Had he already made up his mind to retreat because of famine, disease, and discontent in his own ranks? Did Leo threaten the punishment of Heaven and Hell? We do not know. Suddenly in the meeting, Attila turns his horse, crosses the river, enters his camp at a gallop, shouting hoarse orders. Tents are lowered and folded. Chariots are harnessed. Horse lines are emptied. Towards nightfall, the clatter of hooves begins to die away. By morning, the camp of

[3] "Petrolanus, who desired to see God, now sees him."

the Huns is deserted. Christianity promises men hope and life; on that basis, it claims to dominate all man's life. It confirmed hope and delivered life that day. It would go on to exercise that claim for over a millennium.

All the evidence we have tells us that Attila was a cantankerous, merciless, egotistical, ungovernable, self-willed, ambitious, cunning barbarian with whom ordinary appeals for pity or reasonableness would have absolutely no avail. Yet, no one can doubt that the decision he made at the Po was due in large part to Leo's belief in his mission, and he was able to communicate this to Attila. Up to this time, Christianity had dwelt in the shadow of the Empire. Its kingdom "was not of this world." Only slightly more than a hundred years before that, it had been liberated from the catacombs.

Leo made his two-level vision of history quite clear in sermons preached to the Roman populace after the Vandals had looted but, by his persuasion, spared the people and the city of Rome as a whole, in 455.

> "Who has liberated it (Rome), preserved it from massacre? . . . Ascribe our liberation, not, as the godless do, to the influence of the stars but to the ineffable mercy of the Almighty who has softened the rage of the barbarians. . . . The glory of Peter and Paul is so great that you have become a holy people, a chosen people, a priestly and royal nation, and, thanks to the presence of the Holy See of the Blessed Peter, you have become lords of the world, and by holy religion you are able to extend your dominion further than by earthly might."

Leo was the first leader of Western Christianity who presented his religious beliefs as a total explanation of man and his environment. Fifty years before, Augustine had divided this world into "two cities:" the City of God and the City of Mammon. According to Augustine, all reconciliation was impossible between the two. Now Leo proposed baldly that Christianity was authorized to lord it over both worlds. His action in confronting Attila was a bold and courageous assertion of Christian dominance.

Leo risked his own life and the survival of Christianity. If he had failed, Christianity may never have stepped into the empty sandals of the Roman Empire. Because he was willing to die, he lived and Christianity lived. Because he succeeded, Christianity's dominance held sway over 1000 years. Leo confirmed Christian belief, pulled the papacy out of a historical rut, closed forever the doors of the catacombs, and set Christianity's feet firmly on the road of dominance in Europe.

Symbolically, all but one of those involved in the Attila affair died violently: Attila in 453 by an unknown hand; Aetius, the Roman general who defeated him at Orleans, by the hand of the Emperor Valentinian in 454; the Emperor Valentinian himself by the hand of the future Emperor, Maximus, in 455. Only Leo died in his bed, in 461.

Pope and Nazi

In the early summer of 1944, a meeting took place in the privacy of the Vatican, Rome. The reigning Pope, Pius XII, had been asked by the United Nations Organization to issue a condemnation of Nazi Germany's treatment of Jews and captive European populations. What was to be done? For Roman Catholic Christianity and the Papacy, this meeting was fateful: both would continue, surely, to live and flourish a long time afterwards, yet on the outcome and the decision of this meeting depended the moral stamina of the Papacy and Roman Catholicism.

Present at the meeting were Pius XII; Cardinal Maglione, his Secretary of State; Monsignor Orsenigo, his representative to Nazi Germany; and some of the Pope's closest advisors. Only two sounds penetrated from the outside world: the noise of sporadic traffic beyond the white line dividing Vatican City from greater Rome, and the soothing murmur of the waters that sprayed up to two shining peaks from the twin fountains on either side of the Obelisk in the center of St. Peter's Square and fell splashing, splashing, down on the wide stone basis. The waters sang ceaselessly to the Swiss Guards standing in the shadow of Bernini's colonnades, and they whispered up as far as the windows of the Secretariat of State and the Papal apartments on the fourth floor to the right.

Pius XII was now 68 years of age, self-named Pius (his given name was Eugenio Pacelli) because he wished to work for world peace, born into a family of lawyers, and descendant of a family which had supplied wine to the Vatican for generations. The purpose of the United Nations message was clear to him: ostensibly to do something to save those Jews still alive and doomed otherwise to die in Hitler's crematoria; ultimately, to take the teeth out of any remaining resistance in Germany by breaking the cohesion of its armed forces and of its people behind the lines.

Pius was fully acquainted with the facts, fully acquainted since 1940. Late in that year, Cardinal Sapieha of Poland had sent a secret letter to Pius by the hands of a Polish Jesuit describing the Nazi treatment of Jews and religious people, and asking Pius to protest. Pius had refused.

Once again in 1942, Pius had an interview with Herman von Weisacker, Nazi Germany's ambassador to the Vatican. A secret report written by Georg Gerten had made its way through Orsenigo to the Pope's table. It told of death-marches, of mass shootings, of death by gas, of soap made from Jewish bodies and lampshades made from Jewish skin and decorated with Gothic characters and the Swastika. Pius had, indeed, remonstrated with von Weisacker. And von Weisacker had argued that the reports were exaggerated. Later he cabled to Ribbentrop, Hitler's Foreign Minister: "The Pope will confine himself to general statements and these will hurt no one." Pius did. Only the captives of Hitlerism were hurt.

But a different spirit reigned in the Vatican chancellery in 1942. It was not so much that Hitler had threatened to make Pius a prisoner if he caused trouble. That did weigh, surely: if Pius were taken by Hitler, as Schuschnigg of Austria, as Leopold of Belgium, and as countless others had been, would not the Church lack its leader? But Vatican policy was different then. It came out in phrases heard in policy discussions: "A victory on the eastern front is absolutely imminent . . . the greatest victory for the Church today is the destruction of Stalinism and Russian Bolshevism . . . there is good news from the Russian Front today, they are within sight of Moscow. . . . These Germans are just like the Spaniards in 1527 and the Piedmontese in 1870, we can outlive them. . . . God uses human instruments to destroy atheistic plots hatched by international Jewry and Communism . . . history will reproach the Vatican with having acted out of sheer self-interest. . . . The city has been declared an open one, we will not be bombed . . . we must abide by our side of the agreement. . . . Rome must continue on whatever happens to individual men . . . the Secretariat of State has persuaded the French nuns to remain here in great numbers so that Il Duce will have hostages to brandish in the face of the

French. . . ." In 1942, the Axis powers seemed to hold Europe by the throat, and Japan was rampaging through the Pacific.

Once again in May 1944, Orsenigo arrived down from Berlin. A Russian victory seemed assured. The Anglo-Saxons were allied with the Russians. Within a month, Rome would be in allied hands. Within 16 months, Japan would be on its knees in front of an atomic blast at Hiroshima. Orsenigo had given a detailed description of Hitler's policy for Jewish extermination: facts, figures, locations, names of Germans involved, all were documented and at hand for consideration. By that month of 1944, almost 3-1/4 million Polish Jews had been liquidated. By the end of the war, over 6 million European Jews would have perished in the camps.

Pius knew the facts. This was not the problem discussed at the meeting with Orsenigo and Maglione. The problem was: what to do? He understood that Churchill and Roosevelt were primarily interested in defeating Hitler: "Any stick is good enough to beat a dog if you wish to beat him," Churchill had once growled in retort to someone complaining about his alliance with Stalin's Russia. Jewish survival was a vital but a secondary interest. This held no problem for Pius. He understood.

The issue was specifically a moral one. At that time and in that world, the only authority wielded by the Pope was a moral authority. At that time and in that world, the only possible moral authority was represented by the Pope. Now a genuine and gargantuan crime against humanity was in full swing. As the three men met and spoke, lives were being snuffed out in gas-chambers, bodies were being shoved into ovens, trains were being loaded with human cattle to supply the gas-chambers and the ovens. Should this unique moral authority speak out? Or should it keep silent? If he spoke out, and Hitler took him prisoner, what then? As the meeting wore on, it became clear that Pius would not speak out. If he had spoken now, it would have violated every bone in his body. Pius was primarily a Roman, a politician, and a diplomat. Through such eyes he viewed all problems, moral and religious, and all worlds, the present visible world around him and the future world promised to the faithful after death.

Pius became Pope in 1939 with his geopolitical mind already made up for him. He had one supreme fear: Marxist Communism and Soviet Russia. He had one dream: the resurrection of the long-dead Papal control over the politics and destinies of Europe, no longer by Papal armies and fleets, by excommunications and interdictions, but by a web of interlocking treaties, agreements, concordats, diplomatic and economic pressures. He was direct heir to the European policies of Consalvi, the Papal advisor of Pius VII, in the 19th century. Thus he was convinced that the restoration of Christianity's hegemony in Europe could be effected through the New Order of totalitarianism. He had made concession after concession for this reason. He had remained silent by agreed consent in the hope that finally the essential element would be achieved: Europe freed from the Bolshevik threat. He had calculated that with an Axis victory, the spirit of ancient Europe would once again be born. The domination of the European mainland by the northern Protestant "ascendancy" would cease. Pacelli was a "European" in his own way.

Pius had lived in Germany for seven years (1917-1924), as Papal Legate. He spoke German, loved Germanic order, cleanliness, and efficiency, peopled his personal household with German advisors, servants, and aides. Even after the war, no direct condemnation of Hitler ever crossed his lips. He condemned cruel systems in general terms. His predecessor, Pius XI, three days before his death in 1939, did not hesitate to brand Hitler as an apostate and his system as neo-paganism. This was not Pacelli's way. But he had no use for Hitler..

Pacelli had seen Hitler only once and at a distance. It was in Munich and Hitler was standing in an open car surrounded by brown-shirted guards acknowledging the cheers of the crowds. Pius had not forgotten the appearance of Hitler: his auburn hair, the long head rising on the top of his skull to an almost sharp ridge running from the edge of his forehead to his poll, the congenital sign of the incurable psychopath, the flat ears, the sharply inclined forehead furrowed by long swaths across which ran pulsating waves of emotionalism and mystic rages, the bulbously irrelevant nose above which sat two deeply blue eyes flecked with black, glinting with a faintly green light that flared up with his emotions. The strong mouth set in the center of a triangular face-piece attached by sloping cheeks to smooth temples at the twin round knobs of his cheekbones had a frightening quality.

Pacelli had listened to one of his speeches and found the voice unbearable, had understood that it was endowed with a mesmeric quality that defied analysis but penetrated one's defenses. It grated harshly on the ear but seized subtle hold on the subconscious. It could take one single word, such as *Coventry,* or *Schweinhund,* or *Lebensraum,* and repeat it over and over again, so that it acquired a strange force like a blunt stone knife thrust into the brains of his hearers.

The meeting drew to an end. All protests, Pius had decided, would be couched in general language which could be applied to anyone anywhere who committed any evil. "Those with bad consciences will apply it to themselves," Pacelli had said again and again. Specifically at this meeting, Pacelli discussed the proposed text of a message to Admiral Horthy, the Prince Regent of Hungary, apropos of the Jews who were then being rounded up for the concentration camps. As an example of Pacelli's *Wortketterung,* the text stands uncontested.

> "We have been asked by different authorities to intercede efficaciously, so that in this noble and exalted nation there be no further prolongation or aggravation of the sufferings which a great number of unfortunates have undergone for a long time on account of their racial and national origins. Our paternal heart cannot remain indifferent to these urgent requests, on account of our duty to include all men in our love. We turn personally, therefore, to Your Highness and appeal to your noble feelings, trusting fully that Your Highness will do all in your power to save so many unhappy people from further sorrow and pain." June 25, 1944. P. Pius XII

This tone was not imposed by the extraordinary circumstances of the world war. It was a lifelong trait of Pius XII. In 1956, the American Ambassador in Istanbul cabled Pius at the suggestion of the Greek Orthodox authorities, asking him to protest to the Turkish government against the burnt churches, the massacres, the looting, the desecrated cemeteries, the gutted shops and homes of the Turkish Greeks. Pius waited four months before acting, and then issued an anodyne statement deploring the oppression of innocent people anywhere for any reason by anyone.

Speaking in 1957 to a group of Jewish leaders who had come to him apropos of the Jewish refugee problem, Pius stated that he was against expulsion of innocent ones anywhere on the earth by any power for any reason. For Pacelli, specificity that implied a moral standpoint which, in turn, implied the injuring of delicate diplomatic relationships was an evil and a pest to be avoided for a sacred reason. "Our vocation is to embrace all men in the charity of Christ," he once said.

It is useless to speculate in detail about what would have happened if Pius had taken the moral initiative in 1942, in 1943, or even in 1944. Hitler might have had him arrested and transported to a German prison camp. He might, in his madness, have had him assassinated. He might have been constrained to halt the onward course of his terrible Final Solution. He might have made more violent efforts to liquidate more and more Jews. A protest by Pius might have broken German allegiance to Hitler and produced a successful *putsch* within Germany. It might, on the contrary, have caused Germans in their hour of trial to become ever more Hitler-devoted. We do not know.[4]

But such a moral protest is not measured by the immediate and concrete results it produces. Its sole measure is the exigency of the actual situation to which one must respond without seeking to know the ulterior results. Moral duty confers its rewards and applies its sanctions to the duty itself.

In this respect, we must underline, not an error of historical judgment on Pacelli's part; that was gross enough. It is his erroneous application of the Christian two-level view of history. Ever since the time of Constantine and Leo, Christianity has relied on a secular arm, at least for its defense. When Christianity controlled that arm, as in the high period of its temporal power, it relied heavily on it. What happened in the visible world through power-politics and military might and economic status was paralleled, it was believed, on the invisible plane by supernatural progress and strength. All the political stances of the Christian Church with their mistakes and successes, their partisan politics and unholy decisions, can be traced to this two-level view of human history and to Christianity's belief that it was born to dominate.

All that Pius ever wrote concerning doctrine, monastic perfection, theological orthodoxy, virtue, compassion and heavenly

---

[4] It is to be noted that Pius XII organized *privately* more than one agency to take care of refugee Jews. At a certain moment, convents and monasteries in Italy were instructed to give them refuge. His own summer palace at Castelgandolfo was thrown open to refugees.

rewards is rendered dull and, in the long run, severely diminished by this failure. Even his majesty of presence and the constant impression he gave of being an ethereal spirit enclosed in a fragile tenement of clay, all this is affected by the failure of that supreme moment.[5] If Pacelli had taken a clear moral stance, it might not have quite taken the Roman Church out of the Middle Ages right into the 20th century, to quote one post-War writer. It would, at one and the same time, have made the Roman Church relevant, and been a supreme act of moral independence free from all traces of partisan politics.[6]

There is no doubt that both Leo and Pius XII, separated by a span of some 1475 years, regarded human history from the same angle. The difference, however, is great. One is inclined to say that Leo ran a far greater personal risk and gambled for a higher price—the submergence of a weak and barely developing Christianity. But the real difference lay in another direction. By the first third of the 20th century, the two-level vision of history was inoperative: the human environment had changed radically. The last person to believe in its practical effectivity was Pius. He relied on the stratagems and methods of modern diplomacy. Moral standpoints have no validity in this area. He could not, thus, have taken a moral stand and played the game of international politics as he had learned to do.

Pacelli's two-level view of history has been verified in another way. Today, the visitor to Dachau passes through the Administration Building with its corridors of grisly reminders and its wall-to-wall photographs of mountains of bones, out past the long slabs under each of which lie buried in a common grave the remains of 10,000 people, and finally reaches the Catholic chapel. To its left stands the Protestant chapel. Further on is the Synagogue. To the left is the infamous Blood-Ditch and, beyond, the Crematoria preceded by the Showers where still hangs a sign in German which says: *Please Remove Your Clothes*. All is quiet and peaceful now in Dachau.

[5] To a lesser degree, Protestants and Catholics in Germany share in Pacelli's failure. Responsibility also lies with Christians and Jews abroad throughout the world who did not protest in time.

[6] A. Roy Eckardt points to a recent example of such partisan politics on the part of the Vatican in his *Elder and Younger Brothers*, Scribners, New York 1967, p. 175.

Hitler and the engineers of Dachau, of Belsen, of Buchenwald, and all the other horror-camps lie in their graves; their system and ideology have ceased. The Catholic Mass is celebrated daily in the chapel cared for by nuns. The Protestants hold their services, as do the Jews. This would be Pacelli's defense and answer: the evil was finally destroyed; the truth continued to exist. But the rough headstone speaks for all: *Denket daran wie wir hier sterben. Reflect on how we died here.* The one word "how" expresses a wealth of indictment.

In the history of religions, one of the more repelling aspects is the suffering and pain imposed by organized religion on human beings in the name of that religion and the god it worships. Essential to Roman Catholicism is the belief that death is but a gateway to eternal life and happiness with God. Tied to this fundamental belief is another: truth is eternal. Over the centuries, Roman Catholicism and Christianity in general have become deeply involved in social and political matters. For a period of their history, they claimed to have the key to all problems, religious and lay.

A contradiction has seized hold of Christianity in all its forms due to this historical inmixture. The dead weight of material things, wealth, power, and influence, possesses an inertia that seemingly defies the spirit. History teaches that Christians are capable of behaving like people without any religious principles precisely in order to futher Christianity. The words remain Christian; the actions are unchristian. The total result is catastrophic.

A comparison of Leo's dominance with that of Pius XII's brings this out clearly. We only know this dominance in its effects. Leo's concept of dominance brooked no half-measures: he did not retire and leave Rome to Attila's sword and fire-brand. He, so ran his conviction, was assured of a moral victory even over an unprincipled barbarian such as Attila. Leo assured the material interests of Rome by moral means.

Pius XII, on the other hand, was caught in the rules of the diplomatic game he had chosen. Professing the same universal dominance and practising his diplomacy, the vital material interests of Rome and the Vatican dictated logically that he compromise. His words and thought-molds in this instance would be traditional Christian ones: "the greater good," "the lesser evil," "the eternal character of truth," "punishment by God," "reward by God to the victims of injustice," "eternal life receives them," and so on. But these thought-molds and words expressed a secular purpose and an element in dominance lacking in Leo's. Leo had acted like a Christian of the 5th century. Pius acted like a temporal ruler of the 19th-20th century. Leo's maxim riding out to confront Attila would have been: since death is the gateway to life, I do not refuse to confront Attila merely because he may kill me. Pius XII's maxim in not taking a public moral stand on the Hitlerian Terror, would have been: death is not the end for these poor people; in the meantime, we buy time. Worse could befall us, if we do otherwise. For the just, to die is to live with God forever.

22. Two Assassinations: The Khalif and the Boss

Scenario: It is fitting that one man should die for the People

In noonday stillness, the youth stood at the foot of the steps leading up the sloping side of the *teocalli*. A priest struck one soft blow on the gong. The youth placed himself on the first step, raised the lute to his lips, and started to play. A stream of clear notes went up like a flight of pretty birds and fell in lilting cadences through the bright thin air over the heads of the worshippers. Abruptly, the music ceased: he snapped the lute in half, threw the pieces over the edge of the step, took another from his leather quiver, moved up one step and recommenced his playing. The Toxcatl feast in honor of Tetzcatlipuca, king of the gods, had begun. All was well.

Tetzcatlipuca would be satisfied. Men, when they died, could hope to avoid Hell, a place without light or windows, could hope to reach either Paradise, an evergreen land of perpetual summer, or Heaven, the abode of the sun where the dead became gaily-colored birds. The thin piping melody wove continuously; its interruption at each new step, each new breaking, each new beginning, was done in perfect rhythm. Every second of the music's duration was carefully patterned on the movements of stepping, breaking, taking a new lute.

The *tonalpauhque* priests saw to the exactitude of ritual each year with religious scrupulosity. The youth chosen had a spotless body without blemish, without defect. For one year, he was worshipped as the God. Twenty days before the sacrifice, his long hair was cut; four beautiful girls were given him for his delights. On this day, he played all the lutes he had used during the year of his divinity.

Standing now on the last and highest step, he broke the last lute, threw its pieces over the side, and faced the awesome mask of Tetzcatlipuca standing over the altar. Five priests seized him. Four held his body down rigidly on the altar slab. The fifth plunged a knife into his chest, opened it around his heart so that the steam and the blood gushed up warm before Tetzcatlipuca's eyes. When both stopped, his head was cut off and impaled on the *tzonpantli* pole. The multitude then danced with joy. The light of the sun would not die. The earth would not be devastated by fire. Better one man die for all the people. All was well.

The Khalif

On June 17, 656 A.D., Khalif Othman, successor of the Prophet, Commander of all the Faithful, was assassinated in his residence at Medina. This was a heinous crime in the eyes of all the Faithful. But the prime motive of his assassins was religious: Othman was unfaithful, they maintained, to the precepts of Islam, and he had adulterated the Khalifate with worldly habits and vices.

Othman had become Khalif in 644 A.D. at the age of 70. The Prophet had loved him during his lifetime, had declared his innocence and modesty to be so great that even the angels of Allah felt inferior to Othman. Mohammad had even promised Othman Paradise and assured him that he, Mohammad, would meet him at the Gate and introduce him to its delights, so impressed was Mohammad with Othman's virtue. Othman married two of the Prophet's daughters. Mohammad loved to liken Othman to the Patriarch Abraham.

As a young impetuous follower of Mohammad between 610 and 615 A.D., Othman had been trussed up with a rope like a chicken by his uncle who threatened to let him die in that position unless he renounced his Islamic faith. Othman had persevered. As one of the first companions of Mohammad, he had fled with his family to Abyssinia in 615, and fled again to Medina in 622 to rejoin the Prophet. In 630, at a low ebb in

Mohammad's monetary fortunes, he had provided 960 camels and 50 horses out of his own pocket, so that the Prophet could raid Tebook. Later Mohammad used him as a top negotiator.

He was of middle height, sturdy in build, had been extremely handsome in his youth, wore his hair long and in lustrous waves below his ears. At the age of eighty, he was full-bearded, pleasant, still handsome, and amiable. People always remarked on his modesty and friendliness, but nobody ever mistook his gentleness for weakness or his benign look for vacancy of mind.

Under his Khalifate, Egypt was secured from the Greeks, the conquest of Armenia was promoted, Cyprus and Persia were totally subjugated, Carthage, the capital of North Africa, was taken, and the first Muslim fleet was built. At Medina, he laid out public buildings, established a constabulary, and was responsible for the final text of the Koran such as we have it today. A number of differing Koranic texts had appeared during the previous ten years. Othman had the text revised, and succeeded in collecting and burning all other versions but his revised one.

Discontent, however, started about Othman's 80th birthday. He was the first Umaiyad to become Khalif; he was disliked, therefore, from the beginning by the Hashemite family. The latter, as the family of the Prophet, claimed priority. In addition, Othman's judgements were harsh and unpredictable. For instance, he dismissed Amr ibn al Aasi soon after becoming Khalif, then reinstated him as governor of Egypt when the Greeks attacked, then dismissed him again once Amr had defeated the Greeks.

Graver accustations were brought against him. Chiefly he was accused of worldliness. He violated the fundamental rule of Mohammad who had laid down that one-fifth of all the loot taken in battle should be put in the central treasury of Islam at Medina. Othman apparently allowed a favorite, Abdullah ibn abi Sarh, an Umaiyad, the conqueror of Tripolitania, to keep one-fifth of the treasury's one-fifth. When the other four-fifths reached Medina, Othman gave them to his cousin, Merwan, to dispose of as he wished.

Secondly, he was accused of nepotism. Actually, he did replace Hashemite governors and generals with Umaiyad: Abu Musa Ashari, governor of Basra was replaced with Abdulla ibn Aamir; Waleed ibn Uqba, governor of Kufa, was replaced by Saeed ibn al Aasi. Thirdly, Othman was accused of sacrilege:

in fixing the text of the Koran, he had caused all differing versions to be burned. "Othman burned the sacred words of the Prophet," was the accusation.

Lastly, Othman committed grave errors of judgment. A certain Ibn Masud had been the personal attendant of Mohammad at Medina. Besides, the man had a photographic memory and could recite every word of Mohammad and his Koran by heart, as he had heard it from the Prophet's lips. His version differed sharply from Othman's in places. Othman practically told him to go to the devil. In addition, Othman persecuted a certain holy man, Abu Dharr, who attacked the rulers of Islam for their luxurious ways, their marble palaces, their alabaster baths, their fine clothes, their sumptuous banquets, their concubines, their wives, their slaves, and their greed for money. Othman banished Abu Dharr to a lonely oasis where he died and was afterwards venerated as a saint. Besides, Othman himself lived very comfortably, was well-dressed, not always barefoot, ate well, gave and received presents, and possessed quite a few slaves. In a word, he violated the tradition of the "bare-footed khalifs."

Trouble started in Iraq and Egypt, where the Khalif's relatives were in charge. Revolts broke out and were suppressed. Plots were hatched, demagogues went around the bazaars arousing the people, agitators spread rumors, false and true. The name of the Khalif and his appointees was attacked. But nothing need have come of this. Othman made the Pilgrimage to Mecca in 655 and took the opportunity to consult all his governors.

Ibn abi Sarh of Egypt advised Othman to buy off all the malcontents. Abdulla ibn Aamir of Basra suggested that Othman start a holy war to distract the dissatisfied: "a man fully employed in fighting, in treating his horse's sore back, in picking lice out of his sheepskin coat, has no time for sedition." Muawiya of Syria blamed the governors of Syria, Iraq, and Egypt: "there is no discontent in my province." But Amr ibn al Aasi was brutal and blunt: "You, O Khalif, have subordinated the whole nation to your own tribe, Beni Umaiya. You have gone astray and so have our people. Now, either make up your mind to act justly, or resign from your job as Khalif."

But by now, Othman was too old and weak and compromised to do anything. He retired to Medina. Either he had resigned himself to death, or he did not think that Muslims would kill the Prophet's successor and representative. He did not even ask Muawiya to send military help. Death was not long in coming. The rebels converged on Medina and laid siege to his house. Alone he confronted them, refused to abdicate, promised to correct certain abuses, but would not yield to threats of death: "Death is preferable to me," he replied, "sooner than desert my post."

Othman was now deserted by all his friends who left him, lived in surrounding houses, and watched the end. A few relatives, supporters, slaves, and his women remained in the house with him. Othman tried to preach at the Mosque on the Friday before his death, but he was stoned as he stood in the pulpit and had to be carried back to his house unconscious from several blows on the head. He recovered in time for the end. In the month of May and early June, the heat was unbearable, and no water was allowed to reach Othman's household. Then news reached the besiegers that Muawiya was on his way with troops by forced marches. The besiegers decided to act quickly.

The house was attacked from the front. Othman sat upstairs in his room reading the Koran. Mohammad, son of Abu Bekr and three others climbed through a back window and suddenly burst into the Khalif's presence. This Mohammad seized Othman by the beard and raised his sword. "By Allah, O son of my brother, I take refuge from you in Allah," was all Othman said. All now fell on him and drove swords through his chest and belly. Othman fell forward clasping the Koran to his chest, his blood reddening the pages. His wife, Naila, and his other women threw themselves over his body screaming and sobbing. They did not save his life. They could only prevent his head being cut off by his assailants. Several of Naila's fingers were sliced from her hands.

Three days later, Othman was buried quietly outside Medina. Othman's shirt and the severed fingers of Naila were smuggled to Muawiya in Damascus. The latter nailed them to the pulpit in the mosque and vowed to avenge the innocent blood shed. For five years, the Arab Empire was in turmoil. In 661, Muawiya became Khalif.

Historians are agreed that the assassination of Othman marked the end of a period in the history of Islam. Shortly afterwards, the theocratic idealist state of Islam was transformed into a lay empire. In addition, the traditional feud of the Beni Hashim and the Beni Umaiya played a large role in the affair.

But in Othman's assassination and Muawiya's reprisals against his assassins the religious motive of Islam and its idea of dominance played a major role. If Othman had not violated tradition, as he did, the assassination would probably not have taken place. Muawiya's reprisals (he was of the same family as the assassins) seem to have been motivated by his concept of Islamic dominance: on earth, the Khalif succeeded and represented Mohammad, who, in turn, represented Allah. A sacrilege had been committed against this sacred hierarchy. It had to be avenged. Muawiya, too, had his personal ambitions to foster and his own enemies to liquidate.

The Boss

On Monday, July 14, 1958, King Faisal II, a Hashemite, direct descendant of the Prophet Mohammad, was assassinated some minutes after 5 o'clock in the morning, in his residence at Baghdad, Iraq. For the Faithful, this was either a heinous crime or an act of piety, depending on their government's stand. But the prime motive of his assassins was primarily political: he stood in the way of Islamic nationalism, and he had aligned himself with the West, whereas the leader of that nationalism, Colonel Gamal Abdel Nasser, known to his intimates as the Boss, was now leaning heavily on Soviet Russia, the enemy of the West. The storm had started in a big way, for obviously vital reasons; and Faisal had to go, by death or exile.

At the time of Faisal's assassination, the Boss was half-way through his 40th year. He was born at Beni Mor, "the Tribe of the Bitter Ones," on the edge of the Nile in Upper Egypt. He had greying black curly hair, a deep scar almost in the center of his long curving forehead, an aquiline nose with Assyrian nostrils running between narrowly set, expressive brown eyes, narrow temples, broad cheekbones, wide jaws, long mobile mouth, fine teeth, clean-shaven face but for a thin-line moustache, columnar neck, broad shoulders, spatular fingers, a quick catlike bound to his walk, and a tawny depth to his voice that exercised an undoubted mesmerism on individuals and crowds. Nasser had seized power as number two with one, Mohammad Naguib, on July 23, 1952. Naguib he had relegated to a living death shortly afterwards: he could not afford to let him live; he could not dare put him to death. Naguib was put in a private prison all his own.

Gamal Nasser, by his own definition, is the hero whom the Arab "nation" has sought for a very very long time in order that he lead it to fulfill its role in the world.[1] The Arab predicament is summed up simply and succinctly in seven words: "a role in search of a hero." The geopolitical situation of Islam, or as Nasser puts it, the "Arab nation,"[2] he sums up with equal simplicity. Egypt is surrounded by three concentric circles: the Arab Circle composed of the neighbouring and contiguous Arab countries; the African Circle because Egypt is an African country and Africa shares Egypt's desire to be free and to prosper; the outer circle of Egypt's "brothers in faith who, wherever under the sun they may be, turn as we do, in the direction of Mecca, and whose devout lips speak the same prayers."[3] Now Faisal II of Iraq was Colonel Nasser's chief stumbling block within the Arab Circle.

At his death, Faisal II was in his 23rd year. Small in height, unimpressive in presence, a sufferer from chronic asthma, Faisal nevertheless carried himself with dignity, possessed good intentions, and enjoyed a certain popularity with the mass of the people. In 1954, he secured the services of Nuri es-Said as prime minister. From the start, Faisal, Nuri Pasha, and the Hashemite monarchy were the objects of attacks, slanders, threats, and criticisms over Nasser's Voice of the Arabs radio in Cairo. On February 1, 1958, Nasser achieved by bloodless means the union of Syria and Egypt. In March, Said al Islam, Crown Prince of Yemen, signed a pact of confederation with Nasser. The United Arab Republic was born as a two-pronged

---

[1] Cf. *Egypt's Liberation: The Philosophy of Revolution,* by Premier Gamal Abdel Nasser, introduction by Dorothy Thompson, Public Affairs Press, Washington, D.C. 1956, p. 81 ff.

[2] Nasser never speaks of Islam as such or of Muslims as such. His interest is in the "Arab nation," terms which he uses to cover all peoples anywhere who speak Arabic and profess Islam. Actually the majority of such people in Lebanon, Syria, Iraq, and in the Maghreb are not ethnically Arabs. In Pakistan, Malaya, Indonesia, the percentage of Arab stock is very low or completely negligible. In his *Philosophy of the Revolution,* he used the terms "Islamic" and "Islam" only in historical connections, (cf. pp. 61, 86, 87, 89, 112, of *op. cit.*).

[3] *Op. cit.* p. 111.

pincer; one prong (Yemen) curved dangerously around oil-rich Saudi Arabia, the other prong (Syria) reached eastward to Iraq and Iran. Late in April Nasser flew to Moscow, laid wreaths on the tombs of Stalin and Lenin, and arranged for military hardware, economic supplies, and valuable technical personnel.

By late June, the propaganda blast of Radio Cairo had reached a crescendo. Both Hussein of Jordan and his cousin, Faisal II of Iraq, were called colonialist stooges and associated with French, British, and American "pythons, white dogs, pigs, power-hungry beasts, imperialists, and bloodsuckers." Lebanon and Jordan began to undergo bloody riots. A Nasserist coup was nipped in the bud at Amman, Jordan. Sporadic fighting broke out in Lebanon. The U.S.A. started to ship arms to Beirut.

Iraq was vital to Nasser. With a population of 40 million Arabs living in 2 million square miles, Iraq is flanked by the Islamic states of Turkey (25.5 million), Iran (19.7 million) and Pakistan (84 million). It borders the Persian (Arabian) Gulf giving direct access to the Suez Canal. Iraq's riches are represented by "black gold," the oil which gave 700,000 barrels in 1958. Nasser has called oil "the sinew of material civilization without which all its machines would cease to function.[4]

On June 28, Nasser together with his wife and children, his aides and some friends sailed away from Alexandria on the presidential yacht, *El Houriah* (Freedom), for a 15 day holiday trip to Tito's Yugoslavia. He had had additional radio equipment installed on board the yacht, six extra radio operators had been added to the crew. Direct radio contact was maintained with Cairo, Amman, Beirut, Damascus, and Baghdad. London, Paris, and Tel Aviv were constantly monitored. The stage was set.

At 5 o'clock A.M., July 14, Major General Abdul Karim el-Kassem led a revolutionary army into Baghdad as it slept in tranquillity lit by the first yellow rays of morning sunlight. The take-over was swift, silent, and complete. One by one, the railroad station, the post and telegraph offices, the radio station, and all main intersections were occupied. Then Kassem headed for Faisal's palace. Faisal and his uncle, Crown Prince Abdul Illah, were up early that morning. They had shaved, washed, dressed, breakfasted, and packed their papers in preparation for a flight to Istanbul for an emergency meeting of

4 *Op. cit.* p. 106.

the Baghdad Pact members. The timing was perfect. Faisal and Abdul Illah were dressed for death.

Kassem and his soldiers made short work of it all. Both princes were shot then and there together with Abdul Illah's mother, two nurses, and two palaces guards. The palace was looted. Abdul's body was thrown out the window and dragged through the streets, then strung up naked in public. Faisal's was wrapped in a carpet, smuggled out secretly, and buried in obscurity. The next day, Nuri es-Said was captured as he was trying to escape disguised as a woman. He was stripped naked, impaled alive on a pole and left to rot in the fetid noonday July heat. Kassem proclaimed a treaty of defense with Nasser.

On this same July 14, an aide entered Nasser's stateroom aboard the *Houriah* in the early morning, shook him by the shoulder until he awoke (Nasser sleeps very heavily), and communicated to him the latest reports. Only the date was news to Nasser. All else he knew. On July 15, the U.S. Sixth Fleet put Marines ashore in Lebanon. The United Kingdom flew two crack paratrooper battalions into Jordan. Nasser flew from Yugoslavia to Moscow to confer with Premier Khrushchev, then flew back to Cairo and Damascus. "Let us thank Allah," he told the jubilant crowds in Damascus, "that our holy march is going from victory to victory." One important segment of the Arab Circle was now within his grasp.

"We cannot go back to the tenth century," wrote Nasser in his *Philosophy of the Revolution,* "we cannot wear its clothes, which appear strange and exotic to our eyes, and we cannot become lost in its thoughts, which now appear to us as layers of darkness without any ray of light." [5] This sums up the dilemma of Nasser and Islam. But it underscores the difficulty both have in maintaining the traditional Islamic two-level vision of human history.

According to traditional Islam, Nasser should not make treaties with the Soviet Union, which is professionally atheistic, materialistic, and infidel. He should not sign any treaty at all which is not guaranteed by the sacred law of *Shari'a.* Nor should he accept aid in the form of personnel or money or arms from Soviet Russia or, for that matter, from the West. Nor should he decorate the graves of two arch-infidels such as Stalin and Lenin. Nor should he have a secular parliament, a national constitution drawn up, as it is, on Western models.

[5] *Op. cit.* p. 83.

Nor should he have invaded an Arab country such as Yemen with an army of 40,000 and with his air force: Muslims can make war only when attacked. Yemen did not attack Egypt. Nor should he plot the downfall of any Muslim ruler, much less that of the Prophet's descendants. One could extend this list.

But Nasser has found that classical Islam is incompatible with the exigencies of a modern constitutional state, and certainly irreconcilable with the conditions of a modern dictator bent on acquiring new territories and fresh channels of power. Nasser is bluntly honest about this failure of Islam. Islam presents the annual pilgrimage, the *Hajj*, as a sacred duty which guarantees entry to Paradise. "Our view of the Pilgrimage must change," wrote Nasser, "it should not be regarded as only a ticket of admission to Paradise after a long life, or as a means of buying forgiveness after a merry one. It should become an institution of great political power and significance . . . as a periodic political conference in which the envoys of Islamic states can meet in order to lay down in this Islamic-world-parliament the broad lines of their national politics and their pledges of mutual cooperation from one year to another." [6]

There is here a complete shift away from the two-level view of history always professed by Islam. No longer is the world divided into Islamic and non-Islamic believers synonymously understood with good and evil. No longer are all human events a mere shadow-play of invisible realities in an invisible world. Nasser's viewpoint is a hard-headed, rationalistic one worthy of any Western or Asiatic ruler.

The cycle of decadence is thus completed. The terms, the phraseology, and the concepts customary in Islam are found on Nasser's lips: "Allah," "our creed," "the mercy of Allah," "our glorious faith," and so on. He still utilizes the traditional binary concepts of light and darkness, right and left, high and low. Yet their fundamental connotation has been changed. The final passage in *Philosophy of the Revolution* is revealing:

> When I consider the 80 million Muslims in Indonesia, and the 50 million in China, and the millions in Malaya, Siam and Burma, and the nearly 100 million in Pakistan, and the more than 100 million in the Middle East, and the 40 million in the Soviet Union together with the other millions in far-flung parts

[6] *Op. cit.* p. 112 ff.

of the world—when I consider these hundreds of millions united by a single creed, I emerge with a sense of the tremendous possibilities which we might realize through the cooperation of all these Muslims, a cooperation going not beyond the bounds of their natural loyalty to their own countries, but nonetheless enabling them and their brothers in faith to wield power wisely and without limit.[7]

Terms used here by Nasser such as "creed," "brothers in faith," must be understood without any reference to the classical idea of the supernatural and the invisible world. They refer analogously to what people in Europe and the U.S.A. call the European or the American "way of life."

The motives for the two assassinations are, therefore, quite different. Yet, the language used by Nasser in describing the policy of his personal dictatorship, his nationalistic revivalism, and his defense of the slow undermining of other Islamic governments is sprinkled with traditional words, epithets, and thoughts of Islam. The death of Faisal II was, according to him and his propagandists, the necessary removal of an obstacle on the road of the Islamic nations to their historic destiny.

Nasser, however, as we have seen, wishes in no way to be bound by the ethico-moral sanctions of that Islam or to bow to the theological beliefs of its classical formulas. He has found these unworkable in modern national and international society. As in the ·cases of Pius XII and David Ben-Gurion, their classical worlds do not function today. But the ancient concepts and terminology of those worlds are used by all three.

23. *The Crisis of Dominance*

We have seen in the first three chapters of this section the "official" language and conceptuology that are promoted by classical Judaism, Christianity, and Islam. All three claim to move on the plane of super-history. Concepts and language are geared to that plane. On the other hand, in another three chapters, we have examined the concrete decisions which some of

[7] *Op. cit.* p. 113-14.

their important participants took in three distinct cases. The hard historical realities and their behavior have been noted: these latter-day decisions are not compatible with that official dominance. All three have opted for an ethical behavior that would not be tolerated in the classical periods of each religion; it cannot be reconciled with some fundamental tenets of these religions.

Thus a disconcerting gap appears. Why this gap? At first, when we seek the reason, we hit our heads only against hard realities: Pius XII's desire for survival (personal survival, perhaps; collective Catholic survival, certainly); Mr. Ben-Gurion's need to cope with the harsh reality of reoccupying a contested territory with international legal status; Colonel Nasser's desire to control Iraq.

In these three historical examples there has been a failure. The religious dominance of each did not function as expected. How must we judge this condition of religious dominance? There is no possibility of judging it or assessing its latter-day weakness, unless we see it within the tangible framework of living society. For in the abstract the claimant of religious dominance displays a certain winsomeness.

When described in a book or explained by a professional teacher, the triple dominance of Judaism, Christianity, and Islam can appear attractive and noble. All three foreswear evil of all kind. They profess a desire for men's happiness now and in the hereafter. All three laud peace and mercy, gentleness and humility. They profess to seek no riches, no power, no influence. They claim to aid the spirit of man, to enlighten it, to ennoble it, to bring it to final perfection, even though in the individual history of each religion we do not find that their effect on human society has always corresponded to these principles and proposals.

We can be momentarily mesmerized by the abstract claims of such religious dominance. Its claimant can sound so secure and so objective. He announces an ancient message from beyond the stars amongst the sticks and stones of this aging world, saying in effect: "I have the true and the only religion and explanation of all. All other men should adhere to my beliefs. No situation can arise in space or time which would be irreconcilable with my doctrine concerning the ultimate reality of man's existence, which would not be under the control of my ultimate reality, and, therefore, under my control in a certain real sense."

It is immediately obvious that those typical expressions of religious dominance can imaginably issue from other lips: a military conqueror, a dictator, a Nietzschean individualist, an overman of 19th century German pragmatism. The winsomeness can give way to less attractive accents, and the song of dominance can be heard sometimes with an ominous note, as in the *Internationale* chanted by the Bolsheviks in the glare of Kerensky's rifles; sometimes with an overwhelming pathos and appalling non-violence, as from the gas chambers of Dachau, Belsen, Buchenwald, and Auschwitz; sometimes with the note of twisted righteousness, as in the motto engraved on the belt buckles of the Nazi S.S. man: *Gott mit uns*. Its irreverence can sometimes be almost comical as in the dying words of Narvaez when asked by his confessor if he had forgiven all his enemies: "I have no enemies, Father; I had them all shot." It can be frightening, as in Stalin's words to Churchill who included the Vatican of Pius XII as a factor to be reckoned with: "How many divisions has the Pope got?" It was persistently winsome, perhaps, in Pacelli's later rejoinder: "Tell my son, Joseph, that he will meet my divisions in eternity."

At all events, the situation concerning dominance is a concrete historical one. The problems which trouble us about human dominance in general are always concrete ones driven deep into the stuff and matter of man's earth and man's historical dreams. Hence, while being a useful mental tag for categorizing academically and intellectually a disturbing phenomenon, the term dominance must be seen in its hard realities. We do not see dominance rampant in the visible world; we can, nevertheless, see its effects. We cannot trace on the lineaments of man's face the dominance-trait; we can, however, reason out its existence within him.

To speak intelligibly about the general dominance-trait in man, we must speak of its effects and then probe, with the aid of research, into the nature and the force of that trait. These effects are perceptible realities that characterize man as an individual and as a social animal, as a spirit roving in the realms of imagination and the gleaming light of creativeness, and as a bundle of physical and physiological needs, demands, exigencies, and possibilities. They involve psyche and organism, soul and body. Any attempt, therefore, to understand or grapple with the dominance problem exclusively on one or the other plane (psyche *or* body) is bound for shipwreck.

The paradigm of dominance, therefore, is a multi-level framework. The problem of dominance is the problem of equilibrium between competing elements within that framework. The framework is the multi-level society of man. The competing elements are many, but they all have one specific identity: each element is a *capacity* of societal man. And every one of these capacities has many facets: need, desire, hope, force, want, deficiency.

Each individual member of society is a walking armory of such capacities. Each sub-group in any given society is not merely the sum total of all the capacities to be found in the individuals which compose it. The synergism of combined capacities is at work here, so that $2 + 2 = 4 +$, not merely 4. Each given major society within the whole human society is another synergistic composite, but its magnitude is, again, not to be measured as the sum total of the various individual societies of which it is composed. It is synergetically so much more. Singly and by themselves, individual men, sub-groups, individual societies, and the society of man as a whole, are thus synergistic circles of capacities, making up the framework within which we see the effects of dominance and try to identify its source.

The problem of human dominance is, as noted above, the problem of equilibrium between all the capacities of man as a societal individual. We referred to these capacities as "competing elements." Each capacity strung out along the circles of human society is, by definition, a "perfectibility," a possibility of "betterment" in man. Each capacity can translate itself alternately into the deficiency and need and hope of what is necessary for life at various levels, into the desire for "more" of what man already has, into the insistent command-desire to have all possible fulfillment of a capacity or of capacities.

A discussion of the dominance-trait within this framework and merely as a human trait suffers in the present state of human knowledge from a vast lack: we do not know either the cause, the nature, or the function of the human dominance-trait. We only know of its existence from its effects; these effects have been noticeable since man emerged from the darkness of prehistory.[1] In its simplest and most innocuous form, the dominance-trait is most noticeable in the congenital competitiveness of man. Societal man competes by his very nature. Competition is used here in its broadest sense: competition with nature to offset its disadvantages, to exact a more satisfying result from it than it would spontaneously give; competition with one's neighbors, one's fellow-citizens, one's family, one's fellow-countrymen, to better oneself. Competition implies a desire to be better. To be better implies someone who is to this extent dominated. Competition, therefore, implies a dominance-trait and a dominance-effect.

Because all men are not born with equal powers and qualities, a continuous sifting and shifting takes place: the Alphas come to the fore, the Betas, the Gammas, and the remainder fall into their due place. There is no sub-group, group, or society born that does not give further birth to Alphas. There has thus arisen in all forms of organized human society known to us a system of rights and duties, privileges and sanctions, their development, their restriction, their mutual warring, and accommodations.

The entire economic-financial and political structure of the Western democracies is built today on the validity of the competitive principle. In the next section, we will note that it is impossible in our present stage of knowledge to state to what degree the competitiveness characteristic of the Western democracies is due to a congenital dominance-trait of man, or is in greater part due to the basic Jewish and Christian doctrine concerning the perfectibility of man. Both religions teach that man is placed on earth to better himself, that the earth itself can be better, indeed that it will be bettered and perfected "at the end of days." Neither Islam nor the Indic or Sinic

[1] Lacking above all is an exact knowledge of the relevancy of the various sciences to each other in the quest for roots of human dominance. While general clearing-houses for inter-disciplinary relevance exist, there is no means at present of knowing how two sciences, for example, working along parallel lines could be made to cooperate and collaborate in order to fix with precision the nature and extent of the human dominance-trait. The relation of religion and mental health does receive some attention, but efforts have not been made to focus resources on dominance. A good deal of preliminary work is being done by Robert Ardrey in the field of palaeontology and prehistory. We have yet to bridge the rather specific gap that lies between the animal kingdom and man.

civilizations of the Far East ever developed the same socio-political ideas and practices as the West.

Competitiveness is one thing, however. As such, it does denote a benevolent dominance-trait; its dominance-effects are benign and beneficial. When these are malevolent and undermine the acknowledged rights of man, then competitiveness is rightly said to denote a malevolent dominance-trait.

History teaches us, however, that the framework of human society, as man has hitherto known it, apparently possesses no automatic principle of equilibrium between the elements. In human society and its various parts, there is no categoric imperative automatically stopping one capacity from strangling another. No inherent operative law backed up by powerful sanctions is detectable that hinders men from exceeding their own rights, violating their duties, and infringing on the rights of others. Societal man has not even succeeded in agreeing what all the fundamental rights and duties of men are and how they are to be interpreted. Man's various capacities are not hindered by an irresistible voice of nature, by any voice at all. The total equilibrium of societal framework is, therefore, beset by this problem.

Two main conclusions follow from this. Simple competition, which does not mean the infringement of rights or the abandonment of duties, is as connatural to man as the capacity to think. Man is a competing being. On the other hand, all the malevolent effects of dominance imply a violation of rights of others. Now the fundamental question confronting man on the threshold of the 21st century is: how can he prevent the malevolent effects of dominance? What is malevolent dominance and in what does it differ from benign dominance (or competition)?

As pointed out, we lack the scientific knowledge of man as a psycho-physical composite to pursue the discussion of dominance as a fundamental human trait any further beyond this point. Recent literature on this subject is either unenlightening or hampered by unscientific presuppositions. The work of Lorentz, for instance, suffers from the prior and unwarranted exclusion of any religious reality.[2] It is a presupposition of his thinking and conclusions; it invalidates both. Koestler in his *The Ghost in the Machine* builds his thesis on the neurophysical

[2] Particularly his book *On Aggression* (translated by Marjorie Kerr Wilson. Harcourt, Brace and World, Inc., New York, 1966).

theories of Paul McLean concerning the "three-brain" condition of man,[3] and concludes that, since the basis of malevolent dominance is physiological, what man needs is something in the nature of a "peace-pill," a serum of some sort, that would affect the malevolent dominance-trait. Koestler has the same crippling presuppositions as Lorentz, apart from being overshadowed by the unexplored terrors of dominance which the possessor of such a peace-pill or serum could wreak on men.[4]

The religious dominance of Judaism, Christianity, and Islam supplied three age-old answers to this problem. Judaism teaches that man has, since the disobedience of Adam and Eve in the Garden of Eden, two inclinations in his heart: one good and one evil. Malevolent dominance is the evil inclination of man's heart. Christianity has developed its very essential doctrine of Original Sin: the sin of Adam and Eve entailed for all men a loss of spiritual strengths and qualities by which they could have avoided all sin, especially sins of malevolent dominance. Islam adopted more or less the doctrine of Judaism with some slight modifications. All three religions would offer one type of remedy: spiritual reform of man's habits. Man must accept the total explanation offered by one of the religions, accepting thereby the moral code of that religion. That moral code imposes duties and sanctions and clearly teaches a man his rights.

When we examine Judaism, Christianity, and Islam we find that they are impeded in two ways from being able to cope with the dominance-trait of man: their structure emphasizes the dominance-trait rather than sublimating, transforming, or getting rid of it; they have, as a consequence, fallen into what appears to be an insoluble historical difficulty.

First as to their structural difficulty. We have noted that all three religions look on the world in a bipolar fashion: their world is polarized, and the religions used the dialectic of opposites—their basic binarism—to express this bipolarity. In all their internal and external manifestations, this bipolarity held a prime position and produced the system of absolutes: their individual ideals were absolutely good, the opposite is absolutely evil; their guarantee of salvation was absolutely sure, the guarantee of any other system was absolutely unsure;

[3] *The Ghost in the Machine*, Macmillan, New York, 1957.
[4] A further consideration of such presuppositions is in the next section when discussing religion.

their god was absolute good, the opposite or opposing element was absolutely evil.

The religions, therefore, installed at the heart of their individual systems the basis for a tension and a contradiction: the absolute perfection demanded of their adherents and the tag of absolute evil pinned to its contrary evoked necessarily a series of revolts out of which sprang new polarizations, each claiming—in imitation of the original—to be the final absolute, the absolutely absolute. Jewish, Christian, and Islamic morality thus could father violent excesses of moral passion which, of course, automatically, became excesses of human immorality.

Judaism and Christianity, therefore, schooled the West in essential divisiveness for over 1700 years. Islam schooled the Arabs and the non-Arab Islamic nations in the same bipolarity for the best part of 1400 years. Small wonder, then, is it that today none of the three religions, as originators and perpetuators of dominance, have a satisfactory answer for man's problems, and all are increasingly irrelevant for their solution. This crisis of their dominance is also, as remarked before, aggravated by a historical difficulty flowing directly from the above.

The historical difficulty into which all three religions have fallen is a big one: man as a whole has not accepted any of the three explanations offered by these religions. Man has not, therefore, accepted the ethical teaching concerning the "evil in man's heart," and he does not, as a consequence, submit to the duties and sanctions imposed by any one of the religions. Man it appears, does not accept either the explanation or ethical teaching because the religious dominance of these religions does not appear to function.

In Mr. Ben-Gurion's case, the ancient claim on God's protection did not seem adequate to keep Egyptian planes on the ground and Arab armies in their barracks, or to stave them off if they did attack. U.N. recognition, reliance on a historical right, and Jewish arms, these seemed and were adequate. In Pacelli's case, the clear moral protest was considered dangerous and inefficient. Avoidance of the issue and the destruction of Jews, so that time could be bought, were deemed safe and effective expedients. In Colonel Nasser's case, Faisal's view of Islam did not include the Colonel as the hero taking on the historical role of Islam's leader; but Islam itself would not remove Faisal II. Bullets did.

The men in question realized this. In order to attain their

objectives, they simply acted as if their traditional dominance vision did not exist. The religious absolutism of that dominance held no sway. It did not function. On the other hand, these three protagonists continued to use the language and, as far as one can judge, think the thoughts of dominance. There is thus a confusion of functions. The old absolutism functions as a mode of thought and a type of language; in the concrete order decisions are taken that are out of kilter with that order.

In other words, for all three, the ancient framework of dominance was no longer operative. We connot impugn the Jewishness of Mr. Ben-Gurion, the Catholicism of Pius XII, or the Islam of Colonel Nasser. Such moral judgments concern the inner thoughts and motives of each person; we cannot make such judgments. We can say that the ancient framework, in the eyes of all three, did not apply, that it was irrelevant. This irrelevancy was felt and accepted by all three.

History does teach us that the world of Solomon (10th century B.C.), of Leo the Great (5th century A.D.), and of Khalif Othman (7th century A.D.) differed radically from our 20th century in this one respect: then religious motives were operative (in Attila and Leo, in Solomon and his Jewish contemporaries, in Othman and his assassins), no matter what motives of ambition, jealousy, pride, and cruelty also held sway.

In the world of Ben-Gurion, Pacelli, and Nasser, religion and religious motives held no sway over important domains of man's social and individual life. All three men had to grapple with the solid reality of such domains: religious dominance, seemingly, had no place, no function, no acceptability, and no convenience therein.

A similar judgement imposes itself concerning Paul VI's visit to the United Nations, where he did not preach the Christian message as such; he made oblique references to it; his main assertion was a re-affirmation of the United Nations organization as the only means by which modern man could avoid catastrophe. But Paul, as a Christian, is not alone in this position. No Christian of whatever denomination and no Jew or Muslim has ever proposed to the United Nations Organization that it seriously consider his religious system and its sociopolitical system as the solution to the problems besetting both the United Nations Organization and its member-nations. Inherently, there is a universal agreement that none of the religions has an applicable solution.

The answer, therefore, to our original question as to why religious dominance has failed and why it has no relevancy for the problems that agonize the present-day world, must be sought in that world: some radical change differentiates it from the world in which these religions arose and flourished so long and so abundantly.

The raw fatality of the modern encounter becomes clearer to us in this light. Modern man does not even cling to ancient formulas and thus face his fate, as one eyewitness describes a Jewish father standing at the entrance of the gas-chambers of Auschwitz and pointing to heaven to remind the son in his arms that it was up there they were going. He accepts no florid dedication to the Bull-God that will condemn him to wander insanely in an underground labyrinth until death overtakes him. He rejects the explanations offered by religion, and cannot therefore cast over the frightening array of his problems any veil of intelligibility by using binary concepts or a two-level view of history. All that he rejects. He has made his way laboriously through the forest of such explanations, rites, formulas, thought-molds. All such faith is behind him. He has bound himself by no contract with a remote and salvific god. Man's power is in him, in all men. Life is this power. Man's faith is in this life. Man's hope extends as far as the grave, the endless succession of graves. Man's love is governed, not by that volatile thing called conscience or that nebulous thing called belief, but by the sure norm of eternal law. Man's speech to god is best expressed in the words used by Matsoukas in Harry Mark Petrakis' book *A Dream of Kings:* "Heaven has become for you a shadowed cavern of emptiness and longing. Your glory has departed. May man have mercy on you."

Thus the societal framework of modern man is undergoing a series of stresses and strains unprecedented in the known history of man. The head-on collision and encounter taking place sometimes elicit the reaction that deep in man's nature there is some obscure need in man to hate; man satisfies this need by venting his passions on his fellow-man. Most observers agree that the crisis concerns man's relation to this fellow-men, and that this relationship is severely disturbed if not distorted by the dominance-trait of man. We have concluded already that the misery of religious dominance today is that it seems powerless to intervene: its own explanation of man's condition is not acceptable; men have refused its control.

This conclusion brings us back to the crisis in these three religions that has been mentioned previously. The crisis is nowhere more vividly seen than in the apparently increasing irrelevance of these religions for the solution of present-day problems. All three claim to be most relevant. This is the claim of their dominance. They are, however, very ineffectual and their solutions for these problems are not even considered seriously. This is radically different from past ages when the religious factor played such a role. Something must have changed. Some mechanism in that former world no longer functions.

We know that the religions themselves have not changed very radically. We know, on the other hand, that the world has undergone a vast and profound change, and that this change is still in process. In order, therefore, to assess the irrelevancy of these religions and ultimately to measure their dominance-traits against their essential message, we must now examine the conditions and the trends of the present change.

Book Three

THE HUMAN
ENVIROMENT

Introduction

When we examine the modern environment of man in which
Judaism, Christianity, and Islam find themselves, it is abundantly clear that these three religions are finished as major influences. As predominant systems of thought, worship, ethical
inspiration, and of judgment on human affairs, they are excluded forever from human affairs. But they will not perish
overnight. They will persist in some parts of the planet with
diminishing influence, dwindling numbers, and changing faces.
They will undergo periodic petty renaissances and sporadic
revivals. They will resist the threat of extinction as dominant
mysteries with all the resources at their power and with the
desperation of all ancient experienced things at bay and staring
at death. Under this threat they may yet render invaluable services to man. They may go protestingly. They may depart with
dignity. They will certainly pass with pathos; and their nod-
ding fall into eternal slumbers will needle the human mind with

nostalgia. But, as they are, their dominance is finished forever. Their day is done.

All three have deserved well of mankind at one time or another, in one area or another, for one reason or another. All three produced saints and sinners, triumphs of the spirit and tyrannies of the body and mind. All three sanctified and desecrated men alternately. All had vast plans, ennobling thoughts, terrible excesses of cruelty, and gestures of great love. They fomented memorable acts of human betrayal and magnificent moments of heroism. There is no sky around man's planet under which they did not labor, just as there are very few flags behind which they have not marched, just as there is no century since their birth in which they have not been loved ardently for the beauty in them and hated fiercely for their inhumanity to man. All three made fateful and fatal choices at the one priceless moment that history afforded them. And all three are paying the price levied by the logic of that history. For history never forgives and never forgets.

But their decadence, decomposition, and death today are about to be the saddest part of their story. Nothing so unbecomes them as the manner of their going. They are going because they failed to do the one thing they promised to do: explain man to man, unwrap the riddle in his need to hate, show him he is brother at one and the same time to all men and to the angels. They failed to save him from the evil in him. Their claim of dominance is refuted by cold facts. No one will bother to liquidate them by shedding blood or to insure their end by choking off the means of breathing life. They will not perish in a vast religious persecution. The cosmos itself provides the Great Leveler of Greek tragedy, Time, who will do them to death. Like old men, blind to the obstacles over which they stumble and break brittle bones, deaf to warning voices around them, too weak of limb to reach for fresh support or restoring means, they are slipping into the vast, silent underworld of shades, and they too, will be remembered as fallible things and additional arguments for the inevitable mortality of all humanity.

The writ of their passing from among the sons of men is brief but telling. Their claims to explain all and therefore dominate all were tied to certain explanations of man and of his cosmos: they claimed to provide concepts and words to express those concepts. With both, man could think, they said, in an intelligible framework and speak intelligibly about that framework. They even imposed both words and conceptuology with absolute authority. Today, they provide modern man with neither an intelligible framework nor an acceptable language about that framework or the grand design of religious salvation they claimed to announce. Desuetude cripples their proposed framework. Ineptitude strangles their words. The environment of man has changed. The heart of their dominance has been torn from them.

The central weakness of these religions today, as we pointed out, lies in their growing irrelevancy for modern life. Once upon a time they exercised absolute dominance, at least for their adherents. They offered explanations which were received as authoritative. They elaborated these explanations into socio-political institutions where at all possible. Bit by bit, and decade by decade, their hold on men's minds and lives is diminishing. We find, on careful scrutiny, that it is fundamentally their explanations which are found wanting. They propose a way to think and speak about man's world which man cannot accept. He cannot accept it because in some cases it is out of tune with what man knows as certainly as he knows anything; and in other cases the words and concepts used in the explanations are unintelligible to modern man. In the end, the explanations themselves are unintelligible. If unintelligible, they are inapplicable. They are irrelevant.

This lack of intelligibility and its consequent irrelevance affect not merely peripheral elements of the religions but the very stuff and matter out of which the religions are made. The garments are not merely worn and outmoded. The bodies themselves are effete and aged, beyond apparent hope of recall to youth and vigor. In the next chapters, we will examine those essential elements of the religions which are unintelligible. It must be noted that very often this lack of intelligibility arises, not precisely because the concepts are old, but because they reflect a mentality which has been rejected by modern man, and because they no longer correspond to the realities with which modern man must cope.

In later chapters, we will consider the religious consensus which these three religions affected among men. The paradigm or ground-plan of any human consensus is first of all examined. Then the basic consensus of the three religions is discussed, and it is concluded that this basic consensus is unworkable today. Instead man is indulging in another form of "getting-together" which is best described as anti-consensus. It is a "getting-together," but the principles of that togetherness exclude explicitly the type of consensus which the three religions advocate.

We then examine the crisis of dominance in Judaism, Christianity, and Islam in the light of the foregoing. The dominance of each religion, besides being beset by the common problem outlined above, suffers from particular strains and pains of its own. Judaism and Christianity resemble each other on many points of pain and setback; but Judaism suffers from internal polarization, and Christianity suffers from a prolonged insistence on being what it need not be. Islam is apart. Still trussed and strait-jacketed in outworn ways and inept approaches to the 20th century world, Islam's agony is what Christianity might have suffered between the 10th and 12th centuries A.D.: total inability even to grapple with its circumambient world. For while Judaism and Christianity are at grips with their world but losing steadily, Islam has never even started, and is in danger of cultural and civilizational mummification.

In actual fact, Christianity and, to a lesser degree, Judaism directly formed the consensus of the West such as man has known it for over eight hundred years. If now we conclude that the consensus is for all intents and purposes negligible, what is to happen or what is happening to the consensus of the West? This is the final pathos of Christianity and Judaism. They can do nothing and are allowed to do nothing really effective, either to mend the fragmented consensus of the past or contribute mightily and preponderantly to the formation of a new consensus.

None of this material and none of the conclusions at which this study arrives are meant to function as either firm prophecies of doom or solid promises of perpetuity. If, at times, it is suggested that any religion cannot survive or that its concepts are unintelligible, this is said in view of the present form in which the religion appears or the current formulation which it gives of its particular concepts. To state that a concept or an idea is unintelligible, is not to state that the reality which men have tried to express in that concept has no validity. Our concept of God may be unintelligible. God may, nevertheless, exist.

PART VI

Brothers of the Boulders

24. *Truth and Reality*

The world into which Judaism, Christianity, and Islam were singly and separately born had no acquaintance either with the intellectual method of modern scientific inquiry or with the underlying ideas of truth and reality which the modern scientific mind takes for granted. Even history, the earliest of social studies and the one subject which the ancients could have treated scientifically, lacked in their hands the characteristics it receives from today's historians and historiographers. The condition of human knowledge between 1200 B.C. and 600 AD. can be rightly seen as a myth-faring condition. The term *myth* must be understood as a technical term: *myth* is a mode of expressing one's actual and true thoughts, beliefs, impressions, and not as a simple fable concocted by the imagination with no basis in reality.

From the comparative history of myths throughout the world it is clear that certain identical and fundamental mythical themes are to be found in many lands. Such themes are: the Creation of the World, the Creation of Man, a cataclysmic Deluge, the origin of Death, the End of the World, the Hero myth, the Satan myth, and so on. These are found in geographically distinct areas between which we cannot postulate any direct relationship. The significant trait of these myths as they appear in regional versions is their plasticity.

There is, for instance, an old androgynous myth according to which there were neither males nor females originally but merely one being; this one being was split in two: hence the male and female. This myth reappears in a Greek form in Plato's *Symposium* where Diotima uses it to account for sexual love: the two halves are always seeking their former union. It reappears in the Hebrew Bible, where the writer uses it to express the equality of men and women.[1] Many examples can be adduced to demonstrate this plasticity of the myth. The fact is that the pre-scientific ancients could take such myths and model them to their beliefs.

In primitive times and later in historical times, man always sought to construct a framework of reality, to express the truth about the world which he saw around him. His constructions always went beyond while including the visible and tangible things of his cosmos. In such a cosmos the explanation of anything was not sought in the thing itself. Between 600 B.C. and 1600 A.D., when various technologies were developed and a start toward a scientific analysis was made, the ultimate truth and reality of all material things were sought, not in the things themselves, but "outside" them, "above" them. The pre-Renaissance world was thus a "vertical" world: every object from man to atoms was a pointer, up and away from the material surroundings to an invisible world.

Put simply, the reason "why" things were what they were and acted as they acted was sought elsewhere than in the objects themselves. There was very little, if any, extensive and

---

[1] Cf. *Genesis* 2:18-25. The word *"sela"* has been traditionally translated as "rib." It seems, however, that the word means one complementary part or half of a whole, like one "panel" of a pair of double-doors or swinging-doors. Thus, the woman's substance is equal to, and the same as, the man's, according to the Biblical text: she is identical with him as a complementary half. The text of Genesis (v. 24) concludes: "that is why a man is destined to leave father and mother, and cling to his wife instead, so that *the two become one flesh.*"

systematic inquiry as to how things became, and were what they were, and how they acted. A hierarchic world and cosmos resulted. All the religions, Judaism, Christianity, and Islam, placed man at the center of this hierarchic arrangement. Man, in Bossuet's words, was the pontiff of creation. He lived amongst animals, plants, things, all of which flung harmonious melodies up beyond the veil of matter to the invisible cause and origin of it all, a creative god.

It is an essential trait of these religions to maintain that neither the "why" nor the "what" nor the "how" of anything can be understood fully and really except by reference to their "outer" and "supernal" explanation: the Jewish, the Christian, or the Muslim god. Since the Renaissance, not merely has technology developed by huge leaps and bounds, but a scientific revolution has taken place. Some wrongly confine this to the chemist's test-tube, the geologist's hammer, the psychiatrist's couch. Actually, it affects modern man more fundamentally. For modern man's idea of truth and reality has thereby become totally different from that of pre-Renaissance man.

In pre-Renaissance and pre-scientific times, truth, as an expression of reality, was considered to be found in a series of propositions which satisfied logic and fed the intellect. They were philosophically logical and intellectually satisfying. Since the advent of the scientific method, truth, as an expression of reality, is considered to be found uniquely in the faithful and scrupulously accurate description of natural phenomena: men, animals, plants, inanimate matter, forces. The refocusing of the source of truth is obvious: it is to be sought and found in the physical construction and accustomed mode of action observable in all things which people man's cosmos.

In her collection of poems *Huntsman, What Quarry?*, Edna St. Vincent Millay vividly describes man in the middle of the things of his world:

> *Upon this gifted age, in its dark hour*
> *Falls from the sky a meteoric shower*
> *of facts . . . they lie unquestioned, uncombined,*
> *Wisdom enough to leech us of all our ill*
> *Is daily spun; but there exists no loom*
> *To weave it into fabric.*

Modern man is intent on weaving this fabric from the facts and things of his world. From them he forms an image of space and a concept of time. He develops notions of man, of people as a whole, of the organization which binds them together, and of the events which, while involving them all, transcend them all and move man and his world on in an irreversible flow. He thus forms his ideas of truth and reality.

Every object has an explanation in itself and in so far as that self by its matter and action is related to other material objects. Man's cosmos is now strewn with objects which carry their own explanation—their "why"—within them at arm's reach of man, if he but search, analyze, study. Each object con-validates its own existence. It is self-validating, self-explana-tory. It needs no "outside" or supernal explanation. The truth about its reality can be known by knowing the object inti-mately. Man's world is no longer a "vertical" one in which each object is, as it were, a Gothic spire, shooting up symmet-rically and hierarchically past the heavens, pointing to the ultimate and invisible ground of truth in an invisible world. No invisible world parallels this visible world of man.

Man's world is a "horizontal" world. Objects are either hooded domes to be prised open by man's curious and tireless fingers so that he may examine the entrails of its reality; or they open onto long corridors along which man must walk with painstaking care noting all the details and guide-lines, thus arriving at understanding the cosmic order and the "horizontal" brother-hood of all things. We are brothers of the boulders. We have no longer a hierarchy in the universe. We have an organization.

Every object which man examines and accounts for in his universe is ultimately seen as part of the total environmental system in which man lives. This environmental system man explores with what he calls an equal system approach. He finds that he is ignorant about many problems in his universe. It may be the effect of solar flares on the weather of Earth, or the way in which cosmic rays enter the Earth's atmosphere, or the 10 per cent increase of carbon dioxide in the Earth's atmos-phere over the last 100 years. He organizes, so to speak, his ignorance about these and multiple other problems, breaking it down into every possible subdivision, and then tackling each one of these problematic segments. Once he solves the problem of any particular segment, then he organizes this partial solu-tion with the other partial solutions into the general plan of his knowledge. In this way he proceeds laboriously and by single break-down problems to effect his objective, a total understanding of his universe.

Furthermore, the modern mind has always before it a pragmatic purpose. It is not with abstract contemplation in mind that man surrounds his planet with remote sensing stations, that he bores deep into the earth's surface, that he maps out the ocean floor and proposes to set up permanent observation stations there. Formerly, man used to think that he was in the grip of irreversible processes, that his history was laid out beforehand and was irrevocable. The god or spirit whom he worshipped revealed to him the absolute and immutable truths about this hierarchized cosmos and this inevitable history.

Modern man no longer acts on such a belief. He no longer believes that he is carried along by the stream of history. He wishes to control it, to reverse certain individual processes within that flow of history, to exercise the highest possible degree of societal option, to make the truth of his existence.

Modern man's concept of truth as an expression of reality is, therefore, quite different from the ancient concept proposed by the religions. Reality is not some "outside" and separate order of being which communicates reality to the objects and the contents of earth. If that were so, in order to understand those objects and contents, man would have to understand, at least by knowing, that "outside" reality. This is precisely what the classical doctrine of the three religions hoped to achieve in the "vertical" world. In those conditions, truth as an expression of reality was not merely metaphysical. It had to be the result of a revelation. For what could a man, an earthling, know of the "outside" reality? Hence all knowledge and understanding of things were subjected to the transcendental knowledge supplied by the revelation from on high.

For the modern mind, in the "horizontal" world each object is part of the vast organization that is the universe. Man has a sacred stewardship to discharge in this universe. To discharge it he must combine a thousand sciences and busy himself in the analysis of scores of thousands of practical problems. Only thus can he attain a total understanding and choose the correct way of dealing with his environment.

The results of this modern conception of truth and reality are rich for man's material and sociological progress. For the ancient religions, Judaism, Christianity, and Islam, they are

lethal. Man must jettison a whole gamut of concepts basic to
the beliefs of all three religions. These concepts are essential
for the dominance of these religions. But the dominance flows
away with the rejected concepts. In the next chapter we examine these concepts. But here we must remark that, strictly
speaking, we cannot speak of a "rejection" of these concepts,
except as an afterthought, as a consequence. What has happened partially, and will go on happening to a greater and
more thorough degree, is simply that modern man finds such
basic religious concepts do not work. He finds them unintelligible in the light of what he claims to know for sure from his
science and scientific enquiry. Man finds he has no means of
understanding those concepts of religion. And they do not make
his world and his cosmos more intelligible.

It is here that we notice the difference between this modern construction of truth and reality and the prior construction
of which we have spoken. The latter, as remarked previously,
started off with a mythological basis, developed into an intellectual and logical system always, however, with a mythological basis. The myths were plastic. They could be adopted
to monotheism by the Jews, to polytheism by the Inca, to a
pantheon by the Greeks and Romans, to a postulatory atheism
by late Chinese and Japanese philosophers, to an entire spectrum of outlooks in Congo pygmies, Australian Aborigines,
Norsemen, Mongolians, North-American Indians, Amazonian
primitives, and Celtic Druids.

The modern basis for truth as an expression of reality is not
plastic; it is rigid, unbending, valid in every clime, and unchangeable by human thought and imagination. Laws of
gravity cannot be altered to suit an ethos. The chemical
formula for water remains H_2O, whether it be in the Zambesi,
the Tiber, the Yellow Sea, in the cruets at a Roman Mass, or
washing down an astronaut's meal as he orbits towards the
moon. Hence it is not this scientific basis which is deserted. It
is rather those concepts and ways of thinking of the three
religions which are increasingly found to be irreconcilable with
that basis. Such, unfortunately, are some of their basic
concepts.

More than one eminent scientist and student of man will
emphasize that the modern scientific method tells man *how*
things happen in his world but not *why* they happen. They
will go on to make a distinction between the two views of a

god, the emotional and very personal view, on the one hand, which permits them to believe, and the abstract, general view, on the other hand, which is their rightful title to be called scientists.[2] The two, they maintain, are not irreconcilable or mutually exclusive. Such men bring to this solution the light of a living faith. They furthermore would distinguish their view of such a god on the intellectual level from the preceding views of him: here their concept would be abstract. But the dichotomy between the scientist and the man is really never bridged. For many it becomes a Bridge of Asses. In many cases, when we examine the concept of the emotional and personal view we find that the god in question is not at all extra-cosmic, is in no way outside the cosmos of man taken in its widest and most comprehensive sweep. Such a god is finally understood as an overall stratum of reality capping the visible and measurable reality of the cosmos. He is part of it all. But he is not Yahweh nor Allah nor the god of the Christians.

25. *To Know and Live Forever*

In this chapter, we will examine six concepts basic to the three religions in virtue of which the believer could know how to act in this life so as to merit eternal life after death. These are:

Revelation	Ethical Rules
Permanent Truth	Soul
Personal God	Sin

1. Revelation

Inherent to these religions is the idea of a primordial revelation: Yahweh, God, Allah, chose at a given moment in time to reveal the truth about life and death. In all three religions, this revelation was done through an intermediary (Moses, Jesus, Mohammad), and involved the creation of sacred writings (Old

[2] Cf. for example, Warren Weaver in his *Science and Imagination*. Basic Books Inc. New York, 1967.

Testament, New Testament, Koran). These writings are endowed with an absolute authority and sacrosanct character: Moses received the entire Torah on Mount Sinai from Yahweh; the Christian evangelists and writers were inspired by the Holy Spirit; Mohammad had the Koran dictated to him in Heaven.[1]

Revelation is a traditional religious term for knowledge of a divine kind. By this term, therefore, the three religions describe the way in which the god they worship communicated divine knowledge to mankind or to one part of mankind.

The concept of receiving knowledge through a divine revelation is unintelligible to modern man to whom truth and reality are made known by the scientific method based on the collection of data, the observation of controllable phenomena, and the verification of results by reference to such phenomena. Modern man has no analogue by which he can understand the reception of vital knowledge from a source completely outside his cosmos.

By this it is not meant that such a happening is necessarily impossible, improbable, or historically untrue. What is meant is that the idea of such revelation is unintelligible: modern man has no ready means of understanding it. In the ancient world and the world of Islam, the idea of oracular communications with the world of the divine, the reputation of soothsayers, prophets, seers, and sages, was established beyond all cavil and accepted as an everyday fact of life. True or false, the concepts men easily entertained facilitated the acceptance of the notion of revelation. More than that: men expected such communications and revelations. The idea was, rightly or wrongly, intelligible to them.

The human idea of knowledge always has implied a knower, something which is known, and a means by which that something is made known to the knower. In the modern framework of knowledge, all three have been fundamentally changed from what they were. The knower is no longer a worshipful believer

[1] Both Christianity and progressive Judaism have allowed that the more ancient and rigid doctrines concerning the sacrosanct character of their scriptures were exaggerated and formulated by pre-scientific minds. Not so with Islam. Rare is the Muslim scholar of good standing among Muslims in Muslim lands, who will admit that the text of Koran contains much that is due to merely human ingenuity and weakness. The present onset of Arab nationalism, which has capitalized on Islam, has made it even more difficult for the Muslim scholar to admit to scientific findings in this matter. But this attitude is not of recent vintage.

receiving passively from a source which he reveres. That which is known is not an arcane truth to be had only by the good will and supreme condescension of an independent power on which man depends. The act of knowing is not fraught with either reverence, awe, fear, or unquestioning acceptance. Nor does the power to know depend on some communicated "grace" or spiritual strength which the god grants, again condescendingly and gratuitously.

Man learns from books and machines. He stores his knowledge in libraries, on microfilm and within the miniaturized cells of computers. In 1966 alone, in the U.S.A., over 30,000 computers were operating, processing information for banks, insurance companies, retail stores, airlines, industrial firms, universities, federal agencies, hospitals, medical research centers, the armed forces, laboratories. The imparting and reception of knowledge are being affected by means of computers. Computers design houses, apartments, wallpapers, carpets. It is in the storage and retrieval of knowledge that the computer is becoming supreme. In physics alone, the number of pages printed annually is doubling every ten years. It is impossible for unaided man to keep all such information in order, to digest it, and to have it readily available. The data-search and distribution methods of computers are being tapped in order to solve the problem.

In the formal science of knowing, education, man's idea of knowledge is being affected. Already one group of private schools has established a multimedia center for the transmission of filmed, taped, and televised instruction. The teaching process involves multimedia instant playback of sound or pictures, rapid retrieval, and duplication of information.

Under these developing circumstances, the idea of knowledge is changing rapidly. Before, knowledge was something inaccessible, passed on by knowing beings, the teachers, a sacred thing, from being to being, a conferring of a privilege, a communication. This is changing. Knowledge is not merely considered the due lot of every man and necessary for advancement and personal prosperity. It is now on the human plane not a matter of personal communication but of salaried direction. It is the fulfillment of the learner who reaches for his heritage, and who receives from the non-human sources the elements and facts which teach him what life is all about and what his world means. Within this framework there is very

little, if any, room for the ancient idea of revelation, of apoca-
lypse, of the opening of the veils, of the gift of privileged
knowledge whose validity is not to be questioned and whose
possession warrants the existence of an unseen and all-dominant
world.

The further elaboration of sacred writings as a vehicle or an
organ of revelation is difficult for the modern mind. The book
or the writing was, by its very nature, a privileged thing in the
ancient world. Before the diffusion of books and, especially, of
printed books, men's knowledge came through audio-visual
means. McLuhan has endeavored to measure the drastic
change in man's psychology which frequentation with the
printed word has affected. Essentially, he is correct on this
point: pre-Gutenberg man's psychology was quite different in
its cognitive approach to knowable things. In the ancient world
and primitive societies, such as Mohammad's Arabia, the book
was a thing of mystery: only the few could read it; only a few
books existed, and these possessed secrets which only the initiated could reach and explain.

While Roman Catholic Christianity has sinned less than any
part of Christianity and certainly less than Judaism and Islam,
all three religions maintain the idea of sacred writings as an
integral part of the revelation process. Modern man can recognize as well as any man of any age the inherent ethical beauty
and lofty wisdom of sacred scriptures. But he cannot understand and accept them as the ancients did. The book in general
holds no mystery or awesome quality for him.

2. Permanent Truth

Central to the revelation concept in all three religions is the
notion that the truth revealed to them is permanent, unchangeable, unalterable. Today, the main characteristic of
advancing civilization and the main challenge to human society arise precisely from the never-ending processes of change
which assail man on all sides. In fact, modern man accepts
change in his knowledge and its application as a sign of progress. Man reposes his hope of progress and betterment in such
change. He regards the flux of change as the hallmark of modernity and as being more human than ever. Modern man has
learned to live with ambiguities and tensions arising from this

condition which he daily accelerates more and more. In his building, painting, music, politics, science, he is always looking for other perceptions, other facets, transforming the classic staticism of symmetry and its eternal poise into many-hued motion. Modern man himself, therefore, hangs back from final judgments, from saying definitively "that is that." His direction is not predictable any more than the determinations of his will, any more than the outcome of his actions or his final fate. For all things are possible; a final coherence of all things human; a disintegration of the human fabric; a widening of human freedom and satisfaction to paradisiacal bounds; a closing of responsibilities to the point of puritanism. All is possible, because for him all is changing.

Much has been written about this trait of the modern world. It has been pointed out that the accelerating pace of change is caused both by scientific inquiry and by the constant technological advances registered in almost all fields of human activity. No longer is there any static science which is contemplative, tranquil, immobilized, and leisurely. Day by day, year by year, hundreds of techniques are developed constantly from decades of developing disciplines. The results are channelled down through technicians, planners, manufacturers, communications media, specialists, wholesale and retail intermediaries, educators, teachers, instructors, finally reaching the consumer public. The last, in its millions, produces scores of reactions—physical, moral, intellectual—which in turn provoke chain-reactions throughout the social, economic, and political frameworks of society. Ethical and aesthetic values are thereby affected and modified. Thus the idea of a permanency in truth and in the configuration of reality and man's destiny is not readily accessible to modern man.

Single areas of man's probing give him another idea of truth. He finds that an electron, for instance, is not so much a "thing" as a name or description of a consistent set of things which take place in given conditions. Electrons can be thought of as either waves or particles. The electron cannot be seen or located precisely. This indeterminacy at the heart of nature and this impermanency are basic to physics research. In another direction, the idea of a permanent body of truth is undermined. Scientists can produce "heavy" artificial elements. Such elements are considered to be possible compact, long-lived power supplies for future spacecraft and underwater laboratories, energy sources for artificial organs placed in the body, and radiation sources for medical diagnosis and treatment. New elements such as Plutonium-238, Neptunium-237, and Curium-244 can now be produced as sources of power. The gain in their output, the usefulness, and the stature of such elements, affect man's idea of what is true and what is permanent in his cosmos.

The three religions, however, maintain that they possess an unchangeable body of truths which describe a perdurable and eternal reality and involve the ultimate destiny of man. These notions are not readily intelligible to modern man.

3. *Personal God*

For all three religions, the god whom they worship is a "personal" one. By this term is usually meant that this god is in no way to be conceived as some species of force or presiding influence which exercises no individual care or interest in man, which is incapable of personal thought. "Personal" involves, in its popular concept, the idea of loving and attentive care such as men experience only at the hands of other persons.

An initial difficulty of proper terminology confronts us here. In English, as in all the main Western languages, the word *God* (with capitalized "g") is used in an indiscriminate fashion which we must avoid by some hard and fast rules. First of all, the form *God* is never preceded by the definite article: Western Christians do not say: "I believe in the God," no more than an American would say: "I shall vote for the Richard M. Nixon." For this word *God* in these languages is the equivalent of a personal name and is used in the same way as other personal names (Allah, Yahweh, and so on).

This means that great care must be taken in using the terms *God* and *god*. The first is a personal name; the second is an ordinary noun or substantive. Strictly speaking, therefore, and abstracting from the truth or inaccuracy of the statement, it is illogical and ungrammatical to state: "modern scientists understand *God* as a cosmic force, rather than a personal being." This is as acceptable as saying: "modern classical scholars understand Homer to have been several different people." Both are grammatically untidy and logically false. Homer is a personal name and, in the tradition, implies one person. God is a personal name and has traditionally implied a person. In the second statement, what is meant is that not one person called Homer but several people whose names we do not know, wrote the *Iliad* and the *Odyssey*. If the first statement makes any sense, it means: there is no personal being traditionally known as God; scientists believe that there is merely and really only a cosmic force. Otherwise what was always considered a personal being (God), is identified with what is considered to be impersonal (cosmic force). This identification is annoyingly illogical.

The illogicality becomes confounded more when we find a statement such as: "Peace of mind appeals to me as a rather unpleasant insult of the God of the restless cell . . ." [2] In practical terms, therefore, for our discussions, this means we must only use *God* when speaking of the personal being traditionally worshipped in Christianity who is on a logical par with Yahweh and Allah. Otherwise the simple form *god* must be used. A particular context could require the artificial form "God," to signify that a non-traditional view of *God*, the traditionally supreme being of Christianity, is being advanced.

Alone of all three religions, Christianity had to refine its idea of "person." This happened because of its early fundamental teaching that its god was a trinity of three persons subsisting in one divine nature. Obviously, some rationalization of the notion of "person" was necessary; every person known up to that time to man was tied to one nature. The idea of three persons in one nature required rationalization. But whether we examine the Jewish, the Christian, or Muslim concept of god as a person, all three included in their concept the idea of person as a permanent subsistent, not subject to change, highly individualized.

Modern scientific methods in psychology, psychiatry, and the behavioral sciences have developed a very different notion of person. It arises from the modern scientific method of knowing, which we have described. In this case, the method involves the observation of human acts of will, intellection, memory, emotions. The resultant data present a "person" as a synthesis of various acts and habits, mental, volitional, emotional, and physical. The normal "person" is, of course, a relatively stable synthesis of such acts, so stable that his actions and reactions

[2] Cf. Warren Weaver in *Science and Imagination*, Basic Books Inc. New York 1967, p. 217.

in any given situation can usually be rather accurately predicted. But the "person" in this modern sense remains just a
synthesis of acts which, after all, is subject to change, increase, decrease, and deflection. This is the only concept of
person which the modern mind can understand readily. L. V.
Gordon bases his *Survey of Interpersonal Values* on this concept
of the person, and categorizes the subjects of his examination
into more than fifty clearly identifiable personality groups. The
point Gordon was making concerned the influence of environment or personality. But the concept of person and personality we have outlined is at the base of his work.

Apart from the psychological view of man which the modern
mind has fashioned, the work of modern molecular biologists
raises vital questions affecting our concept of the human person. The processes of learning, remembering and forgetting, for
instance, are becoming more and more the object of research;
already some cogent but not conclusive evidence is at hand to
establish the "chemical" character of these three processes.
The seat of their operation is being placed in individual molecules, which can, of course, be directly affected by outside
means. Dr. David Krech, professor of psychology at the University of California, Berkeley, goes so far as to say: "I foresee
the time when we shall have the means and, therefore, inevitably, the temptation to manipulate the behavior and the intellectual functioning of all people through environmental and
biochemical manipulation of the brain." [3]

The modern idea of person coheres, of course, with the modern idea of reality as an ever-changing, ever-modifiable thing.
The religious idea of a personal god is traditionally either an
anthropomorphic one (god, i.e. is changeable like man in emotions and desires and ideas) or it is part and parcel of a larger
concept of reality: reality as a world completely at rest, static
in perfection. The official thinking of the religions rejects the
anthropomorphic idea of god: god does not change and vary
like a human being. The modern mind also rejects it, because
it simply is not godly. But that mind also rejects the idea of a
personal god recumbent, as it were, in an unchanging substance. This is not, as Warren Weaver says, the god of the
restless cell, of the blazing novae, of the swirling nebulae.

The concept, therefore, of a personal god is also not readily

[3] Testifying before a Senate subcommittee hearing, in Washington, April 2, 1968.

intelligible. The three religions eschew the notion of change, variation, increase, decrease, all of which are the observable variables and traits of a human "person." They maintain, on the contrary, that their god is personal but not in this sense; they predicate of him substantial acts of will and intellect. But substantial for them implies a lack of synthesis and a complete lack of variation. On the other hand, the modern mind cannot think anthropomorphically of such a god, and it rejects the notion of a god who has acts of will and intellect. It cannot, therefore, understand the idea of a "personal" god. It has no ready concept of such a being.

4. Ethical Rules

All three religions present a code morality to be observed by all men for salvation. Observance of it is the condition laid down in order that a man benefit by the particular salvation which each religion offers. It is axiomatic that Judaism and Christianity impose the Ten Commandments and their traditional interpretation of them, in addition to such rules as the 613 rabbinic prescriptions, and the commandments of the Church in the various Christian denominations. Islam imposes five duties on the pious Muslim, besides providing him with a set of prohibitions and rules.[4]

It is axiomatic for these religions that the body of ethical rules which arise from these basic prescriptions are presented to the individual believers as part of the general revelation. All three religions claim divine sanction for their ethical codes. Yahweh, the Christian God, Allah, in revealing the truth, revealed above all else the way in which men should act.[5]

The authority and the sanction of these ethical codes comes, therefore, from the invisible world. For modern man, whose world is quite "horizontal" and for whom all knowledge is de-

[4] The five prescriptions or foundations of Islam are: 1) belief in the one and only God and in Mohammad as his Apostle, 2) praying five times a day, 3) fasting during the month of Ramadan, 4) a pilgrimage to Mecca at least once in a lifetime by those who can afford it, and 5) paying the poor tax.

[5] In each of the three religions, their jurists took pains to weigh meticulously the merits of each human act and to delimit the bounds of good and evil circumscribing each of man's daily actions.

rived from a study of the things in that "horizontal" world, such ethical codes have neither authority or sanction. Modern man endeavors to establish his rules of ethical behavior from an analysis of the objects which he can examine. He accepts no blanket prohibition of contraception merely because of a general commandment "Thou shall not kill." Instead, he analyzes birth-rates, food supplies, health problems, economic exigencies, educational needs, psychological adaptability, social development, foetal stages of growth, and decides that contraception is an acceptable solution. He finds the strictures against divorce abstract and unrealistic. He decides that what religion would call pornography, he can justifiably consider an art-form. He cannot abide clerical or ecclesiastical control, so he expels it from his government. He decides he can educate better than religious groups, so he builds his own schools. His analysis of food indicates no physical impurities in it, no dietetic dangers, so he rejects dietary laws instituted over 2,000 years ago.

Scientists are aware more and more of the moral and social impact of their fast-changing technologies. At a special three-day convocation on Scientific Progress and Human Values this awareness and acute anxiety were aired.[6] Not merely was it stated that the politicians must be aware of the technical character of policy making, but it was maintained that the standards to be sought were to be "civilized standards, involving moral, cultural, spiritual values, the kinds of achievements recognized in the broad agreement upon what were the great societies and the golden ages in the past. It requires value judgement."[7] Some cited the effect of scientific and technological achievement on the family, which has created new moral situations: the home will have to be invaded in order to ensure to the children the knowledge necessary for survival in a rapidly moving world. The family in itself, it was stated, was a fine mechanism for transmitting conventional wisdom, in a relatively static society. It was not capable of coping with the new situation in knowledge and technology.

Modern man is seeking and apparently finding sources of

[6] Marking the 75th anniversary of the California Institute of Technology, held in Pasadena, Calif., October 1966.

[7] Dr. Herbert Jo Muller, professor of English and government at the University of Indiana. It is interesting to note that more and more in Soviet Russia a scientific elite seem to be acquiring a greater voice in governmental policies at home and abroad.

ethical inspiration in the unheard-of quarters of science and applied technologies. For instance, there is a growing persuasion among leading corporation executives that business has a social responsibility to discharge. They think of themselves as environmentalists: their work and their achievements necessarily affect the human environment, thereby creating moral problems of a social kind. Business for them means that they must participate in a "constructive exchange, seeking to establish viable standards and objectives suitable to the country's economic, social, political and technological aspirations." [8] This sense of responsibility and the duties it dictates grow out of the complex web of profit motives and the foundations for a stable society in which the profit motives can function for the benefit of all. The source of the ethical inspiration is not otherworldly.

Modern man's judgments are based on his analysis of concrete situations and things; they are never the result of adhesion to a transcendental rule issued in the name of an ancient revelation. The concept of an abstract law imposed on men and things by an outside agency is unintelligible to him. He really knows only the laws whose validity he can test and prove or disprove. Concrete situations often force the hand even of the religions. Christian missionaries in Africa, for instance, find it impossible to eradicate polygamy from certain areas. They have found it necessary to allow polygamists to become Christians, even though polygamy is strictly forbidden by traditional Christianity. To do otherwise would be to impose unintelligible and inhuman conditions on the natives.[9]

5. Soul

In all three religions, the teaching concerning the soul of man is of vital importance. For without a soul, there is no eternal life. All three aim at eternal life as the ultimate goal. In their classical forms, they taught that each man has an individual soul of his own. This soul is spiritual, i.e. non-

[8] George S. Moore, President of the First National City Bank, at the Annual Meeting of the American Iron and Steel Institute, 1966, in New York.

[9] Cf. the case of Father Hillman in Tanzania as reported in *Time Magazine* for May 10, 1968.

material. It was directly created by the god worshipped in the religion. It is stained by sins and ennobled by virtue. It can never die or corrupt or be brought to nothingness, as the body can; it is immortal; it will always exist. Linked indissolubly with this religious teaching about the soul of man is the doctrine concerning the resurrection of the body and the soul. Again, in their classical forms all three religions teach that on the Last Day all men will "rise from the dead" with body and soul intact, to be judged in the Great Judgement. All the three religions have various doctrines to account for the place in which the soul of a dead man awaits this Last Day and this Great Judgement, when it will be once more reunited with the body.

The doctrine of the immortal soul of individual man is thus vital to all three; without it a man could not be morally good or bad; without it he could not live forever. The body only lives in function of the soul.

It is generally held that the doctrine of immortal souls is a tardy development in Judaism. Neither Saul, nor David, nor Solomon would have believed in such immortality. Curiously, for our minds at least, Judaism developed the doctrine of the soul's immortality after the doctrine of the resurrection of the body. We find no trace of either doctrine in early Biblical literature; the resurrection is expressly denied in some Psalms and by implication in the early Prophets. One of the first apparent references to the resurrection is in the prophet Isaiah,[10] but the meaning of the passage in question can be disputed. This portion of Isaiah is generally relegated to the late 5th or early 4th century B.C. Two centuries later, we find a full-blown description of the resurrection in the *Book of Enoch*.[11] Somewhat later in the *Book of Daniel* we find it further elaborated by the notion of eternal life: men will rise to live forever.[12]

The doctrine of the soul's immortality appears clearly for the first time in the *Book of Jubilees*.[13] From then on it was part of normal Pharisaic teaching. There is no clear indication of

[10] Cf. *Isaiah*, chapters 24-27. Cf. in particular 26:9: "The dead shall live, my dead bodies shall arise," etc.

[11] Cf. *Enoch* 35:5-7.

[12] Cf. *Daniel* 12:3. This book's approximate date is 165 B.C.

[13] Cf. *Jubilees* 23:31. This book is generally dated at some time between 250-150 B.C.

the doctrine before this time. The doctrine of the soul's immortality came to Judaism from Greek sources. Pharisees adopted it as part of their explanation of the resurrection.

In order to understand this state of affairs, we must form some idea of the ancient Jewish mind concerning the composition of man. Man was a "living spirit," according to that mind. But this "spirit" was breathed into his clay or flesh by the Creator. Death resulted when the Creator withdrew the spirit. No sharp distinction was ever driven between this "spirit" and man's flesh. Man was a "living spirit" as long as he lived. Once he died, his "spirit" was withdrawn, his body corrupted, he ceased altogether to be. The real meaning of the ancient phrase "to be gathered to one's fathers," said of many of the Biblical Patriarchs and eminent personages is quite macabre for modern ears: it meant the piling up of their bones in a common grave.

Islam adopted both doctrines from Judaism, as did Christianity. In medieval times, all three religions developed philosophical explanations of both resurrection and immortality. Yet these amounted to intellectual propositions more or less satisfactory to the believer's mind. With the advent of the scientific method and, above all, with the development of psychology and the behavioral sciences, the concept of a "spiritual" principle such as the soul endowed with immortality lost its intelligibility. A new model of man's interior, now preferably called the human psyche or psychology, was constructed. For science, the only existence and character this possesses is that of a synthesis: the various acts of intellection, memory, will, emotion form a pattern which is recognized as the psyche. As far as science can determine, of course, the psyche ceases to function when bodily functions cease. It is not immortal. The further concept of a resident substantial spirit or soul living on after death and forever is not merely outside the scientist's verificatory processes, it is unintelligible to him. Again, the limits and quality of the scientist's horizontal world intervene here. Modern man has no intelligible concept of such a soul.

The doctrine of bodily resurrection, linked closely to the soul's nature and destiny, suffers a like fate. The ancients knew little or nothing about the human organism—its chemical constituents, its functioning parts, its psychology—and even less about the nature of death. Modern man has measured corruption, can detail the chemical changes that take place when bodily life ceases, has a clear idea of what precisely corruption and decay of the human frame connote, and defines human death precisely by the cessation of the observable functions of the body. The three religions define death as the moment when the soul leaves the body.

On the other hand, the scientist cannot accept the "outside" explanation: that a god will "resurrect" the corrupted body. He knows that in a living body today the actual molecules which compose it were not part of it some time ago. In another decade it will be made up of molecules which at present are elsewhere: in African lions, in passion-flowers of the Amazon, in Maine lobsters, in earth in Patagonia, and in the fur of a Polar bear. For the scientist, the body as such has truly ceased to exist. No "shade" or reduced form of the body exists in an "underworld" or in Elysian fields. The body has ceased to exist. He therefore finds the resurrection of the body unintelligible.

6. Sin

Closely connected with the doctrines of soul and body is the religious teaching on sin. Sin is conceived as *the* result of an unlawful action performed by man in defiance of a divine law. From time immemorial, sin has always been likened to a "stain" or a "blot" on the soul, a deformation of its beauty. Various binary concepts have been used to describe it and contrast it with virtue.

Once, however, the modern behavioral sciences were developed and, particularly, once the psychology of the human being was studied, science provided a description of man's acts which leaves no room really for the traditional concept of sin. When the doctrine of the soul's existence was thrown into jeopardy, naturally the corollary teaching on sin as a stain on the soul was affected. In effect, the modern mind can form no intelligible concept of sin in its classical form, as explained by the three religions.

Having thus examined these six basic ideas of the religions, we have found that they are not intelligible to modern man within the framework of his knowing processes and his modern ideas of knowledge. These latter are dependent on man's "horizontal" view of the world. In that world, all objects carry their explanation. If he does not find the object described by these religions or, if he cannot find and examine it, then he cannot form an intelligible concept of it. In so far as the dominance of the three religions depends on these basic concepts, that dominance is lethally affected.

In the high period of their intellectual flowering, all three religions applied themselves to developing an intellectual formulation of these and other doctrines which would be intellectually satisfying, while leaving room for the leap of faith. But this was done with the aid of philosophies which no longer appeal to the modern mind. The intellectual explanations of such teachings couched in the phraseology and conceptuology of particular and time-ridden philosophies do not appeal.

Modern man, however, has not stopped there in his construction of the world: he has assigned to all things in his cosmos a definite place. Not only is he the brother of the boulders. He is cousin of the clouds and integrated with them in a new romanticism which we will proceed to outline next.

26. History and Mystery

Today, man regards himself as an integrated part of his vast cosmos. He is examining the floor of his planet's oceans. He is plumbing the core of the earth. Above all else, he now has hierarchized himself and his planet within a vast time-space continuum which he continually and continuously endeavors to charter. His planet, he sees, is part of a great bun-shaped spiral galaxy whose total mass is something like 200 billion times the mass of the sun, measuring 100,000 light-years in its width. This vast mass revolves about once in 200 million years, and probably it has already revolved about 50 times since the universe came into existence. He has found that his plant is not even at the center of his own galaxy. This center is more than 30,000 light-years from Earth and the direction of its center probably lies near the junction of the Scorpio, Sagittarius, and Ophiucus constellations at approximate galactic co-ordinates of 327° longitude, 0° latitude; in equatorial coordinates it is in right ascension 17 hours, 30 minutes, declination −30°.

Furthermore, his galaxy is one amongst countless other galaxies. He knows that more than a billion other galaxies are within our present telescopic reach. Thus, while modern man has more obvious reason to feel the humility of the ancient Psalmist, he has more reason than ever from his knowledge and scientific method not to think as the Psalmist did.

For modern man, as Harlow Shapley puts it, "the green leaves of the meadow are sucklings of a star's radiation. The rapids in a brook, responding to universal gravitation, perform erosions such as those that have brought down to oblivion the lofty pre-Alps and the primitive Appalachians. The hundred-ton maple tree that calmly dreams through the decades is in the same universe as the Andromeda galaxy with its billions of seething stars. The tree heeds the impulse of gravity according to the same rules as those subscribed to by the stars in a globular cluster. Further, the tree is made of the same complex molecular aggregates as are the birds in its branches, the parasites on its roots, and the philosophers who wonder about it." [1] But the cousinship of all things in this cosmos is not merely spatial and material; it is also in time. For man, as for his earth, as for his galaxy and all the galaxies, time flows irreversibly. An irrevocable law as hard as the stones beneath man's feet and as rigid as the rule of the stars above his head governs man's life and actions: once time passes, it cannot be reversed by the mythical Time-Machine or any other device.

Modern man's view of history, therefore, is essentially summed up in the dictum attributed to Hegel: *"wie es eigentlich geschehen is."* History is what has actually happened. Historians and philosophers of history proceed to build theories on this fundamental conclusion. But the conclusion never changes. Modern man's primary intent is to find out exactly what happened and how it happened, what happens and how it happens; to catalogue its causes with overwhelming minutiae; and to place the records in his archives, where future generations may look back and learn the lessons of man's past. History, in fact, is essentially retrospective.

Although essentially retrospective, the history of the future is viewed by modern man as something to be made. Dobzhansky of Rockefeller University once said that "the future may be influenced and even planned in accord with what man regards as good and desirable . . . the universe is evolving, and man is a

[1] *The View from a Distant Star,* Basic Books, New York and London, 1963, p. 83.

part of the cosmic process, but he need not be a passive spectator. He may become an increasingly active participant in the process of creation." Dobzhansky is here referring to the environmental changes which man now sees himself powerful enough and curious enough to affect. To this extent, future history may be controlled, and to this extent future history may be considered to be anthropocentric.

Yet, if evolutionary biology and the other sciences which are based on full-blooded Darwinism are taken at their face value, modern man has no reason to believe that there is a cosmic process at work. He can go down no road of cosmic history. He can indulge in no wish-fulfillment. He cannot afford to impose for non-biological and non-scientific reasons the appearance of a single teleological intent on the variegated mass of details which he has unearthed concerning the history of his cosmos. For this would be the consummate idolatry, a step backward, a return to an anthropocentric universe which medieval man philosophized, Renaissance man celebrated, and a long line of hard-nosed thinkers from Bacon through Newton, Galileo Galilei, Montaigne, Descartes, Darwin, dissipated as an exercise in self-deceit and an attempted return to ancient myth-making.

In this regard, the theories of Teilhard de Chardin must be regarded as a half-way house. He is not a Christian traditionalist. He is not an ultra-modern. He endeavored to do for evolutionary biology what Thomas Aquinas had done for Aristotelian philosophy—Christianize it. But neither his "Christification" of that biology, nor his careful integration of biosphere and noosphere, nor his immaculate outline of nature's teleology, nor finally the glories of the Omega point which he sang, can be reconciled with the thrust of modern man's spirit.

Modern man's idea of mysteries or the central mystery of his existence and the universe concern rather the microscopic laws that govern all nature. Man seeks to know the relationship between the basic forces in nature: the force which binds the particles of the atomic nucleus together; the electromagnetic force that governs all the interactions between molecules and atoms; the force which separates particles from the atoms; the universal force of gravity. This fascinates modern man and it interests him more than any proposed religious mystery. It is directly related to his spacecraft, the equilibrium of his planet, and the efficiency of his electric motors.

The ancients, among whom Judaism, Christianity, and Islam were born, shared no part of this view. Their visible world, first of all, was oriented to an invisible world. Furthermore, that world of theirs was the center not merely of all creation but of the personal interest, care, and concentrated direction of the god they worshipped. More importantly, human history was for them the drama of this god's unique and sustained interest. We have referred to this drama of human history as super-history for the ancients. In super-history, all barriers created by the succession of time and the distances of space were annihilated. Those moving on the superhistorical plane could be ubiquitous, could make all the yesterdays of man their todays and even their tomorrows.

The ancients were thus intellectually capable of participating in the religious mysteries. A mystery, in this sense, was not an unknown factor, a puzzle, a "whodunit," an inexplicable event. A mystery was an enactment of some event or action which lay outside of time and was not congealed by the stillness of history; the initiates could participate in it, live it in its actuality. The mystery itself did not need to reach through long corridors of time or over the arches of space: by its nature it was ever-present, ever-livable.

Judaism, Christianity, and Islam embedded at the heart of their rationalization of man's condition the enactment of a mystery. In all three, a historical event or a series of such events which took place on earth at a given time and in a given place was paralleled by the mystery which took place on the plane of superhistory. The past tense of the verb used in the last sentence, "took place," is quite inaccurate. In the mystery, there was no succession in time: neither "took place," "takes place," "will take place" are accurate forms. Timelessness is of the essence. For this reason, even after the historical events took place, the subsequent generation of participants could live the enactment of the mystery: by a simple exterior re-enactment of the historical event in time and space, believers living at no matter what distance in time could live the actual enactment. Superhistory intersected always at the point of re-enactment.

It was thus that the fundamental "mystery" of Judaism, the Exodus from the land of Egypt, was re-enacted and lived by subsequent generations of Jews at the Passover celebrations. The participants had no doubt that participation in the Seder gave them mystical participation in that original Exodus, and enriched them as spiritually as it had the Israelites who were saved by the Angel of the Lord and the lamb's blood smeared on the lintel-posts of Hebrew houses in Egypt.

Christianity from the beginning had its mystery to celebrate: the sacrificial death of Jesus on the Roman cross on Calvary. The inner sense of the later Eucharistic celebrations, and of the Mass itself, was that the priest and the participants actually partook in the mystery of Jesus' death on Calvary. Neither Judaism nor Christianity in their classical periods ever considered these ceremonies as merely commemorative meals or rituals.

For Islam also there are central mysteries such as the Hegira of the Prophet Mohammad from Mecca and the Prophet's nocturnal journey to Paradise accompanied by the Angel Gabriel. Every Muslim who makes the sacred *hajj* to Mecca, who worships in the Prophet's Mosque at Medina, and who travels to pray in the Dome of the Rock at Jerusalem, relives and participates once more in these pre-eminently glorious and mysterious moments of Islam and Allah's revelation to his Community.

Before the modern day, the believers in each religion could live the recurrent re-enactments (daily, weekly, quarterly, or yearly) of the mystery. In fact, this was the condition for the re-enactment to be efficacious. The Chosen People of 500 B.C. were not one with the Chosen People of 1200 B.C., according to this mystique, unless a timeless framework of mystic participation made them one with what otherwise was a past event, past people, past actions, all finished, dead, recorded, and ossified in people's memories. The Christian of 1968 is told that he is risen with the risen Christ of April 21, that he has been crucified as to his sins with the sinless Christ, that he is triumphant with the triumphant Christ. Similarly, the Muslim pilgrim at the Ka'aba or the Mosque of the Prophet does not live *again* the mysteries of the Prophet which *took place* in the first third of the 7th century A.D. He lives the mysteries of the Prophet and thus benefits spiritually from them.

It is clear that this notion of history either as a reversible quantum, or as a negligible continuum is totally irreconcilable with the modern mind. There intervenes here the fundamental time bias and historicism of that mind which is anchored to the irreversible flow of time and the opaque resistance of space. Time and space are the twin brothers of death. "Today we live, as we imagine, harder and more excitingly," writes Cyrus

Sulzberger, "and we think less of the abstractions that defeat us. We travel faster. We penetrate the first veneer of space. We seek, as it were, to escape death, by running away. And still we run, feverishly, into a limitless vacuum where death is undisturbed." [2] This sums up the modern attitude to death, to life, and to human history. Life is considered to be the result of solar energy which flowed uninterrupted for billions of years, was diverted in small quantities on to this planet, remains for a while, and then takes up its place once more in the interminable current of impersonal forces. For this reason, one can judge as pointless the current efforts visible in Judaism and Christianity, and to some small extent in Islam, to modernize things.

The claimed primitive Christian rite practised at Emmaus House in East Harlem is one example. Twenty-five men and women gather in a brownstone. The table is U-shaped; at its head sits a Roman Catholic priest with an anti-Vietnam war emblem in his lapel. The blessings begin.

"Shalom! To those working for peace, those who are actively demonstrating, or not demonstrating."

"Shalom! To effective justice."

"Shalom! To the Beatles who have helped us in our liturgy."

"Shalom! To the 12 long days of Christmas."

Then two large loaves of bread are passed around, red wine is drunk from paper cups, and the participants in the *agape* dine on salad, beef Stroganoff and noodles, ice cream, and coffee.

According to the organizers this is *"agape* with the connotations of the Lord's Supper without specifically taking Communion." This is a sincere attempt to relive the mystery without the heart of the mystery. It presumes that the barriers of time and space can be knocked aside to allow identification with Jesus and his followers at their last meal together.

To be classed with this attempt to re-enact the mystery are such events as the performance of the Primordial Jazz Orchestra in Washington Square Church, on Friday March 1, 1968. The orchestra presented "Blues for the Planet Earth" and began with the whimper of kazoos which gave way to the saxophones; then trumpets and trombones started. Finally drums and bass added a rhythmic foundation, thus moving the volume of sound into the traditional riff-driven attack of a jazz band.

[2] *My Brother Death,* Harper, New York, 1961, p. 40.

This is a novel and utterly modern way of worshipping; it in no way connects with any ancient mystery, is therefore out of place in the traditional setting of that mystery, the church. No anachronistic demands must be made of this rite as such.

Such adaptations of the traditional mystery are as near the original as the "Trumpets of the Lord," [3] the musical adaptation of James Weldon Johnson's book *God's Trombones,* is to the original. The former is a collection of dramatized sermons (act of Creation, Death, Exodus, Last Judgment, Crucifixion) framed in traditional Negro spirituals and Gospel songs. Songs such as "In That Great Gittin' Up Morning," "We are Climbing Jacob's Ladder," "In Shady Green Pastures" evoke not the ancient mystery but the spirituality and tradition of the Southern Negro Baptist. No one denies the powerful religious appeal inherent in such dramatizations. Yet it is not a re-enactment of the ancient mysteries.

Experimentation of this kind is to be found sporadically nowadays in Christian churches: the noonclub organized at St. Peter's Lutheran Church in New York where the attractions are coffee and revues on Original Sin ("The Apple Bit"), pride and innocence ("A Little Baloney"), unwed mothers ("Harry and the Angel"), and so on; the use of 76 deep oil cans for floral decorations at Immaculate Heart College in Los Angeles to signify the deep "Christian involvement in the world"; the use of folk music, the "Rock and Roll Mass" record; the "visual/verbal" sermon relying, for instance, on an arrangement of a piece of sculpture covered with balloons which are popped during the sermon in order to demonstrate how God "shatters contemporary secular patterns which separate us from the love of God"; the introduction of pieces of junk, old tires, and broken TV tubes at the offertory in order to signify the "brokenness" of human life and the central position of religious experience.

Another type of effort to communicate with another mystery of faith is represented by events such as the ceremonies and rituals which accompanied the "Cleveland Week of Progress '67," sponsored by the University of Christian Movement. It took place in the main ballroom of the Sheraton-Cleveland Hotel, Cleveland. Students on the balcony hurled balloons,

[3] Produced in Toronto by the National Educational Television and Canadian Broadcasting Company. It had a five-month Off-Broadway run in 1964, and appeared on Channel 13 in New York City, in 1968.

paper plates and rolls of tissue at the people below. Two machines churned out streams of soap bubbles. Colored slides flashed. A saxophone cried. Motion pictures of bread began to appear on a screen at the end of the ballroom. A group of students proceeded to distribute 27 loaves of bread in small pieces to the participants. A nun remarked: "this must have been what it was like at Creation—order out of chaos." In another vein but yet in an effort to bridge mystically the chasms of space and time, the Reverend Ralph D. Abernathy, successor to the slain Dr. Martin Luther King read in public a "letter" to the dead leader asking him to "go from the throne of Jesus and find Jimmy Jackson, the stalwart hero who could barely read and write, and was shot down just because he wanted to vote and was the first martyr for Alabama." [4]

Such efforts are directed to making things up-to-date: to make the Mass modern, to make Church services more up-to-date and appealing, to modernize the Synagogue services. Alone of all three religions no serious attempts have been made to modernize Islam's ceremonies. There is here an inescapable dilemma. On the one hand, the gestures and vestments used at ceremonies have no intrinsic meaning for the worshipper: these trappings belong to a former age and were introduced by people who drew on *their* own *everyday* life. We use today neither the liturgical gestures, nor the chants, nor the vestments, in daily life. They are meaningless for us, except as reminders, as commemorative items.

On the other hand, to drop them is to cut one more concrete link with the past. Again, whether we retain them or change them, the effect is the same: we are still at one large remove from the lived reality. For our very minds and the texture of our spirits have changed. We are incapable by mental bias, emotional approach, and sociological framework, of reliving the enactment. It is according to this norm that we should judge all up-dating undertaken by the Second Vatican Council. Anachronisms and meaningless elements should at all times be avoided. Yet, the mere recitation of the Mass prayers in English, the accumulation of sitting-down, standing-up, kneeling-down, does not affect the vital issue. All are moribund elements vis-a-vis the desired participation in the original mystery. The use of guitars at Mass may arouse the interest of the

[4] At Atlanta, April 7, 1968, in the West Hunter Street Baptist Church. Cf. *N.Y. Times* of April 8.

people. But it and such adaptations in no essential way help the modern mind to relive the mystery. Modern man has no viable concept for such a participation.

Instead, modern man is now developing a view which enables him to indulge in a new romanticism and a fresh mythology forever bounded by life and death. This is, to adapt a phrase of Nietzsche's, a rope which man has thrown across the impassable abyss. For the man of today's age believes in no immortality and seeks no eternity but the perpetuity of his race in children, in perduring monuments both of brass and marble, and in achievements resounding in the ears of yet unborn generations. But the abyss claims each single mortal man. Yet, in the words of John Gunther, "Faith is the strength by which a shattered world shall emerge into the light . . . hope has a soul that raises man above the beasts and sends him searching for a star . . . hope has made men of medicine dedicate their lives and skills to find ways to eliminate disease and free humankind from pain." These are the dimensions of the new romanticism and the fresh mystery-seeking of modern man.

Some reaches for this romanticism and mystery are expressed by naturalists, biologists, and palaeontologists: a Romain Gary addressing an affectionate and telling letter to the elephant ("Dear Elephant, Sir"); [5] Desmond Morris describing the evolution and true purpose of the female breasts; [6] Robin Fox speculating on the origin of the incest taboo, of brain evolution, and supplantation of the estrous cycle in the female primate; [7] Robert Ardrey describing in graphic terms how human civilization, personified as a patient watcher, is rising from his chair and looking out the window to the gathering clouds on man's skies; [8] and Loren Eiseley in his semipoetic account of the nearly fatal clash with Wolf, his shepherd dog, over the bone of a fossil bison. "Do not," something pleaded in the back of Wolf's eyes, "force me . . . We are in another time . . . I will not give it up . . . the shadows will not permit me." And Eiseley asks: "Had I not . . . been about to respond, to hurl myself upon him over an invisible haunch 10,000 years removed?" [9]

[5] *Life*, December 22, 1967.
[6] *Ibid.*
[7] *N.Y. Times Magazine*, March 24, 1968.
[8] *African Genesis*, Dell Publishing Co., New York, 1961, pp. 353 ff.
[9] *Life*, February 16, 1968.

We find this romanticism and above all the mystery expressed in more metaphysical terms by writers like Harlow Shapley or Warren Weaver. Perhaps Charles Lindbergh summed it up best when he wrote: "Surrounded by wildness, I become less aware of my individuality. I see animals about me as earthly experiments with life; and so I feel myself. Each of us represents a life-stream attempting to survive, to take advantage of every opportunity arising . . . With stars above, a planet below, and no barrier between or after, intuition reaches out past limits of the mind into a mysticism at which man shies the name of God." Lindbergh quotes the African tribesman: "We believe God is in everything . . . in the rivers, the grasses, the bark of trees, the clouds and mountains. We sing songs to the mountains because God is in them." [10]

No more trenchant expression of the modern mind could be offered than that of Harlow Shapley, when he stated that: "We do not need to be weak. The two simple mathematical relations

$$E = Mc^2 \text{ and}$$
$$4H = I \ He + radiation$$

have in them the answer to man's questions about the future—whether he is to continue his evolution into a better life, or is to join the other biological failures as fossils in the dead sedimentary rocks." [11]

To be included with the category of insignificant elements and unintelligible concepts is a series of practices, customs, and institutions, still preserved and performed by Judaism, Christianity, and Islam. We shall consider these in the following chapter. Some of these concern directly the god worshipped in each religion, some concern man's participation in the enactment of each religion's central mystery.

27. The Supernatural

The elements to be examined concerning the god of Judaism, Christianity, and Islam, are chiefly four.

[10] *Life,* December 22, 1967.

[11] Cf. Harlow Shapley, *The View from a Distant Star,* Basic Books, New York and London, 1963, p. 106.

We have spoken previously of the "invisible" and the "spiritual" world which these religions propose as the ultimate reality. It would be extremely naive for anyone to think that the religions conceive of this "spiritual" and "invisible" world as somehow or other lying "behind" or "beneath" or "above" the visible and perceptible world in which men live, move, and have their being. It is true that, in the primitive stages of their development, all three indulged in what scholars know technically as *anthropomorphism:* to speak about this "other" world, they used the only vocabulary available at that time, and this was drawn from the world around them and the physical phenomena which modelled and fashioned their everyday speech. Nevertheless, all three recognized early on in their history that anthropomorphisms were, finally, just anthropomorphisms. They all made endeavors to develop a more rarefield method of thought and expression, usually drawing on contemporary philosophies and the language of logicians and metaphysicians.

In spite of this anti-anthropomorphic trend in all three religions, it was and is still true to say that their most valid and acceptable statements about that "invisible" world of their supreme being are negative statements: they can state what that world is not. The reason for this is most obvious: all man's concepts and words are drawn from the physical world around him and are based on man's experience and his impressions of that world. The very key words used to describe this world of the spirit are illuminating: "invisible" simply means non-visible; "supernatural" means beyond or above nature, therefore not nature; even the term "spiritual," apparently a positive term, is merely so by analogy. Derived from the breath of the lips and air coming from the lungs, it reflects the ancient idea of something forceful found in the wind and in storms but which nevertheless is invisible. Because of its obvious connection with life, this invisible force was attributed to the lord of life who was then described as "spiritual," as a "spirit."

But even within these negative limits, some idea can be formed by which to guide one toward a concept of the supernatural. The first characteristic of the supernatural is the absence of material dimensions: the spiritual has neither length, breadth, height, thickness, weight, color, or the successive duration within which all visible and detectable phenomena of man's cosmos move. When we described the god of

Judaism, Christianity, and Islam as extra-cosmic, this was the
attributed meaning of the word *extra*. The supernatural and
invisible are totally in another order of being.

Strictly speaking, we cannot even say that the supernatural
is "outside" nature, "outside" the cosmos. For to be "outside"
something means we are in dimensional relationship with that
something. To have dimensional relationship means to have
dimensions, for otherwise there would be no dimensional relationship. Now the supernatural has no material dimensions.
It is not, therefore, "outside" nature. But for the same reason,
it is not "inside" nature. The supernatural, in fact, is nowhere,
cannot be anywhere. For according to the modern mind of
men, if a being is somewhere, then he or she or it is localized,
is in dimensional relationship with other material dimensions.
His or her or its dimensions are related to certain dimensions
of place and time. By these co-ordinates we locate the object. A
being without dimensions cannot be localized. We cannot even
say "he is not here" rather than "he is here." Both are super-
fluous and senseless.

The second characteristic of the spiritual and supernatural
world of the Jewish, Christian, and Muslim god is that it is
totally alien to man's nature and his world: man, either by
himself or by any possible means he can find in his cosmos, can
never succeed in understanding, contacting, entering, and possessing that supernatural. Hence all the religions stress the gratuitous mercy and love of their god's action in making it possible for men after death to enter that world. The supernatural
is gratuitous. Nobody can enter Paradise or Heaven or rise to
glory on the Last Day, unless the god facilitate him. No one
lifts himself by his bootstraps to the gates of god.

It was relatively easy for early pre-scientific Judaism, Christianity, and Islamic believers to subscribe to this idea of the
supernatural. In the current mythologies of their day and the
ordinary parlance of thought, the presence of the invisible was
part and parcel of a daily life. Analogues, metaphors, allegories, symbols, common parlance, and constant beliefs, all
these facilitated belief. Besides, there was no precise knowledge
of what things were made of, how things functioned. Knowledge for them was pre-scientific. Thus the pre-scientific believers had what for them were intelligible concepts, concepts
that formed the warp and woof of their mentality. The rest
followed.

This is no longer the condition of the modern mind. Avidly aware of what time is, how extensive space is, how things are made and function, modern man has pushed the frontiers of his world out into distant space and back some millions of years and into the kernel of matter. His principle is that all is finally explicable and intelligible, if and when he gets sufficiently close to examine it. He cannot indulge in even the mildest anthropomorphisms of his forebears. He may use the ancient metaphors, symbols, and allegories in poetry, emotional prose, and for purposes of celebration, just as he uses chairs and tables, but has long ceased to think of them as solids as the ancients did. He knows that the chair, in the words of Warren Weaver, is a shadowy, swirling set of vague and elusive electric charges. But metaphors and symbols do not reflect any intelligible concept of a reality for him. The supernatural is the supreme anti-concept of the modern mind.

The same difficulties afflict the ancillary concepts of God, of Heaven, and Hell. The pre-scientific mind used the concept of remoteness, inaccessibility, towering height, profound depth, fathomless reaches in order to say that the god he worshipped was supernatural. But the sky around man's planet, the oceans which ringed his dry lands and continents, and the earth on which he walked—this height, depth, and profundity—were considered to be "open" at the further end. Somehow or other the eternity and the infinity of the god worshipped lay beyond that point. All shadows whispered of him. All distances depicted him. The in-between was impassable and immeasurable. Heaven was where god resided, Hell where he punished the wicked.

Modern man rejects this concept of god's remoteness and inaccessible being. He knows also that there is no Hell at the earth's center. He rejects these things because finally all distances are measurable for him and all remoteness can be brought into a relative proximity, he thinks. And he rejects them, also, because they were foisted on him by these religions before anyone examined space and pierced the earth. The golden rule of his mental self-possession is that all things carry their explanation. To accept a heaven and a hell and a god's remoteness would be to accept explanations which he cannot verify or convalidate.

The traditional concept of God is furthermore unintelligible to modern man on another score. Modern man's cosmos is not an anthropocentric axis, one end set down on the planet Earth, the other resting in Heaven while all around God's stars and planets illuminate man's firmament and indicate the seasons of his yearlong life. Earth is a minute element in a gigantic universe lost in the tangled lanes of galaxies, other planets, other suns. A god uniquely concerned with such a tiny speck and only with the dominant race of primates on that planetary speck seems a gross exaggeration and an impossible idea to the modern mind. It is out of kilter, man says, with the grandeur, the amplitude, and the magnificence of this universe.

Modern man has further difficulties of an ethical nature with the traditional idea of heaven and hell. He cannot reconcile eternal punishment with his new psychology and understanding of behavioral deviations. He cannot conceive of a paradisiacal pleasure which essentially concerns the spirit about which he can know nothing and have no concept. Not only can modern man not think intelligibly about these matters within his cognitive framework; he cannot accept the idea of a static immutability and a changeless wonder, such as all three religions ascribe to their god. To change and reach for ever-widening boundaries are the conditions under which modern man functions and, therefore, thinks.

It is thus that the central personage of these religions, the abode to which, the religions claim, this central personage has destined virtuous believers, and the place of punishment he assigns to evil-doers have become unintelligible and, therefore, unacceptable to the growing mind of modern man. This apex of the explanation which the religions offered is thus lopped off. Their dominance suffers irreparably.

28. Rites of Communication

Once man believes he has communicated with the "outside," the "spiritual" world, he proceeds to establish a ritual of sustained communication. He thus develops a number of institutions which are meant to ensure his participation in the enactment of the central mysteries, the most important of which are Priesthood, Sacrifice, Sacraments and Sacramentals, the Sabbath, and the Religious Year.

Priesthood, Sacrifice

Today, these are relevant only for Christianity. Judaism unaccountably dropped all sacrificial and priestly elements once the Second Temple was destroyed by Hadrian in 135 A.D. In passing, let us remark on the difference in Judaism before and after the Babylonian Exile (6th Century B.C.). Before the Exile, it was the Temple, the Sacrifice, and the Priesthood, which dominated in Judaism. The Law did not hold a central and unique position. After the Exile and more specifically since 135 A.D., it is uniquely the Law (Written and Oral) which Judaism stresses. In this, there is more radical difference between the original conditions and outlooks of Judaism and its latter-day conditions and outlooks, than between the early Christian Church and its 16th and 19th century counterparts.

In Christianity, no element as essential to it as Temple and Sacrifice were to classical Judaism has been omitted. Indeed, Christianity's way seems to have been rather to accumulate non-essentials than to drop essentials. Islam never had a central sacrificial worship and ritual. Animal sacrifices are still made on special feast-days, but these have no vital cultic function for Islam. Islam could do without them and still possess itself in full integrity.

We cannot understand the concept of Priesthood unless we have a clear idea of what sacrifice implied for ancient Judaism.[1] Christianity derived its notions of priestly and sacrificial institutions from Judaism. The function of sacrificial animals in pre-Christian Judaism is quite clear: the sacrificial animal functioned as a surrogate for the offerer, as gift, as atonement, as propitiation, as plea and prayer. Central to the Temple sacrifice of Jerusalem were the twin ideas of praise to Yahweh and propitiation and atonement for sin. The sacrificed animal was the victim. The offerers partook of the flesh of the victim sometimes, in order to signify their identity with the victim.

Underlying the institution of sacrifice, both amongst the ancient Jews and many other ancient and modern peoples who

[1] Much time and labor have been spent telling us what sacrifices meant for prehistoric man. But most of the results are pure hypothesis sometimes bordering on the ludicrous, often brilliant fantasy, all too often expressions of subjective prejudices and bias.

still use sacrifice as a form of worship, is an estimation and concept of blood. Blood was held to be the vehicle of life in living things: to shed it in sacrifice was to offer the life of the sacrificed victim; to shed it sacriligeously or criminally was a great crime. Anthropologists and palaeontologists are generally agreed on this sacrosanct character of blood.[2] The quasi-universal attitude to blood in early times is one of the most strikingly attested traits of early religions. Within this perspective, the character of a priest was monolithic and unitary: his chief and essential and only function as a priest was to offer sacrifice for the people.

Christianity adopted and adapted these ideas of priesthood and sacrifice. Jesus was seen as both the victim sacrificed for men's sins and the priest who offered himself willingly as the victim. In Christian teaching from the beginning, an intimate relationship was set up between the death of Jesus on Calvary and the last meal he had with his disciples, the night before he died. At that meal, Jesus, the Gospels recount,[3] offered bread and wine to his disciples saying: "this is my body . . . this is my blood . . . do this in commemoration of me." Christian teaching was that already the bread and wine Jesus offered to his disciples had become mystically but really Jesus' own body and blood as the victim of men's sins on Calvary the following morning. There was no difficulty about time-sequence, as we have seen, because on the superhistorical plane time is reversible, and, anyway, the events on that plane intersect the events on the natural plane of history wherever God wills.

In summary, Jesus was crucified on Calvary. By the shedding of his blood, he wiped out all men's sins. In the Christian Church, Christians participate in this central mystery by doing the very same as Jesus and his disciples did at the last meal: by having a priest bless and consecrate the bread and wine and by partaking of these; they have now become really the body and blood of Jesus as supreme victim.[4] The priest in sub-

---

[2] Wooley and Hawkins suggest that the use of red ochre in early Paleolithic and Mesolithic graves was a symbolic gesture calculated to usher the dead man into after-life. The red ochre would represent blood.

[3] Cf. Matt 26:26-29; Mark 14:22-25; Luke 22:15-20.

[4] *Transubstantiation* is the technical term in Christian theology for this change.

sequent Christianity holds the place of Jesus in that he enacts the drama of Jesus' crucificial sacrifice and admits the faithful to partaking of the mystical victim.

We must note with emphasis that from the very beginning of recorded Christianity and increasingly down the ages it was stressed that Jesus won salvation for men by the shedding of his blood. This teaching, of course, lost ground after the 16th century Reformation. It nevertheless is a constant theme of Roman Catholicism, High Anglicanism, and all the Eastern Orthodox forms of Christianity.

While such a concept was very intelligible and necessary to the pre-scientific minds and spirits of those early days, it is totally incomprehensible to the post-Renaissance and scientific minds of today. Some have endeavored to make it intelligible to modern minds by analogy at least, by identifying it with the shedding of the blood of a patriot who dies for his country. The analogy does not hold up. The patriot who willingly allows his blood to be shed effects nothing more than a demonstration of his patriotism and love, proves his own nobility and unselfishness, and perhaps encourages his fellow countrymen. He may lose his life in a heroic act (taking a fortified position of the enemy, rescuing another human being in danger at the price of his own life, bringing vital information, etc.). The shedding of his blood, however, does not effect salvation and a safety for his fellow countrymen. If, in shedding blood, he destroys a machine-gun nest or delivers information, for instance, this act may contribute to safety and salvation. This does not effect salvation. Anyway, it is this act and not the actual shedding of his blood accompanied by the suitable interior dispositions of love, devotion, courage, perseverance, which produces those effects.

But traditional Christian teaching is adamant: by the shedding of his blood in love, devotion, courage, perseverance, and submission to God, Jesus actually effected the deletion of all man's sins, actually saved men. The essential function of blood in the sacrifice is quite clear.

The modern mind has examined, on the one hand, the chemical constituents of human blood. It has also studied the functions of the blood within the physiological frame of man. Again, the modern mind treats blood as a self-validating and self-explanatory object, as everything else in its horizontal world. This mind cannot understand how a physical element such as blood can efface an invisible and spiritual entity such as a sin. Nor will that mind accept it as a dictum: the only parallels it knows are drawn from primitive religions whose rituals it has classified and studied according to the behavioral sciences. All doors are shut to its understanding.

Christianity itself has evolved no concept of blood which is intelligible to this modern mind. It merely asks the modern worshipper to accept the doctrine on faith and by analogy with ancient practices of mankind. The net result is a refusal on the part of that worshipper in many cases, simply because he has no means of understanding the sacrificial function of blood in the sacrifice of Jesus.

Christianity has also failed to evolve a suitably intelligible concept of the sacred meal: the worshippers partake of bread (and, sometimes, wine) which is believed to be the body (and blood) of Jesus. By participating in it, the believer is united with Jesus, not merely symbolically and mystically, but sacramentally and really. This sacramental aspect is also unintelligible to modern man, as we will examine below. Meanwhile we must note one of the various trends in the modernization of this participation in the mystery. This is the trend which emphasizes the Mass as a sacred meal and diminishes the accent formerly laid on its sacrificial and priestly character. Thus the modern *agape* and Communion Meal has developed in which union and fraternal love are stressed particularly. This, of course, is nothing but a dodging of the principal aspects of the ceremony: the sacrificial and the priestly aspects. Modern man understands quite well what a fellowship meal is: he experiences this at his club-house, at university fraternities, and in the intimacy of his own home. But thus the ancient value is set aside. An element in the original message of Jesus, fraternal love, has been over-stressed. For Jesus, according to Christian belief, did not die primarily to make men brothers, but to save them from their sins. Brotherly love is a result and outcome of fellowship in Christ's salvation. It is not the principal purpose of Jesus' sacrifice.

One can understand, therefore, the mixed reactions evoked by the recent changes which the Episcopal Church of America introduced into its service in the spring of 1968. The language has been modified and modernized throughout with an ecumenist and activist in mind. "The goal is to emphasize that holy communion (that is to say, the eating of the sacred bread) is a time of rejoicing in God's creation and offering joyful thanksgiving," was the comment of one pastor. We see here the emphasis on the "meal" aspect of the ceremony to the practical exclusion of the sacrificial element.

Neither does the modern mind easily understand the sacrificial function of a priest living, say, in downtown Chicago. That he discharges a series of social functions, as spiritual guide, psychological counsellor, organizer of social events, as custodian and administrator of church buildings and schools, this is quite intelligible. But his priestly function, and, in this connection, the sacrificial aspect of this priestly function, is something for which the modern mind has no acceptable concept. It may be on account of the decline in real understanding of what a priest traditionally connotes that the scarcity of priests has started in the Roman Catholic Church. Ideally there should be one priest for every 800 Catholics, ecclesiastical authorities state. The worldwide ratio is about one priest for every 1,300 Catholics. The situation is getting worse in Spain and France, in Brazil, Argentina, and the U.S.A. Dropout rate is high: in very Catholic Spain it is nearly 50%. U.S. enrollment of candidates for the priesthood dropped by 5,541 in 1966. In France, forty-five dioceses have had to close their major seminaries because not enough candidates applied. It is symptomatic that already twenty-four countries (U.S.A. included) have asked the Vatican for permission to ordain married men as deacons to fill the empty places of priests.

Sacraments and Sacramentals

Only Christianity evolved a system of sacraments. Judaism and Islam together with Christianity developed sacramentals. Sacraments are special rituals performed by Christians; each one consists of an outward gesture or gestures and a "spiritual" benefit or effect which is conferred on the person for whom the ritual is performed. Christianity developed seven sacraments.[5] In Baptism, for example, the rite by which somebody becomes a Christian, water is poured on the head of the person to be baptized, while certain words are pronounced; these are the

[5] Baptism, Confirmation, Eucharist, Penance, Extreme Unction, Holy Orders, Matrimony.

outward signs.[6] Inwardly and in the person's spirit, a special spiritual benefit is conferred by God on that person by which his guilt of Original Sin is wiped out.

Sacramentals are, in general, all the external signs (sign of the Cross, a blessing at meals) and objects (holy water, blessed candles, ikons, sacred medals, mezuza, Torah Scrolls) which the three religions use in order to obtain spiritual effects in their users.

The idea behind sacraments and sacramentals was quite intelligible to pre-scientific minds whose ideas of the invisible and spiritual world permitted them to see these things as vehicles, causes, occasions, or frameworks through which divine light and help came to believers. Again, in the "vertical" world of the ancients, such functions were readily ascribable to such objects and rites. In the "horizontal" world of the modern mind, no satisfactory concept of either sacrament or sacramental has been evolved. The modern mind is oriented to the chemical and material analysis of objects, and it does not readily see them either as evocative symbols of an invisible reality or the causal elements in a system of spiritual life-giving.

Sabbath, Religious Year

The term Sabbath is used here to describe the weekly day of worship which the three religions set aside for special rest and devotion. The origin of this institution in all three religions is to be sought in the account of the Creation of the world given in the *Book of Genesis:* Yahweh created the world in six days; on the seventh day he rested from his labors.[7] The Jewish Sabbath is traditionally on the Saturday; the Christians celebrate it on Sunday; Muslims explicitly chose Friday, in order to be different from Jews and Christians.

The Bible tells how Moses included the Sabbath prescription in his Ten Commandments because "it was six days the Lord spent in making heaven and earth and sea and all that is in them; on the seventh day he rested, and that is why the Lord

---

[6] The water is sometimes sprinkled; sometimes the person to be baptized is immersed in water. Strictly, the water can be poured or touch any part of the body.

[7] Cf. Genesis 2:1-3.

has blessed the Sabbath day and sanctified it." [8] The Muslim Sabbath was apparently instituted for the same reasons as are alleged for the Jewish Sabbath.[9]

The scheme of creation as outlined in the seven-day span by the writer of Genesis is, of course, unacceptable and unintelligible in the light of modern science. Extending over a period of ten billion years, the universe expanded and cooled; stars were born and stars died; slowly our present solar system was evolved. Life started in the form of bacteria and simple plants. About 100,000 years ago man appeared. The fundamental religious reason proffered by all three religions is thus unacceptable and nonsensical to the modern mind. In modern times, however, stress has been laid not on this Biblical aspect, but on the need for a special day when religious worship could be performed in an atmosphere of peace. This does not seem, however, an adequate reason, because the law of Sabbath both in Judaism and Christianity is not observed as a general rule. Anciently, all servile work was forbidden. People lived in small conglomerates. There was little movement, little to do but to rest. The modern urbanized populations, however, have plenty to do, plenty of journeys and visits to make, plenty of amusement to obtain on the first free day of the week. The purpose of the original institution, therefore, seems to be frustrated. The Sabbath institution no longer makes sense in 20th century megalopolis.

The purely provisional character of the Sabbath prescription in the Ten Commandments was underlined recently by the permission granted to Roman Catholics living in Rome to fulfill their weekly obligation on Saturdays rather than Sundays. The chief purpose of the "experimental change," as Angelo Cardinal Dell'Acqua, papal vicar for Rome, stated, seems to have been to capture the crowds of Italians who wish to spend the weekend on the beach. Sporadic permission has been given in the past to change the Sunday obligation to Saturday both in Europe and in the U.S.A.

The term "religious year" refers to the custom adopted by the three religions of dating historical events from the special date on which each one considers itself to have officially be-

[8] Cf. Exodus 20:11.
[9] Cf. Koran 4:150; 16:125.

gun. Thus, this is 1969 A.D. (*for the Christians* [10]), 5730 A.M. for the Jews,[11] and 1347 A.H. for the Muslims.[12] The use of Christian dating is widespread and accepted internationally. There is no difficulty in using it. Nor for that matter do Jews and Muslims find any difficulty in using their particular dating methods within their own areas.

It is rather the principle behind such usages which is unintelligible to the modern mind and which must finally result in a reform of these dating methods. The impulse to date historical events universally from the time of one particular religious event in the past arose in pre-scientific mentalities which were impregnated with an anthropocentric view of the universe. This chronology was limited to a small portion of time in the history of the planet Earth. As such, it reflects a pre-scientific mind. For the moment, nothing in this matter can change, mainly because agreement could not be reached either between the different religions or between the different ideologies and blocs of our world. Besides, science is not ready with another and more cosmic system of dating; the relative age phases of the Earth and of the universe are not yet fixed with any accuracy. At a later date, and when the science of the stars and galaxies is a surer thing, no doubt another chronological system will be adopted. No doubt, that system will not be made to depend on an event of human history which took place as late as either the Hebrew "creation of the world," the birth of Jesus, or the Hegira of Mohammad. Embedded in the cosmos is another method of chronology which man must extract and adapt to his own use.

29. *Neither Black nor White*

Twentieth-century man now finds himself in an era of peculiar change. The change is not one imposed by outside forces over which he has no control. No unknown, inconceivable or

[10] *Anno Domini* ("year of the Lord") dates from the alleged date of Jesus' birth. Actually this date is generally acknowledged to be incorrect.

[11] *Anno Mundi* ("year of the World") dates from the creation of the world.

[12] *Anno Hegirae* ("year of the Hegira"). See page 129.

"outside" elements are pressuring him. Nor is the change, as often it was in the past, an intensification of previous conditions. The change affects man's total environment, and it is initiated by man himself. For the first time in his history, man is in the process of changing his native environment according to his own pre-set ideas. Hitherto, he had merely modified it in accordance with fixed laws which he found imposed on him by that environment. This new induced change in his environment is the first and fundamental break in man's connatural use of binary thinking and self-expression.

In discussing the anti-consensus of modern man, we will see that because the iron-clad dialectic of opposites, to which we have referred, is being dissolved, man's socio-political condition is vitally affected. Here in this chapter we are primarily concerned with describing the phenomena of this development.

The first elements in this environmental change which directly affects man's binary system are represented by the non-natural increase in man's primary sense-perceptions. Briefly, man has freed himself in practical terms from the limitations imposed on him by the naturally narrow range of his unaided sight, hearing, touch, taste, smell. By nature, these have an extremely limited range, are fallacious after a certain point in time and space, and place man at the "receiving-end" of the communications line. Man is primarily a passive spectator. This previous condition is now changing radically. Some examples from the areas of sight and sound will suffice to illustrate this.

Today, by electronic machinery, man's hearing has been lengthened to a world dimension: by modern technology he can hear simultaneously sounds and voices from all around his world and from widely separated places. His religious binary concepts based on the original limitation of his hearing are fundamentally affected. Man can no longer and with the same religious intensity use the images of prayer, for example, as a call "out" from an inner prison of the circumscribed individual, whose voice a single wall could muffle, to evoke a voice which must travel over the wide spaces "in-between." Voice amplification, extension and variation, acuter and more lengthened hearing, the simultaneous hearing by people separated by oceans and continents—such changes and innovations in man's hearing environment rid this sector of its former richness in images. Millions heard the voices of human beings as they swirled many miles above and around the Earth. Thereby the concept of sound, and of distance to be travelled by sound, was changed. Man can with radio-telescopes "listen" to the radio-waves which reach him from the unknown deeps of outer space. Thereby he begins to look on that outer space as his, not the domain of an invisible power.

Isaiah's "voice of one calling in the desert" evokes no sympathetic image in modern man. The only question the latter would have concerns the lack of electronic equipment in the 8th and 7th centuries B.C. The patient waiting for God's voice to speak across huge distances of eternity and infinity, an image used in the Jewish, Christian, and Muslim sacred books and piety, requires a new coloration today: it is the lack of hearing apparatus that strikes man, not God's inaccessibility and not man's littleness or hearing weakness. The consequent virtues of patience, trust, humility on man's part, and of mercy, compassion, and love on God's part are easily highlighted in the anciently used image, but find no stimulus in man's newly fabricated powers.

Man's sight has also been affected. Not only can he see events in far-off lands simultaneously with millions in other far-away lands. He can see where sight was impossible before: through his own body by projecting X-rays through silver nitrate plates; in the night and through clouds by radar; underwater by means of sonic apparatus. Thereby, a series of binary concepts and their accompanying ideas are affected: sightlessness; light; darkness; acuity of vision; enjoyment of different colors and unheard-of sights, of great events and personages; alien minds—for man finds that crowds of people in Buenos Aires, Manchester, Budapest, Cape Town, Hankow, Moscow, and Djakarta, feel the same emotions as he does, and cheer in the same pugnacious way as he does at a soccer game.

More profoundly still, all man's senses have been affected by the amplification afforded by computers. The data of his world need not be entrusted to the slow-moving, relatively unstable criteria of his own senses. He can now build machines which can absorb infinitely more information, in an infinitely faster period of time, can store them, classify them, analyze them, retrieve them, make predictions based on them, offer alternatives arising from varying configurations and combinations of these data, in ways impossible to man's senses. Man's concepts, therefore, of height, length, breadth, depth, color, right, left, are affected. His abhorrence of certain traits such as blackness, roughness, of what is square and crooked, is changed.

The primary data of his senses can no longer suggest to him either the language or the thoughts with which he can think about a god or formulate his religious thoughts.

Man's binary activity is further affected by the "all-at-once" character of his modern sense-exposure. Environmental information today increases continuously and gargantuanly, details overlapping details so that man finds himself obliged to develop what has been called "pattern-recognition," i.e. instant and total configurational awareness. Only by this means can man perceive the new meanings and relationships inherent in his universe. Otherwise he can never hope to master all the oceans of details. The resultant effects on man's art and self-expression and ultimately on his religious expression are ineluctable. Sense-experience at this stage becomes a riot of new combinations: playing tennis with sound-wired rackets that broadcast the bong of the ball and picking up on delicate hearing devices the sounds of mushrooms producing spores are two vivid illustrations of these remarks.[1]

Greater urbanization and the transition from the polis to megalopolis, to technopolis, is another relevant development today. For by these three steps, man walks further and further away from his natural environment, becomes unfamiliar with the primal forces, wind, storms, changing seasons, fire, earth, growing green plants, production of food, and so on. His dependence is not on a god who sends rain for drought, sunshine to ripen wheat and corn, sap and strength to fruit-trees, and fertility to the wombs of cattle. It is on the efficiency of the supermarket, the speed of trucks, trains, airplanes, canning-factories, wrapping-machines, packaging departments, ready-made clothes, the bustling lunch-counter, and the pre-cooked TV dinner.

Man is furthermore locked into a complex pattern of mechanical lanes and alleyways along which his life must run if it

[1] See the account of "Nine Evenings: Theater and Engineering," which was conceived in 1965 as the American contribution to the Stockholm Festival for Art and Technology. It was presented on October 13, 1966, at the 69th Regiment Armory, New York. Cf. *New York Times,* Sunday, Oct. 2, 1966, *Art Notes.*

is to be at all viable: traffic signals, elevator dials and buttons, sliding doors, electric subway trains, bureaucratic procedures. Vastness is no longer mirrored in the face of oceans or the dust of deserts or the velvet mystery of unchartered skies, but in the all-encompassing society. Loneliness and desolation of spirit are translated into the anonymity of subway crowds and the uniformity of mass-production lines and corporation employ-ees. Man's former dependence on his imagination and ingenu-ity, aided by the "outside" help of a divine providence in which he believed, is fundamentally affected by the subtle geometries of urban life: the curve of the highway, the impersonal voice on the loudspeaker announcing destination in general and not any particular person's destination, the up and down escalators, the one-way street. Man has merely to work with the prear-ranged signals, stop when others stop, keep moving with the moving crowds. Thus in the 20th century, an unanticipated and unplanned revolution is quietly reshuffling man's tradi-tional landmarks, reshaping his concepts of daily life, affect-ing his thoughts and his creative abilities, and molding the words he uses and the emotions he experiences. The Psalmist's prayer: "Lord my God, give me thy light for my feet so that they never stray from the path of righteousness" could only be analogously and meaningfully translated for modern man as something like: "Lord, my God, help me make the traffic-lights in time, and let me not sin by unscrupulously getting rid of those who stand in my way to the presidential chair."

There is a temptation to conclude that all these changes represent mere transferences: e.g. the loneliness of the desert which afflicted the ancients is now replaced by the loneliness of urban commuter crowds or the empty streets of big cities at 4:30 A.M. But there are certain qualitative differences: the god worshipped by Judaism, Christianity and Islam was be-lieved to have created the desert, and its stillness contained his peace for the believer; the city streets are man-made ghettos for the lonely person. But the deeper reason for not yielding to that temptation is that modern life implies the destruction of certain binary concepts which were once fixed absolutes for expressing religious thoughts and emotions.

If we take, for instance, the dictionary definition of *black* and *white* we find the following: [2]

[2] Cf. Webster's *New World Dictionary: College Edition,* 1964.

1. opposite to white . . . 2. dark-complexioned.
3. Negro . . . 4. totally without light: in complete darkness, dark. 5. soiled, dirty. 6. wearing black clothing. 7. evil, wicked, harmful. 8. disgraceful. 9. sad; dismal; gloomy . . . 10. sullen; angered. 11. without hope; as, a black future . . .

The dictionary defines "white" in different terms:

1. having the color of pure snow or milk; of the color of radiated, transmitted, or reflected light . . . opposite to black. 2. of a light or pale color . . . a) gray; silvery; hoary. b) very blond. c) pale; wan; pallid; ashen; d) light-yellow or amber . . . e) blank . . . f) of a light-gray color and lustrous appearance; . . . g)made of silver. h) snowy; . . . 4. morally or spiritually pure; spotless; innocent. 5. free from evil intent; harmless; . . . 6. (rare) happy; fortunate; auspicious; . . . 7. a) having a light-colored skin; Caucasian. b) of or controlled by the white race; as, *white* supremacy. c) (nations of racial superiority). (slang), honest, fair, dependable. 8. being at white heat . . . 9. reactionary, counter-revolutionary, or royalist, as opposed to *red* (radical or revolutionary. . . .)

Apart from the basic chemical and pigmentary differences noted above, there is not one of the ascribed meanings given here which can be put forward today in this simplistic way. In fact, these dictionary definitions define *black* and *white* rather as one will find them in past literature and usage rather than on the lips of modern man in his deliberate choice of images. This is one way of measuring the change in man's binary thought.

The binaries have been involved and affected, however, in a more profound way which will be commented on when we speak of the modern anti-consensus in later chapters. Briefly, the use of binaries or dialectic opposites issues poignantly in man's eternal temptation to use rending dichotomies. Man by nature, as we saw previously, has certain patterns of binaristic thinking which make him divide his world into good and bad, true and false, etc. He sees a moral difference in such extreme light that he opts for what he holds as "good" and "true," and he opposes with hostility, coercion and death what he considers "false" and "bad." The modern anti-consensus seeks another, a non-binaristic, unpolarized world. It is not to the credit of the three religions that they fundamentally nourished and encouraged an extreme binarism in human relations. Their dominance in all its forms relies essentially on the dialectic polarization of opposites. This is one reason, as we see in the following chapters, for their rejection by modern man.

PART VII

The Three Witnesses

30. The Procession of the Crucified

The procession of the crucified took place twice in the year 1968.

Jerusalem, Israel. Palm Sunday, April 7, 1968. The Christians are commemorating the triumph of Jesus' entry into the City, despite the growing hostility and murderous intent of the Jews who wished to kill him. The procession is formed at Bethphage on the Mount of Olives separated from the City by the Kidron Valley: twin columns assemble of bishops, priests, monks, nuns, men, women, children, pilgrims from America, Africa, and Europe. All carry palm leaves. The clergy, bearded and unbearded, clothed in black and white and purple, some with headgear, others bareheaded, all solemn and slightly sad-faced on account of the coming sufferings of Jesus; some reading silently from prayer-books, others saying their beads, others lost in meditation. Groups of children are singing Arabic hymns under the direction of Iraqi nuns. Israeli policemen keep their eyes on all from a discreet distance. The sky is blue, practically without a haze of cloud. The sun is bright, warm, pulsating.

The winding path of the procession is lined with thousands of Israelis: some just curious, some interested, some reverential. None of them has ever seen the procession before. Christian tradition holds that some of these Israelis' forefathers had seen the original entry of Jesus 1900 years before and had chanted "Hosanna to him who comes in the name of the Lord!" while others had gnashed their teeth and plotted how to liquidate Jesus. The twin columns wound their way slowly under the bright sun through the Arab village of El Tur where women kissed the hems of the bishops' robes to be healed of their ailments, down through the olive groves of Gethsemani where Jesus had sweated blood in anticipation of his crucifixion, and climbed the hillside to the City, passing by a mound of rocks bearing a plaque commemorating the Israeli soldiers who died fighting for possession of the City in June 1967.

It entered the City through the arched Gate of St. Stephen. In June 1967, the Israeli army had broken through this Gate into the City and captured it from the Jordanians, and one of the Gate's huge doors had been demolished by the fierce firepower. Now Israeli sentries stood above and around the Gate, at ease but watchful. An airplane could be heard faintly in the distance toward the south. Jesus had not entered by this Gate, but by the Golden Gate. It, however, lay in the Haram es-Sharif area now holy to the Muslims and therefore impassable to Christians.

The procession was now walking the Via Dolorosa, the Road of Pain, on which Jesus had trailed in reverse direction carrying his cross to Calvary and death. The procession stopped in the courtyard of St. Anne's Church which was pockmarked by shells; the faithful gathered around the clergy; incense was burned; prayers were intoned; hymns were sung. The Christians reminded themselves that this triumphal entry of Jesus was a prelude to his painful rejection by his people and his horrible and unjust execution for the sake of all men's sins. The Gospel was read. "And Jesus wept and said: 'would that even today you knew how to attain peace. But they shall not leave one stone upon another, because you did not recognize your opportunity to be saved. . . .' " "Imi," asked a small boy in a yarmulka, "is he speaking of the Egyptians?"

The clergy dispersed. The nuns marched the children off in

formation. An Arab beggar, both eyes bulging with chronic trachoma, collected two American dollars, thirty piastres, and five cheese sandwiches wrapped in a plastic bag bearing the name of a supermarket in Dijon, France. The Israeli children chased some remaining blue fumes of incense as playful will-o'-the-wisps. Over in Mea Shearim, the Jewish Orthodox quarter, an old man bent over his printed Bible, his sidelocks swaying with the movement of his body and the murmured rhythm of his syllables: "Jerusalem! If I forget thee, may the skill of right hand perish! Let my tongue stick fast to the roof of my mouth if. . . ." Inside the Dome of the Rock, a worshipper knelt leaning on his haunches, his eyes closed: "Say, O you who are unbelievers! I worship not that which you worship. . . ." The Israeli police sergeant telephoned the Ministry of Culture to make his report: all had gone off without incident. "Tov! Ha-kol baseder," said the voice at the other end, when the report was finished. It was good. All was in order.

Jerusalem, Israel. Independence Day, May 2, 1968. The parade began near Shufat, an Arab village in the northern part of the former Jordanian territory: children of Israel were going to march in a five-mile triumph from the Old to the New City. More than 20 years ago, many present were emaciated skeletons in German prison camps, crucified in over ten European countries. This was their glorious entry now. Four thousand spit-'n-polish troops, marching with the long leg-lope and wide arm-swing of British Army tradition, passed in view of almost half a million Israelis, accompanied by sand-colored troop-carriers, amphibious tanks, self-propelled guns, T-55 tanks, Centurion tanks, Patton tanks, in addition to captured Jordanian 155-mm. Long Tom artillery pieces with which the Jordanians had shelled Tel Aviv, and Soviet SAM missiles taken intact from Nasser's army in the Sinai Peninsula. Thirty jet planes flashed overhead in the formation of a spreadeagled, billowy, silvered Star of David. In the sky also dozens of American Skyhawk fighter-bombers and Bell helicopters droned past. All in all, 300 aircraft brought home the lesson of Israel's press-button victory of June 1967.

Most of Jerusalem's 60,000 Arabs remained at home, some watching glumly through shuttered windows, some standing abashed on their balconies, others still raging with anger and frustration gathered in little knots and spoke of retaliation. As the parade wound into the New City, the newly established Israeli national TV station beamed the images to Amman, Damascus, Cairo, and other Arab capitals. In Damascus, protesting crowds milled around chanting: "Jerusalem is ours!" In Cairo, obedient crowds demanded of Colonel Nasser: "Arms! Arms! Draft us!" But every Arab in every Arab land knew that no combination of untold Arab wealth, preponderant Arab armies, intense Arab diplomacy, bitter and ruthless Arab guerilla warfare, and malignant Russian generosity in arms, technical personnel, and logistical supplies had affected anything whatever except total defeat three times at the hands of these men who claimed the land in the name of an age-old tradition.

That night, while the Copts and the Armenian Christians disputed a small matter of precedence in chanting around the birth-stone of their Savior, Jesus, twelve beacons shone from the barren top of Mount Herzl splaying twelve streams of light, one for each of the Twelve Tribes of Israel, out into the dark-blue-velvet dome of the Eastern night. At the Wailing Wall, a locked-arms phalanx of Orthodox Jews complete with stove-pipe hats, frock coats, and sidelocks, red-bereted paratroopers still carrying their compact Uzi machine-guns, young sabras and tourists, danced and chanted to the rollicking music of *Hava Negila,* while a group of Army girls sat and sang the plaintive *Sharm El Sheik,* a war melody popular in June 1967 when the Israeli tank corps spearheaded to the important Sinai outpost of the same name. In the Holy Sepulcher, a brown-habited Irish Franciscan lay-brother waited impatiently until the Greeks had vacated an altar in order to prepare it for Mass. "I wish to God they'd stop that bedlam outside," he murmured in a soft Kerry accent.

Outside in a Judaean ravine, Israeli infantry and helicopters closed in on a squad of Arab saboteurs carrying explosives and killed thirteen of them. In the streets of Jerusalem thousands of young Israelis danced all night to the traditional Hora and its hypnotic strains, then adjourned to cafes, parks, hotels, and lodging houses to sleep off their fatigue. At dawn, when all was quiet the next day, an Israeli girl exchanged promises of marriage with her fiancé standing beside the black altar of Herzl's monument on the mountain. In the Benedictine monastery atop the wall of the Old City, the sacristan, who opened the windows to the east, heard the persistent wail of the muezzin chanting already from the mosque out over the roofs, the desert, and the river, through the clear air of the morning: "O Believers, prescribed for you in retaliation for the slain: freeman for freeman, slave for slave, female for female . . . slay them wherever you come upon them, and expel them from where they expelled you. . . ." Down in Cairo, Colonel Nasser promised a Holy War against Israel because his fellow Egyptians had given him a 99.98% endorsement vote and because this was "louder than the thunder of 300 tanks in Arab Jerusalem."

Jesus, according to Christian belief, was crucified shortly after his triumphal entry into Jerusalem. His crucifixion has been the central theme of Christianity since its foundation. The crucified one stands with outstretched arms overlooking Christian history since the time of Peter and Paul. In another and real sense, the Jew, who has lately established himself in a newly created home in Israel, has been the crucified one of Christian history. Between Jesus the Jew and the Jew of history there is surely more than an affinity of race. The Jew lies with arms outstretched on the road which Christianity travelled. For Christians made of him the object of their hate and their sacred brutality. Lately, in the 20th century, the crucified figure of Jesus has been reproduced mystically in the Arab populations of former Palestine and throughout the Middle East, which have been in the center of warring armies fighting to satisfy the personal whims of petty dictators and medieval monarchs, or to establish the freshly-cooked ideas of Westernized Arabs who studied in Western universities. The Arabs have been wallowing in conditions of social blight, economic backwardness, and agrarian serfdom, which defy the imagination of any Westerner, no matter what he has seen in the barrios of South America, in the slums of Chicago, or the Negro shanties in Alabama or Mississippi.

Christianity within its own borders has specialized in self-crucifixion, at first to quite a minor degree during the first 1500 years of its life, when heretics and dissidents and accused witches and sorcerers were put to death, as Jesus was. Then, with the breakup of its unity in the 16th century, Christians devised for each other one Hell more horrendous and tortuous than another, indulging in a 300-year round of mutual recrimination, accusation, denigration, and relegation by bell, book, and a candle, to the filthiest categories of human life. No branch of Christianity can be excused from this, because all Christians have indulged in it.

No body of Christians ever answered the insults of other Christians with Christ's answer: "Forgive them, Father, for they know not what they do." They all developed special vocabularies replete with violent words such as "heresy," "heretic," "extirpation," "condemnation," "excommunication," "outcasts," "unclean believers," "vice-mongers." Each one devised its special defenses against the other: social ostracism, civil war, discrimination, calumny, legal non-existence. Rome was the Red Lady of the South. Luther was the Pig of Germany. Protestants were the sons of vipers. Jews were the "race of the devil." Muslims were "benighted and error-ridden barbarians." No body of Christians ever tried to conquer the world with humility and patience and love, and no body of believers ever tried to fan the flames of faith in the heart of man by being authentically believers.

The Jews, in retaliation for their pain and their sustained exile, contributed to the sea of hate, distrust and, in some cases, deformation of the truth. They invented multiform expressions of contempt, condemnation, loathing, and utter rejection of Christians. They even modified some of their traditional beliefs because the Christians had borrowed them in their original form and, in their repugnance from all things Christian, they wanted no resemblance to subsist between their faith and that of the Christians. They returned hate with hate. They, also, cannot be excused and considered totally guiltless. They preached truth and justice, yet they violated both in order to maintain their religion and their Jewishness. Christians preached love but practised officially sanctioned hate, intermingling their loveliest psalms of compassion for their dying Savior with expressions of extreme disgust for the Jews. They developed a conceptuology and an entire section of their art in painting, sculpture, hymnody, drama, so infused with un-Christian feelings that, like many a stained-glass window of magnificent Medieval cathedrals, they can only be removed and replaced with substitutes which are artistically less appealing, are certainly not six or seven hundred years old, but are in perfect accord with their beliefs.

Muslims preached mercy and compassion, but they practised none or very little, assigning both Christians and Jews to the lowest rung in Allah's consideration, and historically meting

out to both a treatment which rivals any cruelties of man in
known history. Down through the ages, this procession of the
crucified one has come: formed, maintained, and augmented
by Jews, Christians, and Muslims. Each one has practiced
green-eyed and malignant jealousy of the others' triumphs.
Each one has prayed with its armies to its god that the armies
of its opponents be destroyed. There is no palliating or explaining away this sin of Judaism, Christianity, and Islam.

The three religions failed in another significant way. None
of them attacked slavery or race prejudice or other flagrant
inhumanities of man to man from the very beginning of their
existence. The Arabs of today sanction slavery as spontaneously
as the Popes of the 19th century sanctioned the creation of
castrati choirs for Papal masses, as readily and blindly as the
Protestant ethic of the white American sanctioned the serfdom
and degradation of the Negro race until the second half of the
20th century. Each religion has practiced the art of climbing
on the bandwagon: only when lay and secular reformers, sometimes lacking any formal religion whatever, raised such a hue
and cry that men's consciences were stirred, did the religions
begin to turn their huge resources toward reform. The Catholic Church in Germany and Italy acquiesced in Nazism and
Fascism at least in the earlier stages of these ideologies. Russian Orthodoxy acquiesced in the despotism and sadism of
Czarist times. Greek Orthodoxy sanctioned the corruption of the
Byzantine court and today is bitterly nationalist in Greece's
disputes with Turkey. No Protestant Church and no Jewish
Synagogue ever officially condemned and attacked the Ku Klux
Klan before 1945 in America, though individuals did. Judaism,
Christianity, and Islam have practiced the double standard in
this matter. Islam's learned men, her wise men, her holy men,
her much vaunted principles of equality, of peace, of humility,
of mercy, of goodness have never been harnessed to effect an
equal distribution of goods to the poor in Arab lands, to wipe
out the conditions of misery in which many Arab populations
live, to decry the falsity of perennial dictators, or to alleviate
the human suffering of the Arab refugee camps.

Thus the three religions have not been witnesses to the truth.
All, it is true, have developed an exalted vocabulary, and a very
impressive manner of announcing their own grandiose claims.
All three have exceled and excel in words, as distinct from
actions. All three have an impressive ritual and have refined

psychological approaches to man. Yet the witness of words, mere words, has never yet changed men's minds, nor has mere theological subtlety helped men to be better men. The witness of the three religions has been faulty, at times perniciously false and erroneous. The three of them have witnessed to the uses of hate for the love of a god. And all three have disposed of the lives and happiness of millions of human beings without any real feeling for human suffering or any genuine concern for the concrete realities of life.

It is clear, first of all, that today all three religions lack any authoritative note for man. They have, as yet, each one of them, sufficient number of adherents to give the impression of continuing strength, and this glosses over for them and for the outside world at times their terrible weakness. For each one of them, when scrutinized closely, is blackened with sufficient failures to prevent any thinking man from believing in them. And, above all, all three persevere in making a claim which cannot possibly be valid and true: that they are, each single one, the true religion.

Each one of them, however, hides from the ultimate test of its validity and truth behind a wall of unknowing and expectation. All three chorus that only on the "Last Day," when the "End" comes, when "God" decides, will it be clear that the "other two" and all others besides were false, and it (the claimant) was all along the true community of the one "God."

In today's world, however, this is no longer sufficient. The religions are called upon to witness, not to the truth, but to what they really are. No cavilling, no subtlety, no refuge in ancient formularies, and no appeal to presumed dignities, will suffice.

It is the contention of this chapter that the only condition upon which these religions can possibly begin again to operate salvifically and effectively for the basic religious truth of their monotheism is that they, first of all, cross the chasmic distances which they have dug between each other and, by force of the faith they claim to have and the grace of the god they profess to represent, come to a humble and strong possession of the truth about one god, his revelation to men, his love of men, and his infinitely merciful and sublime plans for man's ultimate and eternal happiness.

Certain difficulties stand in the way. Certain ingrained inhibitions must be overcome. There is a certain precedence:

they must decide that no one is better than another, no one takes precedence over the other, no one receives the other as long lost son or erring sheep. There are certain differences: they must abandon their fascination with these differences; they must cease to study the differences, "participating neutrally" in the liturgy of differing religions, and trying to appreciate "what the other is trying to do and say." Christians must stop trying to participate in Jewish Seders. Protestants must stop "partaking" in Catholic ordinations and services. Muslims must not seek to imitate the parish and chaplain structure of Christianity which Judaism has imitated so well and so disastrously for its purity. They must cease the ecumenism of difference. Instead, their only hope lies in an ecumenism of identity. They must find a common mystery in which to participate, a common belief to share and, therefore, find the one god in which they all believe.

In this section, we wish to consider Judaism, Christianity, and Islam singly as to the inherent difficulties of their dominance. In Judaism and Christianity, we must consider their present overall trend which can be summarized in the word *activism* (chapters 31 and 33). They both preach comparatively little religion or moral rules or piety. They both indulge mightily in actions: attempted participation in socio-political issues, preoccupation with absorbing organizational problems. They both have a problem particular to them. Judaism's problem is Israel (chapter 32). Christianity's problem is Judaism (chapter 34). Islam presents a totally different picture. Its problems are largely ones of inability, backwardness, utter rigidity (chapters 35 and 36).

31. Stones for Abraham

Jewry today sometimes gives an excellent impression: that it was never so strong and self-conscious since the destruction of the Second Jewish Commonwealth under the Roman Emperor Hadrian in the early 'thirties of the second century A.D. Yet, closer consideration shows that Jewry has no center of gravitation. Furthermore, both Israeli and non-Israeli bodies of Jewry are beset by nagging antinomies which threaten their Judaic character.

One sustained ambiguity today hampers clear understanding, sound judgement, and common consideration both of Judaism and Jewishness: this is the persistent confusion of Judaism, Jewishness, and Israeli nationalism. This ambiguity was excusable 50 years ago. Today it is no longer so, but it still perdures and is the source of many misjudgements.

The lines of division, however, drawn by the finger of history are clear. There is, first of all, a religion called Judaism believed in and practiced by a diminishing group of people, the majority of whom live in the U.S.A. and South America, with small ever-reducing communities mainly in Europe and Israel, and with fractional groups settled elsewhere. This we can call the Jewish Synagogue. Of itself, the Synagogue is essentially supranational, professionally religious in nature, possessing a culture and a way of life all its own.

There is, secondly, the socio-ethnic sub-culture existing mainly within the cultural and civilizational ambient of the West, but with some ramifications outside the West; and this division contains the majority of Jews in our world of the 20th century.[1] This is the Jewish sub-culture; it always presumes a carrier-culture in which it has grown. There is, thirdly, a sovereign, national state called Israel, which has nothing essential to do with the religion of Judaism, but is built on a socio-cultural tradition developed by Jews within Judaism during 1800 years. These three divisions are comprehended under the generic term Jewry, so that when this term is used, both the religion of Judaism, the State of Israel, as well as the vaster Jewish sub-culture are indicated.

This tripartite division of Jewry did not exist 20 years ago, when the lines were blurred between the religion of Judaism, the hopes of return to the Land of Israel, and the Jewishness of Jews. These three elements had not yet been catalyzed by irreversible events of history. But in that 20 years, all was changed. The change, however, has been so profound and so

[1] The 1966 *American Jewish Year Book* gives the following totals: Africa—240,100 (greatest number living in Morocco); Canada—275,000; North America and West Indies—6,036,000 (5,720,00 in U.S.A. alone); South America—6,726,200 (greatest number in Argentina); Asia—2,417,550 (greatest number in Israel—2,299,000); Europe—3,955,400 (greatest number in the U.S.S.R.—2,486,000); Australia and New Zealand—72,000 (only 5,000 in Tasmania).

sudden that only now the first visible traces of that change are appearing. In order to assess the plight of Judaism's dominance we must assign to each of these divisions of Judaism its proper character, role, and exigencies today. In this chapter, we will speak of the first two divisions. The next chapter will discuss Israel and its place among the nations.

It has always been a fundamental tenet of Judaism that the god it worshipped was a god of history. He can do with history as he wills. In the words of Jesus, he can "raise up children from these stones for Abraham." He did intervene in history. He spoke through history. He acted through historical events and personages. His will and plan were manifest in history. Rarely did he personally speak or appear directly. But men and things and the world with its elements were always and irresistibly and unresistingly his instruments, his mediators, and the clay in his hands as the Master Potter. Thus to punish his Chosen People, he used the Assyrian, the Egyptian, the Babylonian, the Greek, the Roman. To restore them from their exile, he used Cyrus of Persia. What was policy action for a lay emperor was, in reality, the omnipotent will of the creating god.

To appreciate the change in Judaism which we have mentioned, we have to realize, firstly, that some Jews, but not the whole Chosen People, were restored to the Land of Israel in the first half of the 20th century. Secondly, these Jews were not restored by the unconscious instruments of this Jewish god but by Jews themselves, somewhat aided by interested nations, who wished to found a secular state. These were instruments and mediators—Lord Balfour, Chaim Weizmann, Theodor Herzl, Baron Rothschild—conscious and unconscious of the full implications of what they were doing. They were, however, instruments and mediators, not for the restoration of the Jewish people, not for the restoration of that Israel or Judaism envisioned in the Bible by prophet, priest, judge, and teacher, but for the establishment of a lay state not tied essentially to Judaism. In this sense, Judaism is still in exile; Zion has not been restored. The State of Israel is neither the community of Samson and Saul, nor the kingdom of David and Solomon, nor the commonwealth of Ezra and the men of the Great Synagogue.

Secondly, we must realize that it would seemingly take an actual intervention of the god of Israel to revert what seems to be the irreversible historical process by which in our time the restoration of the classical Zion has been made an impossibility, and by which, therefore, a central piece in the mosaic of traditional Jewish belief has been eliminated forever. For the Jewish people as a whole will never be restored or permit themselves to be restored to Zion and to Israel, nor will that portion of it now restored to the Land of Israel ever, as far as we can judge, allow the classical Zion to be established in place of the secular state of Israel.

Thirdly, it is clear that the majority of Jews have opted for some form of assimilation, thereby renouncing a part of their Jewishness. The Jew who is a citizen of any foreign country necessarily opts for an anachronistic attitude, or he undergoes assimilation great and small. The assimilation will come in a thousand and one ways: observance of Christian holidays, eating according to Christian habits (and thus neglecting Jewish dietary laws), listening to and absorbing willy-nilly Christian ways of thinking, reacting, self-criticism. It is impossible to resist assimilation unless one swings to an opposite extreme. But in that case, the Jew must live at complete variance with his surroundings. His work days and days of rest, his eating habits, his holidays, his ways of thought, all must be differentiated from those of his ambient. And this provokes the danger, if not the rise, of genuine anachronism and of a ghetto mentality. In short, Jewishness becomes, like the many forms of Christianity today, either a social and group-tag—and this is already a profound form of assimilation—or it creates an insularity and social hairshirt within which Judaism must chafe and suffer and eventually wither.

Christian and Jewish theologians have not been quick and clear-seeing in acknowledging the presence of these realities today, either because of prejudice, historical myopia, or prefabricated theories of history and theology.

What all this implies for the traditional dominance of Judaism is quite clear. Let us examine the first two divisions of Jewry. The religion of Judaism needs the least amount of comment in our context. Today, three main branches of it exist: Orthodox, Reform, and Conservative. Orthodox Judaism is severely traditionalist, maintains the unicity of the Bible as a revelation from the god of Israel, the unicity of the Chosen People, and the classical doctrines of Judaism—immortality of the human soul, resurrection and eternal life, Hell, Heaven, the

Last Judgement, to name the principal ones. It also insists on the importance of the Oral Law and its divine origin.

This Orthodox Judaism no longer stands at the bar of history claiming to be heard and accepted. For it has renounced the Temple and the Sacrifice without explicitly doing so, and it has refused to make its ancient doctrines intelligible and adapted to the modern environment. It refuses as a mass to return to the Land of Israel. And it clamors for a socio-political situation which is unacceptable to the majority of Jews and to all modern men today, and which is impossible physically and politically—*viz.* a theocratic oligarchy without the trappings of such a classical form. Orthodox Judaism, there-fore, cannot present a viable form of religious dominance: its proposed explanations of man and his cosmos are unacceptable.

The doctrine of Reform Judaism is clearly such a thorough-going renunciation of Judaism's classical dominance that it hardly needs further comment here. In American Reform Juda-ism, for instance, in both the 1885 Pittsburgh Platform of Re-form Judaism [2] and the 1937 Guiding Principles of Reform Judaism, the unicity of the biblical god was renounced, the "mythological" character of portions of the Bible was admitted, the sacrosanct character of traditional Jewish prescriptions and laws was renounced. The return to Zion, the arrival of the Messiah, and the restoration of the Temple were renounced; belief in the resurrection of the body, in everlasting punish-ment in Hell and eternal happiness in Heaven were renounced.

Essentially, Reform Judaism tends by its very nature to be-come a secular system of ethics based on Jewish culture, or, briefly, a Jewish ethical culture. Eliminated completely is Juda-ism's dominance. Preserved is that which man today calls Jewishness.

Conservative Judaism evolved as a reaction to Reform Ju-daism and Orthodox Judaism, claiming not to be a *doctrine* of Judaism but a *technique* of understanding Judaism. By em-phasizing *how* it dealt with traditional Judaism and not *what* it did in dealing with it, Conservative Judaism hoped to make

[2] During November 16-18, sixteen rabbis met at the invitation of R. Kaufmann Kobler, rabbi of Temple Beth-El of New York, and worked out a formulation of Reform principles which had been initially discussed and decided in the Philadelphia Rabbinical Con-ference of 1869.

good its basic claim: to be genuine Judaism as distinct either from what it called the Orthodox distortion of Judaism or the Reform renunciation of Judaism.

This, however, was an ingrate and impossible task. It was ingrate because it was not accepted by the majority of Jews in the world and because it necessarily was tied to nationalist Zionism and therefore ended up by supporting the establishment of the State of Israel. This, a noble end in itself, rendered impossible the dominance of classical Judaism. It was impossible because you cannot emphasize *how* to deal with living belief without tampering with *what* is believed, and because, in opting for assimilation, it opted automatically for a Protestant Judaism, for a Protestantization of Judaism, which is lethal for classical Judaism.

The modified marriage contract is an example of how one can deal with belief so as to change what is believed. By inserting in the *ketubah* (marriage contract) a clause making the bride and bridegroom subject to a decision of the rabbinical assembly, Conservative Judaism effectively changed the traditional belief that women should not get a divorce if the husband declines. More than one theological principle and truth of Judaism hangs on this original principle.

That Conservatism, as Reform Judaism, opted for a degree of assimilation is clear, even if it is painful for either of them to admit this in so many words. This has been seen in what we have said already about the reality of any Jew's position who does not live in a state governed by a theocratic oligarchy. Assimilation to a greater or lesser degree, but assimilation, is inevitable. The Protestantization of Judaism is another matter. This is clear primarily in the structure of Conservative thought and action. As in classical Protestantism, itself now evolving to a further step, it is a "church" of rabbinical theologians, liturgists, moralists, and spiritual counsellors who give form to Conservative Judaism. The charisma of the laity has been disbarred and discouraged. Conservative Judaism undergoes another form of assimilation here which is shared by Reform Judaism and, to some small extent, by Orthodox Judaism. For the whole system of parish rabbis, army chaplain rabbis, university chaplain rabbis, seminary decisions, the fostering of youth movements and social gatherings is but a Christian and, in this case, a Protestant structure. Conservative Judaism is indistinguishable from Christianity in this structure.

The task undertaken by Conservative Judaism was, therefore, impossible. It was bound to issue in un-Judaic forms and results. A concrete example of this can be seen in the press statement issued by the Jewish Theological Seminary for the High Holy Day message of October 1967.[3] There is nothing in this message which could not be said by a Protestant, a Roman Catholic, or a Muslim, and without any need of symbolism or allegorical interpretation on their part of what is said. The doctrine is not peculiarly Judaic or Jewish. More than that, there is nothing in the message which is typically Jewish as distinct from Christian or Muslim thought or theology. This may seem perfect ecumenism. It is not perfect or even near-perfect Judaism or, indeed, Judaism at all in its classical form. It is not so much that the god of Israel (or any god, for that matter) is totally unmentioned or that there is no mention of an ethical rule or moral hope. It is rather that, on the basis of a completely secular interpretation of sayings from the prophet Micha, Jews and all men are told to go ahead and build a world of their own choosing. This, of course, has as much to do with the essence of Judaism as the Roman saying "eat, drink, and be merry, for tomorrow we die" has to do with Christian submission to the divine will. This is, in fact, no message of Judaism. It is, however, the message of one man to another in a world which believes in no god nor in a salvation by that god. As such, it is up to date and acceptable to the modern world. But, as in Reform Judaism, all dominance traits are wiped out. In this context, it is easy to understand why Rabbi Joseph Karasick, president of the Union of Orthodox Jewish Congregations of America, denounced Conservatism and Reform Judaism as "foreign ideologies that must be rejected firmly and unequivocally . . . as the theology of deviation, the outgrowth of exile and assimilation." He insisted that the institutions of Israel must "reflect the classic, authentic, and lasting Judaism, namely the Torah Judaism."[4]

When we come to consider the vaster and, today, the highly important Jewish sub-culture, we enter an area to which increasingly all three branches of Judaism are losing heavily. Here we find all grades of assimilation possible and all shades of religious renunciation ever experienced by great religions.

[3] Cf. *New York Times*, October 8, 1967.
[4] Speaking at Jerusalem, Israel, on January 8, at the first world conference of Ashkenazi and Sephardic Jews.

It is by considering this division of Judaism that we also come to form an accurate idea of what Jewishness is today. This idea must, however, be complemented by what is said in the next chapter concerning Israeli Jewishness.

The Jewish sub-culture is intensely alive and involved in local, national, and international politics. In the United States, for instance, it has taken an active part in the Vietnam war issue, in civil rights battles, and other burning causes. Yet it was evident that the vast mass of Orthodox, Conservative, and Reform Jews in the U.S.A. were more than disturbed in June 1967 by the possibility that the U.S.A. would not ensure Israel's safety and survival. It was also evident that these Jews expected the U.S.A. to intervene even militarily to save Israel, if the latter could not sustain the attack by the Arab nations. At the same time, this same mass of Jewry was preponderantly against the U.S.A. involvement in Vietnam. The contradiction and annoying illogicality of this position is patent.

We find that this sub-culture retains the same basic folk-ways, a good deal of respect for learning, a solid but not thorough insistence on inter-Jewish marriage, a sense of a rich historical heritage, and a cultural way of life which is the sum total of Jewishness. More and more, especially in the younger generation, Jews are "more interested in political and social problems, than in religion." The Jew's Jewishness does not impel him to "the institutional forms of his religion." It is marked by a certain ethnic attachment, but is void of cultural consciousness and values.[5] His Jewishness does not have its center either in dogma or commandments.[6] Neither the formal beliefs of Judaism nor its traditional laws appeals to Jewish youth as authoritative.

Jewish youth in America partakes perhaps to a preponderantly greater degree than that of other faiths in "youth" movements, peace-fronts, anti-draft and anti-Vietnam movements. As one Jewish commentator said: "The hippie movement is a response to society at large, and Jewishness does not make much difference. The Jewish kids living in Haight-

---

[5] Quotations from the A.J.C. June 1964 report on the meaning of Jewishness to American Jewish Youth. Cf. also the results of B'nai Brith's findings as reported at the Annual Meeting of the Board of Governors in Washington, December 1966.

[6] Contrary to the opinion expressed in the A.J.C. report cited above.

Ashbury are no different from the others." [7] Jewish youth is very critical of traditional Judaism, describes Jewish communal life as "too middle-aged and respectable," [8] accuses the Synagogue of having "abdicated the central role it can play in the area of the poverty program," [9] and deplores its lack of activism: "You go to synagogue to dance or to pray, but you never consider going there to carry out social action activities," [10] said one student. Synagogal buildings are "seldom used except during Jewish High Holy Days when a smaller building could have been constructed and the remaining money sent to aid Negroes in the South or Harlem or for other worthy programs," was another comment.

The Jewish sub-culture, like its Protestant and Roman Catholic counterparts, is largely activist, although this has been severely criticized by at least one leading Jewish historian.[11] But withdrawal from dogma and traditional belief is also found explicitly among the rabbinical clergy as, for example, the case of Rabbi Richard L. Rubenstein who advocates a post-Christian and post-Jewish paganism: "After Auschwitz, I find I must reject a transcendent God entirely. God is where we come from and where we go, but he is just not involved in the world in any way." [12]

The fact of Israel has produced a pressure area in this sub-culture which is replete with problems of a practical and theoretic nature. On the one hand, the Israeli victory of June 1967 has been hailed as having religious significance.[13] The restoration of the State of Israel "stands second only to the Exodus" in its importance for contemporary religious experi-

[7] From a speech given in San Francisco on November 30, 1967 at a session connected with the Annual meeting of the A.J.C.'s National Executive Board at the Fairmont Hotel.

[8] Joel Rosenberg at the same session in San Francisco.

[9] Judy Lechner at the annual convention of Conservative Judaism's college group, Atid, in New York, Autumn of 1967.

[10] *Ibid.*

[11] Rabbi Arthur Hertzberg of Temple Emanu-El, Englewood, N.J., lecturing at the New School for Social Research.

[12] Speaking on October 29, 1966, at a 4 day conference on radical theology held at the Campus of the University of Michigan.

[13] R. Shubert Spero, an Orthodox rabbi, speaking at the Columbia University Conference under the Sponsorship of the Synagogue Council of America, on February 22, 1968.

ence. This new state "must be understood as the release of the messianic forces latent within the Jewish people," declared R. David Polish,[14] and "is yet to be enshrined in the rhythm of our lives, personal and collective, as a hallowed time, capable of interpretation only in theological terms." These Orthodox and Reform extremes were tempered by R. Edward M. Gershfield's sober statement: "I didn't have to wait for the six-day war to see God at work in the world." Reform Rabbi Eugene Borowitz stated that he found it difficult to put forward theological justification for political sovereignty, in direct contradiction to one central note of Biblical Judaism which is, if anything, tied indissolubly to territorial sovereignty and political independence.

The fact of Israel and its continuing history provides a problematic area for all branches of Jewry. Rabbi Spero could state that the present State of Israel is "a stage in the process of becoming the awaited Kingdom of Priests and Holy Nation." Yet the issue of immigration to Israel is not so clear. Even the World Zionist movement is divided on the issue as to whether its membership should be restricted to those who commit themselves and their families to personal immigration to Israel within five years.[15]

But the fact is that the State of Israel, its victories and vicissitudes are in themselves totally removed from the sphere in which classical Judaism moved and in which Orthodox and Conservative Judaism would like to move. This will be clear in our next chapter.

What emerges from any profound consideration of Jewry in its three branches, especially a consideration of the Jewish socio-ethnic sub-culture, is the effort to see fulfillment in activism such as Jewish aid to Negroes; Jewish collaboration in the wars on poverty, crime, and narcotics; Jewish pressure for peace-talks on Vietnam; Jewish programs to assist Jews of Latin America, Jewish opposition to the draft, to a tax rise in view of the war; Jewish programs for seminary organizations, building, education, youth. Like their Protestant and Catholic counterparts, Jewish rabbis readily interfere in matters which ten years ago were considered to belong exclusively to the competence

[14] At the same conference.
[15] Discussed at the preliminary meeting of Zionist leaders in Jerusalem, Israel, in February 1968.

of the State and of laymen. The Rabbinical Assembly of the Conservative Rabbis voted to suspend its system of obligatory army chaplaincy for all newly ordained rabbis.[16] The counsellor to Jewish students at Columbia University stated that he would advise students to resist induction into the armed forces on moral grounds.[17]

Non-Israeli Jewry, therefore, seems to stand at the crossroads of a great decision. At times, one gets the impression that the big decision has been made, and that this body of Jewry will head down the road of total assimilation through activism in social and political matters. At times, there is a tendency to draw back and to re-examine the core of Judaism. There is also, as we have seen in an earlier chapter, a certain definite gap between the mind of Jewish dominance and the modern mind. That gap does not appear to be narrowing; rather, modern non-Israeli Jewry on the whole seems to be opting for the modern mind and for relegating Judaism's superhistorical outlook to the attic of ancient things.

Two clocks adorn the Town Hall in the former Prague Ghetto. The hands of one clock face move in a clockwise direction around the hours indicated by Arabic numerals. The hands of the second clock move anti-clockwise around the hours indicated by Hebrew script. In one view, the arrangement is senseless: Hebrew script runs from left to right when inscribed on a page. But if the letters are used as numerals to run around the diameter of a clock face, there does not seem to be any good reason to run the hands anti-clockwise. A circle has neither beginning nor end, left or right, up or down. It is the sign of perfect integration. In another way, the arrangement is full of sense, a profound sense: Jewish time moves concomitantly with world time, yet in a Jewish way; and, at heart, what does "anti-clockwise" mean? It denotes the contrary of an established Occidental convention, merely that.

The concomitant, if contrary, method of indicating the same passage of time on the two clocks, however, is a parable in itself, as one writer has remarked. Judaism, side by side with Christianity and other alien influences, undergoes the same

[16] On March 26, 1968, at the 88th Annual Convention at Concord Hotel, New York.

[17] Rabbi A. B. Goldman, in his first annual report to the University's Jewish Advisory Board.

time span, counts that time in the same units. But its reckoning is different.

In this difference lies the heart of Judaism's religious dominance and the root of its crisis in the modern world. Modern history is showing increasingly that the two systems cannot run side by side synchronously but separatedly. Modern life does not permit it. If the struggle to keep them separated and distinct is still going on in non-Israeli Judaism, the matter has already been definitively decided in one way by Israeli Jewry. This we will consider in the next chapter.

32. My Name Is Israel

An incident which took place during the Maccabean Wars 175-142 B.C.) serves to illustrate the deep crisis which Israel presents to Judaism and Jewry. Maccabean forces with their women, children, and cattle were cornered by their enemies on a Sabbath day, when all work and effort were forbidden by the Law. Their enemies appealed to them to lay down their arms and come out.

"Come out and yield yourselves to the King's pleasure. Your lives will be spared."

"Come out and yield to the King's pleasure we cannot. For it is the Sabbath."

The attack began, but the Jews could not offer any resistance. Never a stone flew. Never a hiding-place of theirs was put in a state of defence.

"We will all die innocent men," said the Maccabees. "Let heaven and earth bear witness: it was no fault of ours we died." All perished passively, one thousand men, women, and children, with their cattle.

When their comrades heard about the disaster, the important decision was made: "If any should attack them on the Sabbath day, they should fight back."

In that religious dilemma and in that decision we have the dilemma and the decision out of which Israel came. The dilemma was as follows. If the Hitlerian holocaust had not taken place, Central and Eastern Europe would still be the super-historical center of Judaism. The term super-historical must be carefully understood. For over 1800 years Judaism had relegated the question of a Homeland to the "unknown time," the "last days," the coming of the Messiah. The concrete ideal of Maccabean and Zealot, of the men who died at Masada and at Qumran on the shores of the Dead Sea, was an Israel on earth. But in the Diaspora it became a weightless ideal as light as spidersilk floating on tracks somewhere between the stars (from behind which the god of Israel had spoken in ancient prophecies) and the solid earth (where the Chosen People wandered and waited in exile, expiring in mortality, buoyed up by their promised perpetuity). Israel became a super-historical ideal because it was to be restored at the end of all human history.

The pressure of anti-Semitism in the 19th century and the decisive event of the Holocaust drove Jews to seek a return to the ancient homeland in Palestine. For the super-historical center in Europe there was substituted a place in the sun and in contemporary history: a country for Jews. The Land. The Jewish settlements in Central and Eastern Europe had become by force of time a recognized homeland for exiled Judaism. The area had acquired a certain sacrosanct character. Thereby Judaism had maintained an inner unity based as much on geographical oneness as continuity of cultural and religious tradition. The extinction of this traditional home in exile for Judaism, the splitting up of this main center of gravity into two poles—Israel and non-Israeli Judaism—introduced a fatal dichotomy into Judaism.

Non-Israeli Judaism necessarily becomes polycentric; in Israel, Judaism necessarily becomes nationalistic in a modern sense. Zionism, which built Israel, is a kind of politico-religious Messianism without a Messiah, thought out in terms of immanent political forms but colored by a romantic religious rationalism. But the consensus of the Israeli people is taking on a new form: the personal Messiah of traditional, normative Judaism has become the idea of an immanent power, a symbol of the everlasting progress of the human spirit, or of a future perfection which is the goal of evolution.

Polarization of Judaism was inevitable. No Jew could be indifferent to the newly created State of Israel. For the existence of Israel emptied the word Diaspora of its traditional meaning: the scattering of the Jews abroad from Palestine until the final gathering in of all to the bosom of Israel. The central connotation of Diaspora, a caravansary where the exiles waited until the recall, was wiped out. Diaspora now became synonomous with non-Israeli Jew. And from this Diaspora was banished the traditional idea of the Expectation. For all who refused to return voluntarily to the new State were, in fact, deciding to undergo some form of assimilation. They were in fact refusing any form of super-historical character to their Jewishness. They were opting for historical, national, cultural, and political anchors to the world outside. This was the dilemma of Jewry, and it needs a tighter formulation in terms of Israel and the new polycentric non-Israeli Jewry.

This dilemma can be expressed in the following brief form. Jewry today substantially lives in the Western Hemisphere and in Israel. For the Jew who remains outside Israel, the choice is stark: forego the essentials of Judaism's dominance and become assimilated; thereby Judaism in the West is headed for ultimate extinction. Or maintain Judaism's dominance—in which case anachronism and separatedness take the Jew out of the stream of modern life; Jewry could not hope to succeed in this venture. For Israeli Jewry, the choice is also stark. To make Israel viable in a hostile area, she must be and act as a modern nationalistic state; thereby inevitably she must admit the modern mentality described in previous pages and make it her own; and thereby she forsakes the traditional religious dominance of Judaism. We have seen how irreconcilable these two are. Yet Israel is essential for Judaism's survival. Or Israel could refuse to forego Judaism's dominance; thereby Israel would ultimately endanger her own viability as a modern state; as it is, she is in mortal danger. Let us see in some detail the decision already made for Israel and the crisis which this decision has provoked.

The decision made for Israel can be illustrated in the following way. If we were metaphorically to ask Israel to identify herself, her answer would run somewhat as follows:

My name is Israel. This year I am twenty years old. Dusty-throated professors are still wrangling over the meaning of my name. But I will tell you what it means to me: I share this name with a Land and with a People. For it, for them, for me, it means life, it means home. We are alive. We are at home, the Land, the People, and I. My people waited almost two thousand years for us. When I was born, the Land was rock, and mud, and sand, and desert, and sun, and desolation. My People were abroad, dragooned on earth by spiritual and political tyrants; loaded with social ostracism; punished by the burning pile of fagots, imprisonment, taxation, hate, contempt, fear; destined, they were told, for hellfire as a sanction on their Jewishness in the next life.

They had no place to go, no future to build, no one to hear but the ancients who gave them hopes to forget their belly-aches and formless, fruitless incantations in place of freedom. They are no longer unarmed in the face of terrifying and terrible mysteries. They are not held up to ridicule. They are all individuals, children of this world and this day. They have made of rock and mountain green wooded shoulders heaving up to Judaean skies. They grow citrus, oranges, melons, apples, grapes, where before the desert fox and the scorpion vied in cunning and venom. They mine copper where Solomon mined it. They cast their anchors in harbors used by Hiram of Tyr. Where before dry sand swirled in the hamzin, now fresh water runs, grass grows, cows graze, and milk—yes, milk—runs for little children. They have honey, also, and eggs, and grain, and tomatoes.

They train African youth. They instruct Africans in flying. They teach Asians how to build schools and airports. They have built airports, constructed roads, thrown up skyscrapers. They fly. They drive. They walk. They swim. They play.

Each one of my people can live the history of his race between a dawn and a dawn. He has the long wrongs and bird-swift joys and the endless hurt of his ancestors graven on stone and metal, sung in the language of Isaiah and David and the Maccabees.

I am my people. They are me. Since the morning of time in a forgotten forest until this day, each one of my people has heard the knock at his heart of a god he could meet. He has met him and realized that he was everyman, that everyman was a king descended from kings, an empire striding in power, a strolling continent of awe, knowing adventure, exultation, gladness, glory, gratitude, and that he could walk in complete understanding with a god of this world every one of the 24 hours of every day.

This is something like the answer modern Israel would give if, metaphorically speaking, we could put her the question: who are you? The answer would be this-worldly, assertive, nationalistic, and limited to a full expression of nationhood, citizenship, and freedom. The decision taken for Israel by its founders is now a thing of the past. Only the results and consequences concern us today. That decision was for a modern state and for

all a modern state implies. In the formative years of the decision preceding the establishment of the State, it was a choice
between assimilation or anachronism. For a modern Jewish
nationalism installed on its own territory must develop along
one of two lines. It can adopt the spirit of the Second Revolt
of 132-135 A.D., which was inspired by the ancient theocratic
ideal of Israel. In this case, nothing but anachronism can result. Neither modern Zionism nor the modern Israeli national
outlook has any theocratic element in its make-up. To take the
bones of the last defenders of the Masada fortress and inter
them in modern Jerusalem could be a salute to the last Jewish
fighters for national territorial independence. It could also be
an idealistic hearkening back to a mentality as unintelligible
to the modern Israeli as the outlook of the astronauts of
Gemini 4 in 1965 would have been to the crew of the Santa
Maria in 1492.

Israel, on the other hand, can develop into an ordinary
Levantine state: it can undergo assimilation to the surrounding nationalistic models. Gradually, the hold which the small
percentage of the Religious Party in Israel wields can become
politically innocuous. The laws enforced at present in Israel
out of deference to the Religious vote and the influence exerted by that party can wane and fall into abeyance. Already by
January 1968, there was a merger of three of Israel's largest
political parties: the Rafi (David Ben-Gurion's own party),
Mapai, and Ahdut Haavoda. This new party will command 59
votes out of 120 in the Israeli Knesset, just 2 votes short of a
majority. It is possible that eventually this party will gain control of the Government. The consequences could be great.
Ushering in, therefore, majority rule, this emergent party could
do away with the importance of the 17 Religious votes. The
bargaining power of these Religious votes is all that preserves
the Sabbath laws and other theocratically minded prescriptions
in Israel. Without this dependence on the Religious vote, the
Government can legislate for the non-religious attitudes of the
vast majority of Israelis. The Jewishness of Israelis will emerge
finally as a form of nationalism. It will be as different from the
Jewishness of their Polish or Lithuanian or German grand-
fathers as the patriotic belligerency of a Negev settler is from
the urbane interests of a Wall Street banker.

This situation brings up the immediate question for both
Diaspora and Israeli Jew. It is a simple but a nagging one:

what is Jewishness? Who is a Jew? Is identification with Jewish nationalism necessary in order to be a fully fledged Jew? How can Israeli identification be necessary for Jewishness, since inherent in traditional Jewishness and Judaism is the persuasion that only on the final days of the world when human history has petered out will Israel be restored? And does the creation of Israel not dissipate the Waiting and the Expectation?

Salo Baron, writing on this subject, comes to the conclusion that for him everyone is a Jew who (a) is born of Jewish parents and has not been converted to another faith; (b) is born of mixed parentage, but declares himself a Jew and is so considered by the majority of his neighbors; and (c) by conscious will has adopted Judaism and joined the membership of the Jewish community. For Baron, therefore, the criteria of Jewishness are physical descent, religious commitment, and the individual judgement of a man and of his neighbors.

While this practical answer is intelligible and clear, it leaves large areas of doubt and thought untouched. An Israeli citizen of Tel Aviv and an assimilated Jew of Miami cannot be said to have the same Jewishness, even though both are Jews by physical descent. A Polish Orthodox Jew who lives as far as possible within the prescriptions of traditional Judaism cannot be equated with a French Jew who has (1) married a Christian, (2) rears all his children as Christians, (3) never went or goes to any synagogal service, (4) observes no dietary or sabbatical laws, (5) shares the mind, the milieu, and the opinions of his Gentile wife and neighbors, and (6) considers as outmoded nonsense the teachings of Judaism, its dogmas, and its beliefs.

Here the difference becomes important because for all practical purposes the French Jew has renounced his Jewishness. But he has not formally converted to another faith. Israeli and non-Israeli Jewry would consider that this man is still a Jew, merely because he was circumcised. The basis, therefore, of membership in Judaism is a purely physical one in his case. Israeli Jewry, as in the case of Brother Daniel (Oswald Rufiesen) about whom we have spoken earlier, will not consider as Jewish a Jew who converts to another faith. The contradiction of these positions is manifest, as the two positions are irreconcilable.

It is probable that at a later date in the history of Jewry, this contradiction will be removed, that even the physical mark of circumcision as an obligatory sign of Jewishness will be abrogated. In the meantime, the problem concerns Israel. Is it, or at least will it finally be, a Jewish State? Israel will always have Christians and Muslims among its population. In addition, any sound prognosis indicates that Israel will become increasingly secular. If, by hypothesis, the majority or even a very large minority of Israel's population were non-Jews (Christians and Muslims), and the State became thoroughly secular, would it still be a Jewish state? The basic problem of Jewishness is back again to plague such questions and their answers.

A few things are clear. Israeli Jewry includes only Jewishness, not the religion of Judaism, as its essential mark. Jewishness here implies three things: partial or total physical descent from Jewish parents or conscious option for Jewishness, non-conversion to another faith, citizenship in the State of Israel. But if one can adopt Jewishness by conscious option without having to adopt the religious trappings of Judaism, it is probable that in the future the Jewishness of Israeli will be purely nationalistic.

Non-Israeli Jewry includes, finally, only Jewishness, not Judaism. But Jewishness here implies only physical descent from Jews or conscious option for Jewishness together with circumcision and non-conversion to another faith. The three branches of Judaism and the Jewish socio-ethnic culture are here involved. It is obvious that the day is not far away when the vast number of Jews will not even insist on Jewishness, will not insist on physical descent or on non-conversion to another religion. This will most probably develop outside of Israel and catch on quickly within the State afterwards. For all intents and purposes, the religion of Judaism has no great future ahead of it in Israel.

Yet, the central contention of Zionism is unassailable. Any hope for the persistence of Jewishness in the post-Biblical world of the succeeding decades, and any substantial hope for an authentic revival of Judaism, depend on the viability and the spiritual prosperity of Israel. Neither persistence nor authentic revival can come from the new Diaspora Judaism. Israel, on the other hand, preserves still the deep wound to her spirit which the Christian West inflicted on it. The sufferings of World War II were only the culmination of centuries. This living wound together with other internal difficulties creates some gnawing doubts as to Israel's possibility of succeeding in her historic role. Israel, in whom all genuine hope for Judaism rests, is affected by another sanction of history.

Israel is not only the linch-pin of survival for ancient Judaism, it is the most hazardous adventure the human spirit has devised since the dawn of known history, compared to which the departure of Christopher Columbus across unchartered seas in the 15th century, or the landing of a man on the Sea of Tranquillity in the Lunar world, seem feasible, practical, and almost prosaic. An Israeli poet has described the founding of Israel as an effort to topple an immemorial mountain over into a plain—all for the sake of a simple vine. The tendrils of that vine are young and strong. But the mountain is, after all, a mountain. And the plain is not disposed to receive the mountain.

The difficulties that confront Israel are twofold. Its fate as the living center of Judaism is not a promising one. Its destiny as a distinct national culture inserted in the geopolitical and cultural pattern of the Middle East is, to say the least, overhung with foreboding clouds. Whichever way one turns the question of Israel's survival and future, more than gloomy prospects offend the eye.

We have seen that the ideological and political founders of the State of Israel fully intended it to become a genuine historical process inserted into the flow of human history and benefitting from the irresistible drive of the logic of that history. At another time and in another place, perhaps, Israel might have been easily and rather painlessly achieved as a genuine historical process. The supreme condition for success is that any such proposed historical process should be conceived and born in geographical and geopolitical conditions that will allow it to take root in the human ambient in which it takes place. There may be, as often happens, an initial shock and repulsive reaction. Christianity emerging in the hostile Julio-Claudian world of the first centuries of this era, and the onslaught of nationalisms against entrenched imperialisms in the 19th and 20th centuries, are examples of genuine historical processes that succeeded in this initial task of insertion into the pre-existing ambient.

The modern state of Israel, judged in this light, has so far failed and, as far as human judgment can perceive, is destined to fail as a historical process. From the very start, the linch-pins that should have tied it to contemporary history were missing. It is bound by mere mooring-lines to the solid earth of historical reality. It is still riding on the seas of changing affairs. At any given moment, the lines can be, severed, and it can be swept away into the vortex of historical failures.

Israel as a modern state has not been allowed so far to insert itself into the cultural and political ambient of the Middle East. Israel is, in fact, in a state of perpetual siege: surrounded on three sides by hostile Arab nations, with its back to the Mediterranean. Ancient Israel at its peak under David and Solomon was a reality resting on the politico-economic triangle of Jerusalem, Phoenicia (modern Lebanon), and the shores of Spain. It could import and export to all its natural markets, the regions that lay within or continguous to this triangle: Lebanon, Syria, Iraq, Jordan, Egypt, Saudi Arabia, the Sudan, to call them by their modern names.

Today, Israel is barred from any commercial traffic with them. With the non-Arab countries that lie outside these limits its activity is rendered tortuous and agonizing through the steadfast attempts of the Arab League to apply the Arab boycott. Any nation in the world doing trade with Israel is put on a blacklist and refused facilities by the Arab countries who are signatories of the boycott. Thus one essential underpinning of Israel as a contemporary historical process in the Middle East is absolutely cut away. But the economic difficulty is only one. More essential still to the genuineness of any such historical process is a cultural underpinning. History is not possible without a culture, and culture is only possible through a mingling of diverse human trends. Any cultural center must receive the impact of diverse cultural centers, the impact of different languages, of different customs, of different mentalities. The impact must be a friendly one and allow for intermingling. It is out of this intermingling that the true identity of any culture emerges.

But this is impossible for Israel and for Israelis. If an Israeli turns on the radio he hears either Qol Yisrael, the Israeli State Radio, or some grating Arab voice hurling hate and fulminating fearful threats against his existence. He cannot travel across the border for a weekend in Jordan or Beirut or Damascus. He cannot holiday on the Nile. He cannot obtain the newspapers and periodicals and publications of Arab countries. There is no cultural exchange, no intermingling of a different mentality. He must live and breathe the national spirit of Israel in Israel and keep himself free from either panic or disgust.

One disastrous effect of this constriction is on the national consensus or national idea of the Israeli "thing." No matter how positive the content of the normal Israeli's concept of himself as a citizen of Israel, and no matter how persuaded he is of its historical authenticity and reality, he inevitably relies on a negation for this concept of himself. He is somebody who is not a Lebanese, not a Jordanian, not an Egyptian, not an Iraqi. He is not somebody who is a murderer, a plunderer, a robber, an intruder, an alien occupying territory belonging legitimately to other people (Arabs), or somebody told over the radio that the rightful owner of the house he occupies or the land he farms can still see the house or the farm from beyond the Arab frontier. He is somebody hit by a grenade or by machine-gun fire as he drives a tractor across a rocky hill, somebody ambushed on lonely roads in the Negev by Arab infiltrators, somebody fired upon as he strolls in the evening, somebody always conscious of the tangled barbed-wire, the nettles, the weeds, the shattered ruins of houses and broken-down roads that lie in the silent No-Man's Land greeting him on three sides of his land.

This continual rain of negations, of negative appellations, of negating events, is only further emphasized by sociocultural constrictions. There hangs over his entire life, private and public, the pall of limited horizons in those very areas in which the human spirit can achieve its only true cultural greatness, and through which any individual culture becomes authentically self-conscious: in sculpture, in painting, in music, in dancing, in academic research, in literary composition, in folklore, in political studies, in economic and commercial theories, in the sociological and demographical effects of a mobile and prosperous population, in what has been called the heterosis of intermarriage. Nothing is possible to Israel and Israelis in these areas except among themselves and by spiritual telemetry with the Western world of Europe and America, a costly and therefore not normal element of daily Israeli life.

The total result of inbred ideas, of negative attitudes, of untried cultural, sociological, and national ventures is obvious. What is not obvious, but none the less real, is the total effect on the State of Israel as a historical process: it cannot under present circumstances achieve insertion into a historical context, no matter how sacred its rights to that position and no matter how earnest and persuaded its people be. Israel must live for the moment in a historical moratorium. No profound decision can be taken as to its character and future destiny. The very Jewishness of Israel is also affected by this atmosphere of moratorium. And so Israel cannot function as a pole of gravity for world Judaism, and a matrix of new life for Judaism's spirit.

Thus the dominance of Judaism, both at home in Israel and abroad in its main centers, is faced with a historical dilemma. No less than for Christianity, there is no visible solution for this dilemma.

33. The Open City

On October 27, 1967, the priest and the artist walked into the United States Custom House, headquarters for all 26 of Baltimore's city draft boards. Quickly, they opened the filing-cabinet drawers, took containers from their pockets, unscrewed them, and poured duck blood bought at a local market over the draft records as a "sacrificial and constructive act" to protest "the pitiful waste of American and Vietnamese blood in Vietnam." The following May, arriving at the courthouse handcuffed to the priest, the artist gave the V-sign for victory to the spectators. Inside, the judge sentenced them both to six years in Federal prison.

During his sermon, the Episcopal minister gave his parishioners Ten Commandments for Renewal, of which the following were the important ones:

"Get behind the Poor People's Campaign until all America is rid of poverty."

"Get behind the report of the President's National Commission on Civil Disorders until America is rid of racism."

"Get behind the campaign to register and vote until nine out of every 10 Negroes register and vote every year."

"Get behind the movement to bring cooperation among all

Christian churches until unity comes to the followers of the way of Christ."

The minister also voiced support for the Columbia University students and faculty members and deplored "vandalism by some students and brutality and destruction of property by some policemen."

In Hamburg, Germany, the student hurried into the small Lutheran church shortly after the doors were opened. From under his duffle-coat he took a package of printed sheets of paper: they were copies of the new "Lord's Prayer"; the group leader had ordered 72 of them to be distributed there. Quickly, the student dropped six copies on the end seat of every pew, then left precipitately. The pastor arrived five minutes to the hour to see that all was in order for the forthcoming service. He read:

> *"Our capital, which art in the West,*
> *amortized by the investments,*
> *Thy profits come,*
> *Thy interest rates rise,*
> *in Wall Street, as they do in Europe.*
> *Give us this day our daily turnover,*
> *and extend to us our credits,*
> *as we extend them to our debtors.*
> *Lead us not into bankruptcy,*
> *but deliver us from trade unions,*
> *for thine is half the world,*
> *the power and the riches*
> *for the last 200 years.*
> *Mammon."*

Radio Progreso of Havana invited its guest, Apolinar Hernandez, to read the prayer he had composed in honor of Fidel Castro and in thanks for the life he, an old man of sixty, now led, thanks to the glorious revolution. Hernandez intoned:

> *"Our Father,*
> *who is Fidel,*
> *who is with us sinners,*
> *free us from the power of Pontius Pilate,*
> *who is Lyndon Johnson,*

and from imperialism.
Viva Communism,
Viva Fidel;
he is in the fore,
and we behind him.
We must always be at his side.
Amen."

The New Jersey hostess placed the little loaves of bread, which she had baked that day, on the silver tray beside the bottle of red table wine. "We are ready, Father," she said to a slightly built man in a light gray sport coat, serge trousers, and brown shoes, who stood chatting with some people at the end of the living room. Three young men, squatting on the stairs, started to strum on their guitars, while the eleven men and women standing around sang softly *What a Friend We Have in Jesus.*

Then the priest took the loaves and said: "My brothers, these are your gifts; you paid Mamie the cost of the flour and the milk." He lifted the bottle of wine: "This is also your gift; you all gave your share of its cost." The young men now sang *O What a Beautiful Morning.* The priest took some pencil drawings off the table: "These are Judy's and Mary Lou's and little Joey's; they too love Jesus."

Then placing his hands over the bread, he said: "The Body of Christ who died for us." Quickly, he broke the loaves into little pieces, and handed them around the circle of worshippers. Then he placed his hands over the wine bottle and said: "The Blood of Jesus." The hostess came forward with a trayful of glasses. The priest poured the wine out, and she went around the quiet circle until each person present had taken a glass and drunk the wine. A few minutes later, the priest looked up and said: "Now, my brothers and sisters; go in peace. We have commemorated the goodness of Jesus."

The 150 members of the Catholic Traditionalist Movement picketed for three hours outside St. Patrick's Cathedral, New York. The slogans on their placards were very definite: "Restore our Latin Mass," "Altar yes, table no," "Wake up, Roman Catholics!" Leaflets handed out by the pickets spoke of the "diabolic subversion now undermining the Church," and reproduced a statement of the Council of Trent some 400 years before: "If any man says that the Mass ought to be celebrated in the vernacular only, let him be anathema." And in lectures across the country, the priest-founder and leader of the movement castigated what he called the "guitar-playing priests, mini-skirted nuns, and the entire humanistic, modernist trend of today."

Events such as these are happening not only in the Roman Catholic Church and in the U.S.A., but in Europe, Africa, South America, and throughout the various Christian denominations. In the above examples, we can catch sight of some of the cross-currents and eddies, the contradictions, the brave efforts, the innovative effort, and the reactionary movements which bewilder many, anger the diehard traditionalists, and cause all to wonder and ask: whither Christianity?

The ferment in Christianity at present implies a direct challenge to the dominance traditional in Christianity. The challenge must be understood, not so much in terms of open attitudes and express renunciations of dominance, as in terms of a new indifference to Christianity's uniqueness. Christians increasingly manifest a persuasion that Christianity is unable to answer the fundamental questions that trouble modern man and that its mode of worship does not correspond to the felt needs of the ordinary people. Christians sense this deep crisis within their religion. They notice that the most impressive achievements of Christianity today are not to be found in the realm of religion as it is understood traditionally. There is no efflorescence of popular piety, or spectacular development in theology, or significant numbers of converts, or any successful solution of man's spiritual problems and doubts. The only spectacular aspect of Christianity today is its activism. More and more, its ministers and its people are taking to social and political issues. Once Christianity enters this area, of course, it has left its own bailiwick. It is no longer supreme arbiter. Nor does it claim to be. It takes its place with the other social elements also engaged in solving those problems. It can claim no special charisma; nor does it display any. It becomes one of the many discordant and contending socio-political elements of our civilization. It has, in effect, ceased to maintain those conditions under which it could authoritatively claim dominance. Side by side with this activism, we find a turmoil in Christianity concerning what to do in those areas where once its dominance was exercised absolutely—education, morals, control of youth. The conclusion to be drawn is that, as Christianity stands now, it is being drawn more and more toward a position of renouncing its dominance. Let us see this in some detail.

From one point of view, Christianity's turmoil seems a sign of vitality. Church membership in the U.S.A., for instance, increased in 1967. Roman Catholics reached a record number of 47,468,333. In 1966, contributions by members of 60 Protestant denominations reached more than $3 billion; church construction cost $1.2 billion; Sunday School enrollment figures ran to 7,601,095 for Southern Baptists, 6,758,905 for the Methodist Church, and 6,155,747 for Roman Catholics.

Abroad, an indigenous Christianity seems to be taking root. The picture is bright for many churchmen; in Korea, a network of churches, schools, seminaries, and indigenous pastors now serves the Christian church; in the Pacific islands, the Pacific Council of Churches was formed last year; in Nigeria, three-fourths of all Protestant ministers are black; in Burma and Malagasy, 15,000 and 40,000 new converts were made respectively in the last five years; in Brazil, the Assemblies of God claim 1.3 million members with 1,850 churches; in Indonesia, 10 million people profess to be Christians. Throughout each one of these countries, the Roman Catholic Church maintains a vast service of bishops, priests, nuns, seminaries, schools, hospitals, welfare clinics and medical dispensaries, technical institutes, and universities.

In Eastern Europe, far from being strangled by Communism, Roman Catholic Christianity has held on and flourished underground, ready to emerge from its bondage at the slightest opportunity. Three Czech bishops, forcibly removed from their dioceses 18 years ago, are being allowed to return. The Byzantine Uniat Church has full freedom to function on its own again in Czechoslovakia. Negotiations are in progress to allow Josef Cardinal Beran to return from abroad to Prague. In Poland, Catholic bishops have been bold enough to submit a list of their demands to the present Communist regime.

At times, some signs of resistance are noticeable, such as the seizure of an anti-Church book in Portugal, the suppression of a Roman Catholic labor publication by the Franco government in Spain, the reiteration of a hard-line on Catholic schools in the U.S.A. or on topics such as abortion, contraception, and divorce. But the overall picture is one of adaptation, experimentation, and renewal. It may be a violent interest of the laity in church affairs as the riot at the St. Nicholas Ukrainian Catholic Cathedral in Chicago on January 19, 1968, where church-goers protested the adoption of the Gregorian calendar; or the publication by Dutch Roman Catholic bishops of a catechism which is the latest word in accommodation to, and understanding of, modern man's difficulties with the ancient truths.[1]

The layman is exercising an increasing influence. The Pope has nominated 27 laymen as his special advisors; the American bishops have restored the ancient idea of married deacons and are now seeking suitable candidates for the position; 2,800 Catholic men and women met in Rome in October 1967 to hold their own summit conference; the Roman Catholic diocese of Rockville Centre plans to set up advisory boards of laymen in all the parishes to advise and supplement the pastors' work and efforts.

Although the Pope has gone out of his way to inveigh "the whirlwind of ideas and events" which arose from the Second Vatican Council, he has taken some steps to modernize the Vatican. He has abolished hereditary offices in his City, introduced a 33-hour week, consolidated ancient functions of power in his Roman Curia, provided five-year terms instead of life incumbency, set a 75-year age-limit for all his top officials, and has at times spoken and acted as if the new international synod of bishops might be superior to the Curia in its influence and decision-making. In 1968, the Vatican had virtually discarded its long-standing ban on any Catholic entering the Ma-

[1] At first printing, this catechism sold 75,000 copies. The National Conference of Catholic Bishops forbade its use in parochial schools. In the Netherlands, 400,000 copies were sold by the middle of 1968. A commission of Roman cardinals reported to the Pope that nothing in the book offended Catholic faith or morals. The Catechism voices, indeed, quite conservative and traditional opinions on many subjects. The chief asset it has is its verbal and conceptual discretion: it avoids hard issues, soft-pedals the inexplicable, makes no demands on the imagination, and does not violate either logic or common-sense. Its big departure from traditional catechisms is its pedagogical format.

sonic order. An American professor and priest challenged with impunity the Pope's recent decision upholding mandatory celibacy for priests.

Theologians are turning from the fruitless "God is dead" theology to a theology of hope and a study of man in his present environmental conditions. Greater interest is now being shown in the theology of 17th and 18th century theologians. Marxists participated in a four-day seminar sponsored by the World Council of Churches in Geneva during April 1968. Everywhere there are signs of adaptation. Clergymen have wheeled a beauty queen around town in a cart, opened coffee-bars and canteens for teenagers, instituted psychedelic bands for adults, run housing services for poor people, organized emergency centers, and stocked the basements of churches with bitters and brandy and "rock" movies in order to attract the young people. Instead of preaching the traditional sermon, many clergymen conduct a dialogue with their congregations; some have instituted the audio-visual sermon; some have no sermon at all; the Gospel is preached in such films as the Episcopal Radio TV Foundation's *One Reach One* (one of the episodes: *Love in a Sexy Society*); into a freewheeling paraphrase in Dixie dialect.[2]

Christian ecumenism seems to make new gains every year. Protestant, Roman Catholic, and some Jewish seminaries are tending to merge together and sink their faculties and facilities in one common pool. Patriarch Athenagoras I, head of Greek Orthodoxy, went to Rome and met Pope Paul. For the first time, the Vatican permitted fifteen delegates to attend the Assembly of the World Council of Churches in Sweden, in July 1968. Roman Catholics joined with Protestants in celebrating Reformation Sunday on October 29, 1967. Although the planned Council of Churches of the City of New York failed to materialize (it would have embraced Protestant, Roman Catholic and Eastern Orthodoxy) and the liberal and conservative factions of Presbyterianism failed to agree, ecumenism made other gains.

The Methodists and United Brethren have merged to form the new 11-million member United Methodist Church. Ten Protestant Churches have set up a special panel to study the ways and means for unifying. The Lutheran Council in the U.S.A. has agreed to join as an observer-consultant. The Vati-

[2] *The Cotton Patch Version of St. Paul's Epistles*, by Clarence L. Jordan, Association Press.

can and the World Council of Churches have established three joint working committees of 20 members each to work in the area of world economic development and for peace.

Ecumenism received fresh impetus from a set of apparently separate but certainly interacting events: forty Protestant, Orthodox, and Roman Catholic churchmen met near Moscow in March 1968 to discuss Christian attitudes to modern social and economic problems; in the same month, New York clergymen invited leaders of Eastern Orthodox, Baptist, Roman Catholic, and Jewish communities to visit them in America; Protestants and Orthodox officials and a Jewish rabbi participated in the consecration of a Roman Catholic bishop at San Francisco on January 4, 1968; an Episcopal bishop was consecrated in St. Paul's Roman Catholic Cathedral of Pittsburgh; the Mount Neboh Congregation conferred a brotherhood award on Bishop Fulton Sheen who addressed the Jewish worshippers from a Jewish pulpit on Sabbath; the California Episcopal diocese petitioned Pope Paul to support population control; on April 28, 1968, Protestant, Roman Catholic, Russian, and Greek Orthodox leaders attended the consecration of the new $3.5 million Armenian Cathedral of St. Varkan in New York, where His Holiness Vasken I, Supreme Patriarch and Catholicos of all 4.5 million Armenians throughout the world, officiated at the ancient ritual; the first ecumenical conference since the great schism of 1054 took place at Beirut in April 1968, where Roman Catholic, Protestant, Anglican, and Orthodox leaders united in conference and in public statements. In troubled New York, a new inter-faith group was formed to help ease tensions in various slum and ghetto areas.

A certain unrest is sweeping through the Church, particularly among ministers and nuns. Many young Protestant pastors are leaving the ministry because they seek a more meaningful way to serve men. At least 711 men left the Roman Catholic priesthood in 1966-67. The contemplative orders of Trappists and Carmelites had a drop of nearly 700 members in 1967-68. In France, 47 convents for nuns had to close in the past decade due to a lack of recruits. Membership is down about 50% in U.S. Trappist monasteries. In 1966, 1,827 out of an approximate total of 175,000 nuns in America left the convent.

Roman Catholic priests in the U.S.A. have organized themselves into a nationwide organization, the Federation of Priests' Councils, with a starting membership of 300 priests

from 114 dioceses. Cardinal Cooke of New York wrote a letter
to his priests asserting that he would not transfer priests without prior consultation and that he would be open to suggestion
as to suitable candidates for various diocesan offices. In South
America, the crisis of "priest power" has gone much farther
than elsewhere. In Argentina, for example, the priests have
openly sided with the workers against capital, management
and their allies, the Catholic Church. In Guatemala, a nun and
two priests took refuge with the workers and the guerrilla
forces.

It is in the region of social and political action that we find
Christians most occupied. The World Council of Churches
organized a conference in Beirut, which we have already mentioned. Its object was to study the purely secular subjects of
economics and world cooperation. Protestants, Roman Catholics, and Jewish leaders in New York pledged ten million dollars in March 1968, to be used for helping Negroes toward
self-betterment. The Reverend Albert Cleage Jr. set the tone of
the action: "If the black community is ignored by the church
and synagogue, then Roman Catholics, Jews, and Protestants
might as well close shop." The general assembly of the Presbyterian Church pledged $100,000 of the ten million. Even
so, the major Protestant denominations were described by the
head of the New York City Mission Society as "stingy" in meeting the needs of the "nation's largest ghetto" in the Bedford-
Stuyvesant section of Brooklyn, New York.

Clergymen of all denominations have been prominent in the
controversies over the Vietnam war. Jewish, Protestant, and
Roman Catholic ministers openly encouraged students to resist
the draft and to burn their draft-cards. They picketed the White
House and Secretary of State Dean Rusk's home, petitioned the
President to de-escalate the bombing, to retire unilaterally, to
"go anywhere any time" to negotiate. The Clergy and Laymen
Concerned about Vietnam organization issued a 6,000 word
document in 1968 concluding that American conduct in Vietnam had been characterized by "consistent violation of almost
every international agreement relating to the rules of warfare."
Eight religious magazines made Vietnam the focal point of
their first issues in 1968. The Easter rites of Christian churches
and Jewish synagogues were full of references and preoccupations with the Vietnam war and racial strife at home. The
Pope in his annual Easter message to the world called for peace

in Vietnam and an end to racism. Peace in Nigeria was the object of a joint appeal made by the World Council of Churches and the Roman Catholic Church. The National Council of American Churches announced a plan to expose in detail the suppression of religious liberty in the Soviet Union.

Another trend running through Christianity to which we have referred already is the effort to modernize the ceremonies of its worship and to modify the modes of its morality. An English Mass is sung with calypso beats in St. Thomas the Apostle Roman Catholic Church of Harlem. Sister Tina of the Religious of the Sacred Heart dances a symbolic ballet down the aisle of Stanford University's Memorial Chapel during a service in which the major Christian denominations participated. The Glide Foundation sponsors a three-day retreat for homosexuals and clergymen at which the former's problems are discussed by the latter. Over 70 walk-in and drive-in churches operate across the nation, some of them accommodating up to 300 people in cars. In Seoul, 430 couples are wed in a ceremony organized by the Holy Spirit Association for the Unification of World Christianity, and at which the President, Moon Sun Myung, officiated.

From whatever aspect we look at modern Christianity, it is clear that the stress is on change, adaptation, experimentation, and immersion in the social and political problems of the day. Of course it must be remembered that the vast majority of clergymen have been inarticulate on the Vietnam war: only a small minority of the 400,000 clergymen in the U.S. have made themselves heard on Vietnam, civil rights, and in daring innovations for worship and ceremonies. The majority of Protestant, Roman Catholic, and Orthodox Christians still worship in the traditional way, live in harmony with their clergymen; the latter live in peace with and submission to their ecclesiastical superiors.

Increasingly, however, two developments are taking place: interest in the old issues which separated Christians in the past is waning, and all Christians are beginning to cooperate and work together on one basis or another without the need to agree on basic beliefs or fixed dogmas. But the lack of insistence on belief and dogma cannot be taken as indicating any rapprochement between any major Christian denominations as to these beliefs and dogmas. There thus emerges the activism characteristic of Christianity today. It follows logically that experimentation, moderate or wild, should take place in religious ceremonies.

The modern mind judges church liturgy and the ritual used at church functions in the light of its main tendencies. Firstly, it can see no point in associating a sermon, money collections, and such activities with the performance of a sacred rite or communal prayer. Secondly, it cannot get any meaning out of a series of gestures which derives from the daily habits and customs of the Roman people who lived 2,000 years ago, or people who lived in Europe over 500 years ago. Thirdly, it can see no utility in pursuing an ecumenism of doctrinal difference; it is only interested in getting practical things done for the good and betterment of other men. Fourthly, it does not see how ancient ideas such as transubstantiation, papal infallibility, inerrancy of Scripture, have anything practical to do with life today. Fifthly, it does not accept the idea of a fixed Sunday or Sabbath service. Sixthly, the idea of lavish cathedrals, churches, and shrines has no appeal for it. Seventhly, the difference between the laity and the clergy is purely functional and not one of a charisma or special authority for this modern mind.

The first type of religious dominance to perish in this flux of change is the denominational dominance: the claim of any one sector of Christianity to be the sole, unique, and true church of Christ. The various churches, especially those originally most insistent on their own unique privilege, act and therefore think on an equalitarian basis. But inevitably because Christians work with all other men on an equal par, because they join with other men in confronting modern problems, Christian dominance as such is finally jettisoned. Christianity's explanation, conceptual and verbal, does not explain man's cosmos to him; but Christians can and do work as modern men with other modern men in order to solve man's problems in that cosmos. Christianity now regards this cosmos as an open city: the City of God and the City of Man no longer divide the cosmos between them.

The fundamental reason for this failure of Christianity's dominance seems, therefore, to be Christianity's failure or perhaps inability to explain man's world in sufficiently intelligible terms for modern man to understand and accept it. For Christianity has never been universalized and presented as the religion of man as such; nor did Christianity keep itself pliant, flexible, and ready to adapt to, and to penetrate, every age and development of man. It is, as we noted previously, a Western religion, formed at one stage of Western man's thought and development. It is, in particular, a highly judaized Western religion. We must now examine this Jewishness of Christianity.

34. Brother Esau

It is impossible to discuss the crisis of Christian dominance without reference to Judaism. This is not merely because a bone of contention has existed between the two religions since the beginning of Christianity, but also because Christianity is to a certain extent what it is today on account of its takeover of the essentials of Judaism. One contention of this chapter is that a fundamental revision of historical interpretation is a necessity for Christianity as it is for Judaism. Another contention of the chapter is that Christians must solve their enmity with Judaism, and they can do this without in any degree touching the sacred elements of their religion.

Briefly, the settling of this enmity would consist in discarding what was wrongfully taken over. The Jewishness of Jesus, as explained in subsequent pages, is unessential to the Christian message of salvation; the "Old Testament" or Jewish character of the Christian Church's presentation of its message is unessential to that message. The maintenance of both in emphatic form has driven Christians to un-Christian attitudes. The solving of its contention with Judaism would still leave Christianity at a crisis of its dominance in the modern world. A graver difficulty confronts it: as it is now, it cannot possibly enter fully and whole-heartedly into the life of 20th century man. But by discarding its Jewishness, it would immediately universalize itself and be on the road toward becoming worthy of man.

First as to Christianity's contention with Judaism. We have described the usurpation affected by Christianity in the early days of its existence.[1] Briefly: Christians claimed and claim to be the inheritors of all that was valuable in Judaism as a divine revelation. Christians are the Chosen People (the Church) to whom the Messiah (Jesus) has come; the Promised Land is

[1] Cf. Part II, chapter 10.

theirs, as well as the promises of resurrection and immortality. The Jews, accordingly, should have become Christians; they did not; consequently, they are rejects of God who, because of his love, will finally save them, more or less in spite of themselves.

As pointed out, this attitude of Christians provoked a natural reaction in Jews: the Opposition. Under this technical term, we included all the modifications which Judaism affected, in order to reduce in quantity the similarity between Judaism and Christianity. The traditional Jewish doctrines of Messiah, Scripture, Salvation, Immortality, Resurrection, Liturgy, Sin, were affected. We also pointed out that Judaism emerged from its initial struggle with Christianity crippled with an ethnic and religious particularism which it has carried ever since.

The one question which neither Christian nor Jew has been capable of answering but which was and is of crucial importance to them both, is an extremely simple one: what is the relationship of Christianity and Judaism?

No other single question has so successfully defied formulation as this one. How can Jews and Christians be said to form one body, as Christians maintain? How can they be said to have no relationship, as some Jews would maintain? No other question calls for an honest appraisal and soul-searching examination in such an insistent way as this one. Many other questions have been asked and many other assertions have been made: is anti-Semitism purely a religious prejudice? Are the Jews collectively guilty of Christ's death? Is there a Jewish plot against Christianity? How can Jews and Christians establish a dialogue in mutual trust?

The answers to these and similar questions are usually given readily, and they all presume a certain viewpoint on the nature of that relationship. But very rarely, if ever, do either Christians or Jews examine their basic standpoint. And this refusal of a basic re-examination has led both protagonists to take up self-contradictory attitudes. Pius XI originated the noble phrase: "Spiritually, we all are Semites"—thus asserting a deep bond between Christians and Jews. On the other hand, he reaffirmed an ancient calumny: "Christ received His mortal body from the very people who were to take His life." Dr. Abraham J. Heschel has castigated religious prejudice as "the most pernicious evil of our time which will inevitably lead to another Jewish holocaust unless something is done." On the other hand, he has stated bluntly, when speaking of the Pope and of Catholics: "You are Nazis. I would send you all to Auschwitz." Pope Paul VI has publicly agreed with Cardinal Spellman's statement that "to accuse the Jews of deicide is historically absurd." Yet he has publicly preached that "the Jews resisted and slandered Christ, and finally they brought about his death"—thus re-asserting the historical absurdity.

The unexamined prejudices of Jew and Christian lead to extreme attitudes; both are pitiable forms of theological *simplisme* and historical naiveté. On the one hand, there is the traditional Christian stance: Judaism was voided and rendered meaningless by Christianity, let all Jews become Christians. And this is a ludicrous distortion of important realities, an insane grimace into the veiled face of theological truth. If Judaism was voided and rendered meaningless by the advent of Christianity, then what remains of our spiritual Semitism as expressed in the remark of Pius XI? Something essential for Christianity has perished beyond recall. What is that something essential?

On the other hand, there is the traditional Jewish outlook: declare your past wrongdoing to Jews, resolve to leave them alone in the future, admit their intrinsic worth, their equality in every respect. And this is a remarkable somersault out of the cold objectivity of historical realism into the ether of wishful thinking. The intrinsic worth of Christianity is bound by "hoops of steel" to the intrinsic worth of Judaism. What, if any, is the meaning of the word "equal" in this context, when we speak of two such intimately related worths? What is that intrinsic worth? And would any Jew admit, conversely, that Christianity is "equal" to Judaism?

St. Paul inescapably maintained four things: that God has granted salvation through Jesus to Jews and Gentiles and not to Jews alone, that the Jews as a whole rejected this salvation and sinned thereby, that God has not rejected the Jews, and that in the fullness of time "all Israel" will be saved.[2] Paul could not overcome the following antinomy: God is faithful to his promises, unchanging in his choices; therefore his choice of the Jews and his promises to them cannot be abrogated even by the coming of Jesus; on the other hand, all God's promises are fulfilled in Jesus and his followers, the Christians; therefore,

[2] Cf. Romans, chapters 9-12.

these Christians are in some way or other the Jews, the new Jews. What then is the relationship between the old Jews and the new "Jews" (the Christians)? Surely there can be only one Chosen People, and surely only the Christians can be that Chosen People? But what about God's fidelity and unchanging character?

Paul never solved or explained this question. What he did was simple. He admitted God's fidelity; by implication he asserted that Christians were, in fact, the Chosen Ones; he added that the Jews had sinned, were therefore blinded and could not see the truth, but would do so at the Last Day. He therefore replaced a contradiction with a mystery which we cannot solve until that Last Day.

Paul continued in his writings to use all the symbols, the imagery, the tradition, and the writings of Judaism. In other words, there was a break with official Judaism of the day, with the Jews of the day. Christianity was not considered to be a prolongation and consummation of *that*. Christianity was considered to be the new Israel, a wholly new creation which inherited all that Israel would have inherited, if it had followed Jesus.

The solution was most unsatisfactory. It did not leave the vast majority of genuine and traditionally minded Jews simply in a balance where even good pagans were permitted to rest, but condemned contemporary Judaism and its officialdom to a criminal role. And it confused the terminology and the conceptuology of Christians throughout almost two millennia, injecting a note of officially sanctioned hate in a gospel of love, thus leading them to omit practice of the basic Christian law of love in regard to the very people from which they had sprung and whose rich inheritance they claimed to have received.

This is the only explanation which will adequately account for the uniform development we can trace throughout the 1900 years which have elapsed since that time. No matter what form Christian anti-Semitism took—economic, political, social, intellectual, aesthetic—basically the Christian ethos of the West assumed that in some way or other the Jews were the enemies of their way of life.

In the light of 20th century developments, particularly the sensitized consciences of 20th century man concerning human rights and human relations, the question provides uncomfortable reflection and puzzling questions: what is the relationship between Jews and Christians? The issues at stake are profound. The implications of the entire subject are more far-reaching than many have been willing to admit. We are not dealing merely with an age-old and persistent myopia, nor with a perdurable incapacity to emerge from a theological ghetto. We are discussing first of all the spiritual stance of an entire religion, Christianity, and, secondly, the world outlook of the Western democracies at its root.

Christians will be incapable of reading any sense into an account of this development, unless they are prepared to make a soul-searching revision of history, of the theology of history, and of the entire Christian scheme of salvation. For inherent in such an account is an apparent threat to a series of ancient and venerated thought-molds petrified and hardened by bimillennial age, encrusted with successive layers of Christian theological thought, philosophical speculation, pietistic practice, and social mores. If the conclusions of such an account are accepted by Christians, it would ring down a curtain on an act of history still continuing, cut off the actors in mid-speech and mid-action, as it were, and call for a drastic recasting of vital roles in the perennial dream of man's relationship to a Saviour-God. But, if this took place, to many Christians it would seem as if the very essence of Christianity were being threatened.

The biggest landmark in modern times for Jewish-Christian relations is the so-called Jewish Document or Declaration approved by the Second Vatican Council on October 15, 1965. In this document, the "Christ-killer" concept of the Jew was condemned. It also rejected the notion that the Jews were the object of a divine curse. Jews have been prompt to underline two aspects of this document: firstly, that it came when it came, long overdue and after Christian Hebraeophobia and derivative Nazi anti-Semitism had played havoc with millions of Jewish lives; secondly, that even the opposition aroused by the document was symptomatic of a still persistent Hebraeophobia. Both assertions are accurate; both reflect hard realities. They only make us realize more vividly that the maneuvering that accompanied the three years' odyssey of the Council Declaration on the Jews was symptomatic of a deep revision of old channels of thought, a churning-up of hitherto congealed ideas in the profound chasm that at one and the same time separated and related those twin peaks of historic monotheistic belief, Judaism and Christianity. For an explosive idea had been cast in between them, and the ground prejudice of mutual opposition, of categoric rejection, was moving.

In no other way can we make sense out of the events surrounding the Declaration's birth: the apparently benign purpose on the part of the Catholic progressive movement spearheaded by Cardinal Bea and his Secretariat; doubts, mood-swings and faltering steps on the part of the mass of the bishops; heated rejection for political motives by the Arab governments and Catholic prelates from Arab countries; steady, unrelenting repetition of an age-old attitude by the undying voices of the traditionalistic minority—a *tohuwabohu* of theology, politics, nationalism, tradition, self-examination, lobbying, memoranda, statement and counter-statement, diplomatic pressures, pamphleteering and tract distribution, consultations and caucuses.

It is not, however, the Christian and Roman Catholic opposition to the Declaration or its tardiness which finally cripples it. It is the entire character of the document. Jews have used the words "condescending tone" in this regard.[3] When we analyze objectively what is meant by that, we see that the Declaration is written in the spirit of the Usurpation. To Jews, it speaks with the voice of those who claim to have inherited the essential values of Judaism. The vital and age-old contention, therefore, between Jews and Christians is not removed by this Declaration; rather it is emphasized. We are thus led from a discussion of this contention to examine the claimed "Jewishness" of Christianity and the viability of its dominance claim in the modern world. For Christianity's dominance claim is built on traits taken from its Jewish cradle. This is where we will find an answer to the tortuous question: what is the relationship of Jews to Christians, of Judaism to Christianity?

Both Jews and Christians need for this hard look at themselves an ocean of patience and an uncompromising love of the truth. They need, both of them, a thorough grasp of what Judaism stands for as a perennial ethos and an ethnico-political outlook which the Christian West manhandled and deformed for

[3] A statement adopted by the House of Bishops of the Episcopalian Church, in October of 1964, is far more condescending than the Vatican Declaration. Dr. F. Grant of the same church stated bluntly apropos of the statement: "If I were a Jew, I would tear up the resolution and stamp on it." Cf. *The Witness*, XLIX, 35 (Oct. 29, 1964).

the best part of 2,000 years. Of the Roman Catholic Church and of Christianity in general, Jews need a deep understanding not merely as a continuing institution but as a spiritually evolving entity; and this necessitates an organic view of the Jewish and Christian heritages as they have been split up over the centuries among differing cultures, diverse sociological conditions, and variant human polities that strew the long road of Western thought and development.

The first prevalent ambiguity to be dispelled concerns a double-barrelled term which is in rather common use even today: "Judaeo-Christian." The civilization of the West is often described as Judaeo-Christian. The term can mean ostensibly only one of four things: either this civilization is an amalgam of Judaism and Christianity in more or less equal dosages, both cooperating and dovetailing to form a third thing, much the same as Greeks and Romans produced the Hellenism of the 2nd and 3rd centuries A.D.; or it is predominantly Jewish with an admixture of Christianity in it, in the same proportions as Christianity stood to Islam in pre-Communist Albania; or it is predominantly Christian with an admixture of Judaism in it, on the model of the Hispanidad of Moorish Spain after it had been conquered by Ferdinand and Isabella; or, finally, it is a two-current civilization in which Judaism and Christianity flow side by side, in more or less sustained harmony, never effecting a major confluence, much as Muslims and Maronites in modern Lebanon live and work side by side.

The civilization of the West does not quite fit into any of these categories. The most approximate category for it would be the third listed above; but a special twist or quirk mars its suitability. Western civilization cannot be accurately described as a greater current of Christianity with a small admixture from an accompanying Judaic current, for this presupposes some harmony and mutual adaptation at some point of confluence. Christianity, as a religion and as a socio-political way of life, took over elements from Judaism. It did not allow these to leaven its own self Judaically, so to speak; it forced an adaptation. For Christianity, Judaism was a failure, Jews were outcasts. More significantly, Christianity claimed all that was valuable in Judaism. It could not, therefore, accept such elements as they were in Judaism. It had to "Christianize" them.

Thus we can understand the Christian descriptive titles "Old Testament" and "New Testament": the former was "old" in that it was effete, no longer valid, that all its worth had been subsumed into a "new" and a higher synthesis, Christianity. "Old" and "new" are not simply chronological terms; they are ideological tags. Thus we can understand Christian racism, Christian sympathy for the Arab cause in the Middle East today, and the "condescending tone" which was singled out by Jews in the Jewish Declaration of the Second Vatican Council.

The term "Judaeo-Christian" as applied to the civilization of the West, therefore, can be logically understood, if we take it to mean two things: a Christian civilization which Christianized some fundamental elements of Judaism and made them its own, and in which Jews through the ages have contributed mightily, especially in the scientific, artistic, and economico-commercial fields, to the technological and scientific advancement of that civilization.

If we confine these remarks to religion, the underlying theme throughout the above discussion is obvious: Christianity has developed its own form of "Jewishness" based on a usurpation of many of Judaism's values and claimed possessions of the spirit. The total individuation of Christianity over 2,000 years included such traits. We are touching here at the heart of Christianity as a divine revelation and at the elements which are essential for its integrity. In Medieval phraseology, we are touching "articles of faith," propositions of truths and the truths themselves, which the Christian believer must accept. Unfortunately each major segment of Christianity and many minor ones claim that they can formulate the data of this revelation more accurately than any other segment. Unanimity is impossible at present. We cannot, therefore, draw up a universally agreed upon list of such "articles."

But the question can be approached from another angle. We can range a number of facts which in present day Christianity have been given a certain doctrinal polyvalency, but which are usually found in any body with a serious claim to be called Christian.

The first fact is the fact of *Jesus* of Nazareth. All Christians assign some central function to Jesus. For the ancient groupings, Greek and Roman Orthodoxy and Russian Orthodoxy, Eastern Churches, Roman Catholicism and some Anglican Churches, to name a few, Jesus was true God and true man.

Across the spectrum to other smaller groups we find the extreme opposite opinion that he was man, a good man, an enlightened man, a privileged man, but merely a man. The fact of Jesus is, however, essential to Christianity.

The second fact to be considered is *salvation*. Traditional groups will maintain that Jesus by his death on the Cross effected man's universal salvation from sin, thus enabling him to live immortally in Heaven. The extremely opposed wing will describe salvation from sin not as a result of Jesus' sacrifice and not as the opening of Heaven's doors. Jesus by his life and death gave an example and a moral lesson. But Christianity announces some salvation. In this latter case, salvation would be up to man himself, based on Jesus' example.

The third fact is some species of *continuing presence* of Jesus, of his salvation, in the world of man. Again, traditionalists will point to *the* Church (or to their church as *the* Church) as a visible and living thing. The radically opposed will speak of the "church" as a "spiritual" thing, a communion of fellowship and brotherly love, after the example and moral apothegms and teachings of Jesus. But some kind of Christian presence is essential for Christianity.

There is, fourthly, the fact of *God*. For the traditionalist, this is a personal being completely apart—perfection itself— from whom all things come, and before whom finally all men will be judged. The opposite wing of opinion will vary from a modern pantheism (God is really an underlying force or immanent power or life in the universe) to a vague atheism maintaining that in reality there is nothing but men, their minds, their civilizations, their cultures. Men in each age fashion a god-idea suitable to their age's mentality, much as physicists form in succeeding generations images of matter according as their knowledge and assessment varies and increases and becomes more refined. But the fact of God is essential to Christianity.

There is then the fact of God's *law*. Traditionalists will point to the Ten Commandments, the principles of Jesus, and of his Apostles, the law of the Church (or of their church as *the* Church), and the natural law. The opposite wing will eschew any sharply hewn, definitively announced, unchangeable body of laws. It will advocate instead that human morality is a situational affair: each fresh age and each new circumstance of man's life can call for a fresh and new law even if it contradicts what was held previously. But a moral law of some kind is a fact of Christianity.

One could go on adding to this list rather indefinitely until the entire area of Christian thought had been covered, including sin, hell, heaven, Mary the Virgin, saints, grace, creation, and so on. In the facts just examined, a spectrum of opinion can be found running from one extreme to the other. No matter how many such facts of Christianity we assemble, and no matter from what point of view we examine them—strictly traditionalist, or ultra-relativist and modern—we find *none* that needs a contribution from Judaism. Neither these facts of Christianity nor any other facts considered essential for Christian belief by the major Christian groupings depend for their validity on the "Jewishness" of these facts.

Thus, to take the traditionalist doctrine about Jesus' act of salvation, we can say that it was not because Jesus was or was not the Jewish Messiah that his blood on Calvary was effective in wiping out men's sins. It was solely because he was the son of God who had become man. One of the traditionalist "proofs" of Jesus' divine character and mission has usually been that Jesus was foretold as the Messiah by the Jewish prophets. He fulfilled all their prophecies, therefore.

But this is an argument without force or validity; it lacks any objectivity to impose itself as cogent and conclusive, simply because it appealed to the minds of pre-Christian and Christian Jews of the first century. The ethnic Jewishness of Jesus is incontestable. Forever as an individual he was and (for the Christian who believes he lives eternally) is a Palestinian Jew, a Galilean, born of one woman, with definite pigmentation and stature and psycho-physical characteristics of a man, speaking one particular dialect of Palestinian Aramaic which has since been lost forever as a spoken language. His lifespan was restricted to a certain number of years. He met certain people, ate certain foods, walked certain streets, and suffered the normal ills of health and the accidents that man is prone to. Christianity insists that, apart from sin or any trace of it, Christ was just like any other man in his human nature.

Christianity is forced by its fundamental tenets to maintain that this very particular man, this individualized being, this human person, was the first human being who possessed a human concept of God's plan for the human race. Christianity must admit at the same time that he must have understood this plan with the concepts of a Palestinian Jew of his time. He was like man in all things, substantial and accidental.

But if the Jewishness and other individual traits of Jesus were essential, then no Occidentalization of his message should ever have been allowed, and no loss of those traits should have been permitted. No Latinization of his ethical code should have been performed. No Hellenization of his theology should have been allowed to develop. No use should be made of any language but the one he used, Aramaic. His Jewish individuation, however, was essential, in that there had to be some individuation by heredity, by education, social background, climatic conditions, and a complex web of influences which go to make any particular man.

Similarly with the other facts of Christianity, the Jewishness is wholly unnecessary. The presence of Jesus on earth, the church or body of people who represent him, need in no way claim to have inherited the privileges of Judaism. They can state that they have adopted the Jewish scriptures because of the inherent wisdom in these writings; that they wish to imitate Pharisaic moral teaching, first of all because Jesus taught it and, secondly, because it is excellent; that they adopt the formulation of the Ten Commandments; that the concepts of God's greatness and mercy formed by Judaism suit the Christian ethos perfectly, and so on. To claim, on top of it all, that Judaism is consummated and useless, seems a pointless act.

In this optic, the relationship of Jew and Christian then ceases to be a matter of contention. The Jews, according to the Jews, are the Chosen People. Christians can also believe that Jews are the Chosen People, provided that no conclusion is drawn which would denigrate the Jews or Judaism of any age or of today. Both Christianity and Judaism are monotheistic. Christians know that the Jewish people as a whole did not reject Jesus, for the simple reason that the people as a whole were never given the choice. It is against Christian principles of love to judge motives, and therefore Christians cannot judge those who did know Jesus.

The same god who chose the Jews and for whom they are still the Chosen People could also have sent his son to found another group. Historically that group evolved as the Christian Church, Occidentalized, largely Romanized, embedded in the world.

The current interest being shown principally by Roman

Catholic Christians in Judaism must be understood, moderated, and directed with this mentality in mind. In New York's Roman Catholic parochial schools a new course in Judaism and on the Jew in literature was planned for the autumn of 1968. The Sisters of Notre Dame de Sion and the Union of American Hebrew Congregations plan to sponsor jointly a series of two-week institutes on Judaism for Catholic educators. On January 21, 1968, sermons were preached at all 225 Roman Catholic parish churches in Brooklyn and Queens on the theme of "better understanding and charity towards our Jewish neighbors." Catholic universities have inaugurated courses in Judaism given by resident or visiting Rabbis. As means to stem, influence, and destroy Roman Catholic Hebraeophobia, these measures are both necessary and good. They should not be used to further any ideas that the Roman Catholic Church is the continuation of Judaism.

We come ultimately to the relationship of Jew and Christian, of Judaism to Christianity. There are two possible views of this relationship: as it is theologically and as men (Jews and Christians) have made it. The theological aspect is quite simple. There was originally one Jewish ambient. Out of that ambient was born a man who, Christians believe, was also God, the son of God. He was a Jew. His earliest followers conceived of him as the Jewish Messiah whom latter-day Judaism expected hourly. Jesus himself, we know, avoided any attempt to make himself king or political leader. He is recorded as having spoken of himself as the Son of Man, a phrase in the Jewish Bible which has Messianic overtones, and therefore overtones of kingship. This is a discrepancy which we cannot remove in our present state of knowledge. When his Jewish followers made converts, they naturally spoke of Jesus as the Messiah who had come. As Jews they used the only theological and religious framework, a Jewish one, which they possessed, in order to tell the truths of Christianity.

In reality, all this was unnecessary but inevitable, given the surroundings and men's limitations. Thus, without any essential or vital reason the entire framework of Judaism with its strength and its weaknesses was transformed into a Christian shape. The relationship of Jew and Christian was historical and demographical: the original followers of Jesus were Jews; the foundational events of Christianity took place in the Jewish homeland and involved principally Jews with some Gentiles.

But there was no drama of continuity, no overnight disinheritance of Jewry, no collective guilt, no religious superiority and lordship and stewardship conferred on Christians over Jews, and finally no dependence of Christianity on Judaism for the validity of its main truths.

There remains for the Christian and the Jewish theologian two further questions: what in view of the long association of Jews and Christians throughout the Christian world has become of both of them? Why, secondly, did God act so? The answer to the first question entails long and intricate studies into the development of both Jewish and Christian theology, and does not concern us here directly, except to say that the close similarity of both is revealed in the similarity of their dominance claim and in the failure which is creeping over them today. To the second question, we do not know the answer. We can speculate that Christianity has yet to become universal before it can reach its fullness; that Judaism must be purified before it can act as the religion of Yahweh's Chosen People; and that we cannot know what development of affairs will take place once both those desirable events have taken place. Fundamentally nobody knows as yet.

Here is the place to use the term mystery. The only nagging suspicion that remains is that perhaps both Judaism and Christianity erred at the beginning, and have to work themselves out of that error, before both of them see the true light. The Yahweh of the Jewish Bible and the God of the Christians is not without a certain type of humor and, from what the two religions tell us, is sometimes wont to do nothing about ingrained blindness until its bad consequences make men turn to him.

Christianity, however, even if it rids itself of this unnecessary burden, has a greater myopia to contend with: its Occidentalism. This is a virulent part of its dominance. There is no easy way out for Christianity after almost 2,000 years of confinement to and development within one mentality. The problem is largely Christianity's own making, but is partly due to its nature. For there is a fundamental problem confronting any religion such as Christianity which depends for the fundamental and essential meaning of its central mystery on one individual man who was born at a certain time, in a certain place, lived a personal life as normal men do, and died. It is this: how can the message of this man be universal, be of universal application, be expressed in a human way without being individuated, as he was, and thus suffer the limitations which human individuation brings with it? This was Christianity's problem from the beginning. As we saw, it solved it by accepting totally his individuation, by Christianizing and Occidentalizing his Jewishness. It is this problem that Christianity must solve, if it is to save itself in the lands of the West and finally take genuine hold in lands outside the West.

35. Impossible Service

It is 8 A.M. in the Promenade Ballroom of the Statler-Hilton Hotel, New York. Outside in the city, New Yorkers are for the most part still asleep: this is New Year's Day, January 1, 1968. Inside, it is Idul Fitri for the few hundred Muslims—Europeans, Africans, Middle Easterners, and Pakistanis—who have gathered here. Idul Fitri, the end of the month-long Ramadan when the sacred law of Islam demands fasting from food, drink, tobacco and sexual relations between sunrise and sunset. The women and children sit in a back corner, some in Western dress, some in saris, some wearing colorful shawls; one young woman is in a red miniskirt. The men sit in front and on the floor; some wear business suits, some are dressed in long white robes, some wear Western hats, some wear skullcaps, others are bareheaded. All are seated facing East in the direction of Mecca, and all have taken off their shoes. Led by their Imam, they recite:

> *Allahu Akbaru! Allahu Akbaru!*
> *Allahu Akbaru!*
> *La Ilaha illa Allah!*
>
> (*God is Great! God is Great!*
> *God is Great!*
> *There is no god but Allah!*)

Then the Imam, clad in a white robe with a white turban over a small red fez, goes through his ritual movements, bowing, standing, straightening, kneeling, touching his forehead to the ground. In close imitation of him, each one present performs the same actions.

If the preservation of Islam and its development were as simple as conducting this meeting, Islam would be in no danger of shipwreck today either in the Islamic or the Western world. Its dominance would be supremely safe. This is not so, and the maintenance of this ancient ritual in such modern settings is as symptomatic of an adaptability in Islam to the modern world as the 1968 performance of Gluck's *Orfeo* by an all-Egyptian cast in the 99-year-old Cairo Opera House or the lifting of a four-year-old ban in the same year by the Egyptian government which had prohibited all showing of *Cleopatra* starring Elizabeth Taylor because she had aided Israeli fund-raising. None of all this touches the essence of the problem confronting Islam's dominance.

Islam's dominance today, however, is hedged in by economic, nationalistic, ideological, and geopolitical pressures of a truly appalling kind. Christianity may seem to some the most pathetic of the three religions, and Judaism the most beleaguered. Islam, however, is certainly surrounded by difficulties which it simply cannot surmount without renouncing in the essential principles of its dominance. By definition, Muslims are the Servants. This time, an impossible service seems to be demanded of them. The crisis of Islam's dominance is intimately linked with its geography and politics, and it can be briefly defined.

The homeland of Islam, the Middle East, has imperceptibly become the most potent area of crisis for the Western world. Three important consequences result from this status of the Middle East, because the countries of Islam have become the objects of attention from at least four of the world's powers, France, China, the U.S.A., and the U.S.S.R. Firstly, the inherent bipolarity of Islam's world is shattered; the world of Islam today is irrevocably multipolar. Secondly, into these countries is arriving at indigestible rates the new technology and science of modern man; thereby Islam's "vertical" world is suddenly upset; thereby, also, the incipient nationalism of those countries is under a powerful stimulus, and modern nationalism is not compatible with classical Islam. Thirdly, by means of the technical aid offered to them, Islamic countries now have a chance to crawl out of the industrial and economic backwater in which they find themselves; but to do so means an abandonment of classical Islam.

It is thus that in the Middle East a 1300-year old ideology, essentially non-Western and monolithic, implying a specific socio-political structure, is forced to adopt a technological organization and structure, but this time both structure and organization are modern and alien. Yet both seem vital for survival. Obviously, Islam must reach new perspectives to survive. It must lift its ideology up to those perspectives in spite of two difficulties: the ideology is irreconcilable with such changes, but the changes cannot be made without the ideology, for otherwise Islam perishes. Islam is truly like a modern Sisyphus who, with his shoulder to a stone, strives for the ever-receding peak.

In this chapter, we will discuss the emergent nationalism of Islam's homeland in the framework of the Middle East's geopolitical importance. In the next chapter we will examine the ideological consequences for Islam's dominance. The Middle East as a vital geopolitical area differs essentially from the Far East to which most Western eyes are today turned.

Since 1950, there have been two major shifts in geopolitics. The second of these concerns the Middle East vitally. But the shift has almost caught the West off balance. In the early fifties, the center of U.S. world preoccupations and politico-military policy shifted from Eastern Europe and the Arab countries to land four-square in an area stretching from the Arctic to the Antarctic, comprising about 64 million square miles of ocean, and involving some 40 countries, island groups, and dependencies.[1]

Militarily, the U.S. Pacific Command, centered in Honolulu, consists of close to 550,000 men, 440 ships, and 5,400 planes, backed up by a forbidding nuclear deterrent.

[1] Sovereign countries in the area are Australia, Burma, Cambodia, China, Indonesia, Japan, North Korea, South Korea, Laos, Malaysia, Nationalist China, New Zealand, Philippines, Singapore, Thailand, N. Vietnam, S. Vietnam, Western Samoa. Territories and dependencies in the area include: French Polynesia (Society Islands, Marquesas Islands, Tuamotu Islands, Gambier Islands, Tubuai or Austral Islands, Clipperton Islands), French Southern and Antarctic Islands, New Caledonia, New Hebrides, Wallis and Futuna Islands (France); Macao, Portuguese Timor (Portugal); Fiji, Gilbert and Elice Islands, Hong Kong, Nauru, Pitcairn Island, Solomon Islands (U.K.); American Samoa, Canton and Enderbury Islands, Horedarm, Baker and Jervis Islands, Midway, Palmyra Island, Wake Island, Pacific Trust Territories, islands under provisional U.S. administration (U.S.A.).

Politically, this Far Eastern region involves such diversified channels of influence as the Anzus Treaty binding the U.S.A., Australia, Britain, Thailand, and the Philippines; bilateral defense pacts with Japan, South Korea, Taiwan, Thailand, and the Philippines; British security obligations (which involve the U.S.A.) to Singapore and Malaysia; bases on Okinawa, Korea, Taiwan, South Vietnam; 12 diplomatic missions; [2] massive foreign aid to at least 11 countries; [3] and continued extensive surveillance of the socio-political developments within countries as diversified and as removed from each other as Indonesia and Korea.

To some this interlocking phalanx of manpower, steel, fire, diplomacy, and economic aid betokens a doxology of terror, a miasma of fear, at the very least an unwarranted interference and pointless preoccupation in non-American things. To others it provides the grounds of relief from the worry of ultimate destruction by sudden war or slow subversion and grounds for belief in the future of a free world. For all, it is the lodestone of interest, whether as doomsday machine or gilt-edge security. This complex organization is an expression of the latest "forward strategy": an arrangement designed to check and repel any aggression close to its takeoff point. For the West as well, and indeed for the U.S.S.R. in some vital respects, the basic geopolitical configuration of the world has changed. Its two components, power and danger, once rode on the China

---

[2] In 1966, these were located in: Australia, Burma, Indonesia, Japan, Korea, Laos, Malaysia, Nationalist China, New Zealand, Philippines, South Vietnam, Thailand.

[3] The amounts are 1964 figures and do not include military aid—merely grants, credits, and assistance:

Country	Approximate Amount
Cambodia	$7 million
Indonesia	$32 million
Korea	$157 million
Laos	$39 million
Nationalist China	$45 million
Philippine Islands	$49 million
Ryukyu Islands	$19 million
Thailand	$18 million
Trust Territory of Pacific Islands	$11 million
Vietnam	$221 million

Another $12 million was spent in the Far East and Pacific, unspecified.

Sea, the Pacific Ocean, and over the vast opaque hinterland of mainland China and its zones of influence.

After the European Wars, in less than a ten-year period (1949-1955), the geopolitical interest of the West shifted drastically and rather unexpectedly from the European delta to the Eastern Hemisphere. The events of the Cold War, the Greek Communist guerrilla war, the complete Stalinization of the present Soviet satellites, the Berlin Blockade evoked a defensive umbrella from the West. NATO came into existence. Power and danger were at first centered in Europe. By 1960, Russia, the U.S. and the latter's allies saw the lethal combination of power and danger in the Far East. The power-center (Communist China) was real. The danger (Chinese expansionism) was tangible. And fundamentally the Russian forces now stationed on the Sino-Russian border have the same function as the U.S. Pacific Command, as the dispositions of U.S. diplomatic missions and the allocation of foreign aid.

Now in a space of two years, the geopolitical center has shifted again and is to be found in the Middle East—and yet there is an apparent unawareness of this shift. Unlike the Far East, the Middle East does not include a catalyst as decisive and as febrile as Chinese Communism. And unlike the Far East, no solution such as a Pacific Command will solve the Middle East's problem. Indeed, the crisis developing there is a quiet, creeping crisis. And the prospects of a final solution are more distant and imperceptible than those in the Far East. Both areas stand on the lower disadvantageous edge of the gap, ever-widening and separating the technologically advanced and economically well-developed nations from their less favored sisters. Both regions have the same fundamental problem: to land on two feet into the 20th-21st centuries. And both are becoming less and less capable of bridging that gap.

There are several reasons why the Far East today is still commanding the major attention of the West, despite the fact that the Middle East is already in an advanced stage of acuity. A latter-day ideology, monolithic and essentially Western, has been imposed on an ancient but effete socio-cultural structure, sweeping away an already dead political system, evoking an organization of human means and human beings which will not fit that structure, and laboring to solve its problems of good, human development, and environmental change. The Great

Auk of Communism is running with the Dodo of the Chinese polity. The Far East presents a tangible danger. The Middle East carries an intangible threat, and explosions there are triggered by a series of imponderables. The former implies an enslavement of the body politic. The latter starts and ends with the spirit of man. The problem of the Far East has been easily understood and expressed in terms of the genocide of Tibet, the attack on India, the takeover of North Vietnam, the attempted capture of South Vietnam, Pakistan's flirtation with Peking, the unenviable position of Burma as the Finland of Asia. All these could be measured in terms of manpower, geographical location and extent, political names and parties, subversive acts, riots, assassinations, burnings, and popular uprisings against American business, industrial and diplomatic installations. However painful and costly, these are tangible.

The Middle East is seemingly locked within a Western system of security: its military potential is regulated by the arranged handicaps of the area's arms' race; its territory lies within easy reach of the West by land, sea, or air; its economy is oriented to, and largely organized by, the West. At least one country, the Hashemite Kingdom of Jordan, depends absolutely on American financial support; and a tripartite agreement (by the U.S.A., Britain and France) guarantees the territorial integrity of the existing countries. Unlike Wordsworth's waterfall which was "frozen by the distance," the Middle East appears to be held by proximity.

Yet even within this static security and because of this very system of preserving the balance of peace, the Middle East is in the grip of a far more tortuous problem: the traditional mentality of Islam is faced with an unacceptable alternative— either frustration within the present guaranteed configuration or a step outside that configuration which would apparently lead to chaos. This affects the very soul of the human beings involved. It could erupt and be without remedy or solution.

In the lands of Islam, an ancient ethos and spirit are dying beneath the hammerblows of exigencies springing from a new development in human affairs. That by which millions of men have lived for more than a thousand years cannot subsist as it is. Yet, as of now, there is neither substitute nor successor to the ancient thing which is doomed. The ensuing vacuum is a dark source of eruptive elements, creating vital issues of man.

These issues can be quite clearly stated. It is not merely that the hegemony of Islam which once provided an all-inclusive framework within which millions of people lived, moved, thought, and died has ceased. It is rather that the lands of Islam and, more properly speaking, the Middle East as a geopolitical area, has become, within the space of a few years, the Third Area, as distinguished from the "East" and the "West," on which the viability of present world structures depends.

For the Middle East by its geographical position is the *plaque tournante* on which the fate of both sub-continental Asia and Africa will be decided. In spite of modern air transport and travel facilities, any power wishing to exercise a predominant influence in Africa has to possess overland access from the other continents. This is the Middle East's importance: it provides such routes. The relatively sudden increase of the Russian presence in the Mediterranean and Soviet attempts to obtain a predominant influence with the nations of the Middle East can only be interpreted in this way. One cannot rule out by any means a Chinese Communist interest in Africa and therefore in the Middle East. China, also, must have an outlet for its particular brand of revolution. Africa would seem to be an ideal breeding-ground for it. Neither Europe nor America, obviously, can allow either the Middle East or, ultimately, Africa to undergo a massive dosage of either Russian or Chinese influence. Economic and political objections to such an event are very persuasive.

By common acceptance, the term Middle East denotes an area composed of the Arab East (the Nile Valley, the Fertile Crescent, the Arabian Peninsula), Turkey, and Iran. The center of Islam historically lies in Egypt, Saudi Arabia, Palestine (now split between Israel and Jordan), the Arabian Sheikdoms, Lebanon, and Syria. The area belongs geographically as well as culturally more to the Mediterranean world than to the Eastern, or Oriental, world. It is one of the most open areas on our planet, belonging to more than one "world" at the same time, and partaking of the Afro-Asian, the Arab, and the Mediterranean regions. The Middle East acts upon these regions politically, culturally, and physically; and they in turn react upon the Middle East. Islamic countries are usually numbered around 20. Islam, however, as a religion, is not restricted to the countries enumerated above. There are some 465 million Muslims all over the world, of which 98.5 million live in Africa, 353 million in Asia, and 100,000 in Oceania, apart from 400,000 to be found in the Western Hemisphere.[4] Many people do not understand this widespread character of Islam; they restrict it to the "Arabs," and thus the extent and the importance of Islam, Arabs, and Muslims in general escape them. In Asia and Africa, some 35 countries have Muslim majorities. And throughout West Africa converts accede to Islam at a 9-to-1 ratio over Christianity.

A preliminary question which we must dispose of here concerns the expression *Arab* and *Arab country.* We use the term indiscriminately today without inquiring what group of people can be accurately described by the term. Opinions are expressed by many on this subject. We shall follow Middle East usage in this matter. When Nasser of Egypt and Bourguiba of Tunisia speak of the Arab nation or their Arab brothers in North Africa, Iraq, Jordan, or elsewhere, they are referring to the inhabitants of those countries who share the Islamic heritage to one degree or another.

We find in the Middle East that the country at the topmost rung of the economic ladder does not even reach the bottom rung attained by most underdeveloped modern Western countries. For few Middle Eastern countries or societies have either

[4] The Muslim percentage of local populations in countries located in relevant areas of Europe, Asia, Africa, and the Middle East is indicated here: Aden (98), Afghanistan (95), Albania (53), Algeria (92), Bahrain (100), Burma (2), Burundi (1), Cameroon (20), Central African Rep. (3), Ceylon (8), Chad (50), Congo (2), Congo Republic (1), Dahomey (7), Ethiopia (17), Gambia (1), Ghana (20), Greece (1), Guinea (60), India (11), Indonesia (88), Iran (98), Iraq (96), Israel (11), Ivory Coast (15), Jordan (91), Kenya (12), Kuwait (94), Lebanon (50), Liberia (5), Libya (92), Malagasy Rep. (10), Mali (60), Malawi (30), Mauretania (98), Morocco (95), Mozambique (14), Muscat & Oman (100), Nepal (4), Niger (75), Nigeria (55), Pakistan (88), Philippines (8), Port Guinea (5), Red China (2.5), Qatar (100), Rwanda (1), Saudi Arabia (99), Senegal (70), Sierra Leone (20), Spanish Sahara (98), Sudan (86), Syria (65), Tanzania (26), Thailand (4), Togo (3), Trucial Coast (100), Turkey (98), Uganda (18), United Arab Republic (93), U.S.S.R. (10), Yemen (99), Yugoslavia (11), Zambia (1).

sufficient literacy, a substantive tradition in social justice, a supply of capital, a tradition in technology, or an even temporarily reliable governmental and administrative apparatus. What Walter Rostow has termed the "preconditions for take-off," "drive toward maturity," and "high mass consumption" cannot be verified in any of these countries.

There has emerged in Arab countries a politically conscious generation, rejecting the highly conservative economic and social philosophies proposed by the previous generation. They reject also the parliamentary systems bequeathed them by the post-Ottoman generation of political leaders who had aped rather slavishly the various European models. The new generation is a minority at its very best. Its members are drawn from civil servants, technocrats from private industry, university circles, and army officers. They plan a social and political revolution in the Islamic context. They aim at raising living standards, at state control of the means of production, at wide social welfare plans, at reform of the agrarian laws, and at mass education. This is Arab Socialism.

But in Islamic countries, whatever be their antecedents, whether the population be Algerians, Tunisians, Egyptians, Syrians, Palestinian refugees, Iraqis, Iranians, Jordanians, Lebanese, Turks, or Pakistanis, they opt for an ultra-nationalism proposed, propagated, and maintained by small groups each dominated by one or, at the most, two figures—a Nasser, a Boumedienne, a Habib Bourguiba, a Salah din al-Bitar. This general tendency in the countries of Islam, however, has only underlined and reduced to painful choices the fundamental crisis affecting Islam. For nationalism is a subtle secularization of Islam. And Arab Socialism is another name for a new tide of individual Arab nationalism, in which nationalistic feelings are confounded with *Islamic* feelings: the "Arab nation" is confounded with the Islamic Community of Believers.

The key to the situation lies in the fact that Middle Eastern society has had a pyramidal character from time immemorial. For over a thousand years, its society has been composed of a huge proletariat living in economic, social, political, and military dependence on the junta of bureaucrats, soldiers, politicos, and traditional oligarchs. For centuries, Islam has been not merely the sole reality and religion for this mass, but also the sole way of life. In the ultimate analysis, whoever wishes to obtain the adhesion and the loyalty of the Muslim masses must approach them in the guise of one who is, once more, going to activate the glories and the independence and superiority of Islam. Thus the leaders of the new nationalisms clothe their socialism in the language and the thoughts of Islam. They have no intention, however, of re-installing the old theocratic state; they prefer to talk of the "Arab Nation." But hampering this new "Arab Nation" and its creators is an inner dilemma: how to reconcile the ancient demands of Islamic faith with the new exigencies of survival?

For Islam gazes upon the universe as a holy unity: nature and man, idea and substantial reality, essence and existence, consciousness and reflection, all these are subsumed into a higher unity dominated by the Community of Believers. From the very start of Islam, the orthodox members undertook to provide for all aspects of human existence. The early Christians had no developed social theory or political ideals. Early Islam set out to establish existence within the framework of divine law and revelation. The consensus of Islamic belief aimed at nothing else than a thoroughly Islamic and Islamicized cosmos. Islam believes with Christianity in an inherent purpose of a god in human history.

For Islam, involvement in history is the obverse of their coin; the reverse can only be perceived by faith. It is polished, brilliant, and pure gold. It is the face of God clad in his innumerable attributes, but chiefly resplendent as the all-wise, the all-merciful, the all-powerful. It is in the other world. The Community of Believers has a reality in the world which is supreme in the next, the invisible world. As a consequence, Islam begins with Allah. To Him it shall return.

From early times, the lives of all Believers were to be regulated by the *Shari'a*, the sacred law. All Believers were equal beneath this law. The consensus (*ijma*) of the Community was the source of the *Shari'a*. But it was the consensus of the *ulema*, the learned teachers, which regulated all behavior. It alone was normative. The ulema, after the 10th century, ruled out completely any individual interpretation of the law.

It is abundantly clear, then, that any real genesis of nationalism in the modern sense would be an impossibility wherever Islam in its pristine and primordial state reigned. For nationalism, if at all worthy of the name, implies some form of democracy, or an oligarchic rule by men who govern without reference to the Community of Believers and their beliefs. It is ultimately impossible for the Community to have a say in governing where the law and constitution by which they live can only be obeyed, where all and any revision, amendment, fresh interpretation or adaptation of the law and constitution is impossible. Actually, in orthodox Islam the only possible theory of political power is a monopolistic one; it could be totalitarian either through one individual or through an oligarchy. It could hardly be democratic in a Western sense. Arab or Islamic nationalism, therefore, is ultimately irreconcilable with Islam.

Even a respected thinker such as Cecil Hourani, while diagnosing the ills of Arab nationalism and seeing clearly what Arab countries need, is blind to the real difficulties. Writing in *el-Nahar,* the most influential Arabic newspaper in Lebanon, he states quite categorically that "the greatest source of weakness in the last twenty years has been the introduction into Arab political life of methods of government and of ideological slogans which are unsuitable and irrelevant to the actual conditions of the Arab countries." He goes on to declare that "the most immediate and urgent problems which face nearly all the Arab countries are those involved in establishing the minimum conditions on which a modern society may eventually be built." But then he proceeds to turn a blind eye to the crux of Islam: "For some of the underdeveloped countries of the world, the necessity of finding an outside source for the capital investments and the technical skills they lack forces them to an involvement in the ideological conflict and divisions of the more developed world. *No such necessity exists for the Arab world* [my italics], which has all the material, and many of the human resources, which it needs. There is sufficient capital and liquidity to make us independent of outside financial help . . ."

The precise difficulty for Islam is ideological conflict. Islam cannot adopt the technology and science of the West without adopting the Western outlook on the world. This outlook is already an ideology quite distinct from that of Islam. This inevitable danger is quite distinct from the involvement in either Western, Soviet, or Chinese political ideologies. In the next chapter, we will examine the impact of modern technology and science on Islam.

36. The Cross of Islam

After the death of Mohammad, undisputed transmittor and interpreter of Allah's will, the duty of maintaining the integrity of the Community and of spreading its truth devolved on the Khalifs. Up to the Battle of Siffen, 657, the succession of Khalifs took place according to revelation. After that, Ali, who had been defeated by Mu'awiya, was compelled to submit to arbitration his claim to the Khalifate. Over this dispute three sectarian branches appeared in Islam: the Sunnites, the Shi'ites, and the Khawarij. The first held that the Khalifate was an elective office of the Quraish tribe; the second held that it was a Allah-given office and could not be settled by arbitration; the third group believed that it was open to any believer who was elected by the faithful.

Up to Siffen, Islam was in theory and in practice an idealist theocracy. And Siffen is the first cardinal date in Islamic history. The reign of Mu'awiya started the transition from an essentially religious theocracy to a lay empire. Central Arabians, however, still retained their pre-eminence.

One hundred and eighteen years after the death of the Prophet, the Abbaside dynasty defeated the Ommayads, transferred the capital from Damascus to Baghdad, and assumed lay control over an empire which stretched from Gibraltar to the Indus. The empire was multi-racial, no longer monoethnical. Arab nationalism ceased to be the cement. Islam became the basis of all cohesion.

The first and the greatest period of dynamic expansion had come to an end for this Arab ethos which had swept triumphantly out of the desert-places of Arabia. The decision resulting from the Battle of Siffen marks the end of the first vital burst of spiritual energy. Islam was never again to know such success. It is interesting and important to note, on the other hand, that this step meant the abandonment of Arab nationalism. A certain universalism had taken over. The *Revelation* and the *Shari'a* were both retained within the lines of a lay empire. And there arose the classical structure of Islam: a cosmopolitan religion in which individual nationalisms had no part, because all fitted within the framework of divine history presided over by Allah and infused by his spirit as manifested in the secular government.

Islam thus was able to integrate many elements from Arabia, from Hellenism, from the Semitic cultures of the ancient Middle East, from Sasani Iran, from India. Islam's achievement was that it welded these into a homogenous way, as it provided, too, the drive and power to sustain the empire.

The center of this unifying force was religious law (*Shari'a*), which regulated within its powerful and precise sweep everything from prayer rites to property rights, from women's veils to rulers' swords. The agony of Islam today and the crisis threatening its traditional dominance can be fully appreciated only if we contemplate Islam attempting to find a viable solution within the multi-level framework which modern world developments have imposed on it.

There is no aspect of human life which does not come under the sacred law, the *Shari'a*. All particularities are transcended and included. All finite boundaries are caught up in the infinity of the Community's progression to eternal salvation. All the confines of man's mundane life are a negative paradigm of the eternal here-and-now in which Allah lives and to which the Community is destined. The purpose of man's history is, under Allah's guidance, the attaining of the decreed fullness. Therefore, man in his social, political, international, domestic, economic, commercial, esthetic, and scientific totality has to be governed by the principles of the Law and its prescriptions. There is to be no adaptation of existing institutions, no coloration of practices obtaining hitherto, no acceptance and conversion of ingrained ways of life. For all is transformed or destined to be transformed.

In addition, Islam has been accustomed for over 1,300 years to a bi-polar world. The two poles were and are: Islam versus the remainder. For a long time the "remainder" or the "outsiders" were Christians with an amalgam of Jews and Judaism. These two poles were characterized also as the Faithful versus the Infidels, as Good versus Evil, as the Children of Allah versus the Children of Satan, as Light against Darkness, as the Saved against the Damned, as Heaven against Hell, as Allah against the Demon. This trait of Islam goes deeper; Islam has nothing in its fixed heritage, nothing in its past experience, nothing in its modern make-up which can help it to think in any other way.

As we have seen, the world in which Islam finds itself today is an array of influence-poles: the West, Russian Marxism, Chinese Marxism, Christianity, the positive neutrality advocated by Afro-Asian nations, and so on. The most viable way for Islam, the way of internationalism, presents unacceptable traits to Islam. Genuine cooperation in our emergent internationalism means that the dominance of Islam at least in its principal modes must be sacrificed. No Islamic group or leader can appear at the United Nations General Assembly, for instance, and propose that the assembled nations submit to the message of the Koran and organize their peoples according to the revealed truth of Allah. Yet this is the only accurate way in which Islam could behave among the nations. It cannot do that. More importantly still, not only must it sink its claim to be ultimate of ultimates, but it must *accept parity* with other ideologies, must enter a modern pantheon. Nor can Islam even start defining its past because its present state is only a beginning, and the future for all the countries and peoples of Islam hangs by a thread against which is laid the sword of economic disruption.

Nothing calamitous happened to Islam until it came into contact with the Occident in the 19th and 20th centuries. As a matter of history, nothing could have changed the accepted validity of the solution accepted after Siffen as long as the environmental *status quo* did not change. Islam could cope with newly discovered lands (from the 15th century onward), could progress in science and philosophy, could live side by side with hostile empires. It did all these things. But the essential structure remained firm. The need of a second solution arose and could only arise when at least one of the essential components of its well-being were affected. Thus the second and the latest *crux islamica* arose when the environmental *status quo* and the politics by which it lived were changed.

Nothing essentially and substantively affecting Islam happened between 750 and the start of the 20th century. Neither the clash of empires, nor the Industrial Revolution, nor the rise of national individualism, nor even the birth of Marxist Communism could affect Islam. To all these Islam could bring day-to-day solutions, could even absorb the shock of them, could, finally, outlive them. In most cases it did so. Even when the

military and economic superiority of the Occident made inroads into Islam, nothing essential was affected.

The essential change arrived in the second half of the 20th
century. It is a characteristic of modern man, we remarked
earlier, that he inclines to set up a series of self-validating
truths; he objectifies all things; he analyzes them; he categorizes them; eventually, he can use them for his own betterment or convenience. But the most outstanding use to which
man is putting his recently discovered knowledge is to *change
his environment*. The most important discovery made by Occidental man since the basic invention series—fire, food—was
that man can, should, is bound to remake the environment in
which he lives—under pain of extinction. Man's terrestrial
heritage is found to be in flux, to be perfectible. The development of man's society and its conditions of viability are in the
hands of man himself.

This is an Occidental discovery made piecemeal over a space
of 2,000 years. On the one hand, it violates Occidental man's
Greek Hellenism and its innate principle of static symmetry
and "isness." On the other hand, it should be in keeping with
the Semitic conception of all things visible: a flowing, dynamic,
living, changing, becoming array of creatures, speaking,
dancing, clapping hands, adoring. And this element should be
in the make-up of Occidental man on account of his Judaic
heritage. But it is not so, because modern man objectifies all
single things, thus breaking their inner cohesion as de-objec-
tivized components in a hierarchic creation.

This discovery was made piecemeal, for the Occident started
off with the notion that the universe was static and hierarchic.
Even when new laws were discovered, they were taken as laws
of a static universe. At one stage, indeed, complete staticism
reigned. Between the 16th and the last half of the 20th century,
all this has changed. The physical laws were seen not as those
of a static universe, but as those of a changing, dynamic universe. More than that: man has learned that he himself can
change his environment: the air he breathes, the organs he
uses, the ambit of his senses, the width of his travel, the penetration of his vision, the extent of his hearing, even the laws
of physical behavior and the pattern of his psycho-physical life
and energy.

This, then, is the crisis of Islam: can it adapt itself to this
irreversible change in man's environmental status quo? There

is no question of "coping with" it; it is assimilation and adaptation or liquidation.

The difficulty lies in the nature of the machinery by which this change is being wrought. No longer can it be done by Allah; this change is being brought about by a technology, by material means, and by the rule of external law. Now wholehearted adoption of these latter means signifies that the adopter enters the world of "reason," that he "objectifies" all things, that he establishes a series of self-validating truths within a closed but ever-expanding system. One ceases to judge purely and simply and exclusively according to a revelation made in the early years of the 7th century.

But this is no longer service according to the classical model of Islam. Islam no longer dominates as the source of explanation or of guidance. Islam is relegated, at best, to one part of life. A whole series of practical dilemmas confronts Islam. First of all, as regards internal government and civil affairs. For Islam, a government must be chosen and must rule in virtue of, and according to, the Muslim sacred law, the *Shari'a*. Anything else is anathema. Blasphemy. Yet all Muslim states, with but two minor exceptions, have instituted at least a semblance of the Western democratic process for the selection of rulers. Furthermore, the institutions or government ministries by which government is performed have become counterparts of Western governmental services and ministries.

Classical and authentic Islam neither requires nor permits a code of civil law. All law is religious. Yet all these Arab states have had, perforce, to draw up codes of civil law based on the principles of law and not on any religious motive. Here, we can see an inherent contradiction built into the heart of modern Islam, affecting government, civil affairs, marriage, property, law administration, buying and selling and so on.

Secondly, as regards the outside world. To be modern, Islamic states have to participate in world affairs, in order to obtain some foreign aid or UNDP help, which they all seem to need. They must subscribe to the U.N. Charter, its declaration of human rights, and to all its conventions. But such things have no validity at all for Islam. Yet to survive and to progress, Islam must subscribe to them. The same inherent contradiction exists between the inner consensus (which condemns all this as belonging to the outer infidel world with no credence or fidelity to be paid to its obligations) and the exterior rationalization of the visible, tangible world which they must perform in order to survive in that world.

The most disconcerting thing about the outside world for Islam is that her classical concept of the world as bipolar fails to explain the present world situation. Not one, not two, but at least four poles of attraction confront her: America, Europe, Russia, and China. The world of reality is multipolar. It cannot be described as bipolar. Furthermore, to survive and be successful in this world, Islamic peoples must submit to a rule of external law, a law not based on an original revelation to a prophet, *the* Prophet, but a law made by men for men and based on the pragmatic needs of the men under the law. Such law has no validity for Islam; strictly speaking to obey its imperatives is a form of infidelity and blasphemy. Yet Islamic states must obey that law in order to become part of international life.

Thirdly, as regards modernity and updatedness which are the great need of such developing countries. No modern state can hope to survive today which does not participate in the socio-technological development of the West. But this means a secular and non-religious education, an education which explains all things in the world on the basis of history without revelation, economics without religious law, physical science without the need of a creator, and biology and psychology without the need of a spirituality or a cult.

Again, the same contradiction afflicts Islam. For according to Islam, nothing is really explicable except in terms of its sacred doctrines. Here is really the heart of the matter and the tingling nerve-center of Islam's agony.

To think as a modern educated man is to unthink basic Islam. At its apogee, Islam produced one of the fathers of modern chemistry (Jabir ibn-Hayyan), the founder of algebra (al-Khwarizmi), a towering historian (Ibn Khaldun) rivaling the Roman Tacitus, the Greek Thucydides, the English Gibbon, the German Von Ranke. They produced expert doctors, surgeons, dentists, astronomers, engineers, and physicists of the first order, side by side with poets, dramatists, writers, and musicians. What was it in Islam then which permitted this efflorescence of scientific and humanistic knowledge, and which is there no longer today? Why should Muslims not be able to do the same today—given the education and the money?

In truth, Islam has not changed. These sciences have

changed; their ambit, their presuppositions, their tendency, and their general conclusions are totally and specifically different from their forerunners at the time of Islam's high period. Modern biology and psychology not only take no account of a soul in man; they presume and they act as if man had no soul; they even tend to disprove its existence altogether.

Modern physics studies the material universe from microparticles to interplanetary phenomena. But for physics this is a closed cosmos in which neither God nor any being causally creating all things has any place. Much of physics study tends to disprove the idea of a creator and a supreme being in the traditional sense.

Modern mathematics waves an almost magical wand, and all the absolutes, time, space, the planets, earth, our galaxy, the universe, assume a mere relative existence. In such a world, Islam is not merely blind, deaf, mute, directionless, homeless. It is stifled, suffocated, without light, without sustenance, without starting-point or anchor, and seemingly doomed to extinction.

The present Arab-Israeli impasse illustrates in a painful fashion the dilemma of Islam.

The Arabs cannot abide the presence of Israel standing four-square in the center of their geopolitical seesaw. Superficial readings of recent history ascribe this to the Arab-Israeli war of 1948-49, the exodus of Arab refugees, the loss of territory and, more important to Arabs, the loss of face. All these are factors, to be sure.

Yet, the fundamental reason is other: Israel in the eyes of Arabs and according to Islam is an integral part of the outside world, to which Islam is irrevocably opposed, with which no ultimate peace can be made. Islam can have no truck with rampant infidelity.

Israel, therefore, must go. Yet, what to do? To oust Israel, Arab states have launched within 20 years no less than three disastrous wars, the net result of which has been to increase the territorial possessions of Israel, to reduce Arab military prowess to the smoking ruins of overrun military installations, the multiple rusting graveyards of their tanks in three deserts, the unserviceable airfields pockmarked by the pin-point accuracy of Israeli bomber pilots, the worse than useless state of four national armies totalling more than a half a million effectives reduced to a trounced, defeated, routed rabble, and to put strategically and economically invaluable sites in the hands of the mortal enemy.

They cannot reasonably hope to meet this enemy in the field and conquer. They cannot possibly negotiate with her. Nor is there any hope that they will match her economic growth and power. In education, in technology, in work-effectiveness, in professional excellence, in the will to survive and win, Islam has no real hope; only dreams sustain it.

On the other hand, if we suppose that Islam's adherents resolve to attain the technological and professional excellence of the Israelis by all-out mobilization of their vast wealth potential and their overwhelmingly larger populations, another insuperable difficulty arises. It would be tantamount to suicide—for Islam. To do this they would need to shed the shackles which Islam places on such a program. This would mean renouncing Islam. But Islam is the ideology in virtue of which they wish to obliterate Israel. Yet without economic and technological progress and modernity in politics and social structuring, they cannot hope to compete with Israel. Nor can they possibly exert pressure within the organization of nations.

This dilemma of Arab nations vis-à-vis Israel was reflected in the varied reactions to the Israeli victory of June 1967. Grandiose plans vie with severe breast-beating, ineffectual threats, and economic foolhardiness. Mohammad Hassanein Heykal, one of Colonel Nasser's closest confidants, proposed in February 1968 that the Arabs create a strategic air command, a pan-Arab world airways company, and a variety of other joint undertakings. Colonel Nasser, insisting that another war with Israel was inevitable, bade Egyptians mobilize for the decisive battle against Israel, while the majority of Egyptians are economically and socially underdeveloped, and Egypt had to borrow $140 million from Kuwait, Saudi Arabia and Libya in a one-year-period following the June war of 1967 to help offset losses of revenue from the blockaded Suez Canal. The Palestinian refugees at the refugee camp at Suf in Jordan clamor "Going back, going back, we will be going back to our homes," but there is no power capable of reinstating them. As part of the 600,000 refugees today in Jordan, their educational and economic problems only add to those of Jordan, which lost 38% of its productive capacity and 85% of its tourist income as a result of the June War. Prince Faisal of Saudi Arabia called for a *jihad,* a holy war, against Israel, in order to defend the Holy Places "being dishonored each day" by the Israelis. Jordan petitioned Secretary General U Thant to take urgent steps to end Israeli violation of the same Holy Places. Yet, as the Secretary General and Prince Faisal know, the fundamental issue is political and economic. To cap it all, Egyptian Copts who support the Nasser regime reported miraculous visions of the Virgin Mary at the Church of the Virgin in the Zeitoun District of Cairo; and Coptic Bishop Athanasius commented for newsmen: "We consider them (the visions) a good sign, a symbol of God, who sees what the Jews have done in the Holy Places. God is strengthening the spirit of the people in Egypt and the Arab nations. We are waiting for victory."

Thus Islam and its adherents have been trapped within a watershed of history and caught fatefully between two prongs of an iron pincers—their hide-bound ideology and the incompatible ambient. They are held down helplessly on the unyielding anvil of irrevocable human development, to be battered incessantly by the hammer-blows of economic necessity and political viability within the emergent organization of the planet's nations.

Islam is surrounded by the inescapable walls of hard and basically unacceptable choices. The agony stems from the necessity of making a choice. To maintain its exclusivity and cope with the changing reality: this is the problem. The lands through which the writ of Islam once ran supreme and the peoples who once lived in its shadow are beset by problems they cannot solve: basic problems such as food, housing, transport, power, population growth; more complicated problems such as economic and industrial development; more important but less material problems such as new political forms, fresh mentalities adapted to brand-new ideas; finally more profound and vital problems such as their very reason for living, their interpretation of man's place in the universe, and the adequate substitute for the ancient ideology which is now helpless.

Islam could even foresee a point when its entire formulation and conceptual configuration of reality will be awry, unacceptable, unintelligible, non-viable. Islam could foresee this, only if it allows itself to foresee it, to think of it. Islam may be hurling itself against barriers which it has erected as dogmas and which it considers necessary for the integrity of its belief in the reality of Allah. Breaking through these thought-barriers will mean, in that case, literally the destruction of Islam's ideal in conceptuology and terminology. For this is the price of Islam's exclusivity: that it never change from the fixed molds of the 7th century.

37. The Eastern Twilight

A folk tale of ancient China relates how, in the beginning when the heavens and the earth were being formed, the gods were disputing as to where the sun would rise: in the East or in the West? They finally decided to arrange matters equitably, saying: "Let us have two twilights, one in the East and one in the West: in this way, the East will be in doubt for a little while as to the sun's arrival, and the West will be deluded for a while that they have the sun longer than the East." This is why the West starts off in darkness and finally enters into full possession of the light,—only to be finally dispossessed of the sun towards evening. The East starts off in the twilight of doubt and after a short moment is finally dispossessed of the sun. The image of the Eastern twilight illustrates the general impression which the religious situation in Eastern countries gives today.

This is all the more remarkable because it would seem that it is today, above all other ages, when the religions of the Far East would enjoy a vogue and a noonday popularity in the West. This conclusion arises sometimes from the tired brains and dispirited hearts of Occidental man. He is disgusted by the rush, the smog, the thoughtlessness, the apparent anonymity of modern life in the West. In particular, 20th century man of the West and specifically a small but clamorous section of 20th century youth reject the peculiarly modern jungle created by the confluence of advancing technology, rising standards of living, increased governmental and bureaucratic interference with the privacy of individuals, the spirit of competition on which life increasingly depends, and the invisible but all-embracing umbrella of the nuclear deterrent triggered by fear. This quasi-Orwellian existence and the mentality which it fashions is contrasted unfavorably with the peace, the profundity, and the harmony which reportedly radiate from the religious spirit of the East.

Furthermore, some of those who have had contact with ecclesiastical and clerical influences in their personal lives and who have recoiled from such influences in their social, cultural, intellectual, and political ambient find in Eastern religions a smiling and relaxing freedom from traditional dogmatism. They discover in such religions dazzling parallels with what they consider best in either Judaism, Christianity, or Islam. They receive sporadic intuitions of a greatness they have long desired, and from them they expect initiation into higher regions of the spirit which seem unattainable for anyone encased in the mail-armor of dogma or the strait-jacket of fanaticism and religious prejudice. The motionless face of some colossal Buddha, the eyes half closed, the enigmatical, elusive expression in the posturé of the body, and the smile of Angkor on the lips are taken as mysterious and mystic reflections of the inward blessings and blessedness to be found in the millenniar enlightenment of the East.

We can speak, however, of an Eastern twilight for the religions of the East. Without any doubt, the intrinsic value of these religions has still to be appreciated by the West. Full light and understanding of their riches has yet to come. But the point of the folk-tale is nevertheless felt: it would seem to be a twilight period. The sun may rise on the glories of Eastern religions. Yet, according to all rational considerations, it will be the morning of the magician for the East, a short-lived glory, before the sun shifts elsewhere for its zenith.

The vastness of this subject can be appreciated by remembering the size of the geographical areas, the population figures involved, the variety and the virility of various religions with which the East is associated, and the immensely long and varied historical processes which have played upon the Eastern religions. Modern political, social, and economic factors introduce further complicating factors.[1]

To understand the problem of dominance in Asia, we must first of all draw a fundamental distinction between Confucianism, on the one hand, and Buddhism, Hinduism, and Shinto, on the other hand. For Confucianism does not propose

[1] It is difficult to quote even approximate figures for the membership of Confucianism. Before the advent of Communism in China (1949), the numbers would run past the 250 million mark. There are no exact figures for either Shinto or Hinduism, although the former must certainly exceed 70 million and the latter 150 million.

any religious belief, whereas the other systems mentioned make solid religious claims on the whole man. This is important to remember when discussing the Chinese Communist state and when contrasting Confucianism with the major Eastern religions. Secondly, the central and unresolved question concerning religion and religious dominance in the Far East concerns uniquely the relationship of Buddhism and Chinese Communism. This is as much because Buddhism is the most widespread of all Eastern religions, as because Buddhism is the only system which could offer a viable answer to Chinese Communism. A study of religious dominance, therefore, should be concerned principally with their relationship and its evolution in the social, political, and economic order. The purpose of this chapter is to outline briefly the relationship. Separate and exhaustive treatment of this subject is needed, and it belongs in another place. Buddhism will first be discussed, to be followed by a short treatment of Chinese Communism.

Buddhism. Buddhism's brand of dominance is specifically different in our Western eyes from the dominance characteristic of Judaism, Christianity, and Islam. Apart, therefore, from the forbidding extent of the treatment due to it, it is not susceptible of simultaneous and parallel treatment with the three religions we have been discussing.

A first impression received from an examination of Buddhism—and, indeed, of Far Eastern religions—is that neither Judaism nor Christianity ever made any serious or lasting conquests in Asia. Islam, due to the military conquests of its early days, spread widely in certain areas and as far east as Malaysia and Indonesia. Yet Islam made no significant inroads into the heartland of Asia represented by China, the south-east Asian countries, and Japan. Even Islam's penetration of the Indian sub-continent was partial and seems to have stopped at a certain definite line of ethnic and cultural demarcation. Christianity never succeeded in Asia, although at one stage or another of its history it was protected and fomented by five powerful colonialist empires the Portuguese, the Spanish, the Dutch, the French, and the British.

The total number of Buddhists in the world today is placed approximately at 300,000,000. They worship in 2,000,000 temples, and their number includes about 800,000 nuns and priests in Asia. Buddhism is not monochrome or monolithic but multifaceted and diversified. Gautama Buddha was born, tradition says, in 563 B.C. and died about 490 B.C. His fundamental teaching was simple in its concept, but difficult to implement. He established as man's goal a condition of being which in Western terminology would be described as one unaffected by time, by pleasure, by pain, a world which was without forms, without limits, a timeless void of negative infinity, and an unconscious state of illimitless unbeing. Nirvana, according to the Buddha, lacked the restlessness of details, the limits of particular consciousness, the birth and death of individual existences. To reach this goal, Buddha taught, man should attain the Middle Way by following the Four Noble Truths and by keeping thus to the Eightfold Path.[2]

Within 200 years of his death, Buddhism had split into two main movements. Theravada Buddhism, known also as Hinayana or the Lesser Vehicle Buddhism, was orthodox and strict, following all the original rules of Buddha and emphasizing monastic asceticism. It spread through Ceylon, Burma, Laos, Thailand, Cambodia, parts of South Vietnam, and India. Mahayana Buddhism, known also as the Greater Vehicle, adopted rules which were more suitable for a popular religion. It also admitted non-Buddhist elements from other religions. It took hold in China, Japan, Korea, Vietnam, Tibet, and Mongolia. These areas are still dominated by the two movements.

The basic difference between Mahayana and Theravada Buddhism for Western minds lies in the greater facility which Mahayana offers for salvation. According to it, man is not alone in seeking his salvation in Nirvana. A pantheon of saintly beings, Boddhisattvas—men who are already almost in Nirvana,

[2] The Four Noble Truths are:
1. All existence is suffering. Life is ephemeral.
2. Suffering comes from ignorant craving and the desires of individuals.
3. Suffering ends when all desires are extinguished.
4. To extinguish desires, one must follow the Eightfold Path.
The Eight Steps of the Path are:
1. Right views.
2. Right will and motives.
3. Right speech.
4. Right conduct.
5. Right pursuits.
6. Right efforts.
7. Right mindfulness.
8. Right concentration.

but who voluntarily consent to remain outside that blessed and ultimate perfection—help mankind to attain it. But Theravada stresses personal asceticism, isolated striving, and the aloneness of individual efforts to reach Nirvana.

In India, Buddhism drew heavily on Hindu mythology. In China, it combined with Confucianism and Taoism. In Japan, it blended with Shintoism. Throughout south-east Asia, in Tibet, and in Mongolia, it adopted many of the local animistic and dynamistic elements of previous religions. On account of this intermingling and borrowing, it is impossible to describe Buddhism in simple uncomplicated lines. The official books and teachings of Buddhist leaders, intellectuals, and pressure-groups can be categorized and described within definite limits. But Buddhism as a religion of the people never had, and does not possess today, anything like the doctrinal and practical uniformity which Westerners are accustomed to see in Judaism and Christianity as organized religions.

It is a fact that no Western mind finds it impossibly difficult either to believe in the Four Noble Truths or to set the Eight-fold Path at least as an ideal. Judaism, Christianity, and Islam reproduce in their own words and sometimes with striking verbal similarity many of the Truths and much of the Path. This surface similarity can be most deceptive, leading the "tired" or "disillusioned" Westerner to believe that in Eastern religions he can find a "pure" expression of what came to be known as natural religion during the rationalistic and idealistic fervor of the 19th century.[3]

Where the Western mind cannot be genuinely Buddhist is in the fundamental concept of time, human existence and earthly history which underlies Buddhism as a way of life. Basic to the Western idea of time and of history is the triadic

---

[3] The apotheosis of the "natural religion" movement was the hypothetical "noble savage," much vaunted and sought after by the 18th and 19th century rationalist mind. The "noble savage" was, reputedly, incapable of lies, clean of body, upright in morals, gentle with the weak, fierce with the cruel, living in forest dells beneath leafy fronds with his equally moral wife and angelic children; with no inclination to address himself to a supreme being, only reverencing the sun, the wind, the rain, the lightning, the thunder, as fellows and brothers and as natural forces; untainted by what we call culture, uncomplicated by the "dogmatic religions." Everywhere man searched for the "noble savage," man found just that—a savage.

framework of *beginning—middle—end*. Within this framework man's life has reality and significance. Before it there is nothingness. After it, there is death. Because of this view, the Western mind regarded man's end, death, as the ultimate evil. He sought to prolong earthly life through his religion or his creative ingenuity or both. From religion he expected the panacea of immortality: to reach the Isles of Eternal Youth, the Water of Eternal Life, resurrection after death in the company of a savior-god. Through an ever more skillful and perfected technology he sought and seeks perpetuation of his life on earth.

Buddhism borrowed heavily from pre-existent Hindu mythology. In particular, it formed its concepts of time, history, and the world on Hindu models. From what we can discern in the mass of legend and adulatory reports about Gautama Buddha, he seems by nature to have been a stoical, unimaginative, moralistic man, slightly addicted to all-embracing platitudes, affected by the messianic persuasion of his own powers and destiny we find in other similarly great men, and bent on an almost masochistic flight from concrete reality. In Buddhism, time and history were considered to be an endless continuum of ever-recurring cycles. Eternity is composed of spans so extended and so unreal that individual man is not merely lost in them; he is nothing. Buddhism insists that human existence is not a phenomenon within the *beginning-middle-end* framework. Rather man's existence is an epiphenomenon to the eternal continuum. Man is incidental. For him, therefore, there are no absolutes—no absolute limits, no absolutely identical beings. All is impermanent. What is called existence is suffering and, therefore, evil. There is no such thing as individual identity, personal happiness, personal goals, personal salvation, personal god. No after-life is possible; an epiphenomenon has no real life before, during, or after anything. Man's religious efforts must be to escape from the continuum. He must attain Nirvana.

The Western mind is confronted with an inescapable obstacle in such a doctrine and way of life. Western society, its basic institutions of morality, government, law, commerce, scientific research, education, political durability, and personal achievement are built from top to bottom on certain presumptions: individual identity, absolute rules, fixed laws, the value of human endeavor, the necessity of human effort in science, in exploration, in literature, in art, in perfecting human society on man's earth. It regards birth as blessing, death as curse. It does not exalt a pleasureless and desireless existence as an ideal.

The Western mind is hampered by a further difficulty in understanding Buddhism. Buddhism's ideal is, according to its teachers, ineffable, inexpressible—to use Western terminology. No word, no concept, no image can reproduce the ideal faithfully. Hence all Western man's descriptions of Buddhism's ideal end up in a list of improper and inaccurate negative terms: no identity, no consciousness, timelessness, spacelessness, painlessness, pleasurelessness. If he is faithful to the mind of Buddha, Western man will, as an extremely difficult mental somersault, avoid describing Nirvana as non-human, non-being, non-personal, non-existence, or even by such neologisms as unbeing, unexistence, unhuman, unperson. For Nirvana cannot be defined as the opposite of anything man knows or is. It is not anything. It is not. By the same token, it cannot be described as nothing. It is not a state of non-being. It cannot, strictly speaking, be described as "unknowable," for that is intelligible to man, and Nirvana is not intelligible. But Nirvana is not unintelligible, even in negative terms. Man has to "get away" from human existence and human concepts. The *I* and the *Thou* of the Western dialogue must be forsworn; they are not translated into a "third" or "we," as certain trends of Western mystical thought and speculation have dreamed, and as the Jewish and Christian ideal of brotherhood has proposed.

It is clearly impossible to define the religious dominance of Buddhism in the same terms which we used when discussing Judaism, Christianity, and Islam. Buddhism propounds a dominance all its own: it explains man's origin, his existence, his end, and his ideals in totally different terms, and claims that this explanation is supreme. But its religious dominance is of a specifically different kind from that of the Western religions.

The condition of Buddhism today and the dilemma of its particular type of dominance are also specifically different from the difficulties confronting Judaism, Christianity, and Islam. The latter are exposed to the most lethal of all human elements: indifference. They claim to have the answer to all problems of a practical nature in man's life. More and more they are found wanting. But Buddhism never claimed in its classical period to have such answers. It disclaimed all responsibility both for the solution of such problems and for the problems themselves. Like man, they were epiphenomena, winking shadows in the fluid penumbra of human impermanence and suffering. Buddhism eschewed them. It abdicated any claim to cure society or perfect man's socio-political condition.

Yet, Buddhism teaches, the man who attains Nirvana does not end up in nothingness. Nothingness, after all, is intelligible, at least by contrast. Any attempt to translate the teachings of Buddhism and its practices into Western terms and techniques becomes otiose and recourseless, a seemingly useless and pointless juggling of contradictory and irreconcilable terms void of any meaning. The Buddhist ideal repels the inherent binarism of the Western mind. In its higher reaches, it eschews any absolute "yes" and "no," in addition to all intermediary grades of assent and dissent. Indifference itself is not a Buddhist ideal; it is only a means to the ideal. At this remote and unattainable point, many have seen or tried to see a conjunction of certain Christian and Jewish mysticism with Nirvana, the "summit" of John of the Cross, the Cloud of Unknowing of Juliana of Norwich, and the "ocean" of medieval Jewish Kabbalists. But this is also inaccurate. All such Jewish and Christian mysticism had theological underpinnings and elaborate concepts which Buddhism rejects.

Officially and according to its ideals, Buddhism cannot father a social theory, form a political system, carve out power-blocs within economic and social boundaries, give birth to an intellectual movement, foment a school of music, of art, of painting. It cannot speak of solving social ills or of perfecting social and political systems. Nor should it collect funds, set up bank accounts, indulge in military operations, or inspire reformist movements, university studies, secular organizations, political and literary propaganda, and civil activity.

Any real vogue for Buddhism among the major populations of the lands traditionally Buddhist must wane inevitably, according as modern technology enters the Far East, and according as Eastern populations are subjected more and more to urbanization, technological facilities, the political and ideological stresses of world politics, the world bloc system, the wrangling of super-powers, and the free flow of ideas. Classical Buddhism would recoil in horror from the politicking of South Vietnamese monks, the activities of the World Fellowship of Buddhists with its resolutions on peace, war, and hunger, the building of leper-stations by Buddhists in Japan, and the propagation of Buddhism by the Ceylonese government in

African countries. All such conduct implies an acceptance of
the human condition, the here-and-now of man's earthly life,
which Buddhism in its classical purity rejects.

There remains the complicating factor of Chinese Communism. The fate of Buddhism is linked inseparably with the
course of Communism in China and the undeniably pathetic
inability of Confucianism to cope with the Marxist outlook.
Buddhism also stands in dependence on the fate of Shinto and
Hinduism. The condition and the problems of these religions
cannot be considered profoundly within the scope of this study.

Chinese Communism and Confucianism. Today, due to the
installation of a Marxist system at its heart, mainland China
has become the single all-important geopolitical factor in Asia
and Oceania. To use an ancient Chinese term, mainland China
has become the axle of the universe, as far as the neighboring
countries are concerned: India, Burma, Tibet, Mongolia,
Korea, Japan, Pakistan, and the states of the south-east Asian
ganglion—Vietnam, Laos, Cambodia, Thailand, Malaysia,
and Indonesia. The present fortunes and near-future evolution
of these and other countries in the area depend on what happens in China and what evolution Confucianism undergoes in
China.

Confucianism is built on a presumed principle of respect for,
and an ultimate value attributed to, the individual, his body,
his soul, his this-worldliness (as opposed to his other-worldly
possibilities), his social and family heredity, and the socio-
political framework in which he lives, moves, and acts. Confucianism functions as the good man's moral broker between
man, the individual, and his environment. Confucianism, also,
while not eschewing what was called metaphysics in the West,
with its dependence on the pseudo-Hellenism of the post-Hel-
lenic revival at the time of the European Renaissance, indulges
in what may be termed an absence of this form of intellectual
excursion.

Confucius himself seems to have taken for granted the religious paradigm of reference prevalent in his time. His famous
remark in a moment of bitterness at human rejection ("Men
may not know me, but Heaven does") betrays not merely a
religious belief, but a conviction that he had a personal relation
with Heaven. He was probably disgusted with the ethical gap
between what men said they believed and what they did. Being
asked once how one should serve the spirits, he answered tartly

and reproachfully: "You are not yet able to serve men! How, then, can you hope to serve the spirits?" Being asked about death, he answered: "Do you yet understand life? How then do you expect to understand death?" This pedagogic method could only lead to agnosticism and, when logically followed through, to professional atheism. Confucianism lacks even the residues of any sound religious anchorage and rationalizes man's existence and moral obligations to the gods and to men to such an extent that it totters on the most extreme boundary of what could possibly merit the name of a religious morality. It was bound to lead later on to non-religious developments.

His logical error went even further. He concentrated on the organization of society in accordance with ethical principles. He was persuaded that ethical behavior and moral uprightness could be *taught*. He built his entire concept of man on a static concept of human nature. He refused to seek justification for his ethical system any further than in an experimental consideration of human nature. He started, therefore, from several unjustified presumptions. In a later day and in accordance with another mentality, it was easy to substitute a source for human nature other than the Heaven of Confucius, to re-define human nature according to an arbitrary choice. His pedagogic approach to morality removed emphasis from personal responsibility and the personal conscience as a primary datum. Morality was reduced to aphoristic maxims and unjustified generalities. Without either a metaphysical justification or an ultimately theological backing, his system lent itself to subsequent interpretation and deformation.

For his unseen world it is easy to substitute an abstract theorem concerning human history. His concept of nature was so fluid, so ill-defined that a pragmatic definition could be substituted for what he originally intended as a philosophic and ethical one. He believed that the principles of behavior came down from the ageless past. He taught that *li* should be in accordance with those principles. But thus anyone who could maintain that the ageless principles were different could change the concept of human nature, could dictate a method of behavior in complete dissonance with the teachings of Confucius. As long as Confucianism dwelt in a land largely untouched by modern developments, it could continue undisturbed by modern developments, it could and did absorb all comers. It took the Taoist movement and leavened it. It con-

sorted with Buddhism and maintained its distinction. Its principles were basically those of a primitive society which had
attained a certain level of culture and stopped there. It depended
for its strength and permanence on the continuity of the social
ambient and the perpetuity of a solid, unchanging society into
which very few new ideas flowed. It depended on a society
whose established ways of living and dying suffered no violent
change. The advent of Maoist Communism to mainland China
in 1949 provided exactly the disruptive elements for which
Confucianism had no defense. It spelled the end of Confucianism as a viable ethic and as a conceptualization of life in
accordance with an unseen world.

It is important to note in this connection what are the essentials of Maoistic Marxism today. Its basic components are:
the absolute cult of a single personality, Mao Tse Tung, as
teacher, leader, ideal, provider of thoughts and health and
prosperity for all Chinese; the levelling of all classes below the
hierarchic Party group; the insistent identification of job, bodily vigor, and good health with the highest fidelity to the maxims and teachings of Mao Tse Tung; the equation of conformity to Maoist principles with happiness and with the true
quality of China; the invincibility of Chinese Marxists; the
infallibility of Chinese Marxism; the innate opposition to China
in foreign countries.

There is not one of these components which has not appeared
with or without one or more of the other components
throughout Chinese history. The only real novelty consists in
the identity of the leader, Mao Tse Tung, and the Marxist dictionary of systematic terminology. From early times down to
the end of the Chinese Empire, the installation of the Chinese
Republic, and the beginnings of Communism, Chinese Confucianism proved itself powerless against the absolutism of
Legalism, the personality-cults of Taoism, and the heady ad-
ventures of Neo-Confucianism in all its forms. The following
passage could take its place in the "little red book" of the
Sayings of Chairman Mao, yet it comes from the Confucian
philosopher Mo Tzu who flourished in the first fifty years of the
4th century B.C.

> Everyone upon hearing good or evil, shall report it
> to his ruler. What the ruler approves all must approve.
> What he condemns, all must condemn. When the

ruler makes a mistake, his subjects must remonstrate with him. When the subject has merit, his ruler shall discover it and recommend that he be rewarded. Those who identify themselves with their ruler, and do not form cliques with their subjects, shall be rewarded by their rulers and praised by their subjects.

Mao Tse Tung's absolutism could not be better expressed than in Mo Tzu's exaltation of his own teachings:

My teachings are sufficient for all things. To reject my teachings and to think on one's own account is similar to throwing away the harvest and picking up individual grains. To attempt a refutation of my words with one's own words, is like throwing eggs at a rock. One may use up all the eggs in the world. But the rock remains; it is unshakable.

It is a fact of history that none of the practical steps taken by the Chinese Communist party in the exercise of authoritarianism is new to Chinese life: concentration camps; forced labor; absolute censorship of thoughts, words, books; centralization of all sources of power; elimination of individual freedom; systematized marshalling of manpower; destruction of family traditions. Maoism appears today as a revised form of ancient tyrannies wedded to a modern ideology. The dominance of religion in Asia depends on the evolution of this Chinese Communism. The crux of their relationship is to be seen in the lack of any innate power in Buddhism to answer the questions and solve the problems which Communism claims to answer and to solve. Buddhism, if it remains within its classical purity and adheres to its ideals which have been called lofty and profound, should not even consider such problems. But Buddhists are increasingly under pressure to consider them and to seek solutions. Their Buddhism is accordingly modified and will ultimately be affected. In the statements of activist Buddhist monks and intellectuals, we see rudimentary expressions of a religious dominance peculiar to Buddhism. Whether Buddhism can develop its own answers and translate them into appropriate sociological and political forms is the key question.

PART VIII
The Modern Mind

38. Consensus and Dominance

The three religions share a common structure and set of basic values. These we must now examine as a consensus, in the light of the modern mind. We must also examine the new consensus to which that modern mind seems inclined. For the heyday strength of religious dominance lay in its power and success in developing consensus among its adherents. The religion enjoying such a consensus was then able to proceed in the world of men and affairs, imposing its will, making and unmaking empires, indulging in power-politics and nationalist movements. Consensus and dominance are the two essential correlates.

Structure-lines of Consensus—The dictionary definition of a *consensus* gives three principal connotations to the term.[1] As

[1] *Webster's Third New International Dictionary* gives the following (abbreviated): 1. harmony, cooperation, group solidarity; 2. general agreement, collective opinion; 3. formal statement of religious belief.

410

used in the context of nations and national harmony, it can be described as the collective attitude and opinion shared by the majority of a group as the basis of their harmony and cooperation that is manifested in externals such as sociological and political institutions, religious and ethical laws, folkways, mores, and policies.

This description does not, however, explicitly mention the six main constituents of a human consensus, be it sociological, political, religious, or other. These factors are Source, Occasion, Motive, Focal-Point, Exteriorization, and Ambit. It is relatively easy to classify the human consensus within the framework of these factors.

Fig. 5 *Paradigm of Consensus*

1. *Source:* This-worldly/Other-worldly
2. *Occasion:* Historical/Non-historical
3. *Motive:* Ethical/Theist/Pragmatic
4. *Focal-Point:* Self/Geographic/Trans-Sense
5. *Exteriorization:* Sacral/Social/Political/Intellectual/Sensate
6. *Ambit:* Self/Others/All

The *Source* and the *Occasion* of a consensus are intimately linked. In the history of civilizations, the source can be presented as this-worldly or other-worldly, as the result of a divine mandate or of men's simple agreement to join for a common end. The other-worldly source implies always a superhistorical occasion; into the normal course of visible, recordable human history an event or occasion is inserted which is not a mere mechanical or logical outcome of human history. Thus the Exodus of the Israelites, the birth of Jesus, the Hegira of Mohammad were such occasions. The source was always other-worldly and trans-sense; it could not be perceived by man's senses or in this world: Yahweh, the Christian God, Allah. An example of a this-worldly source would be the Nazi or Stalinist ideology; their participants repudiated the idea of the other world; they maintained that their consensus sprang directly from historical circumstances. A historical occasion would be, for instance, the absolute necessity for *Lebensraum* which caused the migration of whole groups of peoples throughout the history of Earth.

The *focal-point* of a consensus is that center around which the people of the consensus gather, such as their hearth and lodestone. Sometimes this center has been wholly interior to man as in the case of pure Confucianism and its classical consensus. Sometimes it is geographic, as when a central shrine, a holy city, a sacred grove, a revered temple, or a royal city are the focal-points of a consensus. Sometimes, the focal-point is conceived by its participants as totally removed from both men and things and the visible world in which both live and exist. This was the ideal of the Buddha. But the consensus is sometimes focussed on an axis between the interior of man and a trans-sense destiny point, as was the consensus of early Christianity in the first two centuries before it emerged completely from the catacombs and the expectation of an immediate end of the world.

The focal-area may stretch all the way between the interior of its participants and a trans-sense ultimate, but take in a geographical area. Such, in effect, became the focal area of Medieval and Renaissance Christianity beneath the Roman Popes, and of such was the focal-area of the Protestant nations in the first 300 years of their existence (16th-19th centuries).

The *motive* for establishing a consensus can be a purely pragmatic one (e.g., gains in the economic or political order), an ethical one (for the sake of preserving human relations based on laws of ethical behavior), or a theistic one (because of a revelation from a god or a belief in a god). In the latter, the motive can arise from monotheism or polytheism.

The *exteriorization* of the consensus follows no definite pattern, and usually it presents more than one of the six possible components charted in Fig. 5. The consensus can be manifested in a purely religious way (functions, rites, conscience rules, etc.); in a social way, as the enlivening spirit of social functions and institutions; or by indulging in them as integral parts of its life (marriage, celebrations, hierarchy, economic and financial investments, education, etc.); in political ways, as when the consensus takes over a national government; in an intellectual way, as when academic endeavor, scientific research, and learning are harnessed to explaining, furthering, and enlightening a consensus; or, finally, in a sensate way, as when the atheistic and literary activities of participant members in the consensus are infused with their spirit and outlook.

At some stage of their long history, the consensus of Judaism, Christianity, and Islam were exteriorized on all six planes. In the 20th century, the political exteriorization has dwindled to a very negligible degree.

There is lastly the *ambit* of the consensus. The *ambit* is very intimately related to the *focal-point*. Some consensus include only the self, the inner man or inner identity, whether this be ethnic, geographical, social, or cultural. Some consensus are projected to include some other men, as happens with a modern sect such as the Jehovah Witnesses. Others still are projected over an ambit that includes all men.

The force of a consensus, as it appears in history, seems to reside in a complex of inner convictions, possessed by men of a group. These convictions inevitably include a series of intellectual propositions and another series of determinations or resolutions. Emotions are harnessed to strengthen and bolster those propositions and resolutions. In the normal human consensus, this interior complex pours out onto the exterior world, explaining the various phenomena it meets in man's cosmos and dictating how the participants of the consensus should act and react vis-à-vis those phenomena. In tracing the early history of Judaism, Christianity, and Islam, we saw such a consensus in action.

Contrariwise, when a breakdown occurs, in either the propositions or the resolutions, the consensus begins to lose its viability. Its outer force diminishes, the cohesion of its members dissolves. It seems axiomatic in the history of human consensus that when the interior complex is corroded or weakened or shattered, there follows inevitably a decay of those structures in which the consensus had been exteriorized. There are very few examples of a consensus which perished overnight in the blossom of its greatness, which came crashing down at one fell blow, dragging with it the lives and fortunes of all adherents. A ready example might be the collapse of Montezuma's Mexican Empire under the sudden blow of the Spanish mailed fist. But we do not know enough about the condition of that Empire to say that it was in full blossom; it may have reached a nadir.

The history of empires, polities, dynastic and dictatorial hegemonies, and religions contains many more examples of another kind: consensus-groups that gleamed on the human horizon with a special brilliance all their own, then slipped into decay slowly and sometimes imperceptibly, dissolving under the hammer-blows of fierce primitive forces, while their consensus dissolved interiorly for other reasons. We can usually uncover a sapping of the interior persuasions of the consensus prior to a weakening and destruction of its exteriorization in the socio-political world of man.

The Religious Consensus—Judaism, Christianity, and Islam share a common consensus which, of course, each one diversified and particularized for itself. The *source* of the consensus is the god-figure (Yahweh, God, Allah), who intervenes from the other world. The *occasion* is a super-historical one: the temptation and sin of Adam and Eve, the first man and woman. We say that it is not historical because Adam and Eve as they are presented by the three theologies were not subject, before their sin, to the strictures of place and time which are the necessary parameters of any genuine human history.

In Christian theology, the condition of Adam and Eve has often been characterized as *preternatural,* meaning that while they did not enjoy supernatural bliss in Heaven, they were not bound by the limitations of space and time. Jewish and Muslim theology could very well adopt the term: they concur generally in this picture of the first man and woman.

According to this religious teaching, this first pair were immune from death, pain, libido, and unfortunate accidents. Falling into water, they would not drown. They could not perish by hunger, did not need to fear the ferocity of wild beasts, were not injured by a falling tree, or by a stone which struck them, or by a lightning bolt which fell across them. Disease could not attack their organisms. The sun could not scorch them. The winds could not buffet them. Ice-cold weather would not numb them. Work did not tire them. Death never knocked at their door. They lived, in other words, in physical conditions totally different and separate from those we know to be the constant ones of our Earth and our universe.

Their temptation and sin, therefore, as the *occasion* of the triple consensus is super-historical. The *motive* of the consensus was frankly that the transcendent god had revealed himself to men and asked for their loyalty and obedience, in return for which he would guarantee them salvation. The motivation, therefore, of the consensus was monotheistic salvation. The theme of salvation is fundamental to the triple consensus. According to the consensus, man would be saved in two ways: from the guilt of his sins and from the terrible fate of not enjoying Paradise forever with the god. Salvation, for the Jew, is achieved by fidelity to the Law and to the teachings of Judaism. For the Christian, salvation comes primarily through Jesus' sacrifice on Calvary and secondarily through the cooperation of the man who obeys the voice of Jesus' representatives on Earth. For the Muslim, salvation is obtained by fidelity to the *Shari'a*, the sacred law, by observance of the five duties incumbent on the good Muslim,[2] and by wisdom arising from his love and knowledge of the Koran.

Originally, the triple consensus was purely sacral. Very quickly in the history of each religion it extended to the sociopolitical, intellectual, and sensate planes of human life; the *exteriorization* of the consensus was thorough and all-embracing. To be a Jew, a Christian, a Muslim, was to be Jewish, Christian, Muslim in all things from womb to tomb.

The *ambit* of this consensus was quite definite: only the chosen ones, the saved ones, the believing ones, the persevering ones, could benefit by the revelation of the god. Christians and Muslims no less than Jews considered themselves the chosen people, the only ones who were right, correct, god-fearing, upright, enlightened, in possession of the truth, and destined for eternal happiness. All others were wrong, in the grip of evil, in error, doomed to eternal punishment or at least to eternal exclusion from the joy of Paradise. In all three religions, we find at various stages an attempt to include those of the non-chosen who lived according to their lights.

All three consensus, finally, professed a triple *focal-point:* interior worship, geographical centrism, and a sacred place. Judaism created for itself Jerusalem and the Temple in Jerusalem. Christianity, until the 16th century, centered on Rome in the West and Constantinople in the East, with an abundance of secondary centers throughout its length and breadth. Islam centered itself around Mecca primarily, and secondarily around Medina.

But the geographic ambit of the consensus had another very significant aspect—the land on which the believers lived. In Judaism, we know that Israel was regarded as the Promised Land to which Moses had led the Israelites after forty years of wandering in the desert between Egypt and Palestine. Yahweh

---

2 The five are: belief in the one and only God and in Mohammad as His Apostle; praying five times a day; fasting during the month of Ramadan; a pilgrimage to Mecca at least once in a lifetime by those who can afford it; and paying the poor tax.

was the god of this land. The land was His and sacred. It could
not be violated by non-believers or by the sins and sacrileges
of the believers; it was holy and blessed by Yahweh.

Christianity and Islam both retained this geographic idea,
but they refined it to suit their circumstances: these religions
were of much wider demographical spread than Judaism and
embraced many nations. Christianity from the beginning spoke
symbolically of their faith as a Promised Land to which Jesus
had led them. When Christianity took hold of European lands,
they immediately became "Christian lands" bathed in the
light of the Gospel and blessed by God, as opposed to the outer
areas which were considered to wallow in error and to be
engulfed in the darkness of paganism.

Thus the close link between nation (or race), the country in
which that nation lived, and its religion was forged. The consensus invested all aspects of man's life. National ideology and
politics, geographical area, and religious belief were thus indissolubly bound together. This amalgam served as the later moral
justification for the colonization of Africa, Asia, and the two
Americas. Christian lands should radiate the message of salvation out to the lands of the pagans. This state of affairs
reached its climax in the temporal power of the Roman Popes
during the Middle Ages. When the Protestant ethic was born
in the 16th century and a more direct return to Biblical concepts was started, the idea of the Promised Land once more
grew vivid. Protestants, persecuted in one country by Catholics, fled to sympathetic areas from the darkness of Romish
superstition. The great Puritan emigrations to America were
explicitly undertaken as to the Promised Land.[3]

It is certain that the "racism" peculiar to the West vis-à-vis
the other parts of the world is due in large part to a residual
idea of the "Christian" land, as opposed to the "pagan" or
"foreign" or "unenlightened" lands abroad. It is significant in
this context that China was the only non-Western country where
a similar racism and xenophobia arose. China, also, had
originally developed mythological traits in its ancient consensus which resembled the original Judaic idea of a Promised
Land belonging to a particular god and specially singled out to
be blessed for its chosen inhabitants.

Islam, no less than Christianity, developed a similar "ge-

[3] Cf. Chapter 6.

ography of blessings and of curses," as one writer has expressed it. The lands where Islam reigned supreme were, in Islamic eyes, the blessed lands. "Outside" lay the "others," the "foreigners," the "infidels." Racism and a falsely conceived ethnic unity were developed according to which the Muslims were practically equated with the "Arabs." [4]

An important extension of the geographical center element in the consensus was the emergence of local synagogues, temples, cathedrals, basilicas, churches, chapels, shrines, mosques. Basically the notion and intent behind such structures was originally the same as that which prompted the Israelites to build a shrine at Gilgal, at Shiloh, at Shekem, to build the Temple at Jerusalem, and after the Exile to erect local synagogues outside the geographical center of Jerusalem. All were surrogates for the center.

This notion and intent are very anciently found in human civilization: the god or spirit worshipped by man lives "outside" man's ken, "outside" his world. From time to time, he condescends to be present among men, to have a presence among men at one geographical location. That location immediately becomes "sacred," "holy." It is the "house of God and the gate of Heaven." [5] To be "near" the god or spirit in question, therefore, men consecrated this spot and made it holy. Even in such a place, there was always one exact location where the invisible presence was supposed to alight: the Holy of Holies in the Jewish Temple, the Black Stone in the Ka'aba, of Mecca, the Tabernacle in Christian churches. In mosques, the *mihrab*, a semicircular niche reserved for the one who led the prayers, indicated the *gibla* or direction in which the Ka'aba of Mecca lay in relation to the mosque.

Thus the consensus of each religion was an all-embracing complex of convictions, propositions, emotional attachments, geographical centers and areas, political and social institutions infused with the convictions of the consensus, and locked within the basic triad of race-country-religion. Thus the Jewish, Christian, and Muslim consensus appear at their flower. We shall see in detail how this consensus was exteriorized in each religion and what penalties of history have been levied on these

---

[4] There is no ethnic basis to the idea of an "Arab" nation occupying all the lands of Islam.

[5] Cf. *Genesis* 28:17.

religions on account of that exteriorization. Here, we must go
on to examine the constituent elements of the triple consensus
in the light of the modern land.

It is obvious that this consensus of Judaism, Christianity,
and Islam is built on three cardinal statements: that the human race stems directly and uniquely by physical generation
from one man and one woman, Adam and Eve; that their
creator decided to choose from among their descendants one
particular group; and that this group would be the sole beneficiary of the salvation the creator offered. Adam and Eve, the
Chosen People, the Salvation.

It is impossible for the modern mind to accept the proposi-
tion that either all men are descended from an initial pair
(Adam and Eve) or that the first woman was formed from the
first man.[6] Science tells him that between ten or twenty million
years ago the line of evolution which finally led to man
branched off from the main stem of primate evolution. There
is no evidence of a sudden appearance of man with no antecedents, and just as little evidence that the female was formed
from the male. Modern man cannot, therefore, think intelligibly
with such concepts.

Christianity's doctrine of the Original Sin of Adam and Eve
is not found fully developed in Judaism and Islam.[7] Christianity teaches essentially that because Adam and Eve sinned, the
entire human race descended uniquely from them is affected
by this sin. In ordinary Christian parlance, each man born
into the world carries this Original Sin. Christian Baptism
relieves him of it, and thus makes his soul pleasing to God.
Cruder expression of this doctrine holds that Original Sin
passed from mother to son by physical transmission. More

[6] In 1909, the Pontifical Biblical Commission of the Roman Catholic Church decreed that such propositions belonged to the foundations of the Christian faith (*facta quae christianae religionis funda-
menta attingunt*).

[7] Judaism, although it possesses a similar term (*het haqadmon*)
has never stressed it, partly to be different from Christianity. Neo-
Orthodoxy is more inclined to speak of "inevitable sin." This goes
back to the very ancient doctrine of the good and the bad inclinations in man's heart. For practical purposes, this inclination corresponds to the Original Sin of the Christians. Islam recognizes an
innate tendency to evil in man's heart, but does not stress its connection with Adam's sin.

refined expressions avoid saying quite that. Yet the concept of inherited sin or guilt is neither intelligible nor acceptable to the modern mind. Similarly, the Jewish and Muslim doctrines about good and evil inclinations in man do not find a ready echo in modern clinical and behavioral psychology. We must remember that such concepts came very easily to the ancients.

This notion of salvation from sin is opaque for the scientific mentality. That mentality can understand what a morally good or bad action is by reference to the concrete surroundings of man, his familial, social, political, and personal obligations. Sin in this sense is intelligible. The idea of sin as a "spiritual" entity giving such offense to a "spiritual" god that he punishes it by the severe sanctions of hell-fire and eternal torments is not intelligible. In the first place, the "spiritual" character of the sin and its "staining" or "deformation" of the soul appear as images to the modern mind, not as expressions of reality. When that mind seeks to go behind the image and find the reality, it finds nothing intelligible. Jewish, Christian, and Muslim theologians have tried to define sin as a lack, a negation of what should be there: the god establishes an order of things in which A should follow B; man wilfully puts B in front of A for his own purposes and in direct contravention of the god's known will. The god's order has been disturbed by man; man has sinned.

All this, however, does not explain the "spiritual" change in the sinner, and this is precisely what is not intelligible to the modern mind. For that mind, the dangers which threaten and the salvation which it seeks are quite different. It is not man's particular beliefs but man's survival and uniqueness which are at stake. Thus, modern man seeks salvation from dangers of physical extinction which overhang his existence due either, now, to man's misuse of his environment or, in 80,000 years, to fresh ice sheets that could engulf Europe and North America.[8]

Prime amongst the dangers from which he seeks salvation is the ever-widening economic gap between the poor and the rich nations, and the wave of governmental and sociological instability currently shaking the international scene. Man knows that in eighty underdeveloped nations, the income per person is rising by only one per cent and, at this rate, will only

[8] Cf. the address of Dr. Wallace S. Broecker, at the 1968 Annual Meeting of the *American Geophysics Union*.

be $170 per year at the end of the 20th century. On the contrary, he knows that the average income per person in the U.S.A. will reach $4,500 by the same time. The instability of today is disturbing. In the last eight years there have been 164 outbreaks involving 82 national governments. The poor nations are more unstable than the rich: in the former, 32 out of 38 have suffered significant conflicts; all 38 have had an average of two major outbreaks per country. Of the twenty-seven rich nations, a major internal disturbance has afflicted only one on its own territory. Yet by 1975, the children of the poor nations will equal the total population of the rich nations. Before that point, in 1970, half of the world's population will live in the poor nations, but they will have at their disposal only one sixth of the total goods and services in the world.

The *International Biological Program* is organized in order to find out over a period of five years and by means of a cooperative study of plant, animal, and human life, what man and his technology are doing to man's environment. A report of the House Subcommittee on Science, Research, and Development stated that the Program was "not for the sake of learning. It is a matter of survival in the kind of world which human beings come to regard as desirable." [9]

The dangers envisaged come from extensive defoliation and clearing of jungles, diversion of rivers and lakes for desert irrigation, pollution of waters and atmosphere, and the generation of huge amounts of heat by urban and industrial complexes. Affected by these would be man's water supply, the air he breathes, the plants and the animals around him.[10]

The *Center for Science and the Future of Human Affairs* is another organization with fundamentally the same purpose: to effect this pragmatic salvation. The problems facing mankind as a result of the scientific revolution were mooted at a meeting of the Center in March 1968, and the mere recital of them is more than enough to give modern man gooseflesh: total severance of human sexual life from the reproductive process due

[9] Published March 19, 1968, Washington, D.C.

[10] The report cites a calculation that "if all human polluting activity were halted immediately, about 500 years would be required to restore Lake Erie to its condition of 25 years ago, and about 100 years to bring Lake Michigan back to its condition of that same period,—if, indeed, that is possible at all. . . ." Lake Erie is virtually dead. Lake Michigan and others are on their way to the same fate.

to new techniques for the artificial production of children, the predicted widespread world famine of the 1970's, the modification of solar energy reaching the earth by the continuous sedimentation of accumulated by-products in the stable layers of the stratosphere due to the exhausts of jet aircraft, to cite but a few.

Modern man, therefore, seeks salvation from such ills as the 500-mile-long smoke plumes of New York and Los Angeles, from the pesticide-bearing trade winds that bend the palm trees on Caribbean islands, and from the climate-altering influence of lead emitted by automobile exhausts.[11] Modern man will engage in mutual salvation projects such as the international pact for the rescue of astronauts,[12] the *Fund for Education in World Order*, which aims at aiding institutions, promoting research orientation on the problems of war prevention, and world-wide welfare and justice, the *Twentieth Century Fund*'s studies of the major institutions dominating our society,[13] or the *International Conference on Human Rights*. It is not the lack of divine grace in man's soul but the "brain drain" from developing countries [14] which it is planned to offset by a variation of the Trieste Plan used at the Center for Theoretical Physics of Trieste.[15]

It is scientists, not theologians or even philosophers, who advise the President of the U.S.A. on practical problems such as world food supplies, environmental pollution, and the food potential of the oceans. It is not a system of salvation, atonement, and sanctification which bothers modern man and is elaborated by theologians, moralists, humanists, priests, philos-

[11] "Can the World Be Saved?," LaMont C. Cole. *The New York Times Magazine*, March 31, 1968.

[12] Signed on April 22, 1968, in Washington, D.C., London and Moscow by 44 nations.

[13] Institutions such as the military establishment, the Port of New York Authority, pools of capital funds, pension-funds, bank-merged trust-funds, insurance companies, and the combined military-industrial complex.

[14] Discussed in a seminar at the U.N., which ended on April 6, 1968.

[15] Under this plan, young scientists from developing countries are facilitated by money grants to do studies abroad, while also devoting some months of each year to solving the problems of their mother-countries.

ophers, rabbis; he is interested, rather, in the principles of systems analysis and its grand strategy for dealing with man's problems as evolved by the coordinated efforts of mathematicians, economists, engineering managers, social scientists, sociologists, psychologists, and public administrators.

The sacred character and importance of a physical location (shrine, altar, tabernacle) is likewise difficult for modern man. The difficulty stems from the completely different concept the modern mind has of the world and the cosmos and of all objects in them. As we remarked before, there is no room for an "invisible" world of the spirit "lying at the back" of the visible world. That a physical location can be a point of contact with a "spiritual" being is neither demonstrable in terms understood by the scientific mind nor disprovable. It is an assertion that cannot be tested. All that modern man discovers by his analysis of objects and his auscultation of the heavens inclines him to disallow this idea.

Lastly, the concept of a Chosen People and a sacred Land finds no analogue in modern man's experience. It only reminds him of former times in history when such concepts were used to justify terrible nationalisms, hateful xenophobias, and racial prejudices. Modern man can understand an ethnic group as such; he may point out that, with a few rare exceptions in outlying parts of society, there is no such thing as an ethnically pure and homogeneous group of human beings today. But the idea is intelligible to him. When this racial or ethnic character is endowed with a "spiritual" or religious character, he ceases to understand.

In general, modern man is trying to exclude from his society any influence that either religion or ethnic bias may have. Both the real and symbolic use of the triad, race-country-religion, are alien to the modern mind as a basis for establishing society. The fundamental and leading ideas of the religious consensus in Judaism, Christianity, and Islam, therefore, are either unintelligible or unacceptable to modern man. He has already developed a different mentality. He approaches consensus from a totally different angle. We must now examine that mentality and that different approach to the consensus on the part of the West and the Islamic nations.

39. *The Anti-Consensus*

From a superficial analysis of today's world and of man in that world, one could arrive at the conclusion that there is in the making a genuinely human consensus, as distinguished from and opposed to various types of particularistic consensus which have hitherto issued from the historical groupings of men. We find, however, on further and deeper consideration that the picture is not quite so encouraging; the various trends cannot be so easily and consolingly interpreted. In fact, a different picture emerges in which two main conditions prevail: firstly, among human beings as a whole there does not seem to be as yet even the remotest, the most vestigial, or the most embryonic beginning of what man hitherto has needed as a basis for any consensus; secondly, irremoveable pressures are at work ruthlessly destroying what, to a former age, appeared to be the foundations of a human consensus.

One is, therefore, forced to conclude that within these conditions there does not appear at present to be any suitable place for the religious dominance of Judaism, Christianity and Islam. Now without that dominance, one cannot imagine what the future state and functional significance of these religions can or will be.

When we endeavor to apply the paradigm of consensus, we come to what initially is a mystifying and discouraging conclusion: we can make hardly any positive entry. We find no positive *source, occasion,* or *motive* for a general human consensus. Neither can we find any positive *exteriorization,* nor, therefore, any *ambit* or *focal-point.* If men agree in any relatively restricted area, it seems to be either through fear or constraint. The *ambit* is restricted to a transient area. The *focal-point* varies dizzily—egotism, greed, want, and on the personal, national, and international level. Far from finding a historical occasion, we find rather that every year brings new occasions of disagreement among men. And, of course, there is no question of a non-historical, a super-historical occasion. Men do not consult either oracles, priests, the heavens, gurus, popes, or the entrails of animals, in their international gatherings. The first impression is a negative one. Can we speak of consensus, therefore, in any sense?

At the end of our analysis, we will find that there exists

today in a developing form, not a consensus, but an anti-
consensus. The term is not used with the implication that man
is opposed to a consensus, but rather is radically opposed to
all forms of consensus hitherto entertained in thought or in
actual fact by man. This opposition is in part voluntary, but in
large part involuntary; there arises in the human ambient
forces and elements which make such past forms of consensus
impossible for modern man. The irresistible logic of history
is at work, and man is the emergent creature of its fashioning.
Modern man knows only those past and present consensus;
he can measure their effects and calculate their effectiveness.
None of them now appeals to him as practical business. In
realistic terms, men find themselves drawn together both voluntarily and involuntarily today. Yet they have precluded from
the beginning of this drawing together any known basis for it.
We are in the era of the anti-consensus.

The first relevant condition of modern man which is mentioned above is the apparent absence of any genuine move
toward a world-wide consensus. All the consensus known to
man hitherto have issued from and relied upon an "inner" complex of convictions: intellectual propositions, determinations of
the will, emotional attachments. We not only find such an
inner complex lacking; we find that modern man is opposed
to it, has gone on record saying so and acts accordingly. We
find, moreover, that it is physically impossible for man even
to conceive of the desired consensus. There is no subject or
carrier for a world consensus. All the subjects or carriers of
consensus have been up to this time either nations, races,
tribes, particular groups, religious sects, churches or political
parties. But the prior and necessary condition for the birth of
any consensus in such groupings was a pre-existent homogeneity in the carrier-society (the subject of the consensus). This
homogeneity made consensus possible.

The homogeneity was always based on ethnic or racial relationship. Perhaps the most potent consensus and the most
striking homogeneities ever apparent in human history were
achieved by major religions. One thinks of Judaism, Christianity, Islam, Buddhism, Hinduism, Shintoism, and, although
not a religion in the accepted sense of the word, Confucianism.
Yet, it is demonstrable that their consensus never took hold
outside of certain racial or ethnic bounds. The Christian consensus never reigned outside the white races. Islam's consen-

sus only dominated one Semite racial strain. Judaism's consensus has always been confined to one ethnic group, the Jews. Buddhism, Hinduism, Shintoism, and Confucianism have always been confined within certain racial and ethnic boundaries. These most potent consensus, therefore, relied upon a prior homogeneity. Other less potent but still vital consensus in history such as the various nationalisms and imperialisms were obviously subject to the same condition. No matter how profound the *pax romana* of ancient times, for instance, it was conditioned by the carrier-society which, in fact, assimilated to itself as many of its subjugated peoples as possible. Romans did not become Jews or Gallic Celts, Spaniards, or Germans. Some of the latter became Romans, thus ensuring that *pax romana.*

Today there is no suitable carrier-subject for a human consensus in sight. Rather it would seem that every year since World War II the swelling roll-call of the United Nations provides fresh heterogeneous elements which diminish further any initially apparent homogeneity in the United Nations. No prior homogeneity of the classical kind, therefore, exists for a truly human consensus. It appears, under this heading, to be impossible.

This lack is further illuminated by another facet of life today. Above all, since World War II, there has grown up a network of international relations such as the world has never seen before in its known history. To be especially noted in this international life is the *United Nations Organization* and its ancillary associations. On another and less universal level, this internationalism is manifested in the political and military groupings of various countries all over the world. A third level appears in the economic and commercial activity which links many nations together. We must, however, not imagine that this three-level internationalism contains any genuine seeds of the consensus we are discussing.

The fundamental reason for this is briefly but effectively understood by a comparison of the two terms *national* and *international* in reference to the realities they connote. The first word is descriptive of an extent entity, the nation; it has no sense or value as a term unless a nation exists whose possessions, traits, history, and interests can be described as "national." For *international,* however, there is no corresponding reality. We can speak of "internationalism," "international relations," "international men" and so on. But we can never speak, for example, of "internation." Nothing real corresponds to such a neologism as "internation."

The word "international" itself and, if it existed, "internation" is really defined by the use of terms which seemingly negate it: an international exhibition is one in which many nations participate. Nation, of course, implies a particularism which is the opposite of what the modern mind conceives as an "internation"; and by its nature the single nation is not a fit carrier-society for a human consensus. The term "international" really implies a relationship (between nations) and not a subsistent entity. There is actually no such entity.

In the long, intricate history of human affairs and the mutual relations of men in society, it is axiomatic that no relationship has any reality, much less perdurability, unless it is housed in an institution or institutions which by their nature are apt and adequate for such a function. Without such institutions, one cannot even recognize the existence of such a reality or form a clear concept of what it is, or know the exigencies it can exercise upon us. In fact, inter-human relationships have no reality at all except in such adequate and suitable institutions. Now, no adequate and suitable institution exists wherein the human consensus, if it existed, could be maintained, recognized, acknowledged, and obeyed.

There has not been born in the human spirit any feasible idea of such an institution. In all his achievements and developing processes since the earliest times, man has never seen in this world an institution of this kind. In a certain true sense, man's nature as we have known it provides him with no pre-existent and irresistibly real basis for it. Man, by nature, founds a family; this institutional unit comes naturally to him even if at certain stages and under certain conditions he makes its existence a very transient matter. It is an inescapable unit.

Man comes from the family. He finds it already there at his birth. He naturally perpetuates it. Likewise with his societal instincts: man seems to us to be made for the society of other men. Again he is born into it. He finds it already there. He naturally perpetuates it. But this society of man and his societal instinct have always been limited to certain "ceilings." These ceilings again are automatically and a priori imposed by nature, beyond and without the cooperation of man: the linguistic ceiling, the color ceiling, the racial ceiling, the geographical ceiling.

In the case of each of these "ceilings," if man has seemingly risen above them hitherto, we can find no trace of a new achievement. Geographical ceilings originally kept Italian tribes separate prior to the emergence of Roman rule. Their unification was achieved by a widening of the geographical ceiling. Racial and color ceilings intervened and were maintained between white and black Americans. These ceilings can be widened within national boundaries to wider ceilings of nationality (American) and of homogeneity (mixture of the two), as has happened in many other countries. Protestant and Catholic missionaries have succeeded in converting large masses of Africans and Asians to Christianity and, presumably, to the Christian religious consensus. But in so far as this has been achieved, it has merely entailed the substitution of a Western ceiling for the original indigenous ones. For Christianity today, Roman Catholic or Protestant, is wholly and thoroughly a Western religion.

When we return, then, to consider a human consensus as such, we find that as far as we can judge, there is no apparent "ceiling" provided by man's known condition. Any appeal to the obvious fact that all men are *human*, that they share human nature, and that this is the ultimate "ceiling," is shattered to fragments on the irreducible fact that human nature, as such, does not exist—though there are beings, men, who have this nature. But in each case, individual and societal, this nature is completely individuated by a bristling array of factors which preclude any facile reliance on common characteristics to bring them together. The concept of "human nature" is a philosophers' alchemy-stone. In theory it should convert the different base tendencies of man's metal into the fine gold of universal love and brotherhood. In practice, it is merely an intellectual plaything.

We are, then, by nature incapable of even conceiving of a human consensus. We can imagine its benefits (peace, prosperity, kindness, sharing of goods, and so on), forecast its external conditions (lack of national individuality, ethnic divisiveness, religious prejudice and bigotry), and recognize what it is not (militant nationalism, totalitarian ideologies, commercial empires, Big Brother geopolitics, creeping revolutions, dominant religions). But we have no idea of what the consensus itself would be like.

We find, furthermore, that man in his recently developed international and societal developments is apparently *opposed* to such a consensus, if we take for granted that the principal inherent trait of the classical consensus would also characterize the human consensus.

The absence of any prior consensus or set of inner principles is in perfect tune with the modern scientific mind discussed on previous pages. The men of today with this mind are more concerned with acting, experimenting, developing, and changing than with speculation about "spiritual" possibilities and supernatural implications. Their world is not bi-polar as the religions would have it. There is no divinely chosen people or one true church or unique community of believers and destined ones. There is no internal law of a god written in the mind and heart of man; there is only external law and the convenience of peoples and nations. But this leads us to the second pressure-building condition of modern man.

This is caused by ruthless and irremoveable factors making a human consensus impossible today. These pressures arise from the new geopolitical elements which dominate all man's thinking and acting—first of all, the peculiar geopolitical power-balance of our day. Peace is important because it is now within the power of men to destroy each other and, by that act, to obliterate all traces of human civilization. The nuclear deterrent, as a basis for peace, cannot of itself produce a human consensus. By definition, it implies opposing camps which are neutralized by fear.

Secondly, there are the constantly widening differences between the technologically advanced and the scientifically educated West, on the one hand, and the large proportion of underdeveloped and developing nations, on the other hand. The latter will not overtake the West in the foreseeable future. A consensus between these groups is hardly an early likelihood.

There is, thirdly, the multi-polarity of independent nation states which every year since its inception have swelled the roster of member-nations in the U.N. The principle of multi-polarity is inscribed, as we noted, on the mind of modern man and is a principle of the U.N. This multi-polarity implies the steadily maintained opposition between the two Communist blocs (U.S.S.R. and China) and the U.S.A. together with its allies. No one can state with any degree of surety that this opposition will die away as quickly as it arose. Yet without China, the family of man is not complete.

This, then, is the modern mind in relation to any possible consensus of the classical kind. Indeed, it is more accurate to speak of anti-consensus: although none of the member-nations of the U.N. are opposed to mutual peace and agreement bolstered by genuinely held convictions, and all see the advantages which would accrue therefrom, the member-nations have opted for conditions which preclude the birth and fostering of any consensus in the classical sense of the word. We can thus logically schematize modern man's attitude to the classical consensus under the paradigm of anti-consensus:

Fig. 6   *Paradigm of Anti-Consensus*

1. *Source:*   Nuclear Deterrent
2. *Occasion:*   Historical
3. *Motive:*   Fear
4. *Focal-Point:*   Geographic
5. *Exteriorization:* Social Political Intellectual Sensate.
6. *Ambit:*   Member-nations of the U.N.

A moment's reflection will show that there is absolutely no room for any consensus that Judaism, Christianity, and Islam would offer. On the contrary, such a consensus is precluded because it implies an inner law and inner sanctions depending on an "invisible" authority, and because all three are highly colored by the history, the culture, the mentality, and the prejudices of one particular region and, at least in one case, of one particular race of men.

40. *The Encounter*

Our picture of modern man and his mind would not be complete if we stopped at this point. For as we have described them, the picture is a negative one in which no ray of real hope shines, and which makes no fair promises for the future.

There is another side to this rather negative picture of the anti-consensus. It is that modern man is intent on having the encounter, come what may and cost what it will. For two reasons: he is bent on knowing his earth and his cosmos without the mental structures of any aprioristic theory or doctrine such as organized religions imposed on him hitherto; and he has found by bitter experience that these religions have only fragmented his unity as man, have polarized the members of his family until they no longer resemble or behave as family members, and have kept him in a certain bondage. Man no longer desires to have the magic of mythology clothing his world. He is bent on finding himself in the raw clash of the encounter—not with any suicidal purpose in mind, not with any Nietzschean challenge to the gods on his lips, but because it is the only alternative left him. All the dangers of such a procedure he recognizes. Yet he considers the result he desires worth the risk he takes.

We have spoken of the binarism in man's thoughts and how this binarism was installed at the heart of Western man's principal religious systems (Judaism and Christianity) and in one non-Western system (Islam) which derived its structure from the former two. This binarism has been referred to as a dialectic of opposites, and we have noted how it is always used by man to describe his experience. The perennial mythology of man, and particularly of Western man, is the story of how he has always hitherto endeavored to create a world in terms of this binarism. He has labored to form and hold a vision in which the light and the darkness are included, in which the high rests on the low; the strong is strong because of the weak; the bad is bad because of good; order reigns because it harmonizes elements in chaos; being is, because unbeing has no meaning, and there *is* meaning. This is the dialectic of man's existence and his perennial mythology.

Each of the three religions, as we saw, capitalized on this innate tendency in historical man; sometimes, they made a dogma out of the binarism, as Christians did with the doctrine of Original Sin; sometimes, they made it a means of self-identity, as Jews did with their concept of the Chosen People; sometimes, they used it to justify the founding of a vast theocratic empire, as Muslims did; sometimes, they were impelled by it to insert a negative element as a condition of their own faith's authenticity, as Christians did with Jews and Judaism.

We have concluded that the modern mind rejects this binarism as a basis *for its human consensus.* No one is blind to the cruel fact that individual nations and individual men continue to practice the dialectic of opposites. Indeed, this is modern man's deep-seated trouble. The nations which compose the United Nations Organization, for instance, constantly think the thought, employ the language, and perform the actions, of binarism. But in the comity of nations, that place where a human consensus should be formed and should reign, this binarism is absolutely rejected.

No one must be branded as evil. No one must be lauded as the opposite good. No one single member, nor all the members as a whole, must be subjected to a concept of truth which has moral connotations, or must be described as evil even if they commit aggression, perpetuate human slavery, massacre millions, or curb and destroy human liberties. At most, they will be reckoned as having violated a rule of the Organization.

For a concept of truth with moral connotations presumes a final criterion superior to all individual criteria, and a concept of evil presumes a final norm of absolute good. As we said, binary absolutes are excluded. Thus far, the perennial mythology of man is excluded by the modern mind.

By this same act modern man excludes a gamut of human impressions and expressions. On the plane of the human consensus, one can no longer speak of the casual callousness of society or the indifference of man's world. There is no question of seeking an outside salvation against the hypocrisy of human conventions, or the dead boredom of limited human existence. All these impressions and expressions are binaristic, are born of an innate theism. They solve no problems and unlock no doors. Indeed, the only doors they have unlocked in the past allowed destructive elements to enter. Man speaks like the heroine of Ingmar Bergman's *Through A Glass Darkly* who "opened a door," but "the god who came out was a spider" with a "loathsome, evil face" who "clambered up onto me and tried to force himself into me."

Modern man, therefore, on this plane of international relations and consensus, shuns any "internalization." He insists on an external framework: *external laws* without the moral coercion of inner sanctions, and external bonds and agreements without any inner spirit—emotion, attachment, abstract principle, philosophy, or religion.

When we consider the configuration of world politics in the last third of the 20th century, we arrive at the same conclusions but by a different route. This time it is the geopolitics of modern man which provide a clue to the workings of his mind. In today's geopolitics, the unique geographical factor lies in the *incommensurate importance* of the African, Asian, and South American land-masses with their populations and resources, in relation to the technological and scientific conditions under which the countries of these areas can be considered viable member-nations of the Earth. The political factor which makes today's geopolitics unique is the *simultaneous depolitization and de-moralization* of international relations. Both factors produce the human crisis of today, and both explain the tortuous agonies of Great Powers and the gyrating policies of lesser powers.

As to the incommensurate importance of Africa, Asia, and South America, it is clear that the imbalance mentioned above does exist. Population projections, for instance, place four fifths of the world's total population of 7.4 billion in these areas by the year 2000 A.D.[1] Yet in the mid 'sixties of this century, 85% of gross world production comes from one-third of the world's people living in North America, Europe, and Australia, mainly. The other two-thirds, living mainly in Africa, Asia and South America, produce only 14% of the G.W.P. In these three areas, 65% of the people are functionally illiterate, 60% of them have less than a minimum adequate diet; they have only 35% of all world food production, and only 7% of all world industrial production.[2]

Gunnar Myrdal in his three-volume study of India and Asia [3] comes to the same conclusions: burgeoning populations, technologically backward peoples, education and health problems, labor difficulties, agrarian complexes, breakdown of Western democratic systems of government usually replaced by military dictators, represent a growing problem which is not aided by the slowing down of the absolute rate of economic expansion in these areas to well below the level attained ten years ago. It is aggravated by the declining expansion of the industrialized countries.

The depolitization and de-moralization of international relations has been cited as the political factor in our modern geo-

[1] Cf. *Population Bulletin*, vol. xxi, no. 4, Oct. 1965.

[2] Figures are taken from the United Nations Development Program report of 1966.

[3] Cf. *Asian Drama: An Inquiry into the Poverty of Nations*, by Gunnar Myrdal, The Twentieth Century Fund, New York, 1968.

political situation. The depolitization is obvious. Today, the basis for international relations between countries is decreasingly political in any sense known hitherto. The three chief forms of international relations in the past were imperial, military, and economic. More and more, the relations of countries are in the economic area, are less of the military kind, and only a fraction are of the former imperialist and colonialist type. This development has moved one preponderant part of international relations on to an economic and ideological level; it is here for the moment that all major battles are fought and profound struggles are engaged.

The de-moralization of international relations has been amply explained before. There is, actually, no international alliance, convention, agreement, or association founded today which is motivated by a moral or religious theme—even partly. The semblance of such a theme can be heard in the voices but not seen in the joint actions of Islamic countries vis-à-vis Israel: ostensibly, the motive is religious; actually, it is political, territorial, economic. The nearest approach to a moral motivation for international actions and policies, despite what her critics may say, is to be found in the enormous generosity which the U.S.A. has shown to the world after World War II. Never did such a mighty nation give so gratuitously so much to so many with such little hope of anything commensurate in return, as the U.S.A. did between 1945-1966. A disbursement of $125 billion in foreign aid (not including Vietnam war expenditures) is unparalleled in history.

As we noted, however, all international relations today are maintained without allowing any religion or religious system to inject its particular point of view into them. The dialogue of international relations implies, first of all, no obligations. No trust, still less love, is required. The basic requirement is the wish for dialogue. Love and trust would imply absolute norms to which no nation subscribes. Secondly, the dialogue is open-ended and without any overall intention. It is not meant to produce union, unity, or harmony. Thirdly, no participant would dream of revealing his genuine difficulties, fears, and plans to another. Only a greater mutual understanding would issue from such a revelation. No participant wishes to be better known and appreciated in this sense. There might be an agreement on absolute principles, and some of the participants would have to bow to these principles. Fourthly, the dialogue is meant to be simply and solely a consideration of problems and exigencies and of the way in which both might be solved without infringing upon the status of any participant.

An example of the dialogue is provided by the varying fortunes of an attempt by the U.S. Mission to the United Nations to enter on the records of the United Nations Commission on Human Rights a statement summarizing the treatment which the U.S.S.R. meted out to Soviet writers who had criticized the Soviet regime's suppression of certain civil liberties and who had their writings smuggled out of the Soviet Union. On March 6, 1968, U.S. Ambassador Arthur Goldberg delivered a formal protest before the Commission against the Soviet treatment of the writers. At a subsequent meeting, the Soviet representative, Yevgeny N. Nasinovsky, obtained the deletion from the record of the three paragraphs in which the American protest was formally recorded. The voting on this issue was 10 (Iran, India, Madagascar, Nigeria, the United Arab Republic, Yugoslavia, Poland, the Soviet Union, the Ukraine, Tanzania) to 8 (U.S.A., Britain, Greece, Italy, New Zealand, Israel, the Philippines, Argentina), with 4 abstentions.

Both those who voted for and against the motion were quite aware of the facts: Soviet writers were tried *in camera* and were sentenced for thinking differently from the regime. This was not the issue. The issue was the condition under which the Soviet Union would continue the dialogue, and that condition does not include any permissiveness on its part in having the stigma of injustice or oppression attached to it in the written records of the Commission.

The participants in dialogue are not consciously trying to find more and better ways by which they can all live and progress efficiently and happily within *a mutually agreed upon idea* of Earth and man's cosmos. This would imply a staticism at the heart of man's intention. But he has categorically rejected this. His planet as a human habitation and his cosmos as a field of investigation and expansion are *yet to be made*. Man feels constrained to insist on the inherent uncertainty of his knowledge and of his relationship to Earth and to the cosmos. This admission provides him with the stimulus to pursue greater change, greater efforts, further and ever-moving researches.

In this dialogue, however, decisions must be taken. The presupposition of all decision-making is that there exists and will exist for some time to come a series of situations which can be described as typical of the anti-consensus. The anti-consensus situation always arises under the following conditions:

1) a set of abiding, irremoveable, and irreducible oppositions exists, and

2) it is impossible to satisfy both sides of the conflict, and

3) the dissatisfied parties can still continue to make their voices heard and are not bound by an irresistible sanction, and

4) no side is able to push its values or point of view to the destruction of the decision-making or the dialogue, and

5) the inability to reach agreement is not allowed to interfere with some form of coping with the opposition by, at least, minimizing its worst effects.

The text of the U.N. Security Council's resolution of March 24, 1968, on the Middle East provides an illustration of the decision-making we are discussing. The resolution lists the reasons for its judgment (the statements of Jordanian and Israeli authorities, and the information supplied by the U.N. representative in the area), recalls two past resolutions of the Security Council (nos. 236 and 237, of 1967), condemns the Karameh attack by Israel, deplores all cease-fire violations, and calls on Israel to desist from such actions. The Secretary General of the U.N. is requested to keep the situation under review and report back to the Security Council.

In this resolution no rights of either side are invoked, no absolute rules of conduct are alleged, no appeal is made to theoretic rules. Nor is there any sanction implied or envisaged. The only subsequent action provided is the continual review of the situation by the Secretary General. This is a purely informational purpose. When we realize that the Security Council has never condemned the organized guerilla bands of Jordan and Egypt which have taken a large toll in Israeli life and property, we can see that in such resolutions there is no question of right and wrong, of morally good and bad. It is a question of expediency. For some reason proper to the behavior and policies of the Arab countries in the U.N. and of their momentary sympathizers, such a condemnation was considered expedient. It was given. Nothing was changed in reality.

A true picture of the dialogue ensuing from such a mentality cannot be had unless we notice that the participants find, apparently, no difficulty in "doing things together." Even such a basic thing as the original polarity of the Western capitalist and Soviet Marxist systems can be set aside for practical work and achievement. In the last five years the market economies and centrally planned economies of both blocs have been improved and a certain mutual convergence has been noted. There has arisen a species of international economic activity dependent on private and public investment funds. It is to be remarked that the official ideological mentalities have not changed in any essential way. But those who have such ideologies can cooperate with each other in "doing things" in meeting the imperatives of interdependency.

Our picture of the encounter would not be complete without some reference to the U.S.A. in particular. Besides being the leader of the Western world and the most influential single power ever to emerge in world history, economically, politically, and militarily, America is the focal-point of non-Israeli Jewry. It possesses the most vibrant forms of Christianity, and its initial consensus was Christian. America claimed a dominance that was Christian in type, and whose initial consensus had, like all genuine Western Christianity, certain Christianized elements of Judaism. Furthermore, it incorporated principles drawn from 17th and 18th century philosophies.

Philosophic and religious principles in a modified form were fused with a series of socio-political institutions in the 18th and 19th centuries, the golden age of the starting consensus. By the start of World War II, this starting consensus was in the process of change. America was entering its international phase. In spite of American involvement in international affairs since its beginning, its history up to this point could be characterized as pre-international. Within 25 years, serious fissures would split its starting consensus and initiate the consensus change which grips the America of the late 'sixties and which explains the universal malaise felt at present throughout the American body-politic. The starting consensus could not possibly have perdured. It is changing today. The built-in elements of Christian dominance are no longer compatible with the evolving outlook of America.

We cannot foresee the resulting status of the American consensus. We can project the influence which this changing consensus of America should exercise on the evolution of what we have called the human consensus. In this regard, America is the best illustration of what we stated previously: today the issue of geopolitics is linked indissolubly with the question of religion and religious dominance. If the national consensus possessed by the leader of the West changes from a peculiarly Christian type and evolves in a non-Christian way, the behavior and the influence of that leader over world politics is modified accordingly. For Christianity and, to a lesser extent, for Judaism, the consequences are clear. We have seen that internal deficiencies hinder their exercise of dominance today. Now, in the circumstances of America's changing consensus their influence as religions and as species of religious dominance is precluded, by a set of external circumstances, from functioning effectively on the geopolitical scene.

In the light of this main conclusion—that the traditional consensus of America has changed and that no new public philosophy has yet been evolved—we should be able to interpret the contemporary scene in America. When a consensus starts to melt, the first tendency of societal man is to take refuge in external laws in order to ensure the orderliness and good working of his society. But such reliance on external framework with no reference to any inner body of convictions produces a brittle character in the society. It is easily shaken by unusual happenings. Dangerous fissures can appear on its surface. That society will also give birth to sporadic attempts to internalize, to seek new inner motives, and fresh bodies of convictions. Slowly the society evolves either to a new consensus formation, or it eventually disintegrates because nothing binds the various human elements of which the society is composed. We are not in a position to state what will be the new consensus formation of America. We know that as a society it is possessed of great health and vitality. We also know that the formation of its consensus depends to an unprecedented degree on the evolving world situation. For this is the peculiarity of modern America.

A review of America's geopolitical outlook and possible principles of action indicates, then, that with the change in her consensus, there will be a change in her foreign policy. As a leading member of the United Nations Organization she, too, will be impelled to participate more and more in the encounter. In the encounter, there is no room for moral authority, moral obligations, moral duties, or moral leadership, in the traditional sense. America's contribution to the human consensus will not be characterized by any of those Christian principles and outlooks which were part and parcel of her starting consensus. Because those principles and outlooks were drawn up on Biblical models but interpreted in a Christian way, both Christianity and Judaism will be the losers.

Their explanations of man, his cosmos, his origin, his destiny, and his proper mode of behavior, will avail less and less, according as the emerging public philosophy of the American people follows its present development to its logical conclusion. As far as human judgement goes, that logical conclusion will entail an American consensus wholly dictated by her pre-eminence in science and technology, her position as a leader without moral authority and therefore without any moral obligations on the part of others. Both America and other nations will have to find a basis of trust and confidence which is acceptable humanly. The basis supplied by Judaism and Christianity has been rejected.

Each underdeveloped nation today, however small and however big, aspires to modernization. This modernization includes as primary elements, firstly, the benefits of modern science and technology both for its physical conditions of existence and for its national life; secondly, direct and sovereign participation in the ever-growing network of international relations both within and outside the United Nations Organization. It is a historical fact, however, that this science and technology is primarily a product of the West and was developed and advanced in countries and by people who arrived at that stage of proficiency while living under the tutelage of Judaism and Christianity. Hence, it is true to say that in adopting wholeheartedly the Western idea of modernization, non-Western countries and peoples seal the fate of whatever indigenous culture, way of life, or outlook they have developed hitherto.

But the mind of the West has for some time, as we have seen, foresworn the "inner" or "spiritual" motivations which originally moved it. Western Christian man no longer believes that Heaven is above, beyond the skies. Nor that a being called the devil inhabits a place of darkness and torments called Hell, beneath the earth, where eternal fire burns. The atmosphere is not peopled with invisible and airy essences called angels. Pollution is more than enough to cope with. Moral acts do not stain an inner part of man called his soul. Nor is this part of man immortal. Nor is man descended from two people who grabbed at an apple in the morning sunlight of a lost Garden of Eden. Christian Western man uses no holy water to sanctify his ventures, no crucifix to exorcise his heart of darkness, no priest to forgive his sins, no bishop to consecrate his rulers with sacred unction, no Pope to arbitrate between man's warring rulers or to decide oracularly and by divine wisdom the agonizing questions confronting the sons of men.

Modern man has none of this: he needs them not. His world is viable and explicable without this paraphernalia. Above all, modern Western Christian man is not bothered by a Jesus risen from the dead. For him the story of Jesus ends with the latter's death, as all human stories do. He accepts a world without any meaningful Easter.

Western Jewish man, who was co-architect of this civilization, has also turned the corner. He no longer needs a temple in Jerusalem where the High Priest flanked by a priestly order of Aaron offers burnt sacrifices of bulls, cows, sheep, and goats. Fires smoking and smelling of burning flesh no longer pollute the air of Judea. A Holy of Holies penetrated only by the High Priest once a year is not the modern Western Jewish idea of the most precious spot on earth. Nor does modern Judaism await a person called the Messiah who will winnow and thrash and purify all the sons of men with fire and judgment. No messianic age is awaited when the mountains will run down with must-wine, the trees produce incorruptible fruit all year around, the fields ripen with corn winter and summer, the lion lie down with a lamb, and little children fondle the ears of the tiger. The Western Jew does not live in expectation of the day that God assembles all the nations and singles out his Chosen People to sit in judgment and to rule a new heaven and a new earth. Justice, peace, equality, brotherly love, the pursuit of truth and learning and man's betterment—these are the realities and the inherent bearers of man's destined reward for the modern Western Jew.

As a result of this development in Western man, all the branches of his science are described without any reference to an ideology or a belief in any absolute rule of conduct or any fixed dogmatic belief. Western man's sociology is completely value-free. The Western theory of history does not hold man to be a responsible agent in history—economic exigencies or power-politics determine his fate. Nor is there a divine providence which moves from end to end mightily disposing of man according to a prearranged plan.

According to Western psychology, man's behavior, far from being the outcome of Original Sin or any such moral causes, is determined by subconscious urges; all men's actions can ultimately be explained without referring to principles of religious motivation or philosophical freedom. No concept of absolute truth is sought or allowed. No absolute concept of justice regulates law making.

These are the bare bones of the Western mind in so far as it is reflected in the science and the technology which it is teaching the rest of the world. We are now in a position to formulate the encounter. There is de-Christianized and de-Judaized Western man armed with his technology and his science and his foreseeing fear of what can happen in Africa, Asia, and South America. There is African man who has been propelled within the space of twenty-five years into a world as different from his original one as a Zulu kraal differs from the Bank of America. His mind is unattuned to Western niceties. His spirit has not been worked by generations of education in his forebears. Up to the time of his entry into international life, he had his own native systems of morality, and his own norms of good and evil. Now he finds himself dealing with imponderables of economics and politics without any moral or religious guide-line.

The Asian finds the Westerner just as inexplicable. Again, it is the lack of any moral, religious, or even philosophical guideline which amazes him most. Along with the African he is let loose in a moral free area, where he finds the South American deeply resentful of the religion and the system of morality which allowed his continent to arrive at this point of economic social disintegration.

But the sharp point of the encounter lies in the fact that the issues which torture modern man seemingly have only been resolved hitherto by means of moral judgments. The issues of right and wrong, of better and worse, of good and bad, were formerly predetermined by religious systems. The latter are now abandoned by modern man. He is not seeking even a middle road between the former absolutes which he has resolved to exclude. For a middle way presumes the continued existence of absolutes on either side. The position of a middle way is calculated in reference to absolutes. But modern man is not trying to find a middle way. He is avoiding the issue altogether. Instead, modern man is seeking to do things, to get things done, without insisting on who is good or who is bad. His only trust is in programs of economic development, in bureaucratic organization, in the spread of neutral ideas, in anything but moral absolutism.

The inherent risk of this encounter is clear. Man meets man without any safeguard, without any previously guaranteed conditions, without any surety that the innate weakness of his nature will not precipitate a situation in which he will destroy himself. It speaks badly for the evangelical quality of those who preach a Gospel of Love, for those who claim to be the Chosen People of Yahweh and to have His revealed words, as well as for those who claim to be the ultimate community of believers founded by Allah for man's peace, mercy, and salvation, that none of the three has been able to elaborate a teaching and an outlook which would suit man as man. But the inherent religious dominance of each one, with its human egotism, its regional particularism, its racial prejudices, and its historical accretions, has excluded this possibility. This is the final condemnation of the triple religious dominance.

Book Four

HISTORICAL
PROGNOSES

Introduction

In very few places throughout the preceding pages has any course of action been proposed which the three religions could or should follow. Apart from incidental commentary, our main preoccupation has been to analyze situations and to draw descriptive conclusions. The subject matter of this study does not lend itself to concrete proposals, for each one of the three religions has a dynamism of its own which is beyond the conscious control of men; and all three are subject to sanctions imposed by history and which, therefore, are humanly irreversible. All that can be done is to indulge in some restrained historical prognoses based on present conditions. Such prognosis is the object of the present section.

Nevertheless, even in these historical prognoses, care must be taken not to indulge in hard and fast conclusions. There is no way of calculating what direction the human religious spirit will take. In history, we have examples of situations where, even after the event, it is impossible to rationalize and explain to our complete satisfaction the rise of a new configuration of circumstances. Thus with Islam: we find it difficult even today to explain its sudden access to world power and the permanency of its appeal, as we have emphasized when speaking about Islam. With the fall of Rome to the forces of nationalistic Italy, the *Times* of London felt perfectly justified in commiserating with the Vatican because, having lasted through so many vicissitudes, it had finally passed away. Yet seventy years later, this venerable institution wields a far greater influence than it did between 1800-1870.

Within certain limits, historical scenarios of a prognostic kind can lead us to exclude certain possibilities with a high degree of probability at best. Absolute surety is impossible. Such scenarios help also in laying down the general lines of policy for massive bodies such as Judaism, Christianity, and Islam represent.

Any serious historical prognoses concerning Judaism, Christianity, and Islam must be drawn up against a background of social and political events envisioned as accompanying the projected developments of the three religions. A certain limit, however, must be set to the extent of detail with which this background is filled. For not only can and will the next twenty years be full of new facts, events, and surprise twists of fortune for religions and for politics; these years may witness extraordinary happenings, some of which we would be inclined to categorize as belonging to the realm of science-fiction or futuristic writing. In drawing up the six following scenarios, then, futuristic and science-fiction elements should not normally be allowed to enter. This is a consequence of the type of scenario used here.

This device has as its purpose the outlining of foreseeable possibilities on the basis of present conditions. The scenario must be drawn up in terms of factors which we can now understand in view of our present knowledge and experience. For instance, the discovery of intelligent life on other accessible planetary bodies is always a possibility. Such a discovery would be fraught with problems for all three religions. If this life were found in beings who thought and communicated much as man does, then we would have a foreseeable possibility which we could understand in terms of our present knowledge and experience. But at present we do not have at our common disposal such information; we do not know if such life exists. It is often said that, if there is intelligent life on other planets, it should resemble ours. But this is a human anthropomorphism as naive as early Polynesian persuasions that the spirits wore clouds as clothes, or the old Indian myth about the sun having seven tresses. Human intelligence, which goes experimentally from fact to fact collating the evidence and building up its synthesis, is only one imaginable form of intelligence, and it is by no means the most efficient or the most encompassing.

The scenarios used here, in other words, are not meant to titillate the imagination or provide a mental escape for minds deadlocked in leaden certainties. They are meant to function as an ancillary to the decision-making of the religions. By testing some foreseeable results of present trends, one should be able to exclude certain possibilities, recommend certain courses of action, and assess other possibilities as iron necessities which will happen no matter what man does or how he suffers.

At the same time, as we have emphasized throughout this work and especially in the last chapters of Book Three, it is impossible to disassociate modern geopolitics from the fate of the three religions. Likewise, the ultimate development of these religions depends on the geopolitical road followed by the West in particular. This is a major conclusion of this study, and it may be in opposition to a current trend of thought concerning the religions that sees the irrelevancy of the religions for social and political matters growing by leaps and bounds with every passing day.

Tied in to the developing geopolitical configuration of our modern world are certain social developments which cannot be neglected in the scenarios. Some of these developments must be presumed as happening necessarily; others can be projected as possibilities within particular scenarios. The former we will call *Presumed Developments:* the latter will be mentioned among the *Conditions* placed at the head of each scenario.

There are, furthermore, a number of x-factors, political, social, religious, and scientific, which cannot be foreseen, but for which we must always make allowance. They are x-factors primarily and solely because no iron necessity whatever governs their emergence. They depend only on arbitrary choices of individual men and nations, and they are usually one of a set of equally possible alternatives. We cannot predict with any accuracy what choices men will make. Even in the case of the

Christian God, medieval philosophers and theologians never satisfactorily understood how he could know such actions before the choice was made.

The more remote the years for which the scenarios are projected, the more difficult and unrealistic one's assessment of these x-factors becomes. Today the pace of change is so great that even adding five years to one's projection can increase the measure of one's impudence in projecting future events. For this reason, the limit of the scenario time-span used here is the cliché-date 2000 A.D.

Lastly, we must note the proportions to be preserved between a scenario and its commentary. Each scenario needs a commentary attached to it, in which the validity of the projection, its foreseeable consequences, and its total impact can be measured. In principle, this commentary should be longer than its scenario. For the scenario, of its very nature, is supposed to resemble an encapsulated description of a multifarious and variegated historical development caught in precise phrases and not indulging in any meditative or reasoning processes.

The presumed developments in the background of the following scenarios are chiefly two:

1. The birth of the "urban-rural" world in several overlapping stages:
    (1) the full accession of America and the partial accession by some few European countries to what has been described as the technotronic age.
    (2) the arrival of the high industrial age in other European countries.
    (3) widespread breakdown of so-called elective democracies and the substitution of dictatorship or oligarchies throughout sub-Saharan Africa.
    (4) periodic and endemic famines in Asia, Africa, South America, and the Middle East.
    (5) severe political unrest in South America with substitution of military rule for elective governments.
    (6) a development in North Africa and the Middle East characterized by,
         —sustained belligerent animosity between the Arab nations and Israel,

—slow accession of the Arab nations to an Industrial Age of their own,

—continuation of the junta rule in slightly modified form in Greece, for as long as the Arab-Israeli contention subsists as a positive source of war,

—de facto alliance between the U.S.A. and the U.S.S.R. to prevent Communist Chinese infiltration and take-over of this area and of sub-Saharan Africa,

—effective non-functioning of the United Nations Organization.

(7) continual local wars provoked by Communist Chinese attempts to take over the governments of Southeast Asia, Africa, Middle East, and South America.

(8) attempted world-wide population control.

(9) accession of several smaller states to nuclear status of a limited kind.

(10) actual nuclear confrontation without positive engagement between Communist China and the U.S.A. or the U.S.S.R.

(11) admission of Communist China to the United Nations.

2. The birth of the "urban-rural" ecumenopolis:

(1) limited nuclear destruction of Earth.

(2) restructuring of the United Nations along urban-rural lines:

—elimination of the five-power veto in the Security Council,

—elimination of equal voting rights for all member-states in the General Assembly,

—establishment of new agencies, notably

(a) a central assessment office, to examine and assess continually the functional and structural value of the Organization and its agencies,

(b) a Security Council endowed with the physical means of arresting aggression by any member-state either within its borders or against another state,

(c) a General Assembly composed of two groups between which the organizational and functional balance of the United Nations is established: the states considered to be at least well

into the Industrial Age and beyond that point;
and the states still outside it or about to enter it,

(d) an economic development council with vaster
powers and means at its disposal than the
present United Nations Development Program
(UNDP).

(3) relatively quick transition by most European, South
American, North African, Middle Eastern, and Sub-
Saharan states to the post-industrial age.

(4) discovery and control by genetic and psychological
means of the physiological elements in man which
contribute most efficaciously to his dominance-trait.

The main x-factors which must be taken into account are:

1. A nuclear world war reducing civilization as we know it to
shambles, but not, as is often alleged, putting man back into
the caves of the Stone Age. For these caves were more mental
than physical. Mankind's intelligence cannot be retarded in
this way; it can be twisted, rendered helpless, or destroyed.

2. A comparatively sudden melting away of all major differences separating the major Christian denominations and their
consequent union in one major Christian Church.

3. The total collapse of Maoist Communism in mainland China,
and the emergence of either a socialistic or western-style
government.

4. The appearance on Earth of intelligent beings from outer
space who could catalyze the present socio-political hetero-
geneity of Earthmen and create an otherwise impossible racial
unity.

5. A sudden and fundamental genetic jump appearing in the
large-scale birth of human beings whose intelligence would
be as superior to *homo sapiens* as his was to that of his hominid
predecessors.

6. Economic disintegration of the Western capitalist system,
with a consequent sociological and political breakup of the
West.

One or more of these x-factors could become a reality and
thus essentially modify any of the prognoses given in this Section. In speaking this way, we exclude them as high proba-
bilities, leaving them as mere remote possibilities.

The possibilities for the three religions are exposed in six chapters. Each chapter outlines one possible configuration in scenario form. Standard to this form is the use of the present tense: i.e., the scenario speaks as would a live commentator describing an actual scene to his listeners. Each scenario has a number of conditions given at the beginning. The outlook for the three religions can be reduced to six main possibilities. The present ecumenical trend can continue until it reaches saturation point. At this stage, the ecumenical movement could proceed logically to wipe out all individual differences separating the churches and the religions (*Ecumenical Scenario*). This ecumenism could, however, stop short of unity, and then several developments could take place. A reversal to classical dominance of the three religions (*Dominance Scenario*) could provoke a general revolt within the three religions (*Underground Scenario*). An ecumenism resulting in the wiping out of the main differences between the religions could lead to an abandonment of the interior type of consensus and an attempt to rely on an external framework (*Externalization Scenario*). This latter attempt could possibly issue in two results. It could fail; in this case, an effort could once more be made to form an internal consensus (*Re-internalization Scenario*). Alternatively, it could succeed by developing into a truly human consensus (*Human Consensus Scenario*).

41. Ecumenical Scenario

Conditions: —No World War occurs between 1970 and 1980.
—No grave losses in numbers are sustained by the major Christian denominations.
—The government of the U.S.S.R. adopts an attitude of tolerance to religion.
—The Arab-Israeli dispute is settled.

Ecumenism here is taken in its broad meanings: it involves not merely all Christian denominations, but all Jews and Arabs. This ecumenism passes through two stages. In the first stage, the leaders of Christian denominations undertake more and more joint ventures with each other and with Jewish and Is-

lamic leaders. In these ventures, all are on an equal level; direction and leadership is by committee and by carefully
arranged rotation of membership. In this first stage, the ventures are all concerned with solving the concrete problems in
the social and political order: lobbying for government aid to
clear slums, create jobs, provide education, avoid aggression,
curb crime, reform prison methods, wipe out disease, promote
health standards, and rid politics and business of all graft
and corruptive practices. The policies and actions of the various ecumenical groups are so well coordinated that by 1975
they are wielding a positive and definite influence not merely
within national boundaries but internationally to solve problems between countries. They contribute to the popular
groundswell of vociferous opinion which finally forces both the
Arab and the Israeli governments to make a durable peace.
They revert the course of apartheid in South Africa. Chinese
penetration of the Middle East and Africa is checked because
this ecumenical lobby forces the hands of the Western governments and of the U.S.S.R. to divert the necessary funds for
the building of grass-roots economies.

In the meanwhile, between each other, at least the major
Christian denominations, Anglicans, Episcopalians, Lutherans,
Roman Catholics, Greek and Russian Orthodox, Syrian Orthodox, Armenians and Copts, have been engaging in mutual ex-
changes: no more cathedrals or big churches, for instance, are
built; their place is taken by what are called inter-churches,
i.e., buildings adapted to the needs of each denomination for
its services. In certain places, notably Holland and the U.S.A.,
the Jews share the same facilities with Christians. In Arab
lands, all Christian denominations and Muslims slowly but
surely come to share the same facilities. Only toward the end
of this first stage do Jews agree to share facilities with
Muslims.

The end of this first stage (a period of about five years) is
marked by a rather sudden and spontaneously formed unity on
two levels. First of all, on the Christian level, the major denominations named above agree on certain administrative
points. They establish a system of administering seven Sacraments: Christians of all bodies may partake freely of these
seven Sacraments in any of an approved list of churches at the
hands of an approved list of ministers and clergymen. Secondly, the nine agree upon an ethical code essentially composed

of the Ten Commandments and certain common precepts. Thirdly, they draw up a common creed, or list of beliefs. In the matter of authority, jurisdiction, and the right of interpretation, no real agreement is formed. The difficulty is exorcised temporarily by an agreement that the heads of the various churches will never participate in deliberative and executive assemblies: no pope, grand rabbi, patriarch, cardinal, or chief bishop ever attends. It is left up to each church to provide for authoritative decisions and jurisdiction for its members. However, the members can follow the authority and jurisdiction of any of the nine bodies.

Secondly, on the inter-religious plane, a parallel unity is established. Jews, Christians, and Muslims agree to adopt the ethical code of the Inter-Church, as it is called. A fundamental common creed is drawn up, embracing three points: 1) the existence of the god, 2) the desire of this god to save man and his intervention in human history to affect that salvation, 3) the existence and immortality of the human soul. They agree on two Sacraments: marriage and confession of sins. Jews, Christians, and Muslims can get married by ministers, rabbis, or priests. Sin is considered forgiven by the one god, if it is confessed to the congregation or to the minister, rabbi, or priest. Regarding authority and jurisdiction, the same rule is established as in the Inter-Church, except that there is no free moving allowed from Christianity to Judaism and Islam and vice versa. This two-level unity is achieved over a period of three years.

The second stage of this ecumenism starts when a rather natural course of events takes place. Among Christians it is gradually found that the authorities and jurisdictions wielded by the various Christian authorities not merely run counter to each other, but that they entail mutual condemnation. The Roman Catholics, for instance, will not allow divorce or contraception, but all the others will. Certain Protestant denominations are stricter on certain human failings such as drunkenness, homosexuality, prostitution, than the Romans. The Greek Orthodox are more generous with divorces than either the Russian Orthodox or the Anglicans. A certain mobility begins to affect the membership of the various churches, as the members seek the church most suitable for their personal problems and outlooks. The churches become restive and afraid that they will lose too heavily in numbers and thus be diminished in their representative character. They begin to insist on their authority and jurisdictional rights. Each church begins to legislate for itself and establish certain rules affecting its dissident members.

The problem is aggravated by the theologians and philosophers of all sides who discover reasons for and against the authority claims and jurisdictions of each body. Within ten years the situation has been brought to the point that the churches are legislating against each other within the framework of the Inter-Church.

Commentary:

It is very unlikely that the ecumenical movement as such will ever attain even the minimum result in reducing the classical dominance of the three religions. For inherent in the principle of ecumenism is the notion that unity must be sought. That unity is conceived as being absolute in the sense that the initial thrust of Judaism, Christianity, and Islam were absolute. The ultimate and most felicitous result of ecumenism would be union of all the Christian churches, of the dissident parts of Judaism, and eventually of Judaism and Christianity. But this implies the setting up of a unity apart from the unity of man as such. As far as can be judged today, if such a unity were achieved, it would mean the total isolation of unified Christianity, of unified Judaism, or of a united Christianity and Judaism. Disunity is not the most horrendous fault of Christianity and Judaism today. In the sixth scenario we shall see that the only advisable ecumenism today is radically different from the current type.

42. *Dominance Scenario*

Conditions: —A refusal on the part of the three religions to practice an ecumenism of jurisdiction.

—A refusal on the part of the various denominations of Christianity to practice an ecumenism of jurisdiction.

This scenario is valid for either of two situations: the three religions persevere in their total claims of dominance, or they fall back on such total claims after an initial attempt to come together ecumenically. For any ecumenism which remains exclusively or predominantly Christian and does not take in both Judaism and Islam, or which stops short of jurisdictional unity and remains merely with operative unity, is doomed to fail. The individual participants will revert to a former dominance in the full form or they will deteriorate and disappear. In discussing the crisis of dominance in the three religions we have already considered some of the consequences which will befall the three religions because of their sustained dominance. We will describe the most likely of these consequences in the next scenario. Here we are concerned with the general process of decay which will affect any religious body claiming a classical type of dominance.

The process of decay follows a classical pattern of all organized groups out of which the heart of the consensus, the inner conviction of its members, has been torn. Without the subsistence of that inner conviction, the exteriorization ceases to have any meaning or significance. Ritualism, formalism, and activist behavior take the place of inner motivated policies, self-generating dynamism, and, above all, the enlightenment and wisdom as to how the consensus can survive. By the middle of the next decade, the three religions, but especially Judaism and Christianity, are all three immersed in being part of their age, absorbed in justifying their dominance claims by being better than others or, at least, as good as others in aiding men.

An insistence on dominance by Judaism and Christianity, as we have noted, finds no echo in the modern mind. As a consequence, the two religions, while preserving their dominance claims, will turn more and more to activism, swept on by the tidal wave of involvement which is sweeping through modern society, according as social consciousness becomes more sensitive and well-informed, and man's efforts to overcome pressing problems become more febrile. For this is the only way in which they can hope to enter society. All doors will be closed to their stance of dominance.

We have noted the activism of Judaism and Christianity. This is the first and comparatively rapid stage of disintegration. Its chief ill-effect is that it inures its participants to a false sense of security. The conviction of salvation, of belonging to an invisible elect will be deliberately and essentially directed to membership of those who are "doing," "acting," "achieving." There will perish any real esteem for an inner forum in man—his thought and his conscience; this inner forum implied a structure of principles which were reflected in outer laws, of beliefs which were formulated in dogma and creed, of "contact" with the "invisible" which was exteriorized in worship, and of inner personal commitment which was translated into good works on the social plane.

Peace of mind, conviction that one is saved, belief that one is doing right, will no longer be based on the soundness of the inner forum, but on the solidity of exterior activity, the restlessness of its details, the acknowledgment of its excellence, the success of its thrust, and the recorded imprints it leaves in what men hear, see, read, and feel.

The first open sign of decay is the increasing *resemblance* between all participants. For that resemblance implies sameness of actions and purposes. Now sameness of action and purposes implies ultimately a diminution of the unique character claimed by a religious body, no matter what be the differences which it claims verbally. Uniqueness goes hand in hand with the exclusivity of dominance. Both are at stake.

More deeply and seriously still, the recourse to activism characteristic of Judaism and Christianity in this age of the late 1970's leads them to be seen as just two more contending and collaborating elements of the social body. Their effective role, as far as men are concerned, is to do what others, not religious in character, are attempting to do and succeeding in doing as admirably.

There results in the public mind a hiatus between the religious dominance claimed by the religions and the actual role they fill. It does not merely register in the public mind. It affects the religions themselves in their inner dynamism. The latter feeds on dominance. But dominance is increasingly feeble and unable to exercise itself. In the real order of events, men, and things, the claims of dominance become abstract matters, resident in books, official documents, formularies, credal statements, and pronouncements. They become a dead letter. Each religion can produce a hard-core group dedicated to that dominance and for whom the dominance is a reality. But their identity and effective contribution to the religion as a whole is as healthy, as total, and as positive as that of the Neture Karta to Judaism or the Millenarists to Christianity.

It is with the advent of the future superstructure of modern nations that this preserved claim of dominance allied to activism will be put to the test and found wanting. There is no doubt that obligatory birth-control will have to be imposed ultimately by governmental and para-governmental agencies. There is very little doubt that within 20 or 30 years permission will have to be obtained for each human conception and, later, birth. There is very little doubt that human birth from the womb of a human mother will not be the only way in which human beings will come into existence. There cannot be much doubt that control of the human memory, the human intellect, the human will, the human emotions, will be achieved before the turn of the century by chemical means. There is no doubt that in a country such as America, by that time, the vast bulk of the population will be engaged in occupations wholly dominated by the incredible speeds and efficiency of computers and electronic machines, thus affecting its mode of thought, its notion of leisure hours, its habits of mind, its family structure, its longevity, its sense of loyalty, and its identity as men. Classical dominance is static, is built on the Graeco-Roman idea of once formulated truth. That dominance, also, has already taken up intransigent positions on questions which will be decided in ways that directly contradict those intransigent positions. Here the hiatus between the claimed dominance and the reality of life will be glaring.

The dominance of Islam follows an analogous road of decay. But Islam travels alone. It is not probable that Islam will have even a chance at religious activism. There will not be time for that. Islam in Arab and other Islamic lands will leap from its strict classical dominance to an utterly pragmatic viewpoint. The industrial age will overtake these countries and their populations and this ethos of Islam, leaving them no time to attempt survival and preservation of dominance.

Commentary:

As far as we can judge, any religion which practises a classical form of dominance is bound to come to grief today and with increasing speed, according as the world develops. This scenario endeavors to bring this out. There is only one condition under which a religious dominance would be totally viable today: if a religion were in full and practically unique possession, not merely of the truth about man and his nature and destiny, but about the physical constitution of man's cosmos and the nature of matter. In the historical order, the three religions have adopted a certain attitude to such areas of human knowledge as are profoundly affected by the hard-core sciences of today. Under such circumstances, there is no possibility of the religions persevering in a flourishing state. On the other hand, if they revise that part of their dominance which is touched by the new sciences, the dominance ceases to function. Either way, religious dominance is not viable.

43. Underground Scenario

Conditions: —Continued peace between Arabs and
                    Israelis.
                —Sustained "cold war" between the
                    U.S.S.R., China, and the U.S.A. in the
                    Middle East.

It becomes gradually clearer, as the world approaches the last quarter of the 20th century, that the nine major Christian denominations (Anglicans, Episcopalians, Lutherans, Roman Catholics, Armenians, and Copts), together with a small percentage of Methodists and Presbyterians, will reach unity neither among themselves nor with Judaism and Islam, nor will they officially modify their traditionalism in order to adapt themselves to recent conditions of mankind. Judaism is split: Orthodox and Conservative Judaism take much the same position officially as the nine denominations. Reform Judaism, together with the vast body of Protestantism, adapt so completely to the new conditions that they cease to call themselves religions, religious sects, Christian churches, or synagogues. Islam is under siege by the forces let loose in the body of its people: the initial industrialization of its territories, its fourth unsuccessful attempt to destroy Israel, and the influx of American, Soviet, and Chinese influences.

The chief concern of the believers in all three religions—and particularly in those parts of Judaism and Christianity which we have listed as stubbornly holding on to their dominance claims—is for a ritual and mode of thought which are intelligible. This is especially true of the Christian Churches in Africa, Asia, and South America, and of the Islamic communities in sub-Saharan Africa and Asia, where the Western concept of priesthood, sacrifice, church, incarnation, and of history never were intelligible to the Faithful. Ancient South Arabian concepts are found unsuitable to the modern African mind.

Already in the late years of the previous decade, Roman Catholic priests were celebrating underground masses, Protestant ministers and clergymen were conducting unorthodox services, and Jewish rabbis were experimenting with new and more meaningful forms of synagogal service. By 1974-75, the matter has gone much further. Throughout the Roman Catholic Church associates of priests have come into being. The same phenomenon appeared in Orthodoxy (Greek and Russian), in Anglicanism, and to a lesser degree in other Protestant bodies. More turbulent and clamorous associations of laymen were formed throughout Christianity, Judaism, and Islam.

The attempts of bishops, ecclesiastical authorities, grand rabbinates, and Islamic colleges to muzzle these associations and to make them at best consultative bodies failed completely. But these attempts only exacerbated the situation. Slowly at first, but with increasing momentum, there grew in number whole Christian and Jewish parishes where the priests, ministers, and their congregations ruled themselves autonomously, refusing to pay any money tribute to higher authorities, making their own rules, holding their own synods every year, changing and adapting their church rituals to meet their needs of intelligibility.

Jewish synagogue congregations increasingly refused to assist at the traditional services, to observe the dietary laws of Moses, to be held by rabbinical prescriptions, to listen to haggadic readings or to abide by halakhic decisions, to recite prayers that had no relevancy for their daily lives and which they did not understand anyway.

By the end of the 1970's, therefore, the status of Christianity and Judaism was sharp and clear: officialdom, still retaining titles and claims and a small minority of the lay believers, stood apart from the great bulk of those believers who no

longer observed Saturday as the Sabbath, or Sunday as the day
of rest and worship, who had turned over their churches and
synagogues for housing, hospitals, and welfare projects, who
had sold all their gold, silver, and precious ornaments in order
to obtain funds for financing social projects, who gathered on a
variable day at a variable time in a private house or in a
public square to conduct a totally new ceremony.

The Protestants, Catholics, and Orthodox had decided
there was no difference between them that the clergy, the theologians, and the philosophers had not made. They participated
in a simple ceremony, consisting of the Lord's Prayer, a consecration of bread and wine, and a song of thanks and petition.
Sermons no longer were given, because in that day direct personal communication was by electronic means and with each
person simultaneously. Church collections and announcements
were affected through television and within the new system of
money which obviated the need of either paper money or coins.
Celibacy was no longer mandatory for priests. Nuns had dis-
banded. Religious schools had ceased to exist.

Jews shared the same place and day of worship as the Christians—at first separately, then together with them, necessitating
an addition of certain elements to the central ceremony, notably
the mention of Israel in the song of thanks and petition. Muslims on the whole no longer had the muezzin calling from the
tower; nor did they worship on Fridays at the mosque. Mosques
fell into disuse and were made public monuments by the
government. Women no longer wore the veil. Polygamy fell into
disuse because a man could no longer support more than one
wife. Muslims substituted new prayers and evolved a simple
service resembling in many parts the Protestant services of the
early part of the century.

The underground movement in organized religion can only
have a pejorative effect both on the religion itself and on that
part of it which goes underground. The nature of Judaism,
Christianity, and Islam is such that no single part can flourish
brilliantly apart from the mother stock. This has been proven
time and time again in history. Underground movements solve
no real problems, but create many more. They do not necessarily rid religion of religious dominance, except by gnawing
at the vitals of religion, thus doing away with the dominance
by doing away with the religion. This is no solution. Nevertheless, an underground movement could be a real threat to

organized religion, presenting as it does an element of the unusual within the atmosphere of the known.

Those who would indulge in such an underground church
and propagate its life have reduced life's choices to a bare two:
either to sink into the mechanical paranoia of automated existence or to yield and follow the constant temptation of man to
concentrate on the dark periphery of things, the Celtic twilight
of the religious mind, where shadow is substance, where light
is dark, where death is poetry, where stars gleam in every patch
of mud, and Jacob's ladder is set down in Soho, in Times
Square, on the Yellow River, and in a Turkish brothel. They
wish to avoid imitating the clerk-editor in James Stephens'
Crock of Gold who started to transcribe a new paragraph and
never got beyond the first letter: he spent all his time correcting
the proportions of the letter. They would rather listen to the
song of the fairies tripping outside over hills and mountains,
valleys, fields, and meadows, through forests, on their way to
the never-never land of airy fairy dreams and the shining glory
of the Crock of Gold.

Both solutions, the underground solution or the helplessness
and immobility within old forms, are innate refusals to go to
meet man. To pursue the image, it is more difficult to finish the
first letter and transcribe the entire page, while the fairy song
is within earshot, than it is to take to esoteric movement or to
refuse to cope with the situation.

44. Externalization Scenario

Conditions: —Nuclear crisis and confrontation between Communist China on the one
hand and the U.S.A. and the U.S.S.R.
on the other hand, in the Autumn of
1970.

—Continued peace between Arabs and
Israelis.

The ecumenism described in *Scenario 1* did not stop short of
unity in jurisdiction; it went much further. The occasion was
a nuclear confrontation between Communist China and the
U.S.A. The crisis lasted fifty days during which the world hung

in balance on the edge of a precipice. The situation was so grave that those who believed in some religion took to their prayers assiduously. It thus came about that huge public scenes were witnessed in the great cities of the world, in Europe, America, and in the Middle East, especially.

At first, each religion conducted its own rites and ceremonies; each prays, however, together with other religions on special occasions. In the process of examining their consciences and preparing for their death and judgment by the one god in whom they all believed, a dilemma arose. Protestants, Catholics, and Jews almost simultaneously asked themselves one question in the privacy of their own consciences and in their private prayer-assemblies (all was public, those days, within the religions, because the end was felt near, and what did it matter if people knew each other's sins?):

"What will He say about my attitude to Jews and about what the Church has done to them?" the Christian queried.

"How will He judge the hate and dislike I have for Christians and the inferior quality I attribute to their worship of Him?" asked the Jews.

"How can Allah forgive my hatred, dislike, and contempt for the Christians and the Jews? I used to call them infidels, and my ancestors smote them hip and thigh," pondered the Muslim with his fellows.

"I think that we have been un-Christian and unconscionably biased and hateful regarding Muslims," Christians asserted to Jews, "and that includes you Jews also."

The first results were mutual visits of leaders and delegations from one religion to another, in order to ask forgiveness of each other and on behalf of their churches and synagogues and communities. There was much genuine sorrow, promised renewal, and real repentance. But it was natural that they incidentally should discuss the basis of difference between the three of them. The Muslim was amazed to find that the Christian Trinity was not composed of God the Father, Mary the Virgin, and the Holy Spirit; he had always believed this, because Mohammad thought it and taught it. The Christian was astounded that the first man to command: "Love thy neighbor as thyself," was not Jesus, but Moses. The second man to command it was Hillel, who lived before Jesus. Jesus was the third Jew to command it. The Jews were taken aback to find that the Samaritans were purer Jews than they themselves, and that before the Greek and Latin theologians got at the material, the teaching of Jesus was pure Pharisaism—impregnated, of course, with Jesus' own contribution.

They all found that certain insoluble difficulties separated them. But the chief difficulty was simply ignorance and nescience. Prejudice, human pride, and man's inhumanity to man had done the rest. "Jesus may have been the Messiah," conceded the Jews, "but obviously not for us, at least for the moment; he didn't give us the grace to see the light, if he was the Messiah. You cannot blame a whole people for blindness. We simply didn't and do not know." The Christians felt that they had certainly stolen from the Jews both their title and their privilege: "You always were and still are the Chosen People," they admitted with brave smiles, "we just don't know how *we* fit into the picture. That's all. We know that Jesus was the son of God and died for us all."

"Almost certainly Mohammad borrowed from you two, holus-bolus," the Muslims confessed to Christians and Jews, "but he had special revelations, and you were a pretty bad lot around that time, if you remember at all. No matter what you think of his personal life, which wasn't brilliant by modern standards; but then don't forget Samson and David and Charlemagne and Pope Alexander VI."

Mutual concessions are made, and all would have ended there, except for one squat Islamic theologian's intervention. He raised a small pudgy hand and said: "Brothers (this was the normal salutation in those days), aren't you forgetting something? All three religions of ours decry the charlatan lip-service of the hypocrite; sorrow must be shown in acts. What are we to do to show that we really are sorry?"

Much discussion and disputes followed, especially since already Jews, Christians, and Muslims, were praying together, and worshipping together. There were several cases of what the Romans called *communicatio in sacris* and the Protestant Americans called *fraternizing with superstition:* one dying Christian had been prepared for death by a rabbi (the priest was not available); a small child who died of peritonitis was blessed by an Imam.

The main conclusion was that restitution had to be made for past slanders; this was the minimum required as proof and indication of real sorrow and of a resolution not to fall into the same errors. *The Threefold Admission of Nescience* was the result, and it became the first plank of the new development. *The Threefold Admission of Nescience,* or the *Threefold Nescience* as it was popularly called, was a formula that spread like wildfire through the ranks of Jews, Christians, and Muslims. People learnt it in Hebrew, Arabic, and English. It was broadcast by all the stations of the world. It ran:

"We Jews do know that Yahweh blessed the work of Jesus. We know that we are the Chosen People. But we do not know if Jesus was or was not the Messiah."

"We Christians do know that the Jews were and are the Chosen People, but we don't know how we fit in with them and they with us, and the Muslims with both of us."

"We Muslims do know that Moses and Jesus and Mohammad were from Allah. We know that Mohammad was the Prophet of Allah, and we do not know if Jesus was the son of Allah and if the Jews ceased to be the Chosen People."

But this impelled them to a further step. They began to recite this in common; each religion chanting its own part. The ultimatum of the Communist Chinese was to expire on the 1st of January, 1976. All preparations were made for that day: the religions and their leaders of Judaism, Christianity, and Islam, proposed that they all, as believers in the one god, go as one body together to meet their death and, they believed, this one god. Ceremonies were now devised for this. In establishing the ritual, they evolved the well-known triple-rite ceremony: all representatives of the three religions started off together and recited a common creed:

"We believe in one god, creator of all things. We believe that he made man with an immortal soul; that he devised a salvation for man in human history; that man can repent in this life and thus avail of that salvation before his death. We profess to love this one god above all other things and goods, and our desire is to live forever with him."

Then the Jews would start off with a brief expression of their hope in the god of Abraham, Isaac, and Jacob, and in the coming Messiah, and then they eat unleavened bread and herbs. The Christians followed them with a brief statement of their belief in Jesus, at which occasion they blessed bread and wine and partook of them. The Muslims took up after them, stating their belief in Moses, Jesus, and in Mohammed as Allah's prophet. Then all together intoned:

"Tell us, One God, how to love each other, since we have

done it so badly up to this, so that we may be truly your children."

Eleven days before the ultimatum expired the crisis was broken by a revolution within China. Cynics expected matters between the religions to slip imperceptibly back to the old normalcy. But something had happened to the three religions. Each one of them had found that it could afford to worship in common with the other two, when following an external framework of rites and words, but keeping its belief within it, without any denigration, external or internal, of the other two. There thus was born the famous *Externalization Principle* and the *Externalization Movement* built on that principle.

Briefly, this principle was as follows: because the most astounding thing was the substantial bulk of common beliefs the three religions shared, they should externalize this commonality of belief in rites, words, and action. Hitherto, all three without exception had only externalized their differences, their hates, their mutual contempt. They found that the latter course of action was sinful (Roman Catholic Moralists termed it a grave mortal sin), so that they were obligated, not merely to make reparations for the past, but to continue on according to the *Externalization Principle* in the future.

Commentary:

A solid Externalization process could be the best disposition for the further and necessary step of reaching man as such without the trammels of religious dominance. Externalization at least cuts away at the exclusivity of the participant religions, and disposes them to make further sacrifices of their proper personality, for the common good. History, however, has examples of initial Externalizations which failed to fructify substantially. The reason always was that the participants did not proceed further; they remained at a half-way house, neither solidly ensconced in religious dominance nor totally given over to the pursuit of reality among men. Externalization of this kind was more than once imposed on dissident parties in the early Christian Church by the Roman Emperors. In these cases, the Roman Church was powerful enough to absorb the dissidents, once Imperial power made it mandatory for them to agree to an Externalization. Some few lingered on, resisting total absorption. Their achievements were never great. This happens today with dissident Eastern Churches which seek union, say, with Rome, but preserve their own rites and practices. They never increase their membership. They do not seem to be intended for a long and fruitful existence.

45. *Re-Internalization Scenario*

Conditions: —Technetronic age in many European countries,
—Industrialization of Middle Eastern countries,
—Increase of mass education,
—Continued peace between Arabs and Israelis.

The Externalization Movement had one inevitable result. It did bring into being an exterior framework of rituals that corresponded to no one particular religion. But it also impelled members of the three religions to start rethinking their religious position. Already in the world around them, they were solely tried by events. Everywhere a new superstructure was being added to the already industrialized nations: they were entering the technetronic age bit by bit. Industrialization was taking hold of the old agrarian civilizations in Africa, South America, Europe, and Asia.

Better standards of living and, above all, wide mass education was producing a very sophisticated popular mind which questioned, queried, doubted, scrutinized, and examined every jot and tittle of the old beliefs. Great numbers of 1965 babies, now between 10 and 15 years old, simply turned away from religious belief in despair: it was utterly unintelligible and irrelevant into the bargain. Some had already done basic courses in anatomy and biology: the concept of soul was void and empty for them, as well as the idea of a creation of a soul or a body by a god. Others had reached calculus in mathematics and were already acquainted with interplanetary dimensions and galactic structures: the old concepts of heaven, hell, and angels had no meaning. Basic courses in physics, chemistry, history of civilizations, languages, affected the 14-15 year olds. It was above all the obligatory courses in psychology, the new genetic control of misformed or deficient genes, and the modification of human behavior by chemical means, that, as hard facts, rendered useless all the official religious talk about sin, virtue, punishment, purity, honesty and any transcendental value.

Slowly, the commonality of exterior rites in which the three religions felt so happy and secure and united turned the members of the religions to each other for mutual protection, encouragement, consolation, and light. Their thought went far very fast. They came rapidly (or rather exterior circumstances made them come) to the conclusion that all three religions were, indeed, unique developments in human history, that they all had received deposits of faith and revelation from the one true god, whom they all worshipped sincerely in common and in one unified ritual. This became a matter of pride for them.

A special surge of studies started that they termed the ecumenism of identity—as distinct from the old partisan ecumenism of difference that had tended to produce a "cocktail" religious mentality and had tempted weaker but ambitious minds to maneuver for, of all things, a "super-church." This mutual evaluation resulted in a new feeling of pride and confidence in the traditional truths basic to each one and common to all. Really they were returning to the sedimentation of religious dominance in each religion, distinguishing the common and shared traits from what was particular to each religion by itself.

Two developments came about. They developed the idea of a true revelation: there was only one god; all three claimed he had made a revelation to man; he never did the same things twice over; only men did this because they do things badly the first time, even the second and the third time; therefore, the one true god had made one revelation to mankind.

The second development arose out of an immediate dilemma. The question was: where was this one true revelation? The dilemma was this: had each of the three religions a part of that one true revelation? In that case, the one god had made partial revelations to each one. Or had he made his entire revelation to all three? In that case, either all three had deformed that revelation by claiming that their particular religion was quite different from the other two, or they all had been given the entire revelation in three stages.

The latter solution appealed to everybody. It blamed no one for the stupidity of division that had plagued them all in relation to each other and within each one of them. It was their general conclusion that in some way or other, the one god—to whom all three had given different names—had communicated with all of them and told to them the total truth about man's salvation, his origins, his destiny, and the means he ought to use in order to be saved.

There thus arose among the three religions a system of what was called *Common Mysteries* and the *People's Revealed Truth*. The latter contained the essentials: the existence of one god, creation of all things, the immortality of man's soul, resurrection on a last day of human history (when all would be judged), and eternal life with this one god. The *Common Mysteries* were reciprocal. Going on the principle that the central mystery of each religion must be some part or other of the total revelation, they firmly concluded that they could not exclude what they did not understand (this was the influence of the *Threefold Nescience* of an earlier moment), but neither could they understand what they included. They therefore called them *Reciprocal* or *Common Mysteries*.

The Jews accepted as a mystery three elements of Christianity and two elements of Islam. From Christianity, the name "God" as applied to Yahweh, the divinity of Jesus, and the Messiahship of Jesus (therefore his sacrifice on the Cross) were accepted as mysteries by them. From Islam they accepted the name "Allah" for Yahweh, and Mohammad's claim to have had a divine revelation and command to form the True Community of Believers.

The Christians accepted as mysteries: the name "Yahweh" and the fact that Jews were the Chosen People, and would always be that. From Islam, they accepted the name "Allah" and the fact of Mohammad's claim.

The Muslims had the most to accept, but as the Russian Archimandrite Nicholas of Kiev remarked, shaking his huge belly in soulful laughter: "You came when the table was loaded, you must eat up!" The Muslims accepted as mysteries: the name "Yahweh"; the Jews as the Chosen People; the divinity of Jesus and his Messiahship; and the name "God."

It was not required to believe in the mysteries as articles of faith, but to believe in them as true mysteries about which they would ultimately be enlightened by the one god. But it was not permissible to say that they were false or doubtful. They were *Common Reciprocal Mysteries.* The immediate result of this was to confer a new self-confidence and pride on the three religions. They went by the name of *The People:* the Jews had wanted to say "People of Yahweh"; the Christians, the People of "God"; the Muslims, the people of "Allah"; but since the personal revealed name of the one god was a Reciprocal Mystery, they simply called themselves *The People.* A revival of inner convictions came about. New elaborations on the sociopolitical plane were developed. A new religious dominance was born, as myopic as the older ones, but far stronger and more durable. In the meantime, the world outside and around was evolving faster and faster.

Commentary:

This scenario is intended to bring out the probable ineptness of such Re-Internalizations to effect any real unity of belief or to mitigate the bite of religious dominance. In effect, the method of solving both problems is by way of formal agreement on conceptual propositions and verbal formulations. The weakness of this solution is that it concentrates on the human area of knowledge. Knowledge is neutral by nature and therefore disinclined to create of itself the tendency to exercise dominance. Knowledge, as knowledge, is not proud, self-centered, egotistic, destructive, restrictive. Knowledge frees the human spirit, but it does not restrain its inherent leaning to one-sidedness. It enlightens, but can dazzle and make dizzy with chasms of pride. It can, if properly used, provide the appropriate breeding-ground for understanding and therefore for love. But this last step requires more than mere knowledge. For we know that a man can have a Ph.D, can cherish a beautiful wife, breed lovely children, listen appreciatively to Bach and Beethoven in the evening, but spend his days gassing and burning human beings in ovens and gas-chambers.

In the sixth scenario we will see that it is not by way of such knowledge that any solid result can be achieved.

46. *Human Consensus Scenario*

Conditions: —Technetronic age in America and some
European country
—Ecumenical movement embracing not
merely Christians but Jews and Mus-
lims
—Sustained peace with a severe nuclear
confrontation between U.S.S.R. and
Communist China.

The exteriorization spoken of in Scenario 4 need not evolve
into a Re-Internalization. Any form of Re-Internalization is
a completely backward step for classical religious dominance,
if it is to overcome its present-day difficulties. Instead, the only
other road—apart from the steep path of disappearance from
man's world—is the way of the human consensus. But this way
is not characterized essentially by traits drawn from the three
religions as is the road of Externalization. This is the difficulty.

The development of religious affairs in the opening years of
the next decade is as follows. An ultimatum has been sent by
Communist China to the U.S.S.R. concerning the Far Eastern
Russian territories. The ultimatum is for fifty days. Russia
mobilizes. In the ensuing crisis every diplomatic move attempted is rebuffed and checkmated. China seems to want a
war.

The world creeps toward a nuclear holocaust in which all
will necessarily be involved. In the early stages of the crisis
and before the ultimatum, the religious leaders are asked by the
governments of their various countries to keep the population
quiet and confident. This they do. As the crisis deepens and
China-inspired local rebellions and revolts pullulate like long-
hidden pus-pockets across the Middle East, Africa, South and
North America and, in all places, Oceania, a tension enters into
men's global parleying. The religious leaders themselves now
begin to take the matter in earnest.

One by one all the political maneuvers fail: the U.S.S.R. and
China are locked in a seemingly unbreakable stalemate of
steel and fire. It is at this point that the Grand Rabbi has a con-
ference-call with Pope Paul VII, Archbishop Borodin of Moscow, and Tagliatelli, the Protestant leader of North American

Reformed churches (they constitute the steering committee of the Inter-Faith World Council for that year). They decide to hold their first summit conference ever in their millenniar existence. "Why must we be threatened with a damn good roasting," mutters the Archbishop of Canterbury to his wife, "before we all huddle together?" "You will be perfectly splendid there, I am sure, dear," she answers, "but don't forget to take your Ovaltine."

The question which the steering committee has to ask the conference is simple: all around them, the nations are preparing for Armageddon; what should the major religions do?

The scripts prepared for the major religious delegates have been drawn up by their underlings: training-rabbis from the Seminaries and the Rabbinates; post-doctoral theological students from Protestant universities; the "old hands" in the Vatican chancellery; seasoned priests from the Moscow and Constantinople Patriarchates; professionals from the World Council of Churches; small thick-bearded Coptic and Syrian scribes from the desert monasteries and wadi hermitages of Syria, Egypt, and Morocco; bulky Armenian protonotaries from Soviet Armenia, fast-talking imams and muezzins and ulema from Damascus, Cairo, and Medina. With one exception, all the scripts reflect the little minds of their authors. The exception is a Muslim marabout, Abi ibn Qalb, who was dragged from his cave outside Benghazi, washed, fitted with a fresh galabiya and kuffiah, and transported sitting on his little carpet in a Boeing 747 Stratocruiser to Jerusalem, where the religious summit meets in a hurry.

The Christians want to meet in the Holy Sepulcher ("it's full of grace" muttered one cleric to another), but the building is declared dangerous by the military governor of Jerusalem. The Arabs want to meet in the Dome of the Rock, but the Roman Catholics object. Finally, a large marquee is borrowed from the Y.M.C.A. and pitched on the banks of the Jordan. There they meet.

The speakers, in their majority, recommend one thing: all the religions must go about their business; they all believed in the end of the world. Well, here it was coming with fifty days advance notice; the Chinese had been mercifully more explicit than either the Apostle John, the Prophet Mohammad, or the Law of Moses in predicting the End. "Up and about our business," perorates one Baptist from Jackson, Mississippi, "throw your holy water, sing your hymns, scatter your Agnus Dei's and your relics, preach the Word. The day of the End is coming on all sinners."

A motion is proposed: that the three religions of the Book join in public meetings to pray, in the hope that the world will be converted, and that they declare to the world their belief in one god, and in the afterlife. Practically unanimous agreement is expressed on this point, the delegates reading carefully from their notes and pausing for effect.

Abi ibn Qalb coughs and stands up. In almost impeccable French, he pours a stream of comment over the delegates' heads, in a few clipped sentences, throws in some English and Hebrew for the Jews and the Anglo-Saxon Protestants, and makes a definite point: "We all think of ourselves. How right we are. How punished the others will be. Are they preparing our beds in Heaven? Stop this insanity. What are we going to do? We did not come here to discuss how fast we could get away? Push off to eternity in our private little skiffs of salvation? Is this love? Did your Jesus die for this? Is this the mind of your Yahweh, who made the oceans as a drop in the palm of his hand, and stretched the sky like a patch of old cloth? Where is all the mercy and compassion of Allah? Are we all hypocrites or little boys? Frightened little boys. Let us think as men, for men, with men."

This harangue sobers the incipient enthusiasm. The delegate from Lambeth, who had proposed the motion, shuffled his papers and felt for his pipe. His arch enemy, a Neapolitan Monsignore leaned forward to the chairman, Grand Rabbi Itzkak of Jerusalem and whispered: "Appunto—quasi!" But the Grand Rabbi has no pleasantries in mind. He calls on speaker after speaker, the best of them. Slowly they rise. Each one, staring at Abi ibn Qalb, speaks deliberately and with long pauses; Bruno the Pentecostalist from Rio de Janeiro; Whippleston, the Episcopalian minister from Riverdale, New York; Gruntzler, Bishop of East Berlin; Hassan Hussanein of Al Azhar; O'Kelly of Dublin; Gunnar Djarelson of Uppsala, Father Caesar Washington, resplendent in Ghanaian robes; Don Angio Urrutia y O'Callaghan, Bishop of Santiago de Chile, who had lost an eye to guerrilla bullets; Tatsuki Doi, founder of Japanese Fundamentalists; and so on down the line. The reasoning and conclusions of all are the same: there must be no

running away, no pietistic assemblies, no flaunting of damna-
tion-or-heaven, no triumphalism. "Could Abi ibn Qalb expatiate
on his idea?" asks the Thai Methodist in his reedlike voice.

Abi ibn Qalb outmatches his former laconic communication.
He stands up, blows his nose in his kuffiah, looks Itzkak in the
eye and says: "Be one as men, that ye be one as sons of the
Most High." Then he simply sits down cross-legged again on his
carpet, and closes his eyes. It takes the precise logic of Henri
Carpin, monk of Taize, and the unswerving frankness of an
American-born Lett, Bishop Eubakivi of the Last Church of
the Holy Spear, to communicate Ibn Qalb's thought. But once
expressed, the notion catches on. On the fifth ballot, the motion
is carried.

The decision is based on a simple reasoning: in spite of
what the Bible or the Koran or the New Testament says about
the Elect or the Chosen, the fact remains that, if there is a
god—and all present profess to believe in his existence—he
cannot wish the destruction of his children. "Let's leave the
Elect idea to the eggheads," counsels Hugo Karelson of San
Antonio, Texas.

"You realize we are cutting our own throats," rasps the asth-
matic Siedler, the Fundamentalist from Magdeburg. "We have
nothing and are nothing, if we are not the Elect," sobs Monsignore Tarantinelle of Cremona plaintively. "What have we
to say, then?" asks Petrov Alexandrovitch, the Ukrainian
Bishop of Paris who had the best collection of snuff-boxes in
Europe, "do you mean to say that we don't speak their language?" But the objections are overcome one by one, some by
logic, some by emotion, some by pietistic motives, some by
hints wrapped up in the leaden piping of indicated death. The
idea is adopted that they should endeavor to think as the rest
of men do at that moment. Anastasis of Bulgaria, who had
been castrated by Khrushchev's bully-boys, phrased it: "We
must not use a word which neither they nor we can
understand."

"But it's not merely language," pleads a gaunt scrawny Scot
Presbyterian kirkman, "it's that our ideas are just a lot of mental
kilt-swirling, lots a' wind but nae a hankerin' thought." The
discussion proceeds for two days and one night, until guiding
principles are defined by agreement, and a scheduled program
of coordinated action is outlined. The final papers were pre-

ceded by a preamble in which those principles were laid out
clearly. Each principle is followed by a key question which is
later answered.

"The purpose of our common action is to act as men, with
men, for men's sake, and according to the destiny of men. The
greatest obstacle to our even beginning such an action is our
disunity. We are a living proof that there is not one living god;
and that if there is any reality corresponding to our manifest
ideas of divinity, it is a committee of Homeric godlets and
goddesses putting the world together and taking it to bits,
merely because their Great White Father slept with a cow, or
some Greek hero decided to gnash his teeth at them. Our first
endeavor must be to be one among ourselves.

"But we have had various unities in the past which were
unseasonable, unreasonable, and anti-human. When we
found someone as happy as us but different, we hissed 'pagan!',
'infidel!', 'heretic!' at him. We made of the world a crucible, of
life a molten lead bath, of death a sewer-top. We decried man's
human love. We made women child-factories. We made rulers
puppets of God or pawns of the devil. Man today feels himself
an individual, a child of this world. He feels that the world is
his garden, where he can wander, and wonder, and see the sunlight refracting ruby-red smiles on the olive leaves as bright
as polished daggers, or gaze at sister moon riding as an antique
silver ship on a luminous sea, and streaming through the open
casements of the clouds. Man wishes to serve the faceless father of all humanity, whose beauty and whose judgement
await all men. Instead we have tried to deliver him up to some
invisible and unknown Master grinning crookedly at all and
sundry from a twisted mass of impenetrable shadows called
organized religion.

"Man has politely left us with a yawn. He refused to be
subject any longer to teachings which admonished him that
every step of his brought him nearer either to damnation or to
heavenly happiness. There was no longer a god lurking everywhere, waiting to cut him down in his miserable actions and
his human misery, ambushing him to catch him redhanded in
his sin, to greet him with a grim stare when he turned some
corner, to scream at him suddenly from a nearby bush: 'Your
turn now, prepare for the lash.'

"Man has conceived himself as having an angel in his

mouth, turning prose to poetry, conferring on him the gift of tongues, and especially the language of all living things. He can pause and turn an ear to a tree, hearing what one bud says to another. Man walks with music in his ears all the day, not just the cornet in the parading high-school band, or the clamor of drums beating for pointless battles, but the deep music of living, the low sad rhythms of eternity, the high song of the turning spheres, the dim lullaby of the worm in its cocoon. All man's world is in tune. Man is in step with that tune. We have never been in step with that tune. We could not recognize that tune, even if we heard it. None of those unities now avail man or us. How do we become one, now?

"The second greatest obstacle is the opaqueness of all our thought. We have rules of morality. We have rules of belief. We have dogmas, doctrines, and formularies. Man cannot accept them because they are not intelligible. The very names we give the one god are enough to repel man. If there is a god, he is not called 'Yahweh,' 'God,' or 'Allah.' We ourselves do not know what we are talking about when we use terms such as heaven, hell, sin, immortality, resurrection, soul, virtue, providence. These are shibboleths, nonsense-movements, kalophonous syllables redolent of minds long dead and of imaginations we cannot imagine. How do we start speaking with modern man?

"Thirdly, the salvation we all promise seems merely 'pie-in-the-sky.' What does salvation mean? If we have salvation, why is it that after 2,000 years we have not at least taught Western man and the Arabs how to get it? There is some one element in our whole presentation, an element which all share, Jews, Christians, Muslims; and that element triggers the worst in man, does not draw the best out of him. What is that element?

"The answer to these questions provided the delegates with their principles. The last question asked is the most important.

"What is that element? Our analysis showed us that the first motion proposed would have condemned us to an Externalization process, whereby each one of us would preserve his little pigmy ideas; we would present a would-be solid front to the world; and we would march into doom and eternity separated from all mankind by a large chasm of our own digging, and mouthing useless syllables like men shouting into a great roaring wind. In Externalization, a certain subtle surrender of our classical group egotism and dominance is effected; but that

small surrender and that strictly religious Externalization
bring with them inevitably a recrudescence of Re-internalization with the attendant ills of dominance. For it seems to be an
iron law of human nature and most significant for our ultimate
inquiry as to the root-cause of dominance in man, that once a
man starts off with an elaborated framework of transcendental
ideas which he succeeds in systematizing into a social order,
the dominance-trait of man is quickened into life and febrile
activity. Give man a master-idea whereby he explains all and
the sanction of a 'superior being,' he proceeds to act as master. God help men from the 'illuminated,' the 'enlightened.' "

"Our difficulty, Jews, Christians, and Muslims that we are,
is that we have always moved in our own safe little cosmos; a
beginning, a middle, and an end, and a supreme god at either
end, midwife and gravedigger, opening and shutting the little
sliding doors and pinning the tags of good and evil on us. We
are used to a plan in our brain, a fire in our souls; we impose
the plan, and we burn with the fire. We cannot afford now to
come forward with such a plan and such a fire. This is the price
of humility and love. Otherwise, we generate a holy hate, and
we establish consecrated death.

"How do we become one? This is the greatest illusion. We
presuppose we are not one already by that query. More poignantly still, we presuppose that any unity in nature is feckless,
corrupt—for nature is bad inherently, according to our prefabricated plans; and hence the enkindled fire to purge it. In
our historical situation, the problem exists and does not exist.

"It does not exist and there is no question of becoming one
among ourselves; we are already one. Due to our theological
tomfoolery and philosophical charlatanism, we have separated
ourselves from others by artificial barriers; we decried nature—
it had to be saved; we viewed all men, our brothers, with distrust—they were damned until we snipped off that little foreskin, dribbled that cold water on the screaming, mewling baby,
or uttered those guttural Semite sounds over his bowed head
beneath the shadow of the Prophet's mosque.

"Therefore, we are one and we are not one. We must not
strive to be one among ourselves, for the simple reason that if
we form this little brotherhood of the confident, this micro-
cosmic, self-satisfied oneness among us, the Children of the
Book, we create a barrier between us and those with whom we
are by nature one. Let us shun the spiritual masochism of the

ecumenical man, if ecumenism means the union of us believers. We have tried it, and we end by believing only in the
most fallacious thing of all, ourselves.

"No wonder men shun us professionally. They will share
drink and food with us, give us a place in their Cadillac, a
spot in their swimming-pool, a room in their mountain-cabin.
They will clean ghetto streets with us, build stone walls in
place of flattened kerosene partitions with us, wipe away the
tears of hungry children with us, sweat at peace-making with
us. They will not build what we call the spirit with us. They
will open their houses to us, their countries and their families
and their businesses to us. They will not admit us to their consciences, their spiritual pains. No wonder they reject our moral
precepts and laws; they mean enslavement; they mean the
stigma of separation from their brothers. We say: we are
moral; we reckon nothing moral to be alien, from us. They say:
we are human; we reckon nothing human to be alien from us.
Thus in refusing our convictions, they refuse our consensus.
Refusing our world outlook, they refuse our god. Logically, humanly, they are the children of the anti-consensus.

"The mistake we make is to think that they are seeking an
alternative to our convictions, another moral law to substitute
for ours, another god in place of our one true god. They are not
seeking either convictions, moral law, or god. They are seeking
to be human. We do not, therefore, become one by melting
Greek with Roman with Russian with Anglican with Copt with
Armenian with Syrian with Episcopalian with Lutheran with
Methodist with Presbyterian: nor by fusing Judaism with Christianity, nor Islam with the latter two. We do not become one
by establishing little conclaves, congresses and conciliabules,
by conceding thrones one to the other, by giving the kiss of
peace to Christians by pitying the Jews, by succoring the
spiritual wants of Muslims. In this way we will never be one,
we ourselves with ourselves or with mankind. This is not the
way to unity.

"How do we start speaking with modern man? We must not
speak *to* him. We must speak with him. We must not speak of
our affairs with him. We must not speak of his affairs with us.
We must speak with him the tongue of man with man, about
the things that interest him and us as men, not him as a potential part of us, not us as us. The things we used to talk about,
our precious messages from out beyond and our secrets, they

must be unspoken; they are to be done, lived, exhausted as means and modes of being with him more and more. For then the message will not be a word (we are fascinated by the theory of the word, the Greek *logos*, the Semitic *dabhar*). Our secrets will not be safely guarded formulas beneath the hard cover of theological manuals, between the hands of a bishop, the chant of a rebi in the staedtl, the Sura from the tower, the assertive 'He has told us,' couched in Latin, Arabic, or Hebrew.

"We have all failed. We tried to consecrate the human race to one regional mind of that race. We declared Heaven available and Hell inevitable for all those who thought as the men they were: Indians, Chinese, Japanese, Westerners, Arabs, Jews, Gentiles. According to Judaism, all men should think as Jews. According to Christians, all men should think as Christians. According to Muslims, all men should think as Muslims. What desecration! This was our failure. Westerners, Jews, Arabs, we wish to achieve man by transcending him, unlike the Oriental who made a studied effort at slumberous surrender to the reality he knew, unlike the creator, Christians preach, who took man as he had made him and became a man.

"We must take the truth we have colored with our prejudices. We must unthink our desecration of the ancient revelation perpetrated by our nationalism, our earthiness, our strong rebellion. We must not see flaming faith in the Ravenna mosaics, or towering love of a god in the domes of Moorish Spain, or indomitable loyalty in the cities of Conquistadores. If truth we have, that truth shall make us free to meet man as man, as he surely goes to his encounter with or without us. Which shall it be?

"Our program therefore must follow these rules:

1. "We must de-Occidentalize our Judaism and our Christianity.

2. "We must rid our Islam of its Arab and Middle Eastern coloring.

3. "We must examine nakedly the truths we live by without the familiar clothing of our region, our continent, our race, our age, our tradition, our language or our people.

4. "We must endeavor to find what is the truth of Moses, the truth of Jesus, the truth of Mohammad, keeping in mind that if they were alive today, they would not be repeating what they said over 1500 years ago, nor doing what they were doing in

those times; and so we must avoid slavish reproduction of what they said and did merely because they said and did it then.

5. "We must not create a conflated religion, or create any religion at all, but pursue the dictates of our religion as we know it, without the trammels of our prejudice, without the hampering accretions of our histories.

6. "We must no longer see man in a god, because we thus deform him, to make him fit our finite ideas of what a god should be; but we must seek our god in man. Not to adore a man-made god, but to find our god there where he can only reside on earth. For if our god has intervened in human history, he does not dwell in water, air, trees, or lifeless stones, but in man, his beloved. This we believe.

7. "We must act as if the world of man is young, very young, the cosmos of man as yet untrod by him, his powers as yet quite dormant, and his destiny as the pride of our god not yet crowned with maturity; and we must regard all our yesterdays as mere moments in a pre-dawn hush, before the sons of God stand up at his bidding and sing with the stars for the joy of living.

8. "We must walk with man into a mushroom cloud, if into a mushroom cloud he must go. We must plan his world as ours, if he is to live.

9. "We must only learn to love by loving, to hope by hoping, to undo our ills by suffering the ills of man's nature, and become one by finding ourselves together in man.

"It is clear that an inner dynamism of history—the sum of man's actions and achievements, his mistakes and successes— is propelling man along his present path. We cannot arrest him. We must not be afraid. For man is going to meet himself in freedom.

"Modern man is bound for the encounter: he enters this arena, not at the bidding of an ancient urge, not because he goes to glory, and not because he hopes thereby for martyrdom. He is unshielded by the spell of antique magics, and wears no vestments. He is unhopeful of all succor save from what he is. We can descend into that arena with him; we can meet with man as man, and find the one true god we have tucked away in folds of clever reasoning, and have drowned in the venerable words of ancient leaders and new-found doctrines. For there is one last principle of our action.

"Modern man's delight, after all, is not to be a god, although Christianity teaches that 'God's' delight is to become a man while remaining 'God.' We must not confound the mortal part of man with the 'destiny,' the 'despair,' and the 'absurd' of some writers. For it is not to die that modern man thinks of death; it is to live and to live forever. He knows, however, that his outer actions are out of kilter with his wild inner desire to live forever. In his weak moments, that element in him which discovers the traces of the fortuitous and the fragile in his life, sneers at his inner drive as if to say: 'You say you do not need to hope in order to act, but I say that you are a weaver of lying wisps and your end is the grave.' Man's spirit answers tranquilly: 'Maybe. But there awaits me the encounter which includes all I cannot escape and everything I crave to have and be. In former ages, it had many faces. But in each succeeding age, I found that the face was closer to my own. Sometimes, I fled it into religion, but I found it on the altar-stone. Sometimes, I rounded upon it and tried to slay it, only to find that it was impervious to my fashioned weapons. In vanity, I tried to smother it in laughter. In exultation, I would have frozen it in art, wafted it away on music. In my foolishness, I attempted to snare it in lawlessness and unreason. I would have exorcised it with myth and spell and sacramental, with bell and book and candle. I know, furthermore, that when the day ends for me, I shall be tempted, like some blind men, to imagine riches lying in the lengthening shadows, whereas it will only be the lambent gold of a dying sun reflected in the still trees of my twilight. I know that.

"But do not confound me with some lonely puny little animal of your story-telling, who must venture forth without a guide, without a consoler, to create as it were from his own vitals the meaning of his existence, and to write the rules whereby he may live and survive, as some have thought. I am not committed to making a meaning out of my life, because in that case I would be forced to transcend it. I proclaim not my subconscious, but my consciousness, not abandonment, but the will to be with my fellows; not acquisition of facts but the light of truth. I do not tend to something, for I know not what lies ahead. Suicide does not interest me. All I know is where I start and what I am starting, myself. The candle I carry to light my darkness may drip hot drops on my fingers, but I shall carry it firmly, not for the honor of being a man but because I must have light."

The summit conference was finished just one week, when the crisis was resolved by peaceful means. Russia agreed to surrender parts of the Far East, while China for obscure reasons renounced all other claims and returned other property to Russia. The Inter-Faith Council laid plans to implement its resolutions.

It is clear that no matter what any religion may attempt to do today, none of the three religions we have been considering is able to intervene effectively to control the present development of man. Man would be without hope, if his very tendency was vitiated at its root. In this case, "God" would really be dead. The end of religious dominance, such as it has been known in these three religions, could only come if the religions set about ridding their individual beliefs of all that is not essential, of all that has been acquired by historical accident and by regionalisms of various sorts. The above scenario could be verified only at a later date, when the three religions have been shaken severely by internal troubles and external limitations. Unless some development like this occurs, it is very hard to see how the three religions could escape quasi-total eclipse.

Index